An A to Z of Feminist Theology

An A to Z of Feminist Theology

edited by
LISA ISHERWOOD &
DOROTHEA MCEWAN

Sheffield
Academic Press

The publishers are grateful to Harvester Wheatsheaf
(Simon and Schubert International) for permission
to use the entry 'Death' by Dorothea McEwan

Copyright © 1996 Sheffield Academic Press

Published by Sheffield Academic Press Ltd
Mansion House
19 Kingfield Road
Sheffield S11 9AS
England

Printed on acid-free paper in Great Britain
by Cromwell Press
Melksham, Wiltshire

British Library Cataloguing in Publication Data

A catalogue record for this book is available
from the British Library

ISBN 1-85075-747-X

CONTENTS

Preface	ix	Eschatology	53
List of Contributors	xi	Essentialism	55
		Ethical Theory	56
Abba	1	Eve	59
Abrotion	1	Experience	60
Abuse	2		
Alienation	5	Female/Feminine/Feminist	63
Androcentrism	5	Feminism and Postmodernism	63
Anger	6	Feminist Spirituality	64
Apostleship	8	Feminist Theology in the Third World	68
Asian Women's Hermeneutical Principle	9	Flourishing	70
Atonement	10	French Feminism	72
Authority	12	Friendship	74
Autonomy	14		
		Gaelic Women's Spirituality	77
Beguines	16	Gender	78
The Bible as a Resource for Women	18	Gnosticism	81
Biblical Exegesis	21	Goddess	82
Bodiliness	23	Godding	85
		Grace	85
Celibacy	25	Greenham Common Women's Peace Camp	88
Christology	26	Guilt	89
Church History	27		
Circle Dance	30		
Community	31	Healing	92
Complementarity	33	Hell	96
Creation Spirituality	34	Heresy	98
Crucifixion	37	Hermeneutics from a Feminist Perspective	99
		Hildegard of Bingen	102
Death	39	Hymns and Hymn Writing	103
Domestic Sacraments	40		
Dualism	41	Idolatry	105
Dunamis	42	Immaculate Conception	106
		Immanence	106
Ecclesiology/Models of Church	43	Inclusive Language	107
Ecofeminism	45	Interfaith Dialogue	108
Economics	48	Invisibilty	112
Ecumenism	50		
Empowerment	52	Justice	113
Erotic Power	53		

An A to Z of Feminist Theology

CONTENTS

Kingdom	116	Pornography	179
		Post-Christian Feminism	180
Law	118	Power	182
Lesbian Perspectives in Feminist Theology	118	Praxis	183
		Prayer	185
Liberation	121	Presbytera	186
Love	122	Priesthood	187
Lust	124	Process Thought	189
		Prophets	192
Macho/Masculine/Masculinist	125		
Marriage as Sacrament	125	Rabbis	195
Martyrdom	126	Rape	195
Mary	128	Reconciliation	197
Mary Magdalene	129	Redemption (1)	198
Matriarchy	130	Redemption (2)	200
Medical Ethics	130	Relationality	202
Menstruation and Laws of Purity	135	Religious Life	203
Methodology	138	Repentance	204
Militarism	141	Resurrection	206
Ministry: A Historical Survey	142	Revelation	207
Misogyny	145		
Models of God	146	The Sacraments	209
Motherhood of God	149	Sadomasochistic Society	210
Movement for the Ordination of Women	151	Saints	211
Mujerista Theology	153	Salvation	212
Mutuality	155	Sexism	213
		Sexuality	214
New Testament Women: An Overview	157	Shechinah	215
Norm	160	Sin	217
		Spirituality	218
Old Testament Women: An Overview	162	Suffering	220
Omnipotence	164	Suffragettes	222
Original Sin (1)	165	Symbols	224
Original Sin (2)	167		
		Theology	225
Paganism	169	Transcendence	226
Pastoral Theology	171	Trinity	227
Patriarchy	173	Truth	228
Peace Movement	174		
Pollution Laws in Judaism	178	Violence (1)	229

An A to Z of Feminist Theology

CONTENTS

Violence (2)	230
Virginity	231
Wholeness	233
Wicca	233
Wisdom	236
Womanist Theology	238
Women and Liturgical Music	239
Women–Church	240
Work	241
Worship	243
YHWH	245

An A to Z of Feminist Theology

PREFACE

FEMINISM, a woman-centred analysis of society, presents a challenge to theology. Most traditional theology has been androcentric, but has not acknowledged itself as such. This has meant that man's experience has been viewed as divine truth and this has closed the door on diverse experiences. Some ten years ago Elaine Storkey stated that it was now possible to 'ask theological questions and give feminist answers' (Storkey 1985: 85). Feminist theologies have moved on in the last ten years and we have witnessed how the 'new' answers have sometimes become dogmatic. The challenge posed by feminist theologies is that they do not necessarily give absolute answers but provide new ways of questioning. We have also come to realize over the last ten years that diversity is at the heart of our search for equality.

A rich variety of insights have arisen from the different methods and experiences that are now applied to the contemplation of the nature of the divine. Feminist theologies allow us to bring our whole personhood to that exploration. It is like exploring one's own homeland—so familiar and yet so new—seeing the familiar with new eyes, experiencing the fullness and freedom of fresh thoughts.

It is important to go back to unlock original meanings and to go forward by opening up closed definitions and statements. Feminist theological research, using fresh and experience-based 'non-jargon' language, unlocks the riches of our tradition; it enables us to see both the situations which stifle women and those which liberate them. By shaking free from the narrow parameters of technical language we also find that the theoretical concepts it conveys themselves come under scrutiny. We are then able to look beyond the agendas that narrow, contrived language inevitably carries, in order to help people identify *their* truth and live *their* praxis.

Our preliminary discussions about this book helped us identify three areas of importance in our understanding of feminism: space, method and language. We addressed these in the following ways: we created a woman-identified space, not that men were excluded from writing, but their focus had to be women-centred. We also wished, as far as possible, to make this volume a 'biophilic' space, to quote Mary Daly. That is, we have tried to focus on life-giving interpretations which encourage and allow the flourishing of women. This in turn led us to realize that it is not enough simply to create a cosy private space where women feel safe and appreciated. We have to push out into the public realm, which in this case is the theology of the major religious traditions, and make that a safe space for women also.

The individual authors in this volume have used this space to make their scholarship accessible in a variety of ways. Many found it most empowering to use the medium of standard scholarship, while others experimented with new ideas and methods of expression. The result is a riotous explosion of imagination and scholarship. This space is also for the reader. It is one in which she can play with the research and run wild with her own ideas.

The method used in this space is crucial. It is, for the most part, a simple one. It take seriously the full humanity of all people, demands empowerment for the cosmos and aims to expand the space we share. Every topic is understood, deconstructed and reconstructed in this light.

An A to Z of Feminist Theology

PREFACE

The language used to explore this method is also of central importance. The language employed, the vehicle of thought expression, symbol-making and interaction, has to take on board all the new insights, developments, wishes and dreams that come from the application of a new method. Patriarchal use of language consciously entrenches the mind and imprisons it in formulae which can harden into doctrinaire statements and unshakeable principles of belief. By opening up language, we attempt to reach beyond this. This volume shows how creative and expansive the concepts created by feminist language can be.

Thus, feminist theology does not present itself as a unified body of research, but rather as a rich tapestry of life experiences and reflection upon them. This volume sometimes charts new territory and at others consolidates the insights gained. It always celebrates women.

This book is a companion volume to *Introducing Feminist Theology* (Isherwood and McEwan 1993) and to other monographs on feminist theology published by Sheffield Academic Press. We thank every author for her or his care and attention, cooperation and enthusiasm. We hope that you will find the thoughts expressed in these pages exciting and that they will kindle and stimulate new insights. May you find this volume a useful tool in the work of dismantling patriarchy.

Shalom.
Dorothea McEwan and Lisa Isherwood
London, June 1996

LIST OF CONTRIBUTORS

Mario Aguilar, Department of Social Anthropology, University of St Andrews, Scotland.

Philippa Berry, King's College, Cambridge.

Sarah Jane Boss, La Sainte Union College of Higher Education, Southampton.

Geertje Bouwes, Writer and Healer, London.

Fiona Bowie, St David's University College, Lampeter, Wales.

June Boyce-Tillman, King Alfred's College, Winchester.

Lavinia Byrne, IBVM.

Jules Cashford, London.

Julie Clague, Department of Religious Studies, St Mary's College, Strawberry Hill, London.

Dorothy Coxon, Cumbria.

Janet Crawford, The College of St John the Evangelist, Auckland, NZ.

Vivianne Crowley, King's College, University of London.

Sheila Greeve Davaney, Iliff School of Theology, Denver, CO, USA.

Caroline Davis, Campaigner, Movement for the Ordination of Women, Winchester.

Jenny Dines, Heythrop College, University of London.

Susan Dowell, Writer.

Toinette Eugene, Garrett-Evangelical Theological Seminary, Evanston, IL, USA.

Robert Evans, Chester University College.

An A to Z of Feminist Theology

LIST OF CONTRIBUTORS

Marie Fortune, Center for the Prevention of Sexual and Domestic Violence, Seattle, WA, USA.

Matthew Fox, Holy Name College, Oakland, CA, USA.

Monical Furlong, Writer, London.

Alison Gelder, Catholic Women's Network, London.

Anne Gilroy, Jesus College, Cambridge.

Ronwyn Goodsir-Thomas, Writer, Le Bourg, France.

Jeanette Gosney, St John's College, Nottingham.

Jane Goudey, Bangor Theological Seminary, ME, USA.

Elaine Graham, Department of Religions and Theology, University of Manchester.

Carter Heyward, Episcopal Divinity School, Cambridge, MA, USA.

Linda Hogan, University of Leeds.

Lillalou Hughes, Britain and Ireland School of Feminist Theology, London.

Mary Hunt, WATER, Silver Spring, MD, USA.

Linda Hurcombe, Writer, Clun.

Ada Maria Isasi-Diaz, The Theological School, Drew University, Madison, NJ, USA.

Lisa Isherwood, Department of Theology, College of St Mark and St John, Plymouth.

Joan James, Women in Theology, Cardiff, Wales.

Grace Jantzen, Department of Religions and Theology, University of Manchester.

An A to Z of Feminist Theology

LIST OF CONTRIBUTORS

Jane Richardson Jensen, Writer, Bathgate, W. Lothian.

Noragh Jones, Womanspirit Wales, Aberystwyth, Wales.

Ursula King, Department of Theology and Religious Studies, University of Bristol.

Ann Loades, Department of Theology, University of Durham.

Mary John Mananzan, OSB, Institute of Women's Studies, Scholastica College, Manila, The Philippines.

Maureen McBride, RNDM, Cotabato City, The Philippines.

Dorothea McEwan, The Warburg Institute, University of London.

Judith McKinlay, Knox Theological Hall, Dunedin, NZ.

Rachel Montague, Rabbi, London.

Sue Morgan, Department of Theology and Religious Studies, University of Bristol.

Anne Murphy, Heythrop College, University of London.

Elisabeth Nash, Training Team, United Reformed Church, Nottingham.

Diann Neu, WATER, Silver Spring, MD, USA.

Catherine Norris, Britain and Ireland School of Feminist Theology, York.

Marcia Plumb, Rabbi, London.

Myra Poole, SND, Catholic Women's Ordination, London.

Ianthe Pratt, Association of Inclusive Language, London.

Ann Primavesi, Department of Theology and Religious Studies, University of Bristol.

An A to Z of Feminist Theology

LIST OF CONTRIBUTORS

Melissa Raphael, Cheltenham and Gloucester College of Higher Education, Cheltenham.

Mary Ann Rossi, Researcher, Lawrence University, Appleton, WI, USA.

Sylvia Rothschild, Rabbi, Bromley, Kent.

Rosemary Radford Ruether, Garrett-Evangelical Theological Seminary, Evanston, IL, USA.

Veronica Seddon, Catholic Women's Network, London.

Nicola Slee, Aston Training Scheme, Birmingham.

Susan Smith, RNDM, Catholic Institute of Theology, Auckland, NZ.

Janet Martin Soskice, The Divinity School, University of Cambridge.

Elizabeth Stuart, University of Glamorgan, Pontypridd, Wales.

Lucy Tatman, The Women's Studies Centre, Ainslie, ACT, Australia

Maureen Tilley, The Florida State University, Tallahassee, FL, USA.

Linda Vogel, Garrett Evangelical Theological Seminary, Evanston, IL, USA.

Jean Waldron, Writer, Cornwall.

Alison Webster, Institute for the Study of Christianity and Sexuality, London.

Estelle White, Campaigner, Dewsbury, W. Yorkshire.

Alison Williams, Colchester, Essex.

Lala Winkley, Catholic Women's Ordination, London.

An A to Z of Feminist Theology

LIST OF CONTRIBUTORS

Sabrina Woodward, Britain and Ireland School of Feminist Theology, Brighton.

Pamela Dickey Young, Queen's University, Kingston, Canada.

ABBA
Lisa Isherwood

THIS IS the word that Jesus used to describe his heavenly Father, but it is a very earthy word. It is a term of affection used by small children who are sure that their fathers are kind, loving and nurturing individuals. It is a term that has no room for the notion of the almighty and vengeful God who is often found in the pages of the Scriptures; it is a tender word.

In this word feminist theology can find hope. It shows that a woman's personal experience can shape her views of God, and that she can have the courage to call her God by the name she has found. In the same spirit feminist theologians feel justified, from their own experience, in calling God mother, lover, friend and many other names which express a close relationship and a loving intimacy.

ABORTION
Grace Jantzen

THE DISCUSSION of abortion in most Western countries has tended to polarize two positions, which have become known as 'pro-life' and 'pro-choice'. The 'pro-life' stance takes a position of advocacy for the life of the foetus, and holds that termination of a pregnancy is murder. The 'pro-choice' position advocates freedom of choice for women, and for women's right to control their own bodies, including the right to choose whether or not to commence or continue with a pregnancy: there is after all no other medical situation in which a person is compelled to put their body at the disposal of another.

There are a variety of issues at stake in the abortion debate. One that has received considerable theological attention is the question of the status of the foetus. Those who hold to a 'pro-life' position typically do so because they believe that life begins from the moment of conception: this is why abortion is held to be murder. By contrast, a gradualist approach holds that personhood develops gradually as the embryo becomes a foetus and then a child. On this view it is possible to terminate a pregnancy, especially in its early stages, without that termination being murder. Those who argue that life begins at the moment of conception point out that the newly formed embryo is obviously human and alive, and that its genetic composition is complete, already carrying the full potential of adult personhood. Gradualists respond that while this is of course true, it is necessary to draw a distinction between human *life* and human *personhood*: the former is certainly true of the early foetus but the latter is not. And although an embryo is a *potential* person, gradualists argue, it is not (yet) an *actual* person, so its moral status should not be confused with that of an actual person.

This debate is connected with the theological and philosophical debate about dualism versus holism; that is, whether a person consists of two parts, a soul and a body (of which the soul is the more important), or whether personhood should be understood more holistically. Often (though not always) those who believe that life begins at the moment of conception are also dualists, and believe that it is at the moment of conception that God places a soul into the embryo. Some of the early Christian Fathers who held a similar view thought that God placed the soul into the body at quickening, which they believed was at forty days' gestation for a male foetus and ninety days' gestation for a female foetus. However, the whole dualistic idea that human persons are made up of 'soul-pieces' and 'body-pieces' has come in for sharp criticism from feminist (and other) theologians, as inconsistent with Christian teaching on creation, embodiment and incarnation. Moreover, feminists have pointed out that dualism has regularly been taken to imply a denigration of bodies and sexuality, as well as of women and of the earth, which have been conceptually linked with bodiliness.

However, if we enter the discussion about abortion not with the question of the status of the foetus but with the issue of women's well-being and reproductive choice as the first question, the whole debate takes on different contours. Beverly Wildung Harrison, in her book *Our Right to Choose: Toward a New Ethic of Abortion* (1983), has presented a thorough feminist theological analysis of abortion beginning from the recognition that the question of abortion is part of a much larger issue of male control of female bodies for sexual and reproductive

An A to Z of Feminist Theology

purposes. This control is exercised through the churches, the educational systems, medicine and the state; and the question of abortion can only usefully be considered if one recognizes the pressures placed on women by all of these.

Thus, for example, it is no coincidence that the Roman Catholic Church, which officially forbids abortion in any case except to save the pregnant woman's life, also prohibits any means of artificial contraception. This effectively places a woman's reproductive system into her husband's control, since such contraception methods as abstinence, 'natural family planning', or withdrawal before ejaculation can at best work only with his cooperation. There have also been objections, not only by Catholics, to sex education at school, and to allowing teenagers access to contraceptives, while at the same time denouncing teenage pregnancies, single mothers and teenage women who seek abortions. As anyone who has counselled these young women knows, the underlying problems often are problems of meaninglessness, lack of educational or job opportunities, and a huge need for love and esteem which is often expressed sexually. Until churches and governments begin to act effectively to meet these underlying needs, with social, educational and employment opportunities for young people, their condemnation of abortion only places these young women in an impossible double bind.

One of the features often seemingly forgotten by those who campaign against abortion is that it does after all take *two* people's involvement for pregnancy to occur in the first place. Yet women who seek abortions most often do so because they feel—often with good reason—that they would be on their own with the child if they proceeded with the pregnancy. The male partner would be unsupportive or would vanish completely, the church would be condemnatory, and the state would begrudge economic and social support. If the woman already has children, their needs must also be considered. In the present political and social climate in countries like the UK and the USA, especially with the rhetoric against single mothers (but not against the men who abandon them), it is hardly surprising that there should be increasing demand for abortion. And in those jurisdictions (such as some American states) where abortion is either illegal or expensive, neither is it surprising that back-street abortions, often with lethal consequences, should be on the upsurge.

Yet even when abortions can be freely and legally obtained, the idea that women enter into them casually is true in only a small minority of cases. Women who become pregnant usually take their situation seriously, and the decision for or against abortion may be very difficult whichever choice is made. Many women who choose abortion feel deep grief and go through a period of mourning even though they believe their decision was the right one. And women who choose to continue their pregnancy face many years of having to cope with what may be a difficult situation—or else face giving up their child for adoption. Whatever their choices, they need compassionate understanding and supportive social structures rather than condemnation.

Further reading: Bondeson *et al*. (eds.) 1984; Petchesky 1986.

ABUSE
Jeanette M. Gosney

ABUSE IS a word which is being used with increasing frequency as situations which have hitherto been accepted as normal are being recognized as abusive. The prevalence of child abuse has been drawn to public attention in recent years through media coverage of such cases as the Cleveland allegations (1987), the publication of the Children Act (1989) and the establishment of support agencies such as Childline. Abuse includes deliberate deprivation of food, warmth and clothing, deliberate physical harm, verbal abuse with demeans the child, emotional abuse which withholds affirmation and love, and sexual abuse, which is the inappropriate sexualization of a child, including the use of children in pornography, and might involve exposure and touching of genitals, and anal, oral or vaginal penetration with objects or the penis. Statistics vary, but suggest that up to one in 5 girls and one in 12 boys are sexually abused by the age of 18. Sexual abuse within the family is most common, but is often also perpetrated by teachers, pastors or childminders—those who have trusted access to children. The abusers are in most cases male. Ritual abuse encompasses the above and additionally involves

ABUSE

links with satanic rites and sacrifice.

Domestic violence such as wife-battering and marital rape are overt forms of abuse, but abuse at home includes, for example, situations where the wife is prevented from seeking outside employment or is treated as the servant of the husband. Women frequently suffer sexual harassment in public places and at work and are, despite the Equal Opportunities Act and legal measures to remove sex discrimination, still subject to inequalities in pay and treatment. Actual sexual violence or fear of it affects the lives of most women, who feel restricted in their movements or dress, in order to protect themselves. The growing number of Rape Crisis centres and women's refuges point to the endemic nature of violence against women. The portrayal of 'ideal' women's bodies in the press and pornographic material, the prevalence of prostitution, and in some countries the possibility of 'mail-order brides' are other examples of abuse of women.

The old or infirm, whether living at home, in residential care or hospital, can be victims of psychological and physical abuse by their carers, whether relatives or trained professionals.

Any group which is marginalized by the dominant culture suffers abuse. Thus racism, classism, heterosexism, imperialism and religious discrimination are all common manifestations of abuse today. Other people vulnerable to abuse include those who are mentally or physically disabled.

Self-abuse may take such forms as self-mutilation, anorexia and bulimia, drug, alcohol and substance abuse, and suicide.

The use of animals for testing new drugs or cosmetics, the exploitation of certain animals for human profit leading to an endangering of the species, the destruction of the rain forests, pollution of rivers and seas and the subsequent threat to the natural habitats of many forms of wildlife can all be cited as forms of environmental abuse.

Causes of Abuse

Overt causes may include stress, poor living conditions, pressure of work or the economic demands for profit or success. Traditional explanations for sexual abuse have often suggested that it is 'natural' for the man and that women and children 'ask for it' or 'like it'. Physical abuse of children is often explained as parental discipline. Such instances can mean that the perpetrator is exonerated and the victim blamed.

Covert causes point to structural systems and ideologies. Most of the above examples of abuse suggest that an imbalance of *power* is a key issue (for example between a parent and a child, or a man and a woman). Power is abused when the powerful deny others their right to choose, when 'power over' is used to the detriment of another and for selfish gain. The powerless, dependent on the powerful for protection, economic or material support, dare not protest: they are coerced into silence. Complaints by victims, if made at all, are often dismissed as trivial or disbelieved, which further reinforces the taboo on speaking out and obtaining justice and appropriate support. Such treatment is in direct contradiction of the equal value of all human beings and the call to love and respect all creation.

A further underlying and related cause is systemic patriarchy. In a society where authority resides with those at the top of a hierarchical pyramid—whether in industry and business, in the family, in the church, or in social stratification—there is little space for those at the bottom of the pyramid to have influence, however democratic society purports to be. Such hierarchical structures facilitate the abuse of power. The model, it can be argued, is derived from the notion of God as king over his people or Christ as head of the body, the analogy being that people rule as his vice-regents on earth, whether that be as clergy, parents, husband or some other position of authority. Submission to authority is thus indirectly legitimated in the same way as submission to God is required.

Gender is a major factor in many instances of abuse. The traditional notion of man's superiority over woman, of woman's dependence, submissiveness and her emotional 'weakness' in contrast to man's independence, assertiveness and rational thinking plays a significant part in implying that women are 'easy targets'. Male socialization reinforces men's dominant role in society. Traditional Christian biblical interpretation (for example 1 Cor. 11; Eph. 5; 1 Tim. 5) has further inculcated such views, allowing men to rule but prohibiting women, placing the blame for sin on Eve alone (for example 1 Tim. 2). Furthermore, teaching on obedience and the

An A to Z of Feminist Theology

need to endure suffering as Christ did (for example 1 Pet. 2; Jas 1) leaves women trapped, for to protest would leave them guilty in God's eyes. There is also the issue of sexuality: men, it is assumed, will 'sow their wild oats', while women must remain virgins. The portrayal of sex with violence in the media further suggests that men are expected to be able to overcome women's resistance: to fail would be shameful. The woman's body is treated as society's property while her intrinsic human dignity is disregarded.

Effects of Abuse

Many victims of abuse are left with long-term psychological and emotional, as well as physical, damage, although courts have sometimes failed to recognize this and have assumed that the victim has recovered with no ill effects. Victims often require professional counselling alongside any practical and legal support which they receive. Abuse is fundamentally an assault on identity. The vulnerable are dehumanized, treated as objects for the benefit of the powerful. Self-worth is eroded; depression, anxiety, anger, self-abuse and difficulties in relationships number among other effects. Shame and false guilt can also be present, particularly in cases of sexual abuse and cases in which the victim—often called a survivor—feels pressure as a Christian to forgive the perpetrator before she is ready to do so. Perpetrators likewise need help, which may include custodial sentences, separation from the family and therapy.

Theological Reflections on Abuse

Whatever form it takes, abuse is a clear example of sin, the 'structural de-creating of all that is life-filled and wholesome' (Grey 1993: 50). According to Carter Heyward, sin is 'rooted in the social structures of domination', which places abuse in a context broader than that of personal 'sins' (Heyward 1982: 90). Furthermore, Dorothee Sölle writes about sin as 'collaboration with and apathy toward injustice' (Sölle 1974: 83ff.): abuse is sin, but so is failure to work against it. She points to Christ's concern with the abuse of institutional power. Sin can also be defined as alienation, brokenness, 'a rupture of relationship' (Fortune 1983: 79-80). Any form of coercion or violation of right relation must be termed an injustice and a sin against the person, the community and God. Abuse, in other words, is evil, for 'evil is an act of un-love, in-justice', 'breaking the relational bond between and among ourselves' (Heyward 1982: 18).

How can such 'sin' be overcome and redeemed? Rita Brock, Grey, Heyward, Rosemary Ruether and Sölle are among the many feminist theologians who speak of God as the power and source of right relation, rather than using the patriarchal image of omnipotence and 'power over'. For Grey, the Spirit of God is the 'energy of connections' in creation (Grey 1993: 100). Redemption and creation are a unified process: 'the very act of recovering a sense of being created in the image of God is…a redemptive act in reclaiming the lost wholeness and sense of self-worth'. Here is the idea of at-one-ment, reconciliation with the self, with others and with God. For feminist liberation theologians such as Sharon Welch redemption comes through resistance to 'the valorization of absolute power' (Welch 1990: 111ff.). There is an ethical, sociopolitical tone here: the divine qualities of compassion and rage which sustain resistance and foster hope for justice, expressed in and through community, witness to the immanence of the divine, to redemption through power in relation (Welch 1990: 172ff.). Again within an ethical framework, Beverly Harrison writes of the creative 'power of anger in the work of love' (Harrison 1985: ch. 1), which allows redemption *from* a position of victimization *to* life in a community of deeply mutual love. And such redemption is possible *now*. Heyward claims that it takes place when people love, befriend and make justice (righteousness), when people make God incarnate in the world (Heyward 1982: 9). The reign of God is not merely a dream of the future. Personal responsibility for the transformation of society and the coming of the *basileia* of God—taking on the role of 'co-redeemers'—cannot be denied on this understanding. So the call of the cross can be expressed as the call to radical love, where the cross is not a model of how suffering should be borne, but 'a witness to God's desire that no-one should have to suffer violence again' (Fortune 1983: 198). And the resurrection in

Christ is the source of life-giving, shared power, the power of God re-membered in all persons. Repentance recognizes the denial of power in relation—the denial of God. Redemption is the healing of that brokenness, the experience of 'power and intimacy in mutual relation' (Heyward 1982: 11). Such a model deconstructs all abusive power structures and patriarchal patterns—and constructs the true *basileia*, the 'beloved community' as envisaged by Welch (1990: 160).

Further reading: Gnanadason 1993; Harrison 1985; Pellauer, Chester and Boyajian (eds.) 1987; Poling 1991.

ALIENATION
Dorothea McEwan

'ALIENATION', ORIGINALLY a term of political theory, denotes a state of non-involvement, critical detachment, lack of emotional involvement, even estrangement. The dramatist Bertolt Brecht wrote epic plays which required that players and audience followed them without emotional involvement. Reality, according to this theory, is constructed and visible to observers, but it does not really touch them. In politics the word 'alienation' came to mean a state of affairs in which people's wishes and aspirations became so divorced from their leaders' understanding that a serious shift occured which led to ever more pressure being exerted by one group on the other group, eventually leading to the eruption of violence and the break-up of the system. The concept of alienation is also linked to the understanding that people can become alienated from their emotions and relationships and can step outside them to view them 'objectively', in a detached way. The subject–object split, termed dualism, provides a method for ensuring that some people are 'actors' or 'agents' of their history, while others are 'victims' of the circumstances they find themselves in. For the former, the world is a place in which they can live and have their being. The latter, however, cannot view their lives as inserted into life around them, but rather as something which can be studied and analysed as if they were not part of it. Hence we find the 'objectification' of women's lives, for instance in pornography; a mechanism which makes the hurt done to women somebody else's problem.

Further reading: Tong 1989.

ANDROCENTRISM
Mary Ann Rossi

ANDROCENTRISM, THE condition of using the male as the determinant of the human being, is derived from Greek philosophy (Plato and Aristotle), and crystallized in Christian doctrine (Augustine, Aquinas, Gratian). It is inculcated from the cradle onwards in Western society. The process of shaping the lenses of gender is subliminal, and the effect is damaging to all women (Bem 1993).

One example of how androcentric and gender polarizing lenses can shape self-perception is the 'burden of proof' difference. Empirical studies carried out by Bem show that women underestimate, and men overestimate, the quality of their own performance, and that men over-reward themselves, and women under-reward themselves, for any level of their performance.

This androcentric self-perception predisposes females to follow behaviour patterns that subordinate their own needs and desires to those of the men and children in their lives. At the same time androcentrism predisposes men to elaborate many ways of being or behaving that put them in a more dominant or powerful position. With this conceptual backdrop, the heterosexual marriage is the perfect breeding ground for inequality, because it brings a male assumer of privilege together with a female denier of privilege. The androcentric social structure transforms male–female difference into female disadvantage; it also disguises a male standard as gender neutrality (Bem 1993).

The Greeks founded a tradition of misogyny that has shaped the conception of women to the present day. The poet Hesiod (eighth century BCE) records the story of Pandora, who was held responsible for the fall of humanity from the state of paradise. The Greek philosopher Aristotle defines a woman androcentrically as an inferior departure from the male norm. Later Augustine, Aquinas and Gratian draw on Aristotle's definition of woman as defective man to support their definitions of woman as inferior to man.

An A to Z of Feminist Theology

The androcentric message of our society is embedded in the Judaeo-Christian doctrines that are the underpinning of contemporary Western thought. It is also a powerful case study of how those seeking power must sometimes suppress alternative perspectives if they are to shape the cultural discourse in their own image. History is important to the analysis of androcentrism. The replacement of Goddess with a God and the defining of woman as other are the basis for the Judaeo-Christian symbols of male dominance, with a patriarchal male God and a sexual, inferior female who tempts the male from the path of righteousness. Eve's story is at the heart of the concept of woman in Western society. She continues to be a living part of all the cultures touched by her story.

Feminist historians and theologians reject the assumption of androcentric methodology that women have not been a force in history, since they have been excluded from positions of official religious and social leadership. Feminist scholars are searching for women's actual experience, as well as their spiritual history. We must not take the norms of history written by men as the measure of our human experience. We seek a transformation of the intellectual imagination that allows us to see old data in a new perspective, such as the reading of the Leta inscription as 'Leta the Priest', rather than 'wife of a priest', as it is according to androcentric historiography (Otranto 1982).

Women were the central and leading figures in the early Christian movement. Yet the patriarchal church has gradually obscured and obliterated the existence of women like Junia, 'outstanding among the Apostles' (Schüssler-Fiorenza 1983: 47). The name of Junia is changed to the male name Junias in the continuing effort to obfuscate the historical proof of women's powerful presence among the apostles of the early church. This evidence, along with the striking example of the women presiding at the eucharist in the Priscilla catacomb painting (who are depicted with beards in a modern reproduction), and that of Leta the Priest, appeared in the BBC Everyman (*sic*) programme 'Women's Ordination: The Hidden Tradition', viewed by two million people a few days before the historic vote for women's ordination in the Anglican synod of November 1992.

Yet another display of androcentrism is the deliberate and calculated editing of the new *Catechism of the Catholic Church* (1994) to eliminate references to women when using generic terms for humankind. Men are made the norm and definition of humanity, the model of the human race. Women are not human beings; to the minds of church officials, they do not count. While men celebrate seven sacraments, women participate in only six, since they are excluded from ordination in the Roman Catholic Church. Hence all women are by birth excluded from full professorships in the departments of theology in German Catholic universities, since the androcentric prerequisite is ordination, open only to men.

Women were also excluded from the voting bodies of the 1994 synod on religious life. A delegation of American nuns traveled to Rome to protest this exclusion of women from a conference deliberating on the lives of religious, of whom women comprise 70 per cent. The androcentric mindset of the Vatican officials continues to erase the contributions of women of the past and to exclude women leaders of the present.

Further reading: MacKinnon 1989.

ANGER
Lucy Tatman

WHAT, AS Christian feminists, are we to do with anger? To remain caught between the Christian pillar of anger-as-sin and the secular pillar of anger-as-madness is an intolerable option, yet for centuries it has been the only option available to women. In this language, on this page anger is but one letter removed from danger. And yes, to write honestly of anger in the context of Christian feminist theology is very, very dangerous, for within the Christian tradition there is much to cause us anger. As women we have received the blame for original sin; we have been described as 'misbegotten males', and we have been named 'the devil's gateway'. Yet we have been told that to release our anger is to release a deadly sin upon the world.

Why were so many of us, especially but not only White, privileged, educated Western

ANGER

women, taught that anger is a sin? That anger must not be expressed? Did not Moses rage at the sight of his people worshipping a golden calf? Did not Jesus rage through the temple, furious that it was defiled? Righteous anger is well and truly part of the Christian tradition, and feminist theologians have begun to claim women's right to this anger, so long reserved for use by men alone. Why is anger theologically and ethically so important? Because, first, it signals that something is wrong. This is important; anger never simply appears at our table, uninvited. Anger always arrives with cause, with reason—not where there is understanding, mutuality, love and justice, but precisely where and when denial, distortion, destruction and negation masquerade as truth. To express this anger is to cry out for the righting of the wrongs, to cry out the absence of justice.

Anger rises with reason, because something is not right. But anger is also a force, a power, that which provides the impetus for action. In her essay 'The Power of Anger in the Work of Love' Beverly Harrison writes, 'where anger rises, there the energy to act is present' (in Harrison 1985: 14). Therefore righteous anger both points to the absence of justice/love and provides the energy to compel us into the struggle toward justice/love. It is only when both of these qualities of anger are taken into account that the beginnings of a foundation for a Christian feminist theo-ethical analysis of anger are created. At the same time the source, the cause of the anger must be named and identified. The force anger provides is a holy strength only when it is directed toward the cause of the anger. Anger thus expressed demands justice; anger unnamed or mis-directed can be just as destructive as the cause of the anger. Anger carries an ethical imperative, and that imperative is to act. The blessing of anger is that it provides the strength to act: however, if an individual or community does not act for justice then that same strength becomes a curse. When a woman chokes back her anger she risks choking herself to death, for the force released by anger will always find a target, any target. It is not anger that is dangerous to Christian feminists, but the denial of anger. From a Christian feminist perspective anger-as-sin is real precisely when anger is denied, ignored, avoided, covered up—which is, of course, exactly what the church has traditionally encouraged women to do in the name of forgiveness, mercy, charity and love.

But the church is not the only institution in which Christian women live. Society at large has had much to say to women about anger, and a feminist theological analysis of anger must take society's message into account. Emotional, irrational, hysterical, crazed, mad. When a woman fills with anger what is seen is not the woman but the madness. How deeply embedded in our hearts and minds is the fear of being labelled mad? Of being discounted, trivialized, hospitalized or burned at the stake by reasonable, rational, calm and controlled guardians of the social order? History tells us these are real fears. When a woman expresses her anger the probable consequences are disastrous for her. This is the truth; the madwoman lives in the attic and in the corner of our minds: a lesson, a warning and a threat all at once. She is not nice, she is not feminine. She is smelly and dirty and cranky and we have been taught to fear and despise her, to fear and despise those parts of ourselves we recognize in her. But is it her we fear or what society has done to her, what society could do to us if we step out of bounds? Paradoxically, it is the strength of our anger that can carry us past the threat of madness directly to the source of our rage, the cause of our fear.

Christian feminist theologians and ethicists have begun to transform the theological understanding of anger from sin to righteous strength by insisting that the cause of our anger is the root issue. Our anger can and must be responsibly directed to change the conditions which gave rise to our anger. This analysis of anger is a challenge not only to injustices within the institutional church but also to secular, social, political, economic, racist, classist and sexist structures and institutions that perpetuate unjust systems, inequitable relations and the domination of a few over many.

The Christian pillar of sin, the secular pillar of madness—neither option is strong enough to contain the rising force of women's righteous strength, our anger. What does it mean for us as Christian feminists to honestly acknowledge the depth and range of our anger, of the causes of our rage? Does it mean creating an entirely new

An A to Z of Feminist Theology

foundation upon which to rebuild the Christian tradition? Does the righteous demand for justice/love on earth as it is in heaven require us to attempt to transform the entire social order, to root out the real insanities which have been used to keep women silent, obedient, passive? These are dangerous questions, the very questions man-made sin and man-made madness would keep us from ever asking. I do not know your answer to them, but I do know that in this language, on this page my answer is but one letter removed from danger.

Further reading: Chesler 1989; Lorde 1984a, 1984b.

APOSTLESHIP
Dorothy Coxon

WOMEN WITHIN the churches are wanting to redefine apostleship because many of them feel that its meaning has become so refined that it has acted as a barrier to women's full participation in church life.

Patriarchal history has presented us with a very esoteric image of apostleship that is dependent upon the assumed importance of the twelve disciples of the Gospels. The term 'apostle' has become synonymous with 'disciple' in our received Christian history and an aura of veneration and saintliness has become attached to the image of the workmen of first-century Galilee. Mary Evans (1983) has researched references to apostles and apart from the twelve only Paul, Barnabas, James, Andronicus and Junia are described as such in the New Testament. The portrayals of the apostles in stained glass windows and works of art vie with the saints in non-worldly piety or suffering stances. While I do not wish to deny the aesthetic value or denigrate the sincerity of motive and workmanship that went into these works of art, their symbolism has helped to set up an aura of separatism around the idea of apostleship.

The assumption that the apostles were all male has survived two thousand years of Christian history and is embedded in our subconscious; part of religious education through the ages has been learning the names of the twelve disciples while the esoteric example of Acts 1.23-26 has been firmly traditionalized by the Roman Catholic Church.

Elisabeth Schüssler Fiorenza has been foremost in questioning the potency of male apostleship in her scholarly book *In Memory of Her* (1983), in which she suggests that female apostles and disciples were as visible and active as their male counterparts in the formative time of Christianity; E. Moltmann-Wendel in *The Women around Jesus* (1982) also makes claims for the prominence of women in the Jesus group. *The Wild Girl* (1984) by Michèle Roberts is a fictitious account of how things might have been and it is the spirit of this book which epitomizes the present-day battle of women wanting to claim equal apostleship with men. They are wanting to act in the spirit of early Christianity and break down barriers of gender, age, nationality and status; Christ's insistence on the equal importance of each individual in the eyes of God is their justification for this 'creative dissonance' (to quote Ann Loades [1993: 20]) and subversion of the present situation, in which some clergy still insist on the validity of the maleness of Christ and his disciples for theological significance in present-day ministry. The fictitious Mary Magdalene of *The Wild Girl* says:

> Each of us is a disciple. Each of us is therefore an authority and each of us knows God within, as the Lord taught us. Each of us can receive revelation. None of us has power over the others to decide what is the truth.

This is fiction but it carries the seeds of the kind of affirmation of apostleship that many contemporary feminists wish to make. We are indebted to the scholarship of Schüssler Fiorenza, particularly her chapter on the 'Patriarchal Household of God and Ekklesia of Women' (1983: 285-334), in which she traces the erosion of both the prophetic strain of apostleship and women's leadership to marginal positions within the churches. She claims that the second century saw a shift in values from a Christian community based on spiritual giftedness to one based on age and gender qualifications—'the societal status of the patriarchal household' (p. 289).

The strong evidence for women prophets as 'the transmitters of the apostolic tradition' (p. 300) is what many women within the church wish to reclaim; the later claims that only the official hierarchy could communicate God's message are what they want to refute. Those who were last at the cross and first at the tomb are the inspiration for this renewal of the importance of female apostleship or indeed any apostleship that is not defined by ecclesial authority. Although 'patriarchal repression' (p. 334) won there is still light shining in the darkness and women have not given up their struggle to strip the concept of apostleship of its precocity.

The non-conformist churches would make a claim for precisely this kind of widening of the office of authority so that the 'priesthood of all believers' becomes reality. The fact that so many women within the churches of all denominations continue to feel marginalized suggests that the change of focus that feminist theologians are attempting is necessary and valid. It is much easier to be exclusive—to make rules, set up parameters, lay down definitions and so on—than to attempt an inclusive programme. Feminist theologians are not saying that 'anything goes', rather that divine revelation cannot be confined to ecclesial office or bound by gender, and they are claiming a justification from foundational Christianity. The motif that feminists want to retain is the badge of liberating ministry; the 'boys' club' of ecclesial apostolic privilege is what has been challenged. Focus on evidence of female apostolic witness stemming from the 'apostola de apostolarum' (Schüssler Fiorenza) is encouraging; the discovery of roots of sustained 'mustard seed' type growth provides assurance. However, the substitution of a 'girls only' outlook would be to deny the vision of apostleship as a derestricted office of liberating ministry open to those who so wish to spend their God(dess)-given talents. This vision looks back to the good old prophetic days and forward to a future enhanced by the 'Memory of Her'.

ASIAN WOMEN'S HERMENEUTICAL PRINCIPLE
Mary John Mananzan

THE EFFORT to formulate an Asian women's hermeneutical principle is a concrete resolution of the Women's Commission of the Ecumenical Association of Third World Theologians (EATWOT). This effort is motivated by the need to deconstruct the mainstream theologies which are predominantly Western and patriarchal. It aims at defining a perspective as well as a methodology in reading reality and interpreting the Scriptures so as to construct a theology that would contribute to the development of the full humanity of Asian women. This is an ongoing process among feminist theologians of Asia. The following covers the main factors being considered in the formulation of this new hermeneutic, and shows the distinctiveness of Asian feminist theology in relation not only to mainstream theology but also to liberation theology, First World feminist theology and other Third World feminist theologies.

The Situation of Asian Women

The sociopolitical economic reality of Asia is that of continuing injustice and poverty in spite of the emergence of newly industrialized countries and economic tigers. Asian women continue to be subordinated in the home, exploited in the workplace, and oppressed by social discrimination. They are victimized by varied forms of women-trafficking, violence, and particularly dowry debts, wife-burning, female infanticide, prostitution, mail-order brides and so on. However, Asian women have become conscious of the situation and are struggling for their rights. This struggle is the starting point in Asian feminist theologizing.

The Plurality of Cultures and Religions

The Asian feminist hermeneutical principle has to take into account the presence of the great religions of Asia that have influenced Asian culture and have therefore served as important socializing factors for women's consciousness. These are Hinduism, Buddhism and Islam. Although not a religion, Confucianism as an ethical principle is likewise a factor in the socialization of Asian women. Although these religious and ethical principles may have their liberating factors, by and large they have contributed to the subordination and oppression of Asian women. Female infanticide and dowry debts in India are consequences of this. The cult of virginity has led to female genital mutilation and the overprotection of girls, contributing to their confinement in the home. The idea that woman is only valuable in her service to man is the cornerstone of domestic life. Religions have inculcated in women a victim mentality, predisposing them to be victims of violence at home, at work and in society. The notion that women are temptresses and objects of pleasure for men explains the lucrativeness of trafficking Asian women. In some countries, the arrival of Christianity in the context of colonization is an added oppressive factor because it has taken away the egalitarian or privileged status which women enjoyed in their indigenous religions. Thus Asian feminist theological methodology prescribes a critique of culture and religion to demythologize the oppressive factors and to discover whatever liberating elements are present.

Reintegration of Scriptures

In addition to the general and pervasive influence of religions whose values become a significant part of Asian culture, there is the special importance of the Scriptures—the Bible, the Koran, the Veda. These Scriptures are accorded normative status, and it is according to them that believers measure and justify their actions, by them that believers are motivated. Many quotations from the Scriptures are used by priests, Imams, and other religious teachers or authorities to perpetuate the subordination and subservience of women, especially in the context of marriage and family. It is of importance that these Scriptures be reinterpreted according to women's perspectives to enhance their humanity—not to detract from it. Asian feminist theologians do, however, see a limit to this reinterpretation, recognizing that most of the Scriptures emerged from patriarchal societies. It is therefore important that they are not considered as the sole norms for actions and beliefs. Importance is given to women's own oral traditions, myths and legends as inspiration for our spirituality and action.

Liberating Action

Just as the oppressive situation in which Asian women find themselves is condemned by feminist theologians as sinful, emancipatory and liberating actions by women for their empowerment are considered a blessing. Feminist theology is seen not as an academic theology but as an emancipatory endeavour leading to liberative action. Asian feminist theologians consider involvement in women's struggle a prerequisite for theologizing as a feminist. If one is not involved in the struggle, one will merely be reflecting on experience as a spectator and not as a participant. It is important that one does not only write liberating words, but is involved in liberating action.

Collective Theologizing

Asian feminist theologians strive to reflect collectively on theological issues. This is not only to ensure that varied points of view be considered, but is an attempt to move away from the competitive individualism of male career theologians. From these theological discussions composite papers are written. This does not prevent individual feminist theologians from writing their own books or articles, but there is a conscious effort at cooperative endeavours.

Further reading: Aguilar 1988; EATWOT 1991; Fabella 1990; Ruether (ed.) 1985.

ATONEMENT
Lucy Tatman

TRADITIONAL THEORIES of the atonement take as their starting point the notion that the suffering, death and resurrection of Jesus Christ were necessary. His death and resurrection functioned to reunite humanity with God, to bring an end to a state of separation or estrangement that had developed between humanity and God as a result either of the power of evil or of the sins of humanity. The idea of atonement is central to the Christian faith; however, it has been understood in a number of different ways throughout the history of the church. Recent work by feminist theologians, ethicists and pastoral counsellors has brought to light the often devastating implications of traditional theories of atonement.

The oldest theory of atonement is known as 'Christus Victor', and means exactly what it sounds like. Christ was victorious over the power of evil. When he died he descended into hell and confronted evil on evil's home territory.

ATONEMENT

For three days he fought against evil (Satan) on behalf of humanity, and on the third day he defeated Satan. His resurrection from the dead proved he was victorious. Christ had to do this because God knew that humanity alone could not conquer the power of evil. In other words, only God could reconcile humanity with God. It is important to point out that the problem to be dealt with in this theory is not so much that humanity is inherently sinful as it is that evil is inherently powerful. Unfortunately, the message this interpretation conveys is that humanity must patiently endure suffering, abuse, trials and tribulations while waiting for God's saving actions. This theory, in effect, denies humanity any response-ability; at best Christians must trust that after death everything will be all right.

The satisfaction theory of the atonement is similar to the Christus Victor theory in that it, too, denies human ability to bridge the gap between God and humanity. In this theory, however, it is not the power of evil but the weight of human sin that drags humanity down and away from God. According to Anselm humanity had sinned against God and therefore had to be punished. Human sins had to be paid for because God's sense of justice would not allow this debt to go unpaid. However, humanity alone could never provide a satisfactory repayment to God. So God, acting out of his 'mercy', sent his son to be punished on behalf of the sinful. Joanne Carlson Brown and Rebecca Parker soundly critique this theory as presenting God as a tyrant-on-high, a father who did not hesitate to use and abuse his only son rather than work out an alternative plan for reconciliation. Additionally, a dreadful consequence of this interpretation is that humans, particularly women and oppressed peoples, are encouraged to suffer as Jesus suffered, indeed, to try to save others through personal suffering (Brown and Parker 1989).

The last of the major interpretations of the atonement is the moral influence theory. In this theory Jesus' death happened not to defeat evil once and for all or to pay for human sins but to convince humanity of God's love, to influence humanity to be open to God's love and mercy. The almost unendurable knowledge that God was willing to allow God's son to be an innocent victim should suffice to make people repent of their evil ways and turn to God. Unfortunately, in this theory the burden is on the victims to convince the oppressors that what they are doing is morally wrong. On the positive side, this is the first theory to suggest that people can change their ways, can be response-able.

In all three of these interpretations of the atonement God the Son's suffering and death were ordained by God the Father as the atoning path to the reconciliation, redemption and salvation of humanity. The two implicit assumptions in all of these theories are (1) that suffering and death were necessary as either the direct route to God or the revelation of God's love, and (2) that humans were utterly estranged from God. From a feminist perspective the practical consequences of these theories are exceedingly problematic in that Christians have been and still are likewise called either to suffer and wait for God to act, to suffer like God for others, or to suffer in the hope that others might change their behaviour.

But was humanity ever totally apart from God? What if humanity was never originally sinful, never totally overcome by the power of evil? Was God truly incapable of thinking of an alternative to the suffering and death of God's own son? Are suffering and death really a form of love, or are they sometimes the unavoidable consequences of love? What happens to people, especially women, when they are told again and again to suffer patiently, to be like Jesus and suffer, for others? What happens to a person or community when they are told not to fight against injustice but to give their life in the hope that someone else will be persuaded to 'do the right thing'?

These questions are directed at the very centre of the Christian tradition; they challenge and threaten the theological assumptions that hold the cross and all it represents as the sine qua non of the Christian faith. There is no single common feminist interpretation of the atonement; responses range from noting that Jesus died for women as well as men to Joanne Carlson Brown and Rebecca Parker's statement that 'Christian theology with atonement at the center… encourages martyrdom and victimization' (Brown and Parker 1989: 3). In their thorough critique of classical and modern theories of the atonement they reach the conclusion that 'the predominant image or theology of the culture is of "divine child abuse"—God the Father demanding and carrying out the suffering and death of his own son' (Brown and Parker 1989: 26) Brown and Parker are not alone in this critique, for Rita Nakashima Brock also writes of 'cosmic child abuse' in relation to the atonement. She notes that 'the ghost of the punitive father lurks in the corners [of traditional atonement theories]' (Brock 1988: 56).

Theologically, the Father God described by Brown, Parker and Brock is a transcendent deity, one utterly above and 'other than' creation, including humanity. From a feminist perspective therefore, one way of transforming the meaning of atonement is to bring it down to earth, to explore what the immanent and continual presence of God on earth might mean in regard to the notion of 'at-one-ment' (see Heyward 1982 and Brock 1988). One practical consequence of this theological shift is that instead of a 'once and for all' action performed by a faraway God atonement necessarily becomes a theory concerning what it means to live in a faithful community as one person among many, one community among many; even, from an ecological perspective, one species among many (see McFague 1993).

Experiences of brokenness, alienation, separation, suffering and death are human experiences; they did not disappear with the death and resurrection (however it is interpreted) of Jesus Christ. Creating an understanding of atonement that does not posit a need for the suffering or death of anyone but that does respond to the daily reality of earthly suffering, death and ordinary brokenness may well be one of the greatest challenges facing feminist theology today. It is a complex task, involving the weaving together of new understandings of community, sin, suffering, crucifixion, theodicy, redemption, revelation and salvation. It is probable that no one will agree entirely with any one theologian's revision of at-one-ment; therefore it is vital that this task be shared and thereby enriched by the contributions of many women, none ever claiming to speak for all.

Further reading: Brown and Bohn (eds.); Heyward 1989; *Daughters of Sarah* **1992.**

AUTHORITY
Julie Clague

THE WORD *authority* is used in a variety of contexts. Two distinct but related meanings are as follows:

1. *Being in authority*. This term is used to describe the power of an office held by a person or group of persons, established by law or by right, to ensure the smooth running of a society or institution. The duty of such an officer is to manage or govern according to an established set of rules or principles which promote the well-being of those who are subject to the authority. A system of authority is one means of regulating and ordering the network of interactions between citizens living in complex societies structured according to a series of institutions, customs and codes of behaviour. In this context, authority is understood as a requirement for peaceful coexistence.

2. *Being an authority*. Complex societies also need individual authorities—a series of experts with specialized knowledge or abilities—in addition to those who govern. Hence, a teacher, by virtue of her expertise, may be considered an authority by her students. The distinction between being in authority and being an authority is clouded to the extent that it is also common for those who are authorities on particular aspects of human living to also be in positions of authority. As a result, the teacher may require certain sorts of behaviour from her students.

Both meanings of authority evoke an understanding of communal living based not only on a network of relationships, but on a series of hierarchies, whereby differences in status or inequalities between persons are institutionalized, and power is exercised for the common good.

The traditional Christian understanding of authority is also reliant on a hierarchical conception of reality. God, the author of all, is the supreme authority. The Christian church claims authority on the basis of truths revealed by God. All earthly authority is conferred by God (cf. Rom. 13.1). This gives humans authority over nature, monarchs authority over their subjects, parents authority over their children and so on.

Jesus claimed that all authority on heaven and

AUTHORITY

earth had been given to him (Mt. 28.18). His authority is central to any understanding of his ministry, but his was a ministry of service (Lk. 22.24-27; Jn 13.1-17). The early church therefore viewed authority as service to others involving a variety of gifts (1 Cor. 12.4-31; Eph. 4.11; Rom. 12.6-8).

However, the model of authority which evolved within the powerful institutional church seldom resembled the New Testamament authority-as-service model. Rather, a hierarchical structure, linked to male leadership in the form of priesthood, emerged. During the Middle Ages, with the development of canon law, authority became increasingly juridical. The Reformation, in part, reacted against excessive papal authority and questioned ecclesiastical authority, preferring instead the authority of Scripture. The Counter-Reformation set in motion by the Council of Trent paved the way for further centralization of authority, which culminated in the definition of papal infallibility at the First Vatican Council in 1870.

The feminist critique of authority forms part of, and cannot be isolated from, the critique of all that falls under the broad term *patriarchy*. Most attention has been focused on the misuse of authority within patriarchy, as opposed to a rejection of authority in itself. Nevertheless, a question still remains: the extent to which hierarchical structures of authority also presuppose and perpetuate relationships of inequality and subordination—which feminism seeks to eradicate. Feminists favour alternative models of relating based on mutual respect. However, whether hierarchies can ever be fully eradicated is doubtful. Most feminists are therefore content to work towards eliminating the misuse of positions of hierarchical authority.

It has been men who, on the whole, have held positions of authority, and have been described as authorities and have been said to speak with authority. Women, on the whole, have been ruled and have obeyed, have been denied their own voice, and have been denied the opportunity to become authorities in their own right.

The opportunities for a woman to become an authority on a particular area of human living have been severely circumscribed in most societies, often restricted to the private sphere of the home as contrasted with male participation in the public sphere. This division of labour has justified an education differential which has further inhibited both female expertise and leadership. Where women have entered traditionally male spheres of authority their contribution has often been overlooked. In addition to the obvious discrimination which women's absence from authority entails, there is also the possibility that this has resulted in the presentation of a distorted world-view.

In the context of Christianity, the resistance to women as leaders and priests is well documented. Christ has been the role model *par excellence* of Christian leadership; thus priests are described as acting *in persona Christi*. In some Christian denominations, this has led to a distorted understanding of the qualities necessary for authoritative leadership, and the maleness of the priest has been inextricably identified with the office. It is still the case that in some denominations, such as the Roman Catholic Church, women take no part in ecclesiastical authority. In addition, women have been denied the role of authority by their exclusion from the enterprise of theology.

While feminist theologians are united in condemning this state of affairs, some believe women should eschew male roles and masculinist structures. Furthermore, they argue, a church which ignores the gifts of women brings itself into disrepute and loses its *de facto* authority. In other words, the authority of the institutional church is so undermined by the unjust treatment of women that the whole claim to truth on which the religion is based is thereby called into question. This, in part, explains the exodus from the Christian church by those who now identify as post-Christian feminists.

Feminist theologians continue to highlight weaknesses in and limitations of the texts of Scripture and tradition. Increased knowledge of the human element of their composition is both revising Christian understanding of these sources of theological reflection, and relativizing the claim to their authority in the sense of being God-given.

The growth of personal autonomy and a readiness to question the old order may indicate that the authoritative status of (male) political, legal, philosophical and religious systems is weakening. Whether, and to what extent, this involves a wider crisis of authority cannot be discussed here; though it is well to remember the Old Testament message: those entrusted with authority—including religious leaders—who deify themselves and abuse power ultimately meet with destruction.

Further reading: Elizondo and Greinacher 1980; McBrien 1994; Radcliffe Richards 1980.

AUTONOMY
Julie Clague

THE TERM 'autonomy' is often used in contradistinction to 'heteronomy'. However, its importance and scope as a concept in philosophy cannot adequately be captured by its literal meaning or common usage.

Feminist discussion of autonomy is ambivalent. To the extent that the term is used in contrast to heteronomy, feminists favour autonomy. Yet the over-emphasis on autonomy in (patriarchal) capitalist democracies has tended to distort its meaning, hence the feminist use of the term 'relationality'.

Autonomy places emphasis on the person as an individual subject. The autonomous individual is free to make choices and act according to the dictates of an informed conscience, rather than rely on or show obedience to the decisions of others. In this sense feminists (particularly liberal feminists) support the notion of autonomy, though it is realized that many have been or are still denied this freedom.

The right to autonomy enjoyed today stems from the liberal humanism which emerged some three hundred years ago during the Enlightenment period: man has rights and freedoms irrespective of his place in society. Man—for the autonomous subject of Enlightenment philosophy was undoubtedly male—was proclaimed a rational being capable of discovering the truth about the world and even God. Human progress and the perfection of society were thought to be realizable goals.

One might well be sceptical of such utopian vision given the blindness of the Enlightenment fathers to issues such as gender. However, feminists are more concerned that the autonomous (male) subject has come to connote the separateness, individualism and self-interest which feminism rejects. Such an understanding of autonomy has been subject to critical scrutiny not only from feminists but also from communitarians and the movement broadly referred to as postmodernism.

Excessive claims to autonomy lose sight of human connectedness and distort understanding of responsibilities and duties to others and to the planet. The assertion of self-identity over against others becomes central rather than the experience of a life lived in relation. A key feminist insight is the conviction that the whole of human existence is grounded in terms of relationality—to other people, to ideas, to value-systems and so on. The research of Carol Gilligan (1982) suggests that female self-identity is conceived and articulated in terms which do not deny but rather incorporate the significant others who have helped to form and given a sense of identity to the woman.

The Enlightenment project was based on what now seems a preposterous assumption: namely that the way to understand the world was to become detached from all that was in it to become the sort of external, impartial, disembodied observer that God was thought to be. It was assumed that empirical data could be collected from the sciences, history, philosophy or any human pursuit and truth discovered on the basis of reason alone. Moreover, it was thought that this was possible without reference to one's historical, cultural or social position. This is autonomy in the extreme, the desire to abstract oneself into a vacuum of space-time with nothing except one's own educated mind with which to judge and evaluate.

We have learnt and feminists affirm that there is no unique vantage point from which to observe the world-as-it-is 'unhindered' by our own subjectivity. This rests on the rejection of two assumptions of the Enlightenment: that universal objective truth exists 'out there' to be discovered, and that we can set aside our particularity. The quest for objectivity has indeed become the Holy Grail of philosophy.

Rather than a shackle from which to break free, it is precisely one's particularity and subjectivity which gives a person the right to speak and makes what one has to say worth listening to. Realization of this is the birth of true autonomy.

The historical experience of patriarchy has prevented women from becoming autonomous agents in their own right. For feminists autonomy means liberation from patriarchy and the resultant empowerment experienced by those who take control of their lives in their own particularity and subjectivity.

In order to be autonomous the Enlightenment male tried to become a detached god. The postmodern female must resist this, remaining firm in her conviction that true autonomy lies in her own subjective view of being a person in particular relationships. The autonomous decision will not and cannot be made without giving due consideration to the outlook of the other. But the global picture cannot be seen with the eyes of a god. The view that is not hers is a view from elsewhere, and the view from elsewhere can only be seen through the eyes of the other.

Further reading: Arendt 1961; Benhabib 1992; Braidotti 1991.

BEGUINES
Fiona Bowie

Origins

THE BEGUINES could be described as the first European women's movement, growing out of the atmosphere of intense lay piety which swept parts of northwest Europe, particularly Germany and the Low Countries, in the second half of the twelfth century. This was a time of urban growth, accompanied by a decline in the marriageable male population as a result of crusades, local wars, clerical celibacy and recruitment to monastic orders, which, while attracting men, attempted to limit the number of women seeking affiliation. Denied more formal religious status, and unable or unwilling to marry, women increasingly sought to live as recluses in their own homes. From the end of the 1170s onwards we find the term 'beguine' applied to some of these recluses, and increasingly attributed to many thousands of women adopting rather different life styles, living both singly and in community. The term 'beguine' comes from the Old French, *li beges*, or 'one dressed in grey', probably referring to the simple, undyed cloth they wore.

There is a *temptation* on the part of many commentators to try to describe the beguines as an order, with a founder, a Rule and set way of life. While they were genuinely a new phenomenon in the life of the church, the beguines should be seen, rather, as a loose movement, an impulse, springing up spontaneously in many different areas in places as far afield as Austria and Poland, Italy, Sweden and England. Whether living singly, in small groups, or in large, well-organized communities, what the beguines had in common was the desire to lead a life of prayer, service and simplicity, free of male control either in the form of a priest or a husband. They took vows of chastity and obedience (to a beguine mistress as well as to the ecclesiastical authorities), but not of poverty, for the duration of their time as a beguine. These vows were temporary, and each woman was free to leave and resume secular life if she wished to do so. There was no single rule of life, each community drawing up regulations which best fitted its own needs and aspirations. Chaplains were appointed, or churches attended, where clergy sympathetic to their cause could be found (often from among the Dominican and Franciscan friars).

Developments

The beguine movement grew and flourished in the thirteenth century, and drew widespread support and approval from contemporary commentators, such as the English monk Matthew Paris, who wrote of them in 1243.

The greatest development of the beguine movement took place in Belgium and in the Netherlands. In most of the larger towns one or more beguine settlements grew up, known as beguinages (in Dutch, *begijnhoven*), which sometimes achieved the status of separate parishes. These were walled, but not cloistered, villages on the outskirts of the town, usually with access to running water because beguines made their living in the cloth trade. Beguines lived in their own houses, either in twos or threes, or sometimes in larger groups. Many took in children for schooling, some as boarders and others coming in daily. The beguinage also housed female relatives, widows and other sick or destitute women. The most important institutions of the beguinage were the church, which provided a focal point for the community, the infirmary, and the Table of the Holy Spirit, which cared for poor beguines. Beguines who were dependent upon one or other of these charitable institutions would leave their property to them when they died.

Although often well born, beguines were all expected to earn their living and to live simply. They engaged in spinning, bleaching, weaving, dressmaking, embroidery and other activities connected to the cloth trade. They worked in education and in the care of the sick, as housekeepers to clergy and wealthy families, took in laundry for students, and took part in the many industries open to urban women before the rise of trade guilds sought to restrict their economic opportunities.

Spirituality

However attractive, an active but discreet life of service in the company of other women was not the substance of the beguine vocation, merely its outward appearance. It was the religious fervour of the age which acted as the initial impulse for

BEGUINES

this new way of life, and we can see from the mystical writings of thirteenth-century beguines that inner union with God was the goal to which they aspired. Medieval beguine spirituality can be described as 'bridal mysticism', in which the soul comes to Christ, or God, as a bride to her spouse. An intense devotion to the Eucharist was characteristic of the beguines, and the feast of Corpus Christi, formally proclaimed in 1264, was instituted at the initiation of Juliana of Liège, an Augustinian nun with beguine connections.

Since women were denied much formal authority—they could not be ordained, preach or become mendicants—identification with Christ's sufferings offered a popular alternative form of religious expression. Several beguines, including Mary of Oignies, were known to be stigmatics.

Beguines had visions of themselves cradling or breastfeeding the infant Jesus and of mystical union, as well as identifying with his suffering on the cross. In a few cases women felt impelled to write down their spiritual journey as a guide to others, and the works of some of these women, such as Mechthild of Magdeburg, Hadewijch of Brabant and Margarete Porete, written in the vernacular, were widely circulated.

Persecution

Despite popular acclaim, beguines were also viewed with suspicion. As early as 1236 a beguine named Aleydis was executed on a charge of heresy. There were further arrests in 1290, and in 1310 Margarete Porete was burned in Paris on a charge of heretical mysticism for allegedly claiming that a liberated soul in union with God no longer need abide by the laws of the church or the moral law, a charge not substantiated by the writings themselves but characteristic of a supposed sect known as the Free Spirit, which probably never existed (as an organized movement) other than in the minds and handbooks of the Inquisitors.

Church councils at Lyons in 1274 and at Mainz in 1310 expressed a distrust of fringe communities, but the biggest blow followed the Council of Vienne (1311–12), which condemned the beguines on the following grounds:

We have been told that certain women commonly called Beguines, afflicted by a kind of madness, discuss the Holy Trinity and the divine essence, and express opinions on matters of faith and sacraments contrary to the catholic faith, deceiving many simple people. Since these women promise no obedience to anyone and do not renounce their property or profess an approved Rule, they are certainly not 'religious', although they wear a habit and are associated with such religious orders as they find congenial...We have therefore decided and decreed with the approval of the Council that their way of life is to be permanently forbidden and altogether excluded from the Church of God (Southern 1970: 330).

From various clerical commentators it becomes clear that it was less the beguines' mystical theology than their extra-regular status which really concerned the church. It was considered that all beguines should be married, or enclosed in an established order. We may see this as the familiar phenomenon of 'backlash'. Male authority was challenged by these women who were neither wives and mothers nor cloistered nuns. Despite their much admired humility and piety, beguines were accused of libertarian behaviour, and behind the image of female sanctity, the male mind might well have perceived a more threatening and less submissive female power, that of the witch.

Widespread clerical persecution followed the ruling of the Council of Vienne, and many beguines living outside beguinages were absorbed into existing orders as Franciscan and Dominican Tertiaries or, where local support was not forthcoming, had their property confiscated and were forced into marriage. The beguinages and their powerful patrons afforded some protection in the Low Countries, but in other parts of Europe beguine 'convents' became, by the fifteenth century, little more than charitable institutions, to be wiped out altogether by the Protestant Reformation. Beguinages in Belgium and Holland saw a second period of growth following the Counter-Reformation in the seventeenth century, only to decline once more with the suppression and persecution which followed the French Revolution.

Further reading: Baker 1978; Bowie 1989; Bynum 1982; Hart 1980; Porete 1981.

An A to Z of Feminist Theology

THE BIBLE AS A RESOURCE FOR WOMEN
Jenny Dines

HOW IS a collection of ancient texts, considered normative for both belief and practice from the early days of Christianity, yet recognized for the last hundred years as being both androcentric and patriarchal, to be used by women today? On one level, there is no problem: scholars of ancient history or Western culture can study the Christian Bible from a feminist standpoint as they would study any other text; this is also true of academic feminist teaching. In fact, for charting the history of women in the Judaeo-Christian world, and for understanding the causes of the contemporary situation of women, both positive and negative, the Bible is an extremely important source.

Its use becomes problematic when it forms part of an individual's belief system, and holds authoritative status as 'revelation' or 'Word of God'. Then a tension, often of crisis proportions, exists between the claims of Scripture to be 'true' and the realization that the texts abound in instances where women (whether literally or symbolically) are ignored, oppressed or vilified. The problem is particularly acute for women within the Reformed traditions, where the Bible's authority is crucial, but Roman Catholic women, for whom Scripture and tradition together are normative, find the struggle no less real. The wider Roman Catholic canon compounds the problem, with, for instance, the heroic violence of Judith and the misogyny of Ben Sira also offered as normative; even the apparent bonus of personified Wisdom (in the Wisdom of Solomon) shows signs of patriarchal take-over (see Long 1992). Jewish feminists also are struggling to come to terms with biblical tradition (see Plaskow 1990).

Reactions to the problem vary considerably. Some have responded by abandoning the Bible as the basis for a credible belief system. Mary Daly rejects a patriarchal Bible, but uses biblical material, brilliantly helping women to free themselves from its chains by zany verbal clowning, throwing patriarchal texts back into the patriarchal camp with deadly aim (Daly 1988).

Strategies

For those who wish to retain some kind of biblical commitment, or at least dialogue, there are various options, resulting in three main (and not always mutually exclusive) approaches.

The first, a 'remnant' strategy, salvages and re-emphasizes positive elements in texts about women, often hitherto overlooked. Passages oppressive to women are displaced from centre stage in favour of other texts capable of being liberative; so Gen. 1.27 is taken as the key text rather than Gen. 2.23; and Gal. 3.28 rather than 1 Cor. 11.2-16. This has the advantage of revealing a rich variety of positive material, but the disadvantage of focusing on only some texts, and of creating a 'canon within the canon' where the bogey of 'by what authority?' promptly raises its head; the broader question is how to prioritize texts. Sometimes there is an apologetic concern to minimize sexist elements and to find acceptable explanations of apparently harmful texts; this is often the approach of women who accept biblical authority or who want to go on using Scripture for devotional or pastoral reasons.

The second approach looks for some unifying theological perspective from which to organize and prioritize the material. Rosemary Radford Ruether has found this in the prophetic message of liberation, which provides criteria for showing up women's oppression, wherever this occurs (Ruether 1983). This approach has been influential; so, in a different way, has Phyllis Trible's guiding 'thread' of the language of sexuality, which provides a paradigm for divine–human relationships not necessarily marred by patriarchy (Trible 1978). This approach has the advantage of widening the scope to allow for more inclusive treatment than is possible if only texts dealing explicitly with women are discussed, but the disadvantage of ignoring elements which do not fit into the chosen paradigms, such as patriarchal bias within the prophetic texts themselves, or areas where sexual imagery is absent. It also presupposes more theological unity to the Bible than such a disparate collection of texts can sustain, though it is true that motifs and images recur in many texts and many guises.

The third strategy is that of reconstruction, based on the assumption that the androcentric

THE BIBLE AS A RESOURCE FOR WOMEN

bias of the text (see for example Exod. 19.15; Ps. 128; Mt. 5.27) has omitted or distorted the real situation of historical women. This can be rediscovered by reading carefully between the lines, by using historical-critical and sociological methods of interpretation, and by calling on the evidence of extrabiblical texts, archaeology and so on. The most influential exponent of this approach is Elisabeth Schüssler Fiorenza (1983). Carol Meyers has attempted to do something similar for women in the Hebrew Scriptures (see Meyers 1988). This has the advantage of utilizing and making sense of all the biblical material, including the objectionable parts, without accepting their premises; and, although highly critical, it upholds the Bible as a source of positive and inspirational material. Its disadvantage is that it sometimes claims a more utopian situation for women than either exegesis or sociological reconstruction can convincingly sustain. But the attempts do highlight the ideals for which women continue to struggle, a necessary hope for the future even if they cannot be proved to have existed in a paradigmatic past.

Methodologies

A further distinction needs to be made as to exegetical methods, since these may cut across the strategies outlined above. They fall into two main categories.

Historical

In fact, most of the scholars mentioned so far work primarily with conventional historical-critical methods, though often with unconventional results. These include tradition criticism, form criticism and redaction criticism and are used, together with tools borrowed from history, archaeology, anthropology, sociology and so on, in an attempt to understand the text in its original setting, to discover its authorship, aim and stages of development, as the first steps to making sense of the text now (controversially, exegesis and hermeneutics are often held together). It is certainly essential to do everything possible to discover a text's original circumstances, both as a safeguard against distortion from our own presuppositions, and for its own intrinsic interest. The problem is that this kind of historical exegesis is extremely hard to do, since there are many gaps and uncertainties in our knowledge, quite apart from the impossibility of really getting inside the skin of an ancient text without continuing to wear our own as well.

Literary

With this method, the text itself is the centre of attention. Vocabulary, grammatical structures, narrative techniques and 'voices', word-play and patterning are all seen to give clues as to meaning. The text exists in its own right, and may be studied quite apart from its conjectured historical setting (although this may sometimes be a way of ducking the historical issues). Phyllis Trible was one of the first to use this method (1978, 1984). Another approach, reader-response criticism, sees the 'meaning' of the text less as something imprinted on it by its author (even when the latter remains unknowable) than as something which emerges from the interplay between reader and text, within limits of appropriateness which are not always easy to pin down. Literary approaches also allow for the symbolic nature of much biblical language to be more fully exploited, and represent a means whereby scholars from other disciplines, notably literary studies, can make a contribution to biblical studies.

Hermeneutics

Irrespective of exegetical method, almost all feminist biblical scholars have adopted a 'hermeneutic of suspicion'. That is, instead of subscribing to the fiction of an unbiased, objective reading, they acknowledge a personal agenda that starts from the probability that women in the text will not have been given a fair deal, or will, in any case, be evaluated from a man's point of view only. They start from questions such as 'Why does this woman have no name?', 'Why has this woman, up till now a central character, suddenly disappeared from the story?' and so on. This means confronting an androcentric worldview with a feminist one, and so deconstructing the world of the Bible to show how it performs against feminist criteria of equality, justice and so on. Given the number of attempts still made to 'redeem' and utilize the Bible, such a hermeneutical approach is important, so that options for the Bible are not grounded in false ideas about the text. Lone Fatum urges more thoroughgoing deconstruction, using the hermeneutics of suspi-

An A to Z of Feminist Theology

cion, before the work of reconstructing is undertaken; otherwise texts may be misread, even apparently 'friendly' ones such as Gen. 1.27 and Gal. 3.28, which Fatum thinks are profoundly patriarchal (1989). She warns against the implicit apologetics within even the most radical approaches, the desire to show that there is something usable lying behind the androcentric text, so as to remain within the tradition.

This raises again the question of authority, which is the nub of the problem. For feminists who start with a conviction of the Bible's claim on them, the solution must come from within biblical Christianity itself: some internal criterion or credibility has to be found according to which the Bible may be accepted and sense made of it. Many writers have struggled to reconcile their deeply held feminism with their biblical commitment; Mary Ann Tolbert (1990) has done this from a Protestant perspective and Sandra M. Schneiders (1991) from a Roman Catholic one, to name only two of many.

Others, while retaining an allegiance to Christianity, and an interest in the Bible as part of the inescapable heritage, acknowledging that much of the vigour of the Christian feminist movement has sprung from it, sit more lightly to the idea of a normative, exclusive canon. New possibilities for handling biblical texts open up when the centre of gravity shifts. Criteria for judgment and action can be grounded in praxis, resulting in autonomous convictions, such as the need for theology to be cosmos-centred rather than humanity-centred; or the innate equality of women and men; or the interrelatedness of all life-forms; or the belief that God is part of the unfolding life of the cosmos and cannot adequately be described in the formulas of classical theology. Some at least of these convictions are shared with people of other faiths, or who are not conventional 'believers', in dialogue and action in which the Bible may, where appropriate, act as friend and ally, but no longer as puppet-master pulling the strings. Among those who have opted for this more 'secular' approach, Sallie McFague takes seriously a point of departure in the modern 'ecological, nuclear age' for her critique of theology based on biblical worldviews and imagery (1987). Similarly, Anne Primavesi works 'backwards' as she rereads Genesis 1–3 in the light of an ecological paradigm, in contrast to the usual method of making Scripture the starting point (1991). This is also the approach of liberation theology, which starts from present experience, analyses it, and reads Scripture in its light.

Resources

If the Bible is to remain a source for women, in whatever way, what resources will help to make its use liberating rather than enslaving? There continues to be so much good material produced by feminist writers that it is difficult, even invidious, to pick out particular names. What follows is the merest sample.

Particularly helpful for initial study is *The Women's Bible Commentary* (Newsom and Ringe [eds.] 1992) and, for more detailed treatment, the Feminist Companion to the Bible series edited by Athalya Brenner (Sheffield Academic Press). Important new ideas on biblical subjects are often aired in the *Journal of Feminist Studies in Religion*, in *Semeia*, in the *Journal for the Study of the Old Testament* and the *Journal for the Study of the New Testament*. Among more recent publications, special note should be taken of *Searching the Scriptures. I. A Feminist Introduction* (Schüssler Fiorenza [ed.] 1994). This is a large collection of essays to mark the centenary of *The Woman's Bible*, covering many aspects and including contributions from black as well as white feminists, and writers from Latin America and Africa as well as North America and Europe.

The way in which the Bible is used will continue to depend on the individual's wider theological beliefs and commitments. The most challenging and creative work at the moment is perhaps coming from writers exploring the implications of a feminist critique of all Christian theology, not just the Bible, starting from their experience as women facing the crises, challenges and hopes of today's world, and daring to hold the mirror of true justice, equality and love to the biblical texts which, whether we like it or not, have helped to fashion who we are.

For further: also Cady Stanton 1985 [1898]; Collins (ed.) 1985; Russell (ed.) 1985.

BIBLICAL EXEGESIS

BIBLICAL EXEGESIS
Judith McKinlay

TRADITIONALLY BIBLICAL exegesis has been understood quite literally as the task of drawing meaning out of a text, with the basic exegetical tools of trade being the questions posed by the reader. Exegesis is thus a dialogue, or a questioning conversation, with the text, a search for as much as can be known, in a quest for meaning that leads the exegete not only to the text itself, but also to its context and relationship with other texts. The questions asked by the exegete may include, for example, those of wording, of syntax, of historical background, of source and genre, and of literary structure. However, the very questions asked may carry in themselves, consciously or unconsciously, certain interests, which, in turn, will dialogue with the interests already coded within the text. Feminist scholarship works with this awareness that neither text nor question is necessarily interest-free, and that such interests may well include those of gender.

It is with this understanding that the feminist exegete goes to work, choosing and asking questions of the text and of its context. A consequence of this growing recognition that both within the text and within the reader's task 'a gender code' may be operating as a significant purveyor of meaning has been that some quite particularly focused questions have been asked and fresh responses elicited. However, this is not to deny the need for the engagement of a whole range of traditional exegetical tools.

The following summary of different critical questions will cite examples drawn from the results of a wide range of recent feminist studies.

One of the first tasks of any exegesis is to examine the text in the language of the earliest manuscripts, and where there are significant differences to weigh these against each other. For instance, later interpretation may have differed significantly from the earliest recorded readings, one of the now classic examples of this being the reading of the Greek form Ἰουνιαν in Rom. 16.7 not as the name of a woman, Junia, but as that of a man, Junias. Likewise, a comparison of different manuscripts may indicate that such gendered interpretations began very early, as in the case of the Western Text's downplaying of the role of Priscilla in Acts 18. Other textual questions may highlight interesting dynamics and prehistories; for example, why is the first verb in Numbers 12 feminine singular? Was this once a Miriam-only text, with Aaron come-lately? If this is so, then other critical questions will immediately follow. Redaction criticism, for example, must ask pointed questions of the interests of the editorial role here. Historical criticism will also note the challenge, and recognize that the very mention of Miriam as challenger allows a glimpse of a woman in a role not often evident in the Scriptures; it will also ask questions of the context of the writer or compiler. Who is it that calls Miriam 'prophet': thirteenth-century Israelites on the bank of the reed sea in Exodus 15, or a much later writer who quite deliberately chose this title with the full Deuteronomic understanding of prophecy? Intertextual questions of literary relationships will have a place here too, bringing the seeming contradiction of Num. 11.25 into the conversation.

Questions of the interpretation of particular words may also uncover gender implications. For example, are the 'wise' women in 2 Samuel 14 and 20 wise by nature or wise by function? Some word-study solutions remain elusive; debates continue over the 'humanness' as against the 'manness' of אדם in Genesis 2, just as they do over whether the meaning of an etymological root, such as רחם, 'womb', remains within the interpretive range of its related term רחמים, 'compassion'. Or the question may be asked when and whether 'wisdom', either in its Hebrew or Greek form, is to be read as a lower case abstract noun or as a personified symbol of the very presence of God.

Tradition criticism follows the use and reuse of traditions and motifs. Tradition-critical studies have, for example, traced the path of the 'wisdom' figure, personified as the gift and presence of God, as it appeared and reappeared in First Testament and intertestamental works, before being adopted in the Second Testament as a christological motif.

Form criticism, which takes account of genres and asks questions of their life settings, connects like passage with like. It is form criticism that

An A to Z of Feminist Theology

BIBLICAL EXEGESIS

brings to attention the notable similarity between Deborah's song in Judges 5 and Miriam's in Exodus 15, and by asking questions of their Israelite life settings allows another glimpse of women fulfilling particular religious functions or roles.

Redaction criticism, which considers the way in which different units or traditions have been seamed together, asks questions of textual compatability and of the activities and perspectives of editors or redactors. Is 1 Cor. 14.33b-36, where women are required to be silent in church, an integral part of Paul's letter? Is it compatible with Paul's views concerning women elsewhere, for example with his statement in Gal. 3.28, or his apparent acceptance of women as colleagues (Rom. 16.1-12; Phil. 4.2-3)? Does the text read smoothly without it? If so, are there any manuscripts where this is missing? The more speculative question might follow as to why an editor might include it here.

Source criticism arose partly from the perceived 'problem' of passages that appeared to be duplicates or even triplicates. Why, for instance, would patriarchs on three separate occasions attempt to pass their wives off as sisters to foreigners (Gen. 12, 20, 26)? Presupposing different source material was one possible solution, and allowed an understanding of different communities transmitting the same story in different versions, in this case preserving the same attitude to women. In each version the story focuses on the patriarch's predicament, brought about by the woman who in turn becomes the foil in the plotted resolution. The results of source criticism also enable a text to be read within a particular theological perspective. Gen. 1.27-28 illustrates the Priestly concern with ordering into categories, where all, including human beings, are created to perpetuate their kind. Such a theology is equally concerned with boundaries and categories of holiness and purity, so that many of the related Levitical laws have considerable implications for women.

Questions of historical context are closely interrelated with many of those above, the close relationship between purity laws and a society's concern with boundaries of identity being a good example. However, some texts offer different readings if placed within different contexts. If the book of Ruth belongs to the post-exilic world of Ezra–Nehemiah, in which mixed marriage was an issue, then Ruth as a Moabite makes a very particular point. If, however, it is an earlier story, that 'foreignness' may lead to quite another interpretation, for a foreign wife choosing to follow the God of her husband and husband's family contrasts strikingly with a foreign wife like Jezebel, who remains loyal to her own gods even in Israel. Deuteronomistic writers were very clear in their position regarding those who did not accept Yahweh as the one god. Or was this a story written by scribes, teasing out the apparent hidden causality of God behind or within human actions, so that it is Ruth 'the character', rather than Ruth 'the foreign character', that is important?

Setting texts from one era and context with those of another may highlight ongoing developments. The injunction of 1 Tim. 2.11-12 that women should learn in submissive silence, and neither teach nor have authority over a man, when taken together with the 'household codes' of certain later writings (Col. 3.18-19; Eph. 5.22-33), would seem to point to a change in attitude to women's roles when compared with those recorded in the book of Acts or Paul's letter to the Romans.

Archaeological findings or suggestions may provide further background material, adding to those of the historical context. For example, there are notable biblical texts (for instance Deut. 7.5; 12.3; 2 Kgs 23.4, 6) that report the breaking down and burning of 'asherah' pillars and vessels, as signs of a syncretistic worship that is to be eradicated, although at the same time it is clear that the worship objects of certain kings of Israel included such a female symbol (see 1 Kgs 16.33; 2 Kgs 21.7). Recent archaeological finds at Kuntillet Ajrud have uncovered inscriptions that refer to 'Yahweh and His Asherah', although whether this is evidence of syncretistic worship or a popular Israelite piety that included worship of a consort depends on interpretation.

Quotations of literary context or canonical setting may also open ways to understanding. The book of Ruth read among the 'Writings' in its Tanakh placing after Proverbs, and especially after the poem of Prov. 31.10-31, may be a dif-

An A to Z of Feminist Theology

ferent reading than one in a context of Judges and the books of Samuel, as in the later Christian canon. Literary settings within a book may also be significant. For example, does the 'woman of worth' poem of Proverbs 31 provide the human face of personified Wisdom hymned in the first nine chapters? And further, if they are put together, do they provide the framework for understanding what comes between, the lens through which the Proverbs collection as a whole is to be read?

While questions posed by literary criticism may highlight the crafting of the work, they may also draw attention to the underlying structural concerns. A reading of the Jael–Sisera encounter in Judges 4 which is alerted to the organizing shame/honour dynamic will have a sharper gender awareness.

The recognition that texts are interest-laden, that they carry certain ideologies, whether those ideologies be political or religious, has led in turn to the recognition that the gaps and silences in the texts also require an exegesis. Why does Sarah have no place in the Akedah of Genesis 22? Why does Dinah's mother have no say in the matters of Genesis 34? Why is the woman who anointed Jesus in Mark 14 not remembered by name? Why is Mary Magdalene not included in the list of apostolic witnesses in 1 Corinthians 15? Why do we know so little of the women with Jesus during his ministry, if, as Lk. 8.1-3 states, they were there at the time 'serving/ministering'?

The final step of any exegesis is to gather together all that has been gleaned from the various critical investigations, and to read the passage with the insights gained, always allowing for the fact that this may not be a definitive reading, and that various possibilities of interpretation may need to be held in tension.

As with so many aspects of biblical study, questions are being asked not only of texts themselves but also of traditional definitions, including the traditional definition of exegesis. The understanding of exegesis that was taken to imply that meaning was potentially or even essentially inside the text, so that the text was a repository, merely awaiting someone to come and draw the meaning out piece by piece, led to a polarized distinction between what was thus drawn out, understood as 'what the text meant', and the result of a further step of interpretation which then produced 'what the text means now'; a distinction which Krister Stendahl notably drew in 1962, and which has brought much debate and discussion in its wake. Recent studies of the process of reading and interpretation have put the 'pulling meaning out of the text' concept in much more doubt, with the growing recognition that meaning arises from a dynamic relationship between the text and the reader, in response to the questions that the reader asks, so that questions and answers are interrelated, with the result that it becomes harder and harder to draw firm lines between exegesis as the first step and interpretation as the later. And while 'eisegesis', or the reading of one's own agenda into the text without warrant, continues to be regarded as unacceptable, we are now more aware that we all approach texts with our own presuppositions and interests, consciously or even unconsciously, so that the line between unwarranted agenda and presupposition is no longer as clear as some would have it. As exegetes we must question the text and question ourselves, in a text–reader dialogue that will continue as long as texts are to be read.

Further reading: Bal 1987; Fee 1983; Fewell 1993; Hayes and Holladay 1987; Schüssler Fiorenza 1984; Trible 1993.

BODILINESS
Elizabeth Stuart

AT THE heart of Christian feminist theology is a rejection of the dualism which has underpinned the Christian tradition for nearly all of its history. Dualism is the belief that human beings consist of two separable natures: body and soul. The body, like all matter, was regarded as fallen, corrupt and prone to sin, endangering the immortal soul which would hopefully one day break free from the constraints of the body and ascend up to the divine who was pure spirit. Therefore, the body, like all nature, had to be tamed and subdued. Women were regarded as being ensnared in their bodiliness to a far greater degree than men and they too had to be tamed and subdued for their own good and the good of the men they might tempt into sin. From its earliest days the feminist movement has been concerned with women reclaiming power over their own bodies. Feminist theology has focused on reclaiming the body, and indeed all matter, as the primary locus for the experience of the divine. The doctrine of the incarnation of God in Jesus of Nazareth, for so long regarded as a unique event, becomes in feminist theology a paradigm for all human experience. The process of doing theology should begin and be constantly grounded in our experience of embodiment. We have to learn to recognize the interconnectedness of all matter and the pain and damage caused when that interconnectedness is denied or ordered in wrong relationship. God is experienced as the erotic power manifest in relationships based upon justice and mutuality which creates a passion for justice in all relationships. Some feminist theologians have developed metaphors of the world as God's body and God as passionate lover of the world. Salvation is the restoration of health to the torn body of the earth, of which our bodies are a part, the restoration of a proper ecological balance or justice. The life of God's body is now at stake because of the ecological crisis: its salvation is in our hands.

The reclamation of our bodies from the abusive hands of the networks of power we name patriarchy necessarily involves the reclamation of our sexuality. In its broadest terms, sexuality is the name we give to our sense of erotic yearning, our desire to connect in embodied right relationship with others—this expresses itself in our desire for friendship and sometimes in our desire for intimate bodily knowing of another. Sexual encounters between people locked in unequal power relations are profoundly disempowering for the person with less power. They are symbolic of wrong relationship. However, making love in the context of mutuality can be a symbol and sacrament of erotic power, a foretaste of wholeness, with embodied reality through right relationship which propels us out to change those structures of our society and world which prevent others enjoying such right relationship. In feminist theology sexuality ceases to be sidelined as an ethical or moral problem, as it is in patriarchal theology, and takes its place at the heart of a relational, body theology.

In feminist theology the death of our bodies is not something to be feared or overcome but rather is seen as part of the natural process in which we return to the earth—God's body—which gave birth to us.

Further reading: Heyward 1989, Jantzen 1984, McFague 1987, 1993.

CELIBACY
Susan Dowell

CONSECRATED CELIBACY—as a lifelong, self-chosen discipline—was instituted in the Christian church in about the second century CE. Although not made an absolute requirement for priesthood in the Western Church until the eleventh century, celibacy has always been required of monks and nuns.

The spiritual and political power that had accrued to monasticism from the fourth century became a major target of the Reformers in the sixteenth century who denounced the celibate system as both corrupt and unbiblical. As part of a renewed emphasis on 'worldly holiness', marriage was revalued as an 'honourable estate', normative for laity and clergy alike.

The scriptural authority for this change lost force with the rise of secular rationalism in the eighteenth century and the churches' continued emphasis on sexual restraint fuelled the rationalists' claim that Christianity, in all its forms, devalues the natural instincts and affections between men and women. The work of later thinkers, notably Freud in the late nineteenth century, gave rise to an understanding of sexuality as integral to human personhood, something which cannot be repressed without serious damage to individual and collective well-being. Itself originating in the Enlightenment as a social analysis based on women's experience, feminism has stressed the connection between celibate traditions and the subordination of women.

A radical reassessment of celibacy is taking place today, both within the church and in society as as whole. This has come about partly in response to feminist critique, and partly from a number of developments within modern thought (for example in ecology and ecofeminism) and contemporary church culture (signalled by the Second Vatican Council), which have combined to highlight the damaging consequences of traditional celibate culture.

The most coherent and useful reassessments have been historically based. There is a broad consensus among scholars that sexual and body phobias are not products of biblical religion but grew out of Christianity's later contact with Hellenistic dualism. Christian celibacy was originally understood in terms of freedom from bondage to the corrupt and coercive sexual mores of the Imperial world. Abstention from sexual activity did not presuppose a rejection of sex as a meaningful and godly expression of love.

The extensive retrieval of women's history which feminists have undertaken over the last twenty years—for example, the realization that most of the women who made a significant contribution to pre-Reformation culture were either nuns or women living in celibacy within or after marriage—has been crucially formative of a more positive assessment of celibacy among feminists generally and has led to specific attempts to reclaim celibacy for feminism.

Feminist theology has affirmed some elements of the Christian celibate tradition as liberating for women, but with some important qualification. First, while women have received high praise, honour and even equality as consecrated celibates they have always done so under different circumstances from those of their male counterparts. Writings from the patristic era, particularly those of Jerome, suggest that women celibates were required to obliterate rather than discipline their sexuality. Secondly, the shift from countercultural theory and practice after the fourth century further widenened the 'gender gap'. The move towards enclosed communities, set apart from the world and governed by an (all-male) church hierarchy, has meant in practice that female celibates have been largely denied the freedom and prestige of their male counterparts.

In the church, renewed interest has been shown in the countercultural potential of celibacy; it can be practised both as a protest against modern materialism and as a means of establishing non-exploitative relationships between the sexes in an aggressively eroticized culture. A revived understanding of celibacy-as-charism is, however, clearly incompatible with celibacy-as-law, and there is a growing consensus among mainstream and feminist theologians that the intrinsic value of celibacy cannot be recovered while it remains a compulsory component of priesthood.

Further reading: Brown 1986; Cline 1993; Dowell 1993; Ruether 1974; Ruston 1982; Schneiders 1993.

CHRISTOLOGY
Rosemary Radford Ruether

CHRISTOLOGY REFERS to the theology about the nature of the person and salvific offices of Jesus of Nazareth, affirmed as the Christ, the messiah or saviour of humanity from sin. Christianity from its beginning affirmed that women as well as men are included in the salvific work of Jesus, the Christ. In Paul's letter to the Galatians, 3.27, the saving work of Christ is said to overcome the differences of status between Jew and Greek, slave and free, male and female, 'for all of you are one in Christ Jesus'. Thus it would seem that Christology should be the Christian doctrine that most explicitly affirms women's full equality with men in creation, redemption and the church.

However, in the actual development of Christology, this doctrine has been used to reinforce women's subordination in the church and hence in society. Even in the late twentieth century the Roman Catholic church has solemnly proclaimed that women cannot be ordained to the priesthood because, by their very nature, women cannot 'image Christ'. The symbolism drawn from patriarchal marriage in Eph. 5.23, 'For the husband is the head of the wife just as Christ is the head of the Church', has also been construed to exclude women from ordained ministry. The priest is said to represent this 'headship' of Christ over the church as a necessarily male office, comparable to that of the husband's rule over the wife in the family.

Feminist New Testament scholars generally agree that the original Jesus movement was egalitarian, or at least was a countercultural movement that leveled class, ethnic and gender differences. This was understood, not just sociologically, but as the herald of a new redemptive humanity. Paul's statement in Galatians is generally seen as reflecting an early Christian baptismal formula that proclaimed oneness in Christ, beyond gender, class and race, as the new identity in Christ which Christians 'put on' through baptism.

The Gospels represent Jesus as an iconoclastic prophet who confronts the claims of special privilege of the religious leadership classes by lifting up marginal people as those who understand and believe his message, while the religious and political elites reject and seek to kill him. The story line of the Gospels is one in which Jesus is rejected successively by his family and the synagogue leaders of his home town, by the religious leaders in Jerusalem, by the political authorities, by the crowds in Jerusalem, and finally by his own male disciples. His women followers are left as the believing remnant who are last at the cross and first at the tomb, the first witnesses of the resurrection who proclaim the good news to the other disciples.

Despite these egalitarian and countercultural patterns that seem to have empowered some female leadership in the early church, by the end of the first century Christianity began developing a patriarchal pattern of leadership that marginalized women. Christian ministry became modeled after the patriarchal father in the household (1 Tim. 3.1-7). The exclusion of women from ministry, and from all public leadership roles, was argued from women's inherent subordination in the order of creation and, further, as punishment for women's sin of insubordination which caused the 'fall' of humanity and the expulsion from paradise.

In the fourth century, when Christianity was assimilated into the Roman empire under Constantine, an imperial Christology developed in which the Lordship of Christ over the universe (Christ Pantocrator) was seen as mirrored in the Lordship of Caesar, the Roman emperor, over the empire. In this imperial Christology Christ become the arche or principle of all hierarchical relationships, the emperor over his subjects, nobles over commoners, masters over slaves, the father over his household, men over women, and finally the mind over the body.

Medieval scholastic theology took over the Aristotelian anthropology which defined women as inherently deficient and lacking in the fullness of human nature. Thomas Aquinas used this anthropology to argue that Christ had to be male in order to represent the fullness of human nature, and that only men could represent Christ in the priesthood. A patriarchal Christology was constructed in this way in which women's subordination was reaffirmed, rather than overcome, in Christ.

Christian feminist theology thus finds the

An A to Z of Feminist Theology

reconstruction of Christology both the most central and the most difficult of its tasks. The teaching and practice of Jesus himself are generally not seen as the major problem, since these are generally seen as critical of social and religious hierarchies and affirming of women. Yet the fact that he was male, and is conceived of as the sole and exclusive mediator of the saving presence of a male-identified God, presents stumbling blocks. Feminist theology seeks not only male affirmation of women's dignity, but the possibility of experiencing female mediatorship of a female-identified divine presence.

Thus many feminist Christologies wish to go beyond the simple affirmation that Jesus' own egalitarian message and practice contradict the patriarchal construction of his identity. They also seek to dissolve the exclusivity of the relationship between Jesus and Christic salvific work. Feminist Christologies stress the redemptive community, as an ongoing and expanding movement of emancipation of women and men from systems of domination, as the location of the Christic reality. In the context of such an understanding of Christic community, it is possible to encounter Christ 'in the form of our sister'.

Feminist Christology also deconstructs the patriarchal concept of the Trinitarian God as 'Father, Son and Spirit'. Feminists turn to a wisdom-centered understanding of the divine transformative presence in history that evokes the feminine symbol, Sophia, as its central focus of God–human relationships. The Wisdom-God can be seen as mother and father in a way that goes beyond mere gender inclusivity to emancipatory transformation of gender symbols. Jesus, then, can be seen as Sophia's son, or as the one through whom we encounter Sophia-God.

The combination of a depatriarchalized Trinity and an inclusive community as the locus of encounter with Christ's saving being and work removes the exclusive male-centred focus of traditional Christology in favour of a Christology that is in process of continually unfolding in the emancipatory struggles of humanity, including the emancipation of women and men from patriarchy.

Further reading: Brock 1988; Johnson 1992; Odell-Scott 1991; Ruether 1981.

CHURCH HISTORY
Janet Crawford

IN CHURCH HISTORY as traditionally defined, studied and taught, as in the study of history generally, the focus has usually been on development measured by tangible and discrete events and on significance determined primarily by power, influence and visible activity in the world. Church historians have concentrated on the growth of the institutional church, or particular aspects of it; on the lives and works of emperors, popes, bishops, and theologians; on theological controversies, councils, canons and decrees. This understanding of the content of church history was introduced as early as the fourth century by Eusebius of Caesarea, the 'Father of Church History'. At the beginning of his *Ecclesiastical History* he defined his subject matter as 'the many important events recorded in the story of the Church, the outstanding leaders and heroes of that story in the most famous Christian communities; the men of each generation who by preaching or writing were ambassadors of the divine word'. The only women mentioned in Eusebius's history are those who, like Blandina and Biblis, overcame the supposed weakness of their sex to win, with their male companions, the martyr's 'crown of immortality', and those who, like the Montanist prophets Priscilla and Maximilla, themselves 'wandered from the truth' and also led others astray, 'making havoc of Christ's flock'. Following Eusebius, the vast majority of church histories have been histories of men, written by men. Although it is certain that the church has always consisted of women and men, historically it has been represented as an institution governed by men and women's participation has generally been marginalized, trivialized, or ignored altogether. All too often in the writing of church history, in Patricia Hill's words, 'The women have simply disappeared' (Hill 1985: 2). When women have been included in church histories it has usually been as peripheral figures, significant only in relation to significant men. Occasionally individual women have been included in their own right, exceptional women such as saints, mystics and queens, but their lives are observed and evaluated from the male perspective of the author. Of women as a group

An A to Z of Feminist Theology

CHURCH HISTORY

within the church little has been recorded.

Among the reasons for the discounting of women's presence in the church by male historians are the following.

1. As traditionally defined, church history has focused on public events from which women were usually excluded. Life in the domestic sphere to which most women were confined has not been considered worthy of historical attention.

2. The belief that women are inferior beings, incapable of causing things to happen, passive objects rather than active agents, a belief which historically was legitimated by many influential male theologians, contributed to a lack of male interest in women's history. There can be no history of women unless women are taken seriously and for most of the past this has not been the case.

3. The androcentric assumption that male experience is normative, that the concerns of women and men are the same and that both sexes are affected similarly by the events of history takes for granted that men's history includes women and so no separate attention is given to women.

4. The concept of the 'eternal feminine', of the timeless, ahistorical and unchanging nature of 'woman', has ignored the diverse and changing experiences of actual women.

5. The problem of sources. History depends on the interpretation of data preserved from the past but for most of the Christian past information about women is less abundant than information about men. In general men acquired literacy before women but even women who were literate were usually excluded from the realm of public discourse. Also, for all the reasons given above, data about women were frequently either not recorded in the first place, or not preserved. For the most part, all that are left are tenuous traces of women's presence in the church. According to Elizabeth Clark, 'The great mass of unexceptional women remains unknown and probably unknowable, barring the discovery of new sources' (Clark 1990: 19).

Contemporary interest in 'women's history' as distinct from the history of men is closely linked with movements towards the equality and liberation of women. *Women Church and State*, perhaps the earliest attempt at 'an historical account of the status of women through the Christian ages', was written by suffragist Matilda Joslyn Gage in 1893 in order to refute two arguments used against women's claims for equal political rights with men: that the subjection of women was divinely ordained, and that under Christianity women enjoyed a higher status than ever before. Gage herself was effectively written out of the history of the women's suffrage movement as too radical although her pioneering and polemical work was reprinted in the 1980s.

In the 1940s two works that were to become paradigmatic for 'women's history' were published. French philosopher Simone de Beauvoir's *The Second Sex* was to become a feminist classic. The central thesis of the book is that throughout history women have been subordinated to men and thus have 'no past, no history, no religion of their own'. A number of later studies have documented and analysed social and cultural forms of discrimination against women, their ideological justification in Christianity and the resulting subordination of women in both church and society. This type of 'subordination study' has attracted attention from both secular feminists struggling against societal oppression of women, and Christian feminists seeking to understand the roots of their own experience of discrimination and oppression within the church. The period of the early church has drawn particular attention, because it was so formative in the development of Christian theory and practice. The risk in this approach is that it may be too polemical and one-sided in its emphasis on women as victims of male domination. Subordination studies may fail to recognize and do justice to women as active agents in history.

Suffragist, sociologist and historian Mary Beard's *Woman as Force in History* was fiercely criticized by the male historical establishment when it first appeared, but twenty years later it was recognized by feminists as a pioneering work. Beard argued that, far from belonging to 'the lumber room of history', women had played a great role 'in directing human events as thought and action' and had been 'a force in making all the history that has been made'. Following Beard, who is credited with having invented the concept of 'women's studies', much

CHURCH HISTORY

study has been directed to making women visible in history and to documenting their presence and their contributions. In the field of church history the period of the Middle Ages has proved to be particularly fertile for this kind of research. Focusing on the lives of exceptional women who form some sort of female elite, the approach that stresses 'presence' and contribution risks assuming that the experiences of this elite are somehow illustrative of the lives of ordinary, unexceptional women. Also, the result of this approach may simply be to add women to men's history while not challenging or changing underlying concepts and assumptions about the nature of history itself.

Since the rise of the contemporary women's movement, or second wave feminism, in the 1960s and 1970s, feminist theory and scholarship have contributed to significant changes in the understanding of and approach to history. The work of pioneering feminist historians Gerda Lerner and Joan Kelly challenged the androcentric nature and assumptions of traditional history and asserted that the role of women in historical events—or their absence from them—was a proper subject of historical investigation. Lerner defined 'women's history' as a methodology, a world-view, 'an angle of vision which permits us to see that women live and have lived in a world defined by men and most frequently dominated by men and yet have shaped and influenced that world and all human events' (1979: xiv). Women's history has the dual goal of restoring women to history and restoring their history to women. Scholarship in women's history has grown rapidly in both extent and depth and there is an increasing theoretical complexity. Although there are differing approaches and methodologies in women's history, feminist historians generally share certain assumptions and principles, which are also relevant for church history.

1. Feminist historians continue to challenge traditional definitions of history. As the definition changes, so does the content. Feminist historians of the church insist that women have always been in the church, that women's history must be restored to the history of the church, and that this history must be reclaimed as the history of women and men. Thus feminist historian and theologian Elisabeth Schüssler Fiorenza 'claims the Christian past as women's own past, not just a male past in which women participated only on the fringes or were not active at all' (1983: xx).

2. Feminist historiography challenges the notion that the history of women is the same as the history of men, asserting that the history of women is unique while at the same time integral to and consistently intertwined with the history of men.

3. Feminist historians assert the need to distinguish between androcentric images of women, which are generally prescriptive rather than descriptive, and the reality of women's experience. In reading androcentric texts, a 'hermeneutics of suspicion' is needed, for, as Schüssler Fiorenza argues, 'it can be shown that ideological polemics about women's place, role, or nature increase whenever women's actual emancipation and active participation in history become stronger' (1983: 85).

4. Another premise of feminist historians is that all historical scholarship is inherently imaginative and that there is no such thing as a purely objective reconstruction of the past and no history that is merely descriptive. According to Schüssler Fiorenza, the image of the historian as 'objective reporter' needs to be replaced with that of the historian as 'quilt maker', piecing together surviving scraps of historical information into a coherent overall design or interpretive model (1987: 35). From a feminist perspective an adequate design or model for church history would be one which took women's historical experience and agency seriously and which understood the history of the church as a history of women and men.

In the study of women's history within the church, much of the focus so far has been on reclaiming women's presence in and contribution to the life of the Church, and on analysing and denouncing the theological foundations of women's subordination. Because of contemporary controversy over the role of women in the church, particularly over the ordination of women, much early scholarship was concerned with women's leadership in the church in different historical periods. An important example is *Women of Spirit: Female Leadership in the Jewish and Christian Traditions*, edited by Rosemary

An A to Z of Feminist Theology

Radford Ruether and Eleanor McLaughlin (1979), in which they argued that, although excluded from institutional church leadership and ministerial office, women in the past had claimed other leadership roles. They were clear that this history was written and researched for a purpose: 'Women should appropriate their history, not merely to deplore their past exclusion but to vindicate the insights of this alternative tradition and use it to reshape and enlarge the vision and life of the church history' (1979: 28).

In recent years there has been a significant increase in historical studies on women in the church. Many of these have been written by historians of women—male as well as female—who do not see themselves as church historians. Some church historians, particularly women, have also focused their attention on women though not necessarily from a feminist perspective. Individual research, however significant, has tended to be specialized and fragmented. The focus has generally continued to be either on women's subordination in the church, or on their active presence in the church.

Thus much of the study of women's history in the church is basically adding women to what is still essentially a history of men. There is as yet no major study of how relationships between women and men in the church have developed over its long history.

Women's history raises new questions for historians, including church historians, but so far there have been no widespread efforts among traditional church historians to incorporate the category of gender, or the new questions, concepts and findings of women's history into their own studies.

Further reading: Coon *et al*. 1990.

CIRCLE DANCE
Lillalou Hughes

The best way to still the mind is to move the body (Gabrielle Roth).

CIRCLE DANCING was introduced to Britain at the Findhorn Community in Scotland in the 1970s by Bernhard Wosein, a German ballet master. The dances are drawn from many countries and cultures—from Greece, the Slavic countries, the Jewish and Celtic traditions—and are created for celebrating rituals, meditation and rites of passage. They are an ancient way of expressing emotions and releasing tension. Some dances are very old, some are new; circle dance is borrowing from the past and creating for the future, using folk and contemporary music.

Bernhard Wosein's aim was to show that everyone could dance and that it is not necessary to be an expert to enjoy these vibrant, ceremonial and social dances. He believed that circle dancing enabled people to experience joy and inner peace.

Circle dance allows the expression of feelings through the many moods of the dances. In our society, which makes the constructive expression of emotion quite difficult, we need to create a context in which we can freely express ourselves. The dance has the potential to take us beyond the limits of our society and rigid roles. This is often difficult, because few people in modern Western society dance spontaneously, and are afraid of being thought eccentric if they dance for no apparent reason.

The circle is the symbol of unity. While the roundness of the dance represents nurturing, in our society, which seems to be more linear in nature, preferring straight lines and hierarchies, the circle of the dance is an enacted symbol. Circles connote the smallest and largest elements of our world, from tiny cells to planets, and convey the sense of the cyclic nature of life and movement. In dancing the circle we experience our bodies as part of that dynamism of life—we experience the depth of our being. The dance is a dramatic representation of human beings' understanding of themselves, the world around them and the deity they worship (Wosein n.d.).

The sacred dance traditions of the world endeavour to repeat the encounters with the divine. By dancing the human–divine encounter humans are put in touch again with their creative origin. This is the aim and essence of all religious or sacred dance. For the dancer the scheme of the round dance is based on total participation, a rapt concentration of one's whole being, while stepping along the perimeter of the circle as it turns around its central point.

In our world, where spirituality and sexuality seem so far apart, the dance points to a union. By expressing our spiritual quest through our bodies we inevitably do so through sexuality and gender. The dance aims to put us at ease with our physical selves.

Circle dancing can embrace all spiritualities and all peoples. Wherever human endeavour becomes a collective effort, a phenomenon occurs that amplifies the energies available to any individual to move from ordinary to expanded consciousness (see Moss n.d.: 116-18). In coming to the circle participants may feel unbalanced, unharmonious, and stuck. They seldom leave the circle unchanged. Linking hands starts the process that the dance continues—and we can feel uplifted and reconnected with people and the world around us. We can feel safe, supported, valued. We can trust ourselves to be spontaneous and let our emotions show. This is a very healing experience. Those who are 'down to earth' seem to find pathways into their intuitive and spiritual natures, while those who are cerebral seem to discover a sensual and earthy side in their characters.

The body itself is a creature of rhythm; it has a heartbeat, and many other subtle pulses as well. There are rhythms of renewal and decay; there are rhythms in the brain, in sleep, and in emotional life too (Gilchrist n.d.). Circle dancing is about rhythm, one's own rhythms and those one creates with others. Moods can be changed by dancing to a particular rhythm, and it appears that different rhythms stimulate certain body centres (Gilchrist n.d.).

Circle dance is first and foremost a group experience. Our competitive industrial way of life is pushing the bodies and minds of many people over the edge into despair, disease and suicide. Circle dance groups have a part to play in re-establishing the cultural balance. They provide a place in which people can let go of the rat-race and other forms of alienation and experience connection with others in a non-verbal, non-cerebral way.

Awareness is important. This means awareness of ourselves and what is happening inside us, as well as awareness of others, and awareness of the interplay between all of these. When the group is moving together with absolute oneness there is a subtle, subliminal level of communication which occurs but is difficult to express verbally—and it only happens when all are tuned to one way of moving.

One of the ways in which circle dancing is used successfully is in liturgies. Traditionally these are based on words, with faith and worship expressed in a very cerebral fashion. It is enlivening to use our bodies in worship, to bring the whole person to God. There are dances which fit every part of the liturgy—dances for greetings and for meditation, dances based on biblical texts, dances for peace and for festivals.

The circle dance tradition is a living one, concerned more with experiencing dance personally, in an atmosphere conducive to absorbing the inner qualities, than with nuance and form. This is understood by feminist theologians who are enabling women to see theology as something they experience rather than something they discuss. Feminist theology envisions theology as circular and weaving and not as the linear progression to and from God that patriarchal theology has suggested. Another insight is that we are embodied and so our bodies cannot be ignored on our journey with God. This again goes against most patriarchal understanding of God and the human body. Circle dancing is the enactment of the basic principles of feminist theology—bodies weaving and circling to a closer experience of themselves, each other, the world and the divine.

COMMUNITY
Alison Gelder

'COMMUNITY' MOST often appears in feminist theology in association with another descriptive term: for example, community of equals, faith community, dialogical community, moral community, redemptive community. Thus we are not talking about 'the community' but about numerous overlapping particular communities.

Community forms an essential backdrop to much Christian feminist thought. Developments of the concept of the social or situated self are used by Christian women in reflecting on the communal nature of creation in Genesis. Feminist writing about community centres around ideas of mutuality and caring. This focus appears in theology in discussion of the Trinity. As a paradigm of Christian community the

Trinity is interesting to feminists because it is neither hierarchical nor a family.

In writing about community feminists draw upon women's experience of sisterhood and sense of being a social group—whether based on biological differences from men or on common historical experiences. This is very similar to the concept of solidarity in Roman Catholic thinking about community. There are also strong similarities between feminist, anarchist and liberation theologians' descriptions of ideal community: no dominion, hierarchy, coercive power or privileges of gender, race or wealth; freedom and justice for all and by all; individuality without individualism; equality without sameness. The key words to describe community in Christian feminism are mutuality, interrelatedness and compassion.

Christian community, as described in Scripture and experienced in history, frequently fails to measure up to this description. The radical afamilial nature of Jesus' teaching in the Gospels is either lost or deliberately buried by the second century. From the Christian Scriptures and other non-canonical early church documents it is clear that the first Christian communities represented a new kinship structure which was open to women and in which traditional hierarchy was turned upside down.

But against this the household code (cf. Ephesians, Colossians, 1 Timothy and 1 Peter) sees church, family and state as models of a patriarchal household with slaves. The church becomes the household of God and oppressive social and political structures are Christianized. For this line of thought the focus on community leads inevitably to conservatism and maintaining the status quo, marginalizing radical alternatives.

The patriarchal, hierarchical church of the household code trajectory did not naturally succeed other models of Christian community; rather it repressed them. However, anarchistic rivals to the main tradition recur throughout the history of Christianity; for example, Gnostic, hermit and monastic communities, Waldensians, Cathars, Hussites, Anabaptists, Quakers, base communities and women-church.

Among the models of community recovered or renewed by Christian feminism three are particularly noteworthy. First there is the concept of an exodus community. Women are an exodus community coming out of patriarchy, marked by liberation from oppression and seeking a promised land of love and justice. Secondly, there is the concept of an inclusive community. Biblically this is rooted in the symbolism of Mary as she proclaims the Magnificat to Elizabeth (Lk. 1.46-55), and more generally in Luke's Gospel in which the marginalized (and especially marginalized women) are central to the Christian message. This aspect of community has been taken up by Third World women, and in feminist spirituality. Third is the concept of community of choice (rather than community of origin). This is reflected in the work and lives of women who have moved away from the church community of their birth to one which is more woman-centred. This may mean a move to another denomination or to a non-denominational group. For post-Christian feminists it has meant a move to a non-Christian community. While people in communities of choice do not necessarily share a common history they do share values and interests which have often arisen from similar life experiences. Friendship plays a vital part in creating and sustaining communities of choice.

In both Scripture and theology community is linguistically and metaphorically female. It lies with humanity as opposed to God, body as opposed to mind and woman as opposed to man. This association between women and community can be pressed further in that community, especially church community considered as household, falls within the private or domestic sphere rather than the public, political sphere. This is where women should be able to be at home, strong, in their element, building and nurturing community. But this is also the arena where hierarchy prevails over democracy and natural order over equality. The dilemma facing Christian feminism here is how to retain the mutuality and solidarity of 'private' community while embracing the democracy and equality of 'public' community.

One way in which this is attempted is through the creation of new models of community. The idea of sisterhood as a form of community which includes all women has been strained by the persistent failure of women to recognize

An A to Z of Feminist Theology

each other as sisters. More recently the issue of difference has become another problem for sisterhood. Women of colour, poor women and lesbians have all challenged the hegemony of white, middle-class, educated, heterosexual women in feminist thought.

Another new model of community adopted and developed from mainstream feminism is that of network. Here small groups and isolated individuals are connected by means of one-to-one communications, publications and meetings. A form of community of choice, networks are a practical way for Christian feminists to seek support, grow in strength and confidence and offer solidarity to others. At their best they operate as communities of affirmation for large numbers of women, many of whom may never meet each other in person.

The sense of community which underpins much feminist theology is of overlapping, particular, diverse, inclusive communities; of community created positively as a condition for liberation and to provide an environment to foster compassion.

Further reading: Benhabib 1992; Friedman 1989; Schüssler Fiorenza 1983; Zappone 1991.

COMPLEMENTARITY
Alison Gelder

COMPLEMENTARITY IS a word which has been twisted, distorted and rigidified by Christian opponents of feminism. It is used to assign roles to women which are oppressive because they curtail women's ability to select and pursue aims and prevents them from being fully human. The language of complementarity is the language of a power relationship. The fact that being complementary is about completing a whole is ignored. Complementarity is based partly on the obvious physiological differences between women and men, but mainly on the Bible, on traditions of biblical interpretation and on historically based Christian practice. It has led to the assumption that the sexes are not whole without one another.

Biblical claims that women and men were created to complement one another begin with the account of creation in Genesis. This is a serious problem for biblical feminists, and is also an issue in Judaism and Islam. In Gen. 1.26-28 God creates both sexes at the same time, in God's image. None of the other creatures in Genesis are sexually differentiated, so the physiological complementarity of men and women may be a significant aspect of the image of God.

In Gen. 2.22-23 the woman is created after the man. Does this mean that woman is the pinnacle of creation? or that she is automatically subordinate to man, the first-born? The woman is created when God removes Adam's side (arguably a better translation than 'rib'). Adam is split in half to become two people. Woman is an *ezer* for Adam, a helper, who is an equal not a servant—a co-worker. The most important fact is that the man and woman are alike, not that they differ from each other. Rigid complementarists argue that woman is made from man, for man, after man and named by man, all of which are said to indicate her inferiority.

The story of the temptation in Gen. 3.1-13 is something of a paradox in so far as rigid complementarity is concerned. Here the woman is the protagonist and the embodiment of questing humanity, while the man is passive and obedient to his wife. Or is the woman silly and disobedient? Much ink has been spilled over the relative guilt of Adam and Eve, but clearly both share responsibility for the Fall.

Some anti-feminist writers make rigid complementarity a post-lapsarian consequence, but do not indicate why this consequence of sin must lie unchangeable until the Second Coming while others, for example the need to work the earth to make crops grow, can be tackled now.

Passages in 1 Corinthians (11.3-16; 14.33b-36), Ephesians (5.21-33), Colossians (3.18-20), 1 Timothy (2.11-15) and 1 Peter (3.1-7) can all be made to say that the submission of women to men is divinely ordained, and that it is wrong for women to take leadership roles. Many points may be made to challenge this interpretation, of which the most widely applicable is the extent of disagreement among scholars about both the meaning and interpretation of these passages (particularly 1 Corinthians, Ephesians and 1 Timothy). Such uncertain and contested ground cannot provide a firm base for definitive

An A to Z of Feminist Theology

rules about roles considered to be fitting for women.

The biblical texts on which rigid complementarity is based are the same texts which are or have been used as proof-texts for woman's inferiority to man and for her position as a secondary or incomplete image of God. They are inextricably linked. So Augustine believed that a woman was only the image of God together with her husband and Aquinas, drawing on Aristotelian biology to support his beliefs, that woman was the image of God in a secondary sense. On this point Calvin was in agreement with Aquinas. All this argument, of course, has taken place within the context of patriarchy, thus justifying the application of a hermeneutic of suspicion to the conclusions drawn about both female inferiority and rigid complementarity.

Many of those who argue for rigid complementarity share a fear that openness about roles for both sexes will lead to the elimination of sexual differences. Often socially constructed characteristics are assumed to flow from a biological or scriptural root. They also come close to the heresy of dualism, setting up false dichotomies: male as mind is closer to God, female as body is closer to earth.

Historically some qualities have come to be associated with women or femininity and others with men or masculinity. In fact, all qualities are human. If women are self-giving, serving, gentle and faithful, this is not to say that men cannot also be, or strive to be these things. Similarly, women are able to show strength, courage, leadership and singleness of purpose.

In addition to Aristotelian biology, biblical stricture and patriarchal tradition, aspects of the call for rigid complementarity suggest fear of women and envy of giving birth. Thus the importance of motherhood is emphasized alongside the dangers posed by feminism.

There are differences between women and men—both biological and as a result of socialization. The differences should be recognized, celebrated and learned from as part of the greater diversity of all humanity.

Rigid complementarity is a type of apartheid. It pays lip service to a form of equality between the sexes but sees nothing valuable in women beyond their difference from men. It is inextricably linked with false claims about inferiority of women. It works to prevent both women and men from developing full humanity and more perfectly imaging God.

Further reading: Hull 1989; Moore 1992; Newsom and Ringe (eds.) 1992; Oddie 1984.

CREATION SPIRITUALITY
Matthew Fox

CREATION SPIRITUALITY is a way of life that is in the feminist tradition of philosophy insofar as it is cosmological (not anthropocentric); it espouses interconnectivity (not competition); it practices compassion understood as celebration and healing by way of justice-making; it honors creativity as the most divine of human activities; it is non-dualistic (matter is imbued with spirit); it recognizes creation in all its aspects including sexuality as a spiritual theophany; it seeks wisdom instead of mere knowledge; it sees relationship as the essence of all things; and it begins with original blessing instead of original sin.

Creation spirituality is about creativity and co-creation—creation with all other beings in the universe and with the 'Source without a Source', the Godhead. Creation spirituality is also the oldest tradition in the Bible. The Yahwist or 'J' source of the Hebrew Bible (ninth or tenth century BCE) was creation-centered, as were the prophets and all of wisdom literature—Job, the Psalms, Wisdom, Sirach, the Songs of Songs, Ecclesiastes. Creation spirituality is the tradition that Jesus knew so well, he who was first called 'Sophia' or 'Lady Wisdom' by the earliest sources in the Christian Scriptures.

Patriarchy espoused the fall/redemption or dualistic tradition of Augustine ('man but not woman is made in the image and likeness of God' and 'spirit is whatever is not matter') in preference to creation spirituality, but there were movements and bold prophets who opted for creation spirituality in the Western church.

Creation spirituality is the tradition of St Benedict and Scholastica. Celtic Christianity, as represented for example by the Irishman John the Scot, was especially imbued with a creation spirituality consciousness, as is clear in its sense

CREATION SPIRITUALITY

of cosmology, its love of art (consider the Book of Kells), its love of wilderness and animals, its passion for gender justice. Indeed, it is because Celtic Christians settled along the Rhine and into northern Italy that we have this heritage so richly expressed in the Rhineland mystics such as Hildegard of Bingen, Francis of Assisi, Thomas Aquinas, Mechtild of Magdeburg, Meister Eckhart, Julian of Norwich and Nicolas of Cusa. Creation spirituality fueled the twelfth-century renaissance that gave birth to Chartres Cathedral and 500 other churches in France alone all dedicated to Mary, the goddess newly rediscovered in Christianity (and all containing the Green Man as well).

With the breakup of cosmology at the end of the Middle Ages and the emphasis on individualism and nationalism that characterized the sixteenth century, cosmology was effectively silenced in theology. By the time Europeans 'discovered' the native peoples of Africa, the Americas and Asia, they had lost creation spirituality and thus failed to recognize the wisdom they had encountered in these peoples. Science and religion split in the seventeenth century and so cosmology was replaced by pietism and rationalism in Protestantism and by increased privatization of spirituality in Catholicism or by a deep psychologism (witness Ignatius's *Spiritual Exercises*). The fact that creation spirituality has been resurrected in America in the last half of the twentieth century is not altogether surprising, since the native peoples' spirit and religion is still alive there, the women's movement is strong there and today's science is acknowledging mystery once again. When science and mysticism come together with artists to name the mystery we have a living cosmology.

Creation spirituality is about adult religion. It is about developing the mystic and the prophet in each person and in culture itself. The mystic says 'yes' to life, celebrates, undergoes awe and gratitude. The prophet says 'no' to life's imposters and enemies, interferes with cultural injustice and struggles to make the yes possible. The prophet is 'the mystic in action' (William Hocking).

Creation spirituality critiques the very naming of the spiritual journey—or the definitions of holiness—that a patriarchal tradition has given us. The starting point of the journey is original blessing: all beings in the universe are holy, good, sacred (cf. Gen. 1). Yes, humans sin. But to begin with a theology of 'original sin' does not lead us out of our sin. Low self-esteem does not drive out demons; it only sets us up for addictions, violence, crime and inertia. Besides, original sin is a thoroughly anthropocentric starting point for religion. To begin with it reveals the bias that the fall/redemption tradition has against the rest of nature (Augustine was the first to use the term 'original sin', which is not a biblical or Jewish concept). Creation spirituality consciously moves from Hellenistic mysticism to Jewish mysticism. (After all, Jesus was a Jew.) Nowhere is this move more evident than in the conscious and deliberate rejection of the naming of the spiritual journey that Plotinus and Proclus gave us as: (1) Purgation; (2) Illumination; (3) Union. Where is the mention of creativity in this journey? of delight? of pleasure? of Justice?

In contrast, the creation spirituality tradition names the journey in four paths: (1) Via Positiva: awe, delight, wonder, gratitude, joy; (2) Via Negativa: darkness, silence, pain, suffering, grief, emptying, letting pain be pain; (3) Via Creativa: creativity, birthing new images, new expressions of God; (4) Via Transformativa: compassion understood as both celebration and healing by way of justice-making. The four paths are not climbing up a ladder ('climbing Jacob's ladder' has dominated as an archetype for the spiritual journey during the patriarchal era) but are closer to dancing a spiral dance or 'Dancing Sarah's Circle'. That is to say, it is earth-based, eye-to-eye, non-competitive, interdependent, with humor, surprise and the body at its core ('Sarah laughed'). Creation spirituality is also earthy and sensual and praises all the chakrahs as integral to spiritual maturity including the sexual one.

An operative theological category in creation spirituality is *panentheism*, all things in God and God in all things. This is distinct from theism, which teaches that God is out there up in the sky; or atheism, which is a rejection of theism with nothing to take its place; or pantheism, which teaches that God is only what is and denies the surprise or transcendence of God (in creation spirituality transcendence is about surprise, not about being 'up' or 'over').

An A to Z of Feminist Theology

CREATION SPIRITUALITY

Creation spirituality is never anti-intellectual or anti-science. Hildegard said that 'all science comes from God' and Aquinas said that 'a mistake about creation results in a mistake about God'. Scientists are important to spirituality because they tell us about creation and therefore more about its primary artist, God. In addition, creation spirituality puts great emphasis on art work as heart work. *Art as meditation* is the primary spiritual praxis of creation spirituality at the psychological level (justice-making being the primary spiritual praxis at the social level). In art as meditation we enter into a relationship with clay or color or sound or muscles in dance or earth in gardening or body in massage and *in that process* we come to awaken our senses, ground our selves, center our beings, focus our energies. We learn to con-temple, to contemplate, to deepen our spiritual selves by making connections. The creation mystics encourage our cosmological selves when they insist that 'the soul is not in the body but the body is in the soul'.

Creation spirituality is deeply ecumenical. The wisdom literature of the Bible is always universalist—wisdom is not sectarian. Therefore creation spirituality reaches out to the wisdom and mystical traditions in other religions, for there is only one 'underground river' (Eckhart) of the Godhead, though there be many wells into the river: Sufism, Judaism, Taoism, Buddhism, native religions, goddess religions or Christian mysticism. Going down a well, we come to common waters. That is deep ecumenism, a sharing of spirituality (not theological position papers) at the level of prayer and spiritual praxis.

In creation spirituality mysticism is not enough. We must take the energy released in mystical experience to heal others, to celebrate, to make compassion happen, since *there* is our divinity, as Jesus put it: 'Be you compassionate as your Creator in heaven is compassionate' (Lk. 6.36). And in compassion 'we imitate God' (Aquinas). Here, too, the deep Jewish roots of creation spirituality are evident, since for the Jew compassion is the ultimate divine attribute. We also find here a deep link with today's science, since interdependence is the new law of the universe that science is preaching (Hildegard said 'all things are interdependent'). The struggle for compassion, the prophetic urge to say no, to interfere, to offer alternatives, to birth new relationships—this lies at the heart of the mystic/prophetic struggle. Mysticism becomes a test of authentic prophecy (a prophet who does not celebrate is a fanatic and soon burns out); and prophecy or justice becomes a test of authentic mysticism.

While not slighting the importance of the historical Jesus of Nazareth, creation spirituality also honours the tradition of the Cosmic Christ. Jesus is clearly a prophet who calls his followers to interfere as he did. He paid the ultimate price for his prophecy and his death and resurrection were indeed redemptive and salvific. They heal us still. But the Cosmic Christ represents the mystical archetype that filled Jesus and that Jesus unleashed in his followers as well. The Cosmic Christ is the Cosmic Wisdom of the Hebrew Scriptures. It represents the divinity in all things and the light in all things (Jn 1)—Hildegard of Bingen says that 'every creature is a glittering, glistening mirror of divinity'. Using the language of science, we can say that the Cosmic Christ is the photons or light waves in every atom in the universe. (Perhaps Jesus is light as particle; and the Cosmic Christ is light as wave.) This means that the Christ is encountered in all beauty and all harmony. But it also means that the Christ is encountered in all suffering. Thus Christ is being crucified all over again when the rainforest is destroyed or the soil or the water or the ozone or the food or the health of our children. Cosmology and ecology go together (*eikos* means 'home' in Greek and the whole universe is our home). And 'environment' comes from the French word *environ*, and a time of an environmental revolution implies a time of panentheism, finding the sacred *all around us* and 'through and through us', as Mechtild of Magdeburg put it.

Creation spirituality is not about asceticism understood as controlling one's passions but about putting 'a bridle of love' on our passions (Eckhart). In other words, it is about steering our passions as a bridle does a horse so that they serve a greater vision, the bringing about of justice and celebration, that is, compassion.

Some people complain that creation spirituality ignores sin and redemption, but nothing could be further from the truth. The question is: what are the real sins of our species? Certainly

An A to Z of Feminist Theology

ecocide and geocide and genocide and matricide and sexism and racism and colonialism and adultism and classism are among our most serious sins, as well as the traditional 'sins of the spirit' that are behind these other sins such as acedia (inertia), arrogance (once called pride) and addiction (once called gluttony). All these creation spirituality addresses both in theory and in praxis, with ways out of our misery and self-hatred and sin.

Creation spirituality has a special relationship to liberation theology. Indeed, it has been called a liberation theology for the *anawim*, including women, homosexuals, the earth creatures that are suffering at the hands of the colonial powers, so called 'third-world' peoples and certainly 'first-world' peoples whose principle enslavement is addiction to drugs, alcohol, consumerism, television, denial itself. Art as meditation plus a living cosmology provide the avenues for redemptive grace to flow (cf. Job). The oppression of creation spirituality mystics through the centuries by the powers that be, including ecclesial and academic powers (the latter resent and misunderstand the emphasis given to the right brain in educating people in mysticism) is evidence of how creation spirituality has paid a price for its prophetic contribution to society and church.

Because creation spirituality honors the universe as the primary sacrament, it honors all good *work* as a sacramental work. Every worker is a priest or priestess bestowing grace on fellow creatures and fellow citizens by his or her good work. Our work is a primary arena where the divine flows and heals and joy and celebration come about.

Further reading: Fox 1979, 1983, 1985, 1988; Swimme and Berry 1992.

CRUCIFIXION
Lucy Tatman

IT IS not possible to write of *the* Christian feminist theological interpretation of the crucifixion. Differences of interpretation arise not only with regard to the meaning of the crucifixion of Jesus as a historical event, but also in relation to the meanings this event has for our lives now, in the late twentieth century. (My use of the word 'our' in this context is meant to be inclusive of all people who take seriously the burden and the blessing of the crucifixion event/memory as a part of their religious heritage.) It is crucial to note, however, that the four distinct Christian feminist interpretations presented here do not necessarily stand each in opposition to each other, but are able to support and complement each other, honoring the validity and necessity of a multiplicity of perspectives and interpretations for the creation of an honest and accessible theological 'ground'.

Rita Nakashima Brock expresses one commonly held feminist interpretation of the historical crucifixion in this way: 'His dying [was] a testimony to the powers of oppression. It [was] neither salvific nor essential. It [was] tragic' (Brock 1988: 98). According to this view Jesus died because those wielding the power of the state were threatened by his life, by his insistence on justice for the oppressed. The crucifixion itself neither was nor is about redemption or salvation; rather, it is a paradigmatic example of what happens to a person who does not passively accept injustice in her or his life or in the lives of others.

However, when one shifts one's gaze from the cross to the ground beneath the cross, another aspect of the historical crucifixion comes into focus. The disciples had either entirely (Matthew, Mark, Luke) or mostly (John) deserted Jesus by the time of his death. But there beneath the cross was a faithful gathering, the beginnings of a community which refused to allow the crucifixion (both the literal event and its metaphoric representation of injustice and oppression and death) to be the final word. This *basileia*, or sacred community, came into being when the women and outcasts beneath the cross refused to allow the suffering and destruction they witnessed break them apart. They brought Jesus back into their community through their memory of him and his actions and their 'visionary-ecstatic image of resurrection' (Brock 1988: 100). This sacred community, this site of resistance and strength in the midst of oppression and injustice, has survived to this day, though its existence has been threatened more often than it has been supported by the institutional church.

A third interpretation of the crucifixion is

CRUCIFIXION

more accurately expressed as a critical evaluation of the ways in which traditional theological interpretations of Jesus' suffering and death have been used against women and oppressed peoples, actually perpetuating suffering, passive acceptance of injustice, and brutalities often committed in the name of God. Women of all races and classes have been exhorted 'to suffer as Jesus suffered'—not to resist violence and oppression but to accept it as our lot in life and as a ticket to a heavenly afterlife. Given the continuing history of violence against women and the domination of the two-thirds world by the superpowers and multi-national corporations (who have a vested interest in maintaining the status quo) it is therefore imperative that interpretations of the crucifixion be read *suspiciously*. In whose interest is it that I or you suffer like Jesus? In whose interest is it that you and I devote our lives to carrying a cross of suffering and death, rather than struggling to achieve justice on earth? The cross has been used as a weapon against the marginalized peoples of the world; this is not to say that the cross and crucifixion of Jesus can never be an empowering image or memory, but it is to say that Christian feminists must read 'crucifixion words' through critical lenses before resurrection of meaning is possible.

How is it possible for the crucifixion to be an empowering memory and image today? For whom does this image hold healing, strength and hope? In order to answer these questions it must first be acknowledged that the crucifixion story as remembered by the Christian church *includes the resurrection*. The suffering and death of Jesus is not the end of the story. Secondly, it must be acknowledged that the church traditionally affirms the divinity of Jesus. God was crucified; God suffered pain and death on the cross. And it is this image of a God who suffers with humanity, who personally knows what it is to experience abuse and pain and torture yet who is not defeated by these unjust acts, that holds a promise of hope and empowerment for many. Womanist theologians such as Jacquelyn Grant remind White feminists that the living memory of a co-suffering God, Jesus, who knows what it is to be oppressed and whipped and killed by 'the masters', has been and continues to be an incredibly powerful source of strength and resistance and hope for many Black women in the United States (see Grant 1989). Additionally, contemporary images of a crucified Christa have evoked strong reactions amongst Christian feminists. 'Christa', by Edwina Sandys, is a sculpture depicting a naked woman with outstretched arms, wearing a crown of thorns. While the sight of yet another battered woman causes some to despair, for others, especially women who have survived incest, rape and assault, the sight of a Woman God *who knows what they have experienced* has powerful, healing consequences.

At this time it is neither possible nor desirable to put forward one Christian feminist interpretation of the crucifixion, for to do so is to deny both the complexity and the power (for good and evil) of the crucifixion event/memory. This brief evaluation of 'crucifixion' has not done justice to the efforts of the many women of all races and classes who have taken seriously the centrality of the crucifixion in the Christian tradition; it is my hope, however, that it will spark more conversations, none ever claiming to be the final word.

Further reading: also Heyward 1982; Ruether 1989; Thistlewaite 1989.

DEATH
Dorothea McEwan

DEATH, 'THE great leveller', is of crucial importance to religions preaching a dualism of values: self-denial in the here and now will be made good and crowned by high favours and achievements in the thereafter. The biological fact of annihilation of the living organism is recognized by the legal concept that death cancels debts. In both these instances, the understanding of death is that of an event which closes a person's life.

When precisely this has happened is a matter of considerable debate and speculation for physicists and ethicists. Where previously the time of heart failure was considered the time of death, the end of life is now defined by the end of activity in the brainstem. No doubt, with ever more sophisticated precision instruments, this might in turn be found to be too crude a measurement and might be overtaken by another measurement. Modern medicine can sometimes alleviate the pain and suffering of dying. The ebbing away of life has been sanitized and largely put into the hands of medical experts who, while charged not to shorten life, do everything in their power to dull the pain so that many people no longer experience suffering or have to witness the suffering of a relative or friend.

But death, the precise moment of the 'end of life', is not just a measurable event. Death is connected with renewal. The irrevocable rupture death brings is also a universal theme of resurrection, analogous to the cycle of nature, leading to a renewal of life. Creation myths from around the world echo this view, the organic understanding of a necessary link between life and death, of the necessity of death to make place for life.

Immortality and rebirth are concepts which are important in dualistic patriarchal religions because they justify obedience to hierarchical structures in the here and now. Feminist writings have exposed these concepts as based on the notion of self-perpetuation beyond death, an egotistic mindset in contradistinction to a value system of relationality and life-affirming views.

In the understanding of many cultures there was a realm of death, an underworld where the dead live. Humans are mortal and stay in the underworld permanently. In the history of the Jews, especially the experience of the exile and God's promises to an obedient people, these views shifted to a different scenario, the awakening from the dead. And when Greek philosophical theories of the immortal spirit/soul flowed into Christianity, the immortality of the soul was purchased by baptism.

Death as the gateway to the underworld became death as the gateway to eternal life or eternal damnation. This traditional Christian view of welcoming death as the harbinger of glory or just damnation, of just reward for injustices suffered on earth, is contrasted in feminist theology with a revaluing of one's personal life. If there is celebration of life to the full in the here and now, which is no more seen as a 'vale of tears', there is no need any longer to console the living with a vision of a glorious afterlife.

Here traditional theology is at its most argumentative, since there is neither hard evidence of an afterlife nor of its glory. Death is itself glorified as the gateway to these supposed glories, the 'reward in heaven'. Life in the twentieth century is a cheap commodity. The hecatombs of 'ultimate sacrifices', the women, men and children murdered by warfare, callous neglect and man-made disasters, seem to underpin the view of the cheapness of life. Life is so bad, the argument runs, it can only be better after death.

But this view reveals that the misery and injustice are accepted and tolerated, rather than being recognized for what they are and fought against. Death was courted in early Christianity as a fast way to salvation, the awful torture of being thrown to wild animals for the entertainment of the masses being seen as an achievement for which one was promised the martyr's palm. Galen, in the latter half of the second century, said of the Christians: 'Their contempt for death is patent to us every day' (Brown 1990: 33). This view gave way in the same religion to another attitude of mind, that of enduring unjust situations, not complaining, 'turning the other cheek' in the sure knowledge of a place in paradise after death and a reunion of the just.

A variety of attitudes ranging from active bravery to passive cowardice, or even an interpretation of obedience that bracketed both, intermingled with philosophical concepts of the Stoa, was underpinned by the notion that what we experience here is nothing in comparison to the two extremes of experiences in the afterlife, be it paradise or hell.

Death, viewed as the physical and spiritual consequence of the sin of men and women, alienation from God (Gen. 2.17; Rom. 5.12-14; 6.23; Eph. 2.1-5), can be overcome and can become an instrument of victory (Jn 5.24; 8.51; 11.25; Rom. 5.17-21; 6; 8.6-11, 38-39; 1 Cor. 15.26, 54-56; 1 Jn 3.14; Rev. 21.4). The 'second death', after the last judgment, the final verdict of eternal damnation (Rev. 2.11; 20.6, 14; 21.8) obliterates death: for those, who 'live' in the fullness of God, there will be no more death. For those who do not, it is a terrifying 'death' sentence of fatwa, an expression of 'gross inhumanity', because it 'reaches to an eternity in hell' (Lennon 1994: 3).

In a feminist theological interpretation, death is no longer the liminal event ushering in eternal condemnation or happiness. Once the crutches of dualism are removed, the dualistic punishment and reward mode, death is no longer seen in the guise of the great leveller in the religions. This process of removing the crutches of dualism is a core agenda of feminist theology. Importance is placed on the task of making life in all its facets enjoyable and enriching, and on keeping alive the memory of the dead, of claiming and reclaiming memory as a tangible link with them. The metaphor of 'dying to the world', which is synonymous with sexual renunciation, from early Christianity onwards had disastrous effects on the churches' teaching on the body. The body came to be seen as in need of control, public control by the clergy. This warped the religion's understanding of the body, of sexuality, of 'renunciation', but again and again women and men have spoken out against it in the relational understanding of process thought, liberation and other contextual theologies of the twentieth century.

The concept of death as the great leveller, as the equalizing mechanism, as retributive justice, is a fallacy. It is a construct to keep people dependent and obedient in spite of the crippling effects unjust structures have on their lives. Death is not so much a compensating gift of providence, but a release. It is up to the individual to live life to the full in the here and now and to enable others to do so. This is not a recipe for hedonism but for responsible stewardship to develop the talents and gifts freely bestowed on each individual. Relationality, just relations, which overcome the social death of uncaring, unsharing egotism, will be the true manifestation of life to the full, where death has lost its sting forever.

Further reading: Ruether 1983; Sölle and Steffensky 1983.

DOMESTIC SACRAMENTS
Noragh Jones

SACRAMENTAL MOMENTS are not confined to formal religious occasions when we receive sacraments such as the eucharist from an ordained minister or priest. Our spiritual journey is not separate from the everyday world, but is in the world and of the world. The experience of grace comes when we have a heightened awareness of the symbolic meaning of our everyday domestic realities, so domestic sacraments occur when perfectly ordinary daily activities become relational and transforming for those taking part in them, through the cultivation of mindful attentiveness. It is possible to enjoy grace while we are sharing a meal with family or friends, especially when the gathering celebrates a new phase of life, a mood of reconciliation, or survival after suffering when we have come through in spite of everything. To be open to the experience of domestic sacraments we need to develop an appreciative awareness of the ordinary things that make up most people's daily lives. Every moment of the day from getting up in the morning and looking afresh at the world, through the frustrations and satisfactions of our daily encounters at home and outside, offers a possibility of relating to other people and to the world around us with a scrupulous attentiveness that confirms the other rather than distorting their humanity by trying to turn them into our instruments or our mirrors.

Domestic sacraments are a way of getting back to the original spirit of the eucharist, which was a transforming process, a celebration embodied in our everyday life stories. When Jesus sat down with the disciples at the last supper he took bread, blessed it and shared it out among all present. When women (or more rarely men) perform the sharing out of food at domestic mealtimes to everyone around the table, they too symbolize human communion and the nurturing spirit which sustains the rhythm of life.

The shared meal of bread and wine representing human communion was a significant spiritual ritual before Jesus' time, across many cultures, and for Christians in the early centuries it was still a very domestic celebration of grace. People gathered together, irrespective of gender or race or social standing, in ordinary homes, each bringing bread for the eucharistic table, and sharing in the transforming process of eating together and drinking from the communal cup. Since the sacraments were formalized in the Middle Ages into the seven official rites of baptism, the eucharist, marriage, holy orders, penance, confirmation and extreme unction, they have been in danger of becoming spiritual consumer goods for passive worshippers. Modern sacramental theology tries to revalue sacraments as active celebrations embodied in our own everyday life stories, which go beyond the formal church rituals to embrace the sacramental potential of everything in our world. The problem now is to reintegrate the sacraments into the continuing human story, so that their symbolic meanings are woven into our everyday lives and open doors onto the sacred.

Appreciative awareness of domestic sacramental moments is a way for us to find meaning in our ordinary lives, a way into the symbolic meanings of the loves and losses, the birthing and dying, the sufferings and resurrections that all human beings experience in their lives. In the context of domestic sacraments grace becomes a creative invasion of our preoccupation with self, a healthy hunger for meaning in our everyday home lives which offers us a continuing integral part in sacramentality.

Further reading: Cowan 1987; Philibert 1987.

DUALISM
Sarah Jane Boss

THE TERMS 'dualism' refers to a system of conceptual organization in which two or more objects are placed in a relationship of binary opposition to one another. The term is thus too general to be used without further qualification. In the writings of feminists, 'dualism' usually signifies a relationship of domination, in which the superior party perceives himself or herself to be significantly different from, and in opposition to, the subordinate. At the same time, the superior treats all members of the subordinate group as though they were the same as one another, and thus fails to recognize their individual differences. A white racist, for example, will fail to take account of the shared humanity which characterizes both white and black people, and will simultaneously ignore the personal differences between individual black people, seeing them as 'all the same'. The dualist sees the world in terms of pairs of opposites, and thereby misses both the unity and the diversity of the world which he or she inhabits.

Recent feminist research has examined the dualism of gender and its relationship to dualism of other kinds. Thus, Susan Griffin has given a detailed phenomenology of the dualism of 'nature' and 'culture' in her feminist analysis of pornography (1981). Likewise, Helen Weinreich-Haste has argued that 'the dualism of gender map[s] on to very basic beliefs about the relationship between the human being and *nature*' (1986: 117). In many areas, man's relationship to woman is 'metaphorically parallel to his relationship to his emotions, his spiritual life, and most significantly, knowledge and understanding of the natural world' (1986: 117). Weinreich-Haste's research suggests that men and science are both perceived as 'rational', while women are perceived as being 'emotional' and 'closer to nature'. Moreover, within the same framework of understanding, nature is itself the object of scientific investigation and technological control.

Historians also have supported the claim that the domination of women by men has been closely tied to humanity's domination of nature. In science and medicine there has been an increasing tendency to regard the world in terms of dualistic categories. Thus, concepts such as 'mind', 'spirit' and 'activity' have been associated with the male, while 'body', 'matter' and 'passivity' have been associated with the female. These associations have been greatly intensified in the modern era, when the rapid development of capitalism (and other forms of 'growth' economy) has created a more antagonistic relationship between humanity and non-human nature.

However, several of the world's major religions oppose the view that there is any ultimate duality in the nature of the universe, for instance between good and evil. In Christian orthodoxy, all things are part of the creation of the one God. Nevertheless, it has been common for Christians to adhere to the dualisms that have been described above (see Daly 1968).

Rosemary Radford Ruether writes that the categories of classical Christian theology 'have been distorted by androcentrism. This distorts all the dialectical relationships of good/evil, nature/grace, body/soul, God/nature by modelling them on a polarization of male and female' (1983: 37). Sara Maitland also describes dualism as a 'heresy' which 'means splitting the wholeness of God's creation into divisions labelled "good" and "bad" ' (1983: 19). This raises the possibility that the problem of dualism within Christianity could be addressed by means of immanent critique: that is to say, that the beliefs of Christianity could be used critically to bring about change within the Christian tradition itself.

DUNAMIS
Lisa Isherwood

DUNAMIS IS the word used by Carter Heyward (1982) to refer to the raw, innate and dynamic power which is often fearsome and is the birthright of all the created order. She contrasts it with *exousia*, authority, which she sees as the false understanding of power. Authority assumes that power can be granted by one to another, while *dunamis* shows quite clearly that it cannot, since it is within us all and has to be claimed by us rather than bestowed. *Dunamis* shows that power is a process, a life-transforming strength into which we grow.

An A to Z of Feminist Theology

ECCLESIOLOGY/MODELS OF CHURCH
Mario Aguilar

SINCE THE time of Christ, groups of Christians have developed and put into practice many different models of the so-called 'church'—the community of believers. All of these Christian churches have at one time or another claimed that they have the authority of being 'the' community of believers that Christ willed in order for men and women to proclaim him as the Lord. It is in the context of that variety of models and the rethinking of the Christian tradition that the feminist model first appears. In the context of a wider ecclesiology, and many Christian traditions, a feminist model is one among many. Nevertheless, for Christian feminists this particular model is the closest to the first community of the Gospels because it has the characteristics that the first community of believers (apostles and disciples, both men and women) had. Therefore a feminist model tries to reflect first of all on the important place that all believers had in the first community, the early church. In that group, the centre was the person of Jesus as the Christ, and therefore every one of the community members was in relation to the centre and not dependent on the authority of others. Ministries, including the Petrine office, were seen as services to the community, and not ritual roles associated with power and control.

Women played an important role in the events that surrounded the life, death and resurrection of Christ. They were not passive agents who followed only cultural patterns, but were given a leading role in the proclamation of the kingdom of God and the values of that kingdom present here and now and not only in the future. That first group of believers preached the lived realities of the kingdom of God rather than setting up an organizational hierarchy. It is in keeping with the preaching of the kingdom of God that a feminist model applies that equidistant relation of every believer to the centre. Everyone has her or his own role to play in the community. Women are disciples, announcers and receivers of Christ's revelation in the community.

In the New Testament different cultural models of every society were adapted in order to proclaim the gospel in different circumstances. The model of church was one in which different peoples and individuals could feel at home among the community of believers and certainly could feel that God was addressing all of them in the mission to create community with others and with God.

A feminist ecclesiology recognizes in its reading of history that as the church expanded and became more structured, the first model of the New Testament changed completely. From a circular model (Christ at the centre, with all the believers around Christ), it changed into a model comparable to a pyramid. That pyramid has some believers on the top, who provide the norms of behaviour and sometimes of belief for the rest of the believers in the name of Christ. In most Christian churches those in leadership are men, and therefore women either do not have a place in the guiding structures of the community, or if they have such a place, are supposed to express their feelings, discoveries, anxieties and hopes in the manner dictated by men in the community.

A feminist model therefore aims at creating a more caring community in which women can express themselves freely. While many churches would assert that women are certainly welcome and part of the community, this requires that they follow a patriarchal model. The feminist model points to the richness of a caring, inclusive model rather than a model of control and exclusion. Within the pyramid model, on the other hand, control is exercised by one group of individuals over another, in fact by the minority over the majority. A Christian group then becomes a patriarchal society, rather than a community of believers in the New Testament tradition.

The model of church of the New Testament is therefore somehow different from the current model of the Christian churches. A feminist ecclesiology challenges the manipulation of the so-called Christian tradition that has been a pattern in the history of the Christian churches. It has been asserted by some traditional theologians that the place of women in the Christian churches has been determined by the early church and that therefore Christian tradition does not allow for changes. That sense of tradition is certainly contrary to the 'sensus fidelium' whereby, in the first centuries of Christianity, changes took place because they reflected the understanding and needs of particular communities. The church was not grounded in fixed principles or static norms. Many of those Christian traditions were local and therefore culturally constructed, and could not have been applied to a universal Christian practice. Theology as 'faith seeking understanding' has pointed to the fact that changes in tradition express the faith and creativity of different communities rather than a lack of faith and orthodoxy. It is in that sense that the denial of dynamism in the Christian tradition brings feminist theologians to suggest that the problem of changing tradition lies not only in the structures that dominate the Christian churches (such as a male clergy), but in the way that theology is being done, studied and written.

Theology has been dominated for centuries by a speculative and rational way of explaining the Christian faith. Theology has been seen as closer to the intellect of an individual rather than to the heart, meaning the feelings and emotions of believers. It has for centuries been developed in libraries and through the reading and re-reading of books. In that sense theology has been an instrument of control by those who have the proper (traditional) theological method (with knowledge of the Scriptures and tradition) and the proper rational answers to the mysteries of God. Those theologians have been instruments of control in a patriarchal society in which until this century male clerics were seen as the only interpreters of God's message and revelation.

In contrast, feminist ecclesiologies rely on the importance of human experience for theology. Such experience, and especially that of women, has been neglected and considered without importance in the churches. While human experience has been important in the ways that liberation theology has developed, it has still been framed in a traditional ecclesial structure provided by a patriarchal society.

The experience of women in their daily lives becomes the place in which feminist theology is carried out. Women, whether they are part of Christian communities or not, represent the place in which God speaks to men and women of today. Women represent the voice of God, and in their experience challenge the limited roles that the Christian churches give them to do theology, and to recognize God in their own lives. Collections of women's human experiences become then collections of theological writings because they manifest the action of God in this world of today through human experience. It follows that the God of human experience cannot be confined to the passages of Scripture chosen and interpreted by men only. God therefore changes position in feminist ecclesiologies. God is not above human interpreters, but walks and speaks through women and their daily experience.

Patriarchal society has stressed the fact that the Christian God is male, and communicates with men first, who in their turn share their experiences of God in the gathering of the believers. Many cultures in the world express their belief that God is female and that she is present in the experience of women. It follows that if God is projected as male and female, God speaks in the Christian assembly to men and women and through men and women. That assertion has important implications for the ritual practices of the Christian churches. Can women find the 'Our Father' meaningful if it addresses God as male? Can women find the reading of the Christian Scriptures meaningful when the language in the modern texts is not inclusive? That problem of language has caused many women to leave the Christian churches, because they cannot identify themselves with the words that seem to place them in subordination.

The problem of women's gifts and charisms in the Christian churches needs to be re-examined in the study and the writings of feminist ecclesiologies. The eucharist, that centre of unity for a Christian community, is for the most part presided at by male ministers. The issue of the ordination of women has painfully divided Christian congregations. A feminist model of church empowers all members of the community to preside at the eucharist. The fact that Jesus was male does not justify the exclusion of women. The Roman Catholic Church has closed the doors to any future discussion on this point by the papal letter of Pentecost 1994.

The principle of equality in feminist ecclesiology aims at fostering gifts and charisms, and gifts and charisms are given to individuals, they are not gendered by a male tradition.

A feminist model of church is not to be studied from books, but is a manifestation of the human experience of women and men who want to unite themselves with God and with each other in communities in which their gifts and prophetic charisms are recognized. As a new feminist theology grounded in the daily human experience of women emerges, the creation and implementation of a feminist model of church becomes an ever closer reality, which nevertheless already challenges the existing patriarchal Christian churches all over the world.

Further reading: Dickey Young 1990; Isherwood and McEwan 1993; Ruether 1983, 1985; Schüssler Fiorenza 1983.

ECOFEMINISM
Anne Primavesi

THE TERM 'ecofeminism' was coined by the French writer Françoise d'Eaubonne and introduced in her book *Le Féminisme ou la mort*, published in 1974. She used it for a particular kind of ecological movement in which women's consciousness of oppression is the main driving force. As a philosophy, ecofeminism brings together a wide range of interconnected concerns, including issues of gender, race and class, while stressing the crucial role played in environmental degradation by the logic of patriarchal domination.

As a form of global activism, ecofeminism aims to educate consumers, environmental organizations and policy-makers about the complex web of interrelationships between all living organisms and their environment. It teaches the interdependence of human and environmental development and engages in courses of action appropriate to the environmental context. It educates by offering a feminist critique of the interrelationship of social and political forms of domination, in particular that of man over woman and nature. It focuses on the logic of this patriarchal domination, whether in language, in culture, in the political and earth sciences, in religion and in psychology, in policy-making and allocation of resources.

Ecofeminists see, for example, that both women and nature suffer common subjection to the destructive technologies of modern patriarchal society. These technologies function most overtly and oppressively within the realms of war and militarism, capitalism and industrialism, genetic and reproductive engineering (Mellor 1992). They function covertly but no less oppressively in mind/body/spirit pollution inflicted through patriarchal myth and language on all levels of societal interaction (Daly). They further the economic colonization of women, of 'foreign' peoples and their lands (Mies and Shiva 1993).

Ecofeminists highlight the connections between environmental degradation and the feminization of poverty. Women, as members of and carers in poor communities, are the first to suffer the environmental effects of industrial and military pollution. As primary producers and processors of food for those communities, they are the first to feel the effects of unsustainable development programmes resulting from decisions and policies over which they have no control. However, even where there is agreement on common factors in their oppression, as in the Official Report of the Women's World Congress for a Healthy Planet held in Miami in 1992 (Women's Environment and Development Organization 1992), ecofeminism does not presuppose a unitary voice for women. Its theory making and activism are necessarily global and diverse, since the character of the oppression it seeks to unmask and resist is multidimensional.

The ecofeminist response is intended to be positive. It seeks to celebrate women's affinity with the natural world and to use it to break down the conventional boundary between nature and culture. It aims at an alternative culture: one which is more peace-loving, non-hierarchical and therefore able to address issues in a wider social, personal and ecological context.

The boundary between nature and culture still continues to be a place of tension within the ecofeminist movement. On the one hand, there are those who reject any essentialist notion of the relationship between women and nature, seeing this as colluding with a patriarchal construct by which women are identified with nature in order to exclude them from culture.

ECOFEMINISM

On the other hand, some see it as a relationship to be fostered, one which can serve as a catalyst for a new consciousness capable of halting destructive practices which threaten the well-being of life on the planet. There are others again who fear that the focus may shift from the politics of women's liberation towards ecological activism in which women are again marginalized and their particular needs and exploitation are forgotten.

Wherever the ecofeminist response occurs, it has a spiritual dimension, one which often places it in a critical relationship with traditionally patriarchal religious institutions. In 1972, Mary Daly made the link between ecological crisis, social domination and Christian doctrine. She contrasted the Christian ethic of 'missions' (to convert 'pagans' or 'barbarians' often over their dead bodies) with that of 'the cosmic covenant of sisterhood' which embraces our sister the earth and all of her non-human inhabitants and elements. This, she says, has the potential to change our environment from a culture of rapism to a culture of reciprocity, one in which we will look upon the earth and her sister planets as being *with* us, not *for* us. She went on to translate parts of d'Eaubonne's writings and to interpret their insights.

Also in 1972, the Christian ecofeminist theological critique was taken up by Rosemary Radford Ruether. In a liberation theology done from a 'feminine, somatic and ecological perspective', she has concentrated attention on the basic dualities which, she claims, all have roots in the apocalyptic-Platonic religious heritage of classical Christianity. These include the alienation of the mind from the body; the alienation of the subjective self from the objective world; the subjective retreat of the individual alienated from the social community; the domination or rejection of nature by spirit. As these symbolic patterns underpin patriarchal religion, we need reshaping, she says, from these alienating dualisms to a symbolic vision of salvation as a continual conversion to the center, to the concrete basis by which we sustain our relation to nature and to one another. We must reshape our basic sense of self in relation to the cycles of life.

Sallie McFague argues for the deconstruction of models and metaphors oppressive and dangerous to the planet. Since Christian tradition has contributed a number of problematic images, it is incumbent upon its theologians to analyse 'the universe as God's body', an ancient organic metaphor which in one form or another was central to Western sensibility until it was replaced by a mechanistic model in the seventeenth century. As a physical image stressing divine embodiment it underscores what the Christian tradition has seldom allowed: that matter is of God and is good.

Ellen Bernstein, director of the Shomrei Adamah project, focuses on the vision of the sixteenth-century Jewish Kabbalist mystics, working for *tikkun olam*, the repair of the world through the integration of the 'four worlds' of Action, Emotion, Intelligence and Spirit. She creates resource material for holy days which honour their seasonal rhythms and ecological roots, connecting Jewish environmentalists to their biblical sources of ecological wisdom.

These and other strands in religious traditions are woven by some ecofeminists, such as Starhawk, into a contemporary spirituality framed by postpatriarchal conceptualizations of the female body. This philosophy of spiritual feminism declares that in both human and divine terms the female is as much the norm as the male. It places the onus for change in society on the recognition of the spiritual as a major element and claims for women a right to their own autonomous spirituality, one not mediated through men's views and actions.

Such spiritual feminism is usually associated, by those outside it, with the Goddess movement. They also assume that the term 'the Goddess' must mean a female equivalent of the traditional God of Judaism, Christianity or Islam. In fact, 'the Goddess' is a shorthand term for a more varied set of concepts coming from three major sources: the feminist movement, native and classical religions and forms related to Judaism and Christianity. From whatever source, the concept of 'the Goddess' within women, of the sacrality of female sexuality (not to be confined to fertility) and of freeing the female divine, is part of a contemporary movement to reconstruct the world. By aligning oneself with the seasons, with the elements, and thereby enhancing self-value, the spiritual and empower-

An A to Z of Feminist Theology

ECOFEMINISM

ing dimension of our relationship with the earth is emphasized (Long 1994).

This honouring of the power of the female and its embeddedness in nature is perceived by some feminists as regressive. Charlene Spretnak ascribes this reaction to the acceptance and internalizing of the patriarchal dualism of nature versus culture. This, she says, has been rejected from the outset by Goddess spirituality. Its central understanding is that the divine is immanent, not concentrated in some distant seat of power, such as a transcendent sky-god. The Goddess is a metaphor for divine immanence and the transcendent sacred whole. As such, she is used to express ongoing regeneration within the cycles of her Earthbody and contains the mystery of diversity within unity.

Joanna Macy has made a major theoretical contribution to the evolution of an environmental ethic informed by Buddhist and environmental philosophy. She interprets the primary teaching of interrelationship in an environmental context, developing her ideas of the 'ecological self' based on analysis of the co-arising of knower and known, body and mind, doer and deed, self and society. This 'self' she describes as a metaphoric construct of identity and agency: the notion around which we focus our instincts for self-preservation, our needs for self-approval and the boundaries of our self-interest. The conventional notion of this self is being and must be replaced by wider constructs of identity and self-interest through a process she calls the 'greening of the self'.

Stephanie Kaza takes the Buddhist concept of experiential knowing based on embodied mindfulness as consonant with the feminist validation of subjective knowing which has been consistently denigrated by Western patriarchal cultures as self-centred and distorted by emotionality. Integrated, experiential knowing, which includes both the object of knowing and the knower herself or himself, is necessary for understanding the complexities of the environmental crisis. The Buddhist and feminist emphasis on direct experience of the environment is informed by the body as mind, rather than body or mind as separate. Through this grounding, the practitioner gains a legitimate voice with which to speak personally and specifically of environmental relationships and how they are ignored, sabotaged or otherwise denied.

This legitimate voice is heard also in those women's movements which derive largely from Hindu thought as interpreted by Gandhi. The feminist ethic they weave together from these sources and their own experience has some characteristics identified by Devaki Jain. They share them with their Buddhist and ecofeminist sisters worldwide, but base them on Gandhi's this-worldly approach to revolution and solidarity with the poor, the unskilled and unemployed.

The first characteristic is their practical desire for peace, demonstrated by their support of peace movements and their rejection of militarism. This is one of the founding insights of ecofeminism: the interconnectedness of war on nature and the hidden, daily war on 'others', however characterized and by whatever means. It is not accidental that one of the first public manifestations of the ecofeminist movement in America was the Women's Pentagon Actions in 1980 and 1981.

A second characteristic is their sense of responsibility and their care for each other and for the survival of the whole. Women's traditional ethical norms are neither individualistic nor group centred. Rather they tend to consider the individual in the context of the group. These norms are manifest in the Chipko movement, the Appiko movement and the Girnar movement centered on the preservation of forests in India. Arising from the same sense of community and context is the Green Belt movement in Africa, in which the scientist Wangari Maathai has enlisted thousands of women in rural areas to plant millions of trees, educating them while doing so in the role of forestation in sustainable ecosystems.

One of the most influential figures in ecofeminism today is the Indian scientist Vandana Shiva whose critique of Western science, its methodologies and effects, is focused on new developments in biotechnology, genetic engineering and reproductive technologies. Her main focus now is what she calls 'the seed movement', a fight against the technologizing of seed production by transnational corporations (TNCs). She calls this 'patenting of life' a violation of ethical and eco-

An A to Z of Feminist Theology

logical principles, and in the autumn of 1993, with the farmers' union of Bangalore, South India, organized a protest against it attended by more than half a million people.

The ecofeminist awareness of the inequalities and injustices in today's world structures unites women and men who work to redress those inequalities in diverse ways informed by different spiritual and philosophical visions of just and fruitful relationships.

Further reading: Adams (ed.) 1993 (especially bibliography); McKinnon and McIntyre 1995; Plumwood 1993; Primavesi 1991; Ruether 1992; Warren 1994.

ECONOMICS
Elizabeth Nash

ECONOMICS IS commonly defined as the scientific study of the production and distribution of wealth or of the relationship between scarce resources and the uses which compete for them. Such a definition is neither about feminism nor theology and yet economics is relevant to them both. Wealth means welfare, prosperity or riches. The way in which wealth and resources, both scarce and plentiful, are distributed throughout society is a reflection of the values of that society. Economics cannot be value free.

Economics and Scientific Method

The claim to scientific method is significant to economists, but it is hard to show that economics follows such methodology. An economist does not observe actual behaviour, seek a theoretical explanation and then prove the theory by repeated observations of the behaviour. The forecasting record of economic models has never been good. Economists take a small part of the real world and build a simplified model of it in order to understand how things are related to one another. The simplification means that many factors are excluded from the theories. For example, the law of supply and demand would suggest that doctors are paid high wages because there is a shortage of them and nurses low wages because there are too many of them. In fact neither is the case. Wages in the medical professions are more likely to reflect position in the medical power hierarchy and whether the job is traditionally held by men or women than they are to reflect economic theory.

The claim to be a science also raises questions about the nature of the 'laws' of economics. Despite modern understanding of the nature of the world, the term 'scientific' might seem to imply a law that cannot be changed. It is not true that the laws of economics cannot be changed by human beings. The principles of economics are not like the laws of physics; they depend on the behaviour of human beings who, if they chose to behave in different ways, would change the principles. Indeed, 'New Science' is moving in the same direction and we are beginning to understand that all scientific law depends on human observers and their behaviour.

A Feminist Critique

The feminist critique of economics begins with the understanding that since the majority of economists have been white men they have used themselves as the model for humanity. The simplified models they build are based on the white male as norm. This has led to three major flaws:

1. Economists have analysed only the parts of life which have price tags hung on them or which could be converted into money. This has meant that a large part of economic activity, the part in which women are active, is ignored. This happens despite the fact that the economic world depends on workers being fed, clothed and cleaned, new workers being brought up and old workers cared for.

2. The power structure, in which power is largely held by white men, is assumed to be the norm and to have no effect on economic theory.

3. The exploitation, both past and present, of the resources of the countries of the South and the exportation of poverty from the developed nations to the South is not given its full value in economic theory.

A Theological Critique

A theological critique begins from the perception that there is a relationship between God and the whole of God's world, including the economic world. This means that, first, the value

ECONOMICS

framework of economics needs to be recognized and set in a theological context. For example, the objectives of industry need to be analysed for their contribution to 'abundant life':

> As long as industry is organised primarily, not for the service of the community but with the object of producing a purely financial result for some of its members, it cannot be recognized as properly fulfilling its social purpose.' What is needed is new understanding of what the economic activity is for. What is needed is to conceive social life from the viewpoint of continuity of life (Swantz 1989: 9).

Secondly, there is a theological hierarchical power model with God at the apex and angels, men, women and the rest of the created order descending below God. It is the model which the Christian church has used for its own structures. In the secular world it has been used to reinforce hierarchical power structures which threaten the environment, the majority of human beings and the survival of all life. Feminist theology regards this as a distortion of Christian theology. Economics, like theology, needs to look for new models of operating using co-operation and ensuring that proper value is given to each part of creation.

Economics is of fundamental importance to all human beings because it has a profound effect on our lives. From both a feminist and a theological perspective economics needs to be reshaped so that all areas of work, all people, the whole created order, the power systems and the value framework are included in its models.

How to Create a Feminist and Theological Model of Economics

A feminist and theological model of economics begins by analysing the whole of the economic world, including the parts which currently have no monetary value, in terms of 'why?'. It is not enough to describe some countries as developed without being clear why they are developed and at whose cost is their development. The attempt to understand why women across the world do more work for less pay than men requires an analysis of community and family values, of the social construction of women and men, of the religious framework of societies in addition to the monetary implications. The question why, rather than a description of what is, raises the issue of justice and fairness which is fundamental to the theological perspective.

Then there is the need to recognize and understand the five key building blocks of our present economic system. They are:

1. The profit motive, which is the engine of a capitalist economy but which is based on selfishness rather than the highest of human motives and actions.

2. The sexual division of labour, which values work and pays for it according to gender.

3. Racial discrimination, which both individually and structurally values people and their contribution to society according to their skin colour.

4. The global division of labour, which encourages business to locate its employment where workers are paid the least and controls of safety and care for the environment are not enforced.

5. Military power, which is the biggest area of international expenditure and which both economically and materially enforces the current power structure.

The third step is to ask: what sort of a world do we want? What should the resources of the world be used for? Who should own land and property, how should everyone's basic needs of food, clothing and shelter be met, what access should people have to education and health care, how should income be distributed, what economic rights should people be guaranteed, what is the place of plants, animals and the environment? The role of women and of black people, the interests of the powerless as well as the powerful should be considered. The tasks of governments in the local, national and international economy should also be included. The answers to these questions can be found through careful theological study. The Bible is a plentiful source book on this subject, with for instance, references to the year of the Jubilee (Lev. 25.10-23), care in society (Deut. 24.17-22), or lack of it (Amos 2.6-8, 5.10-13), Jesus' comments on wealth (Mk 10.23-25), sharing and wealth in the early church (Acts 4.32-35; Jas 2.1-7, 14-17), and the economic contribution of women to Jesus' ministry (Lk. 8.1-3). We should not all agree on the answers to these questions, neither as feminists nor theologians, but it is important to explore the questions thoroughly before seeking economic answers.

The final task is to work out how to go from steps one and two, our understanding of the current situation, to step three, the way we want the world to be. The gap between the two is enormous, and it is by no means clear how to go from one to the other. There is no single correct route. The collapse of the capitalist economies under the weight of their own necessary inequalities or the advent of major revolution or the destruction of the environment are possible routes to alternative economies but they will bring chaos, destruction and disaster. If other routes are possible they will include:

1. Building a new value system, replacing the values of our current society (exploitation, patriarchy, violence, consumerism, exclusion) with the values of a just society (respect for everyone, solidarity between people, stewardship of the earth, non-violence, co-operation, participation.)

2. Living the new value system. A just economic society calls us to choose our lifestyles to match. 'Live simply, that others may simply live.' Unless this happens, there will be less potential for change, and for meeting people's needs.

3. Building new structures, which will create new ways of working and new organizations for the production and delivery of services, such as co-operatives, credit unions, women's organizations.

4. Transforming existing institutions, so that new values reshape the patterns of doing and relating in existing institutions, decision-making becomes participatory, reward systems more just, not biased on grounds of race or gender, conflicts are settled non-violently and co-operation replaces competition.

5. Organizing and designing the process of change. This means organizing, campaigning, demonstrating, boycotting. It takes time, money and effort to create economic and political change.

6. Standing against what is wrong. One part of working for change is preventing policies and actions which reinforce the status quo or take us backwards. It is not possible to be neutral. To be silent is to stand on the side of the status quo and the powerful (see Religious Network for Equality for Women 1988).

Since economics is the creation of human beings and not a set of immutable laws it is properly subject to an ethical analysis, in a theological context, from a feminist perspective. Economists have not sufficiently recognized the value judgments they make and the ethical issues involved. Feminism demands a whole new look at a subject that has been structured in a male way, and the theological critique creates a framework for reviewing the ideas and decisions resulting from economic theory. This whole analysis shows the need for a change in economics itself. For such change to happen, those who recognize the need for it will have to take action. Some actions will be very small, at individual consumer level, some will change hearts and minds and some will reconstruct economics. 'The earth is the Lord's', including all the wealth and the scarce resources. Economists should be answering the question of how these are distributed in the light of feminist theology. Economic theory can be made to reflect a theological and feminist understanding of society.

Further reading: Blumberg (ed.) 1988; Omerod 1994; Pahl 1989; Waring 1988.

ECUMENISM
Lavinia Byrne

SINCE ITS earliest origins, the Christian church has had to struggle with the fact that its members have many gifts and that, in spite of their diversity, they are called to form one household or *oikonomia*. The gift of communion is a gift of the Spirit (2 Cor. 13.13; Phil. 2.1). It will be characterized by community, communion, sharing, fellowship, participation and solidarity rather than by competition or hostility on the one hand, or convergence and a blanket uniformity on the other. In recent years the ecumenical movement in the United Kingdom has mirrored this theological insight by undertaking to follow the Swanwick Declaration of 1987. Here the thirty churches which now belong to

ECUMENISM

the Council of Churches for Britain and Ireland established that 'our churches must now move from co-operation to clear commitment to each other, in search for the unity for which Christ prayed, and in common evangelism and service of the world'.

These churches belong to the Anglican, Baptist and Congregational, Lutheran and Reformed, Methodist, Orthodox, Pentecostal and Holiness, Roman Catholic traditions, as well as the Religious Society of Friends and the Salvation Army. The Council of Churches for Britain and Ireland exists to help these churches to find strength and encouragement in the sharing of worship and prayer, in undertaking joint ventures in mission and evangelism and in responding together to the needs of the human community in these islands and throughout the world. Recognizing that there are still matters which divide the churches, the CCBI provides a forum within which these can be faced more openly as churches grow in understanding and trust. In particular the CCBI links together the work of the four national ecumenical instruments: Churches Together in England; Action of Churches Together in Scotland; CYTUN or Churches Together in Wales; and the Irish Council of Churches. It also co-operates with other inter-church agencies such as Christian Aid and CAFOD. Among the joint ventures of the churches is the Ecumenical Decade of the Churches in Solidarity with Women 1988–98.

Origins

1975 was the United Nations International Women's Year and gave rise to an international decade for women. At the closing conference of this decade, which was held in Nairobi, a Methodist bishop declared, 'what we need is a churches' decade for women'. The World Council of Churches launched this in 1988; its British launch came at Easter with a large service in Westminster Abbey. The year 1993 marked the middle of the Decade and afforded us the opportunity to assess how well it has been implemented in the British and Irish context. So far the best response seems to have come from women themselves. It should be noted that the Ecumenical Decade on Evangelism/Evangelization has moved more rapidly to the front of people's minds because it has received more active financial support from the churches. In many local communities and among women's groups, however, the Decade has provided a rich focus for study days, seminars and conferences, liturgies and the creation of artefacts such as the Durham Quilt and the Manchester Mosaic.

Aims

From the beginning the aims of the Decade have been quite clear:

1. Empowering women to challenge oppressive structures in the global community, their country and their church.

2. Affirming—through shared leadership and decision-making, theology and spirituality—the decisive contributions of women in churches and communities.

3. Giving visibility to women's perspectives and actions in the work and struggle for justice, peace and the integrity of creation.

4. Enabling the churches to free themselves from racism, sexism and classism; from teachings and practices which discriminate against women.

5. Encouraging the churches to take actions in solidarity with women.

It puts the following priorities before the Christian community:

1. Women's full participation in church and community life.

2. Women's perspectives and commitments to justice, peace and the integrity of creation.

3. Women doing theology and sharing spirituality.

These aims serve as a powerful reminder to the churches that the ecumenical requirement goes wider than the sharing of church property or even shared worship. True ecumenism is best served when the radical questions about the human family as a multi-faith, multi-racial and mixed gender community lead to positive action undertaken collaboratively. In this way, in the words of Dr Mary Tanner, Moderator of the World Council of Churches' Faith and Order Commission, *koinonia* will surely become more visible as we learn to be more attentive to each other's experiences and insights and become together a communion in dialogue, never again giving up on one another'.

Further reading: Best (ed.) 1988; Byrne (ed.) 1992, 1993; Gnanadason 1993; Oduyoye 1992.

EMPOWERMENT
Carter Heyward

IN FEMINIST liberation theology and relational psychology, empowerment refers to the relational process through which persons experience their creative, liberating power, or capacity, to survive, affect others creatively, and make a positive difference (see Heyward 1982, 1989; Harrison 1985; Starhawk 1987; Jordan *et al.* 1991; Williams 1993). While, for psychologists, empowerment is a human transaction, for feminist theologians, it is a simultaneously divine and human process which strengthens both Creator and creature.

As a relational process, empowerment involves mutual change and growth, not merely the granting of power as a status or privilege. In a feminist liberation theological framework, power is a creative, liberating relational energy, not a personal, professional, or political attribute or possession (Heyward 1982). This power is the root of love and justice-making in history. Moreover, this power is not only 'from' God; it *is* God, and therefore can be termed sacred. When we are empowered/empowering creatures, we ourselves are 'godding'.

Framing 'empowerment' and 'sacred power' in this way is a departure from orthodox Christian understandings of the goodness of God's power and the depravity of human power. Whether power is more or less creative or destructive, liberating or harmful, it is a social force, a relational energy that belongs to no one.

Relational power is destructive when people are dominating and controlling others. This 'power-over' (Starhawk, 1987; Heyward 1989) is the basis of wrong-relation, or injustice. Relational power is creative and liberating when it is being generated mutually for the well-being of all. In feminist liberation theology, empowerment refers to the creative, liberating process of generating mutual relation, or 'power-with'.

In particular relational situations, if power is to be understood as more or less creative or harmful, it must be analysed: static, unchanging power-dynamics in any relationship are not right and invariably hurt, diminish or oppress people and other creatures.

Empowerment then refers to a process of relational transformation, in which persons experience themselves and others as open, growing and changing in and through their relationships with one another. A psychological effect of empowerment is relational expansiveness: those who experience themselves as open, growing and changing in a particular relationship often will experience themselves this way in other relationships and in the larger world (Jordan *et al.* 1991). Empowerment is a process in which one's sense of personal identity is enlarged to include the quality of one's relationships with others in the world. In this way, being a 'person' means not simply being 'oneself' but being-in-relation-to-others. Empowerment relativizes our self-understandings. We are not autonomous, separate beings but rather are persons only in relation. Our well-being is always relative—in relation—to others.

Among Christian feminist liberation theologians, Jesus is often remembered as a brother through whose life God, our power in mutual relation, was manifest abundantly. We remember then not who, or what, Jesus was in himself but rather who he was in relation to others and who they were in relation to him and one another. The christic, or liberating, power evidenced through Jesus' relationships is incarnate among us in right, mutually empowering, relation with one another. As such, empowerment is a christic process, sacred and liberating. Among feminist liberation theologians, this Christology has emerged through the work of such women as Dorothee Sölle, Rosemary Radford Ruether, Beverly Harrison, Carter Heyward, Rita Nakashima Brock, Sallie McFague, Delores Williams, and Kwok Pui-lan.

As a basis of Christian faith, empowerment signifies more than a reaction against the human powerlessness of neo-orthodoxy and the individualism of liberal religion. It reflects a radical experience of divine incarnation as the social/relational basis of our lives. Increasingly among feminists, empowerment is understood as a relational process involving not only humans but all members of creation and the sacred energy that connects us (McFague 1993). We are connected in and at the root of who we are. This root is God, our power in mutual relation. This sacred power, as we draw upon it through active commitments to justice and compassion, and through meditation and prayer, constitutes our moral agency, our shared capacity to create justice where there is oppression; to show compassion where there is hatred or indifference; and to bear faith, hope, and love where there is despair and fear.

EROTIC POWER
Lisa Isherwood

'EROTIC POWER' is a term that originated with Audre Lorde (1978) and is also used by Rita Brock (1988). It grounds their ideas in reality, suggesting that the ability to bring about transformation lies within us, in our deep desire for union with others. Erotic power relates to our deepest passion and can be applied to all areas of life, not just genital sexual expression. It is a drive for justice and it fuels our commitment to create justice between one another.

Brock claims that erotic power saves both us and Christ because it is found in the heart and therefore opens us to the divine reality of connection. It saves us because it shows us this possibility, and it saves Christ because it thrives on connectedness and therefore removes him from the relationship of dominance and control in which he has been placed by a male theology concerned with hierarchy.

Erotic power also saves us from the sterility of living in our heads alone and places our knowing ability back in relation to our whole selves. The Bible warns that a people who lack imagination will perish and so erotic power opens us once more to all our ways of knowing. *Agape* has been stressed as the highest form of love but for Brock it is too objective; *eros* engages us in a whole way with our world. *Eros* is often confused with lust, but this is too narrow a way of understanding it; lust may not be grounded in mutuality and empowerment while erotic power always is. Erotic power shows us that we experience at a much deeper level than we conceptualize and so we should trust experience more than logic.

Erotic power is a kind of power that is qualitatively different from the one with which we are familiar, a power which could mean the redemption of the entire universe. Erotic power propels us beyond the narrow model of 'power over' oneself, others and the universe into a place of sensual connection. This empowered physicality enables deeply ethical relations with the rest of the created order.

Further reading: Heyward 1982.

ESCHATOLOGY
Lisa Isherwood

ESCHATOLOGY IS a major part of most religious systems, since what will happen at 'the end of things' is a preoccupation for many people. The Bible has an array of eschatological opinions for feminist theology to consider. The main stream of eschatological thought in the Hebrew Scriptures is known as prophetic eschatology: this expresses Israel's conviction that it was an elected people with a part to play in God's judgment over the universe. This was for the most part a historical understanding although the idea that there would be a Judgment Day did develop later; it was probably a development that occurred when the people felt that they had no historical hope. If God were to establish his supremacy it would have to happen outside history and put an end to history as we know it. This kind of eschatology does not suppose that the exact end can be seen by the prophets, but rather that they can deduce from the contemporary situation how things are likely to turn out.

Even though Israel is seen as God's chosen, this election carries with it responsibility and punishment for failing in one's duties. Isaiah developed the idea of the 'remnant', or the few of the elect who would be saved; these are the righteous few who keep the covenant with God and grow close to him. Deutero-Isaiah declares that the secrets of the eschatological age are worked out between God and the angels and then spoken to the prophets. The struggle between God and the evil ones is already over and the false gods are helpless. This of course is placing eschatology on an entirely different plane. It has been argued that there was no

ESCHATOLOGY

eschatological thought in pre-exilic literature because God was in control of his land and could therefore predetermine all the punishment and reward in the course of the people's history. The exile, however, brought this neat pattern into question: the people were righteous and yet suffering, so either God had lied or his promises would come to fruition in another dimension. The only confidence righteous Jews could have was that a reward would be forthcoming in a time to come.

By the time of Jesus Palestine was a place of intense eschatological expectation. Once again the people were in political captivity and so the notion that the righteous would find reward in history was in question, although there was a general feeling that God would somehow manifest his power and save the righteous. The Qumran sect believed that there would be a final confrontation, but they also thought that they were already exempt from judgment due to their pure lifestyles.

The Gospel writers were not only sure that something would happen; they knew that something already had. The reign of God was manifesting itself among them, but very little seemed to have changed, and we find a tension in their writing between the notion that something would happen and the notion that something had already happened. The Synoptic Gospels show this clearly in their talk of the Second Coming, Jesus has already achieved some liberation and reward for the righteous but he will come again in order to complete his task. The early followers of Jesus did not think this time was very far away. The Gospel of Mark presents the whole story of Jesus as an eschatological struggle with evil: Jesus defeats the devil by performing exorcisms and miracles, as well as defeating ignorance, which is the hallmark of the devil, in debate. Luke has the heavens rejoicing and the lowly being raised, which is what we would expect in a world under the direct rule of God. Matthew, the most Semitic of the writers, does not emphasize all these elements of realized eschatology, but he does call Jesus 'Emmanuel', or 'with us is God'. So there is an acknowledgment that, while changes are happening now, they will all be brought to greater fullness by the Second Coming.

The author of the Fourth Gospel was obviously aware of this train of thought, but was also writing much later, when the expected Second Coming had not occurred. While this Gospel contains all the elements of future eschatology—references to the parousia, judgment, resurrection and future salvation—there is also a strong sense that all has already been accomplished. Bultmann believed that all the future eschatological references were the work of a redactor, but this seems to be overstating the case. We can say, rather, that the Fourth Evangelist took the traditional material and used it in a distinctive way. For example, Jesus tells us that he does not judge us (Jn 3.19), but that the light has come into the world; so his presence provides a model against which our actions are judged. This shows the eschatological tension: we are judged now by our actions even though there may be events still to come. The same is true of the resurrection narratives: we are told that the time will come but also has already come when the dead will hear the voice of Jesus and have life (Jn 5.25). The tension here is great. C.K. Barrett has suggested that this passage refers to the raising of Lazarus which is to come, but others are not convinced by this argument. It could mean that the dead are already being raised on some other plane, or that some kind of awakening is happening in the hearts of those who are physically alive while spiritually dead; if the text is taken at face value it contains a promise of something beyond what is occurring now, which constitutes an eschatological perspective.

Feminist theology rejects dualism and so has to dismiss the notion that all will be well in some other realm at the end of time. Indeed as a liberation theology it cannot, nor does it wish to, live with that kind of luxury of thought. Feminist theology is committed to transforming the reality for people on this earth and for the earth itself. In this respect it is like the pre-exilic literature in emphasizing that justice will be done on this earth and in this history. Where it differs dramatically is that it places God so deeply in the process of the earth's becoming that there can be no promise of outside intervention; last-minute intervention on behalf of the just is not a possibility, because God cannot be that distant from creation. The notion of covenant is perhaps relevant here; we have to work with the divine and allow it to come to birth in and between us. All of us have to do this because if we fail there is no guarantee, as of old, that a 'righteous remnant' will survive.

In some feminist thought there is a shift from seeing personal survival as necessary towards understanding that with the rejection of dualism and the acceptance of personal experience as the ground of what is real, personal survival after death is unlikely. We are part of a greater whole, the cosmos, and we are no more significant than any other part; why, then, should our continuation after death be different from that of the rest of the created order? We too will continue as part of the whole, as 'divine compost'. This is not to suggest that we should therefore see the survival of the species or the creation of justice as unimportant; rather, we should see them as important in themselves, and not because they will lead to our personal salvation. Feminist eschatology requires living for harmony and justice; living in order that we may contribute to that reality, not living as though all has been achieved or will be achieved in some other dimension.

ESSENTIALISM
Janet Martin Soskice

'ESSENTIALISM', IN feminist contexts, refers to explanatioarguments are widely rejected by feminists. The rival theoretical position is sometimes called constructivism, and has been most succinctly and influentially expressed in Simone de Beauvoir's remark that one is not born, but rather is made, a woman.

There are different kinds of essentialism. The most familiar and most summarily dismissed is biological essentialism, which argues from biological distinctions to certain social conclusions (for instance, 'because of the nature of female reproductive organs, women are by nature more sexual creatures than men'). Many of the arguments from biological nature to social role, invoked on issues as diverse as women's suffrage and ordination, now seem risible. But as well as biological essentialism there are various forms of psychological essentialism, some of which have been invoked by feminist theorists, for example in suggestions that women are by nature more nurturing or caring than men. Psychological essentialism shades into biological essentialism when it is suggested that the differences noted are inherent and universal features of males and females. But there is a softer version of psychological essentialism which suggests that while the differences we see (for instance, women being more given to caring and nurturing) are not the product of biological nature so much as of socialization, nonetheless in a particular culture one can say that women or men generally 'are' this way. (Carol Gilligan's *In a Different Voice: Psychological Theory and Women's Development*, with its suggestions that women incline to an ethic of care rather than an ethic of justice, generated much debate in this regard.) It is more difficult to develop a consistent critique of this soft psychological essentialism, without ruling out argumentative strategies feminists themselves use; for instance, without eliminating feminist appeals to 'women's experience'.

Diana Fuss, in her important and illuminating book on essentialism (1989), suggests that rather than disparage 'essentialism' categorically, it is more useful for feminists to note that there are different types of essentialist argument; these include appeals to a pure or original femininity, insistence on an autonomous female voice (as in *écriture féminine*), and even the essentialism involved in feminist politics, which must make its case on the basis of some identifying solidarity, even while wanting to say that women are different one from another. It is not obvious that essentialism in this last sense is vicious and, as Fuss points out in criticism of deconstructionist anti-essentialism, dismissal of essence can displace 'the class "woman" which feminism needs to articulate its very politics' (1989: 24). Fuss suggests that the problem is not essentialist argumentation per se, but the end to which it is put.

A number of French feminists have been dismissed by English-speaking feminists as essentialists; notably Julia Kristeva with her explorations of the maternal and Luce Irigaray with her apparent invocation of female anatomy (the two lips). Their defenders (for example Whitford 1991) argue that these writers are concerned by the extent to which the texts of philosophy have been dominated by the male symbolic order and see a need, provocatively, to make this dominance evident by explorations of a female symbolic. To move too quickly from a dominant masculine order to a putatively androgynous one may once again silence and efface women.

Further reading: Jagger 1983; Kristeva 1980; Zrigaray 1985.

ETHICAL THEORY
Linda Hogan

THERE IS a sense in which all feminist theory has an ethical dimension. The formulation of appropriate biblical hermeneutics, the reconceptualization of theological categories, the debates about inclusive language and the ordination of women, all involve us in ethical questions. In addition to this feminist theology has been engaged in reconsidering the content, method and epistemology of ethical theory with attention to current philosophical and theological concerns.

The feminist contribution to specific debates is, undoubtedly significant. One thinks of Sarah Ruddick and Mary Condren on issues of war and peace, Rosalind Petchesky and Gena Corea on new reproductive technologies, Susan Thistlethwaite and Katherine Zappone on issues of poverty and violence. In addition to these specific contributions, a major reformulation of ethical theory has taken place. This is highly significant because the reconceptualization of notions of autonomy and relationality, of particularity and difference, of moral knowledge, far-reaching implications for our analysis of specific ethical issues and responses to particular problems.

Methodology

Alternative ways of knowing and doing arise out of feminist experience and praxis. Indeed one of the distinguishing features of feminist ethical theory is that it claims, as a legitimate starting point for action and reflection, the concrete experiences and praxis of women and feminist men living under patriarchy. In affirming this starting point feminist ethical theory intends to accomplish a methodological shift, since it claims as its primary resources not sacred texts and traditions, but contemporary experience and praxis. This is not an advocacy of the abandonment of feminism to the unmediated subjectivities of women's lives. Women's experience is a central resource certainly. But since it is basically fractured it requires reinterpretation, evaluation and critique. Feminists must be able to acknowledge and arbitrate between competing subjectivities since women do not share a uniform experience or material reality. Experiences are resources but not in an unmediated, atheoretical sense.

Embodiment

As a consequence of the adoption of this methodological stance the content of ethical theory has undergone substantial review. Beverly Wildung Harrison's work has been central to this process. In *Making the Connections: Essays in Feminist Social Ethics* (1985) she mentions attention to embodiment as one of the central features of feminist ethics. In line with a number of theorists Harrison argues that in the dominant ethical tradition 'moral rationality too often is disembodied rationality' (Harrison 1985: 129). Rooted in a theology which promotes a dualism which denigrates the body (and in consequence women, who are more identified with carnality), this rationality promotes a disengaged objectivity as the most appropriate posture for academics to adopt. In contrast however a feminist ethic must begin with 'our bodies ourselves', must eschew all dualistic impulses and promote an understanding of moral knowledge which is body-mediated. This is a natural consequence of a revised notion of the moral subject which appreciates human beings as embodied and does not treat the body as merely an accessory.

Autonomy

Another significant feature of feminist ethics, perhaps the most central, has been the insistence that women recover their autonomy, particularly in the ethical realm. Although published in 1960, Valerie Saiving's 'The Human Situation: A Feminine View' (repr. in Christ and Plaskow [eds.] 1979) remains a powerful statement of the experience of many women. Saiving argues that one of the primary features of women's lives under patriarchy has been our failure to take responsibility for our situation. Encouraged to be passive by a theology which construes sin in terms of 'pride, arrogance, will-to-power…the unjustified concern of the self for its own power and prestige', women have abdicated responsibil-

ETHICAL THEORY

ity and understood themselves as victims. In contrast to the conventional sense of sin women are likely to sin in an entirely different way. The temptations of women are better suggested, Saiving claims, by such things as 'triviality, distractability, lack of an organising centre...dependence on others for one's own self-definitio...underdevelopment or negation of the self'.

There is a certain extent to which this analysis of the female situation is outmoded. Nonetheless the expectation that women become more self-effacing and self-sacrificing has resulted in a reluctance to trust women as competent moral agents. The autonomy towards which we all strive in the moral arena is neither demanded nor welcome in relation to women. It is in this context that the 'right to choose' cliché can function in a positive manner in feminist ethics. It highlights an essential quality of all moral decision-making, which is that responsible choice is central to moral agency. We must be both required and encouraged to make responsible decisions about every aspect of our lives without hiding behind unquestioned assumptions about women's nature or women's traditional roles.

One of the basic demands of feminist ethics, then, is that we acknowledge the principle of autonomy, which is an essential element in our understanding of personhood, in all areas of moral decision-making. Because social expectations of how women should behave have been more akin to what is expected of children rather than adults, autonomy has not been encouraged, particularly in the sexual arena. One of the central contributions of feminist ethics thus far has been its insistence that autonomy in the moral sphere is essential if women, individually and collectively, are to be respected as responsible members of society.

Such an insistence on moral autonomy for both women and men brings with it the language and theories of rights. Both politically and theoretically women have appealed for the extension of all rights to women. This has been a tremendously important element of the feminist enterprise worldwide. The promotion of self-sufficient, autonomous and independent women has been a central aim of feminist ethical theory and praxis.

This rights-based ethic, which stresses independence and impartiality, does however sit rather uncomfortably with another predominant view in feminist ethics. The 'ethic of care' debate has exercised feminist ethicists and psychologists since the publication in 1982 of Carol Gilligan's *In a Different Voice: Psychological Theory and Women's Development*. Arguing that there are two distinctive modes of moral judgment, care and response, which are gender related, Gilligan suggests that women, in general, function with an ethic of care and relationality and do not concern themselves primarily with issues of strict equality or fairness. This ethic of care is a distinctive approach to decision-making, not a retarded development of the more usual ethic of justice which prizes the values of impartiality and equality above all.

What emerges from an ethical theory which arises from and is accountable to women's experience is not one but two distinct approaches to the nature and purpose of morality. On the one hand many feminists are appealing to an ethic of justice as the location from which women may rightfully claim equality and the extension of rights, on the other hand there is a clear sense that the traditional experiences and roles of women as carers need to be revalued and reappropriated.

This brings us to the heart of one of the disputed questions in feminist ethical theory. One of the major problems with Gilligan's thesis is that it is not clear whether she is advocating a type of biological essentialism, another version of the Freudian 'biology is destiny' thesis. There is a conflict in Gilligan's own work. Joan Tronto (1993) suggests that at times Gilligan seems to support the position that 'caring is the activity through which women achieve their feminity and against which masculinity takes shape'. On other occasions she suggests that this alternative voice is 'a function of [women's] social, cultural and economic positions'. However one understands Gilligan on this matter it is clear that her work has made a significant contribution to feminist ethics, not least because it has become a key theory against which, and in dialogue with which, many ideas have been forged.

Similar themes arise with Luce Irigaray's *An Ethic of Sexual Difference* (1993), which in itself appears to be a validation of her basic thesis, which she terms the 'sexuation' of discourse. She suggests that in attempting to draw attention to and redress 'the dereliction of the feminine in language and thought creating worlds is our task. But it can be accomplished only through the combined efforts of the two halves of the world: the masculine and the feminine.' This provocative position obviously has profound implications for those of us who are attempting to explore the relationships between gender, value and praxis. Mary Daly's *Gyn/Ecology: The Metaethics of Radical Feminism* (1978) posits a somewhat similar position.

There may not be a deeply rooted conflict between the ethic of justice (to which feminists have traditionally appealed) and the ethic of care, adopted by increasing numbers of feminists, although clearly there are some points of dispute, and not merely about strategy. What is much more pressing, however, is the continued consideration of the issue of biological essentialism. While feminist theory should not become an undifferentiated, amorphous mass, a consensus on this difficult issue would be welcome. In attending to the experience and praxis of feminists, theologians have employed two distinctive approaches to ethics. Underlying this is an unresolved dispute concerning the relationship between gender difference and biological factors. Since this is a debate which touches all areas of feminist theory it is essential that ethicists pursue their work in dialogue with feminist scientists, psychologists and anthropologists.

Difference and Particularity

The acknowledgment of the plural, fragmented nature of human experience is one of the consequences of the historicization of reason. Feminist theologians have been among a number of groups who have been critical of the assumption, which lies behind much classical theory, that male experience provides an adequate and normative description of human experience. In attempting to break this hegemony, feminist theologians in the 1970s and 1980s had begun to describe and define women's experience. The irony has been that feminist theology, which intended to provide a more inclusive description of the category of human experience, has been criticized, particularly by womanist and mujerista theologians, precisely for failing to do this. For example, in her influential *Black Womanist Ethics* (1988) Katie Cannon goes some way towards formulating an ethic of survival which arises out of the 'real-lived texture' of black women's lives.

A theology which posits a methodological commitment to prioritizing women's experience and praxis, and which is sensitive to racial, class and other differences, must recognize what Emily Culpepper calls 'women's different primary emergencies'. Difference emerges as a key hermeneutical principle. Coupled with this is a recognition that location and context do considerably alter one's perspectives, values and judgments. Taken together these interrelated positions, which have been vital for the development of feminist theology, also raise difficulties for the understanding of moral knowledge.

The essential question is: how, if at all, is it possible to engage in cross-cultural criticism? If it is acknowledged that white Western women have, up until now, defined the content of the category of women's experience, and if it is recognized that all truth claims are in some ways dependent on one's location, then it follows that it is difficult to make any kind of ethical judgment apart from one's own point of view. If respect for difference and pluralism in terms of values is central to feminist ethics then it seems virtually impossible to posit any kind of ethical objectivity. Does feminist ethics have a realist or a relativist epistemology? Is it possible simultaneously to respect the integrity of another tradition to protest unambiguously at what appears to be inequality in another culture or tradition? Such are the questions which continue to exercise feminist ethicists in the attempt to formulate a theoretical position which is faithful to the diversity of feminist experience and praxis.

Similar questions arise for all ethical theory 'after modernity'. Lisa Sowle Cahill (1993), Martha Nussbaum and Sharon Welch have all addressed this complex question in their work. Although no resolution seems likely in the near future, attention to the question of the type of epistemology to which feminist ethicists subscribe is vital.

In conclusion, then, in embracing the methodology of the primacy of experience and praxis, feminist ethicists have revolutionized both the content and method of ethical theory. The ethic which arises from this experience has emphasized the values of embodiment, autonomy, relationality, difference and particularity. While embracing these values have been significant for women's lives they also raise particular theoretical issues which require attention. In pursuing such questions feminist ethicists have also contributed enormously to debate which is emerging from other quarters.

Further reading: Benhabib 1992; Jantzen 1992; Nussbaum and Sen (eds.) 1993; Welch 1975; Zappone 1990.

EVE
Jules Cashford

THE STORY that has been called 'the Fall of Man' in Genesis 1–3 stands at the beginning of the Judeo-Christian tradition as the drama which follows the creation of the universe and reveals the fundamentally flawed nature of human beings. From this story the ideas of 'original sin' and the 'fallen universe' came into being as categories that attempt to explain the human experience of a life of exile in banishment from the divine. Many commentators, both Jewish and Christian, have in addition censured Eve for being the first to break the commandments of God and for subsequently misleading Adam, from whom, they state, she originally came. Some further commentators, Paul among them, have generalized from the sin of Eve to the character of woman, and have justified the imbalance between men and women by appealing to the hierarchical relationship between Adam and Eve. Paul understands this hierarchy as given first in the contrasting modes of their birth, and secondly in the differing interpretation he makes himself of their otherwise apparently identical actions:

> But I suffer not a woman to teach, nor to usurp authority over the man, but to be in silence.
> For Adam was first formed, then Eve.
> And Adam was not deceived, but the woman being deceived was in the transgression (1 Tim. 2.2-14).

There are many responses one might make to this, the most important of which is that this is a literal reading of the story which concretizes the symbols and turns myth into history, losing thereby the meaning and the grandeur of the poetic vision. If the story is read symbolically, it becomes a myth of the birth of consciousness, which dramatizes the moment when humanity becomes conscious of itself as a moral being—'knowing good and evil'—and severing, inevitably, at the same time, its instinctive participation with the source—'seeing that they are naked'. As symbol, the story dramatizes a tragic vision: the call of a moral destiny as an individual entails the loss of an original wholeness. For consciousness, which can now look upon life and the beginning of time, has also to look upon death and the ending of that time. The resolution of these and all the other pairs of opposites has now to be achieved at a higher level—in Christian terms, this is a symbolic way of understanding Christ as the second Adam and the cross of the crucifixion, made from the tree of life, as counterpoint to the tree of knowledge.

In a literal interpretation of the Genesis story, however, the whole meaning is changed. The mythologist Joseph Campbell points out that the story, when read literally, creates a 'nervous discord' in the mind, setting the heart and the brain against each other. For it takes the life-affirming images of the preceding millennia—the garden, the tree of life, the act of birth, the woman and the serpent—and makes of them ambivalent or destructive images which work against humanity. The serpent, for instance, was, from the Neolithic age onwards, in Mesopotamia, Crete, Egypt and Greece, an image of the dynamic and transforming power of the goddess and the god. Whether female or male, the serpent was always an image of rebirth—shedding its skin as the moon sloughs its shadow—portrayed climbing up the tree of life as the ever-dying ever-renewed sap of life rising from an unquenchable source. What happens to the psyche, Campbell asks (1976), when the meaning of these archetypal images is reversed? The image and the word, the feeling and the interpretation, are likely to be, at some deep level, out of harmony with each other.

When Adam names Eve—after Yahweh's curse—'the Mother of all living', he is unwit-

An A to Z of Feminist Theology

tingly invoking the role of the old mother goddesses who stand behind Eve. The story of the begetting of life through the rib was in origin a Mesopotamian myth of the Goddess Nin-ti, a goddess of childbirth whose name meant both 'Life' and 'Rib', and who made the bones of infants in the womb from the ribs of their *mothers*. Reversing this image, with Eve being drawn from the rib of Adam, has invited literalists through the centuries to describe Eve (and often woman) as a 'secondary creation', 'inferior substance', not made in the image of God—as Milton phrases it in *Paradise Lost*, 'He for God only, She for God in him'. Eve is therefore less 'divine'—less rational, less moral, more instinctive—and so more liable to sin: the 'devil's gateway'. As Luther said, if the serpent 'had tempted Adam first the victory would have been Adam's. He would have crushed the serpent with his foot and would have said: "Shut up!" '. The serpent is often painted with the face of Eve, as though it were a reflection of her own deeper nature. By this time she has become both temptress and tempted together and Adam but the unfortunate accessory to his wife's passions. But when Eve is further allegorized as 'the body', instincts and matter, and Adam as 'the mind', reason and spirit, then values enter our language of discourse as absolutes, losing their capacity for exploration and change.

There are two myths of the creation of human beings in Genesis, written at different times. In the Priestly text (Genesis 1 and Gen. 2.1-4) man and woman are created together and both are in the image of God: 'So God created man in his own image, in the image of God created he him; male and female he created them' (Gen. 1.27). This Priestly text is believed to have been begun in the seventh century BCE and reworked after the exile in Babylon in the fifth and fourth centuries BCE. The second creation myth is the Yahwistic text (Gen. 2.4-25), in which the exile from the Garden is related. This has the man created first, and when no suitable 'helpmeet' can be found for him among the animals, a woman is created from the man's body—the woman the man names Eve. This Yahwistic text, although placed second, was actually written first, possibly 400 years before, around the ninth century BCE. Some commentators, in an attempt to reconcile apparently differing theologies of the two myths, created their own first woman, Lilith, whose equality and independence provided an explanation to both early and remarkably late theologians as to why the marriage had to be replaced.

On the other hand, these other ways of imagining a beginning to the world and an origin to human beings might return us to the human imagination, and with that to wonder how best to work with a myth that is both so embedded in our culture and yet has been so fraught with misinterpretations. Perhaps the image of 'Original Blessing', proposed by Matthew Fox in his book of that name might offer a perspective on what we may have lost by focusing on the sinfulness of Eve and Adam—reminding us of the capacity of all symbols for continual self-renewal.

Many feminist theologians, however, do not believe that this particular symbol can be renewed in any way that is life-giving for women. Eve the temptress seems to be an image deeply ingrained in the male psyche. Many women would rather that we abandoned Eve altogether as a mythological figure who has chained women to 'biological destiny' for too long. Once again Eve is interpreted literally as woman in a biological way. Many women who do not feel maternal or who have not experienced motherhood as compassionate feel constrained by this image. Those feminists who do wish to reclaim Eve envisage her as a dynamic and creative woman, one who sought knowledge and was eager to share it. Her disobedience is viewed positively. She could not understand why knowledge should not be sought and so she could not be confined to her station by a patriarchal God who demanded her ignorance.

Further reading: Baring and Cashford 1993; Frye 1982; Hillman 1978; Pagels 1988; Phillips 1984.

EXPERIENCE
Pamela Dickey Young

WHEN FEMINIST theology first began to articulate the shortcomings of traditional theologies, one of the central criticisms was lack of attention to women's experience. Traditional theologies assume a generic 'man' whose temptation was to the sin of pride and whose salva-

EXPERIENCE

tion was to be found in self-giving love. But, as Valerie Saiving was the first to ask (1979), does this reflect only the experience of men and not of women? And her answer is that, at the very least, most of women's experience is not taken into account in theological portrayals of 'man's' experience. 'Women's experience' becomes the way to talk about including women in theology: as specifically included within humanity for the purposes of theological anthropology and as theologians who formulate theologies that are attuned to the possibility that there might be differences (perhaps inherent, perhaps socialized) between the everyday experiences of men and women that affect the way theologies are written and heard. 'Women's experience' is a way to talk about women's reclamation of the power of naming and articulating their lives rather than having that done by someone else.

Judith Plaskow (1980) develops the notion of women's experience, building on Saiving in contrast to Niebuhr and Tillich. Whereas Saiving tended to think of women and men as inherently different, Plaskow points out that societies create expectations and roles for women that affect the messages women internalize about themselves. These messages influence women's experience and, in turn, require feminist interpretation, interpretation that views women's traditional status and roles with the suspicion that these are creatures of patriarchy and serve to bolster male privilege. 'Women's experience' is a complex and multi-faceted term that includes women's bodily experiences, women's socialized experiences (the messages of society about being a woman), women's feminist experiences (feminist analysis and critique of women's socialized experiences), women's historical experiences (the records we have of women's writing), and women's individual experiences. Some feminist theologians concentrate on women's experience in terms of what they take to be inherent differences between women and men, others on women's experience as culturally created, that is, the ways in which it has been informed by social, political and ecclesiastical definitions of womanhood.

Any theology that takes feminist critique seriously uses 'women's experience', both the recorded experiences of past women and the experiences of women in the present, as source material for theological thought. In addition, 'women's experience' becomes the norm or one of the norms by which the adequacy of theology is to be judged. The appeal to women's experience as normative is made in a variety of ways. At its most basic, appeal to women's experience as normative means that any proposed theology that treats women as less than fully human is judged inadequate, and that any adequate theology explicitly and consciously asks whether and how women are included in its model. Feminist theologies take women's experience as a central and uncompromisable norm. For the most part this norm, arising out of feminist analysis, is articulated in terms of whether a theology contributes to the liberation of women from oppression or the opposite.

'Women's experience' is a term that stands for the specificity of female experiences. It is this very notion of specificity or particularity that leads to the recognition that women do not have one 'experience' but many, and that the term 'women's experience' might be every bit as false a generic as 'man's experience'. Women of colour began to develop womanist theologies, based on their experiences. Chicana women have developed mujerista theologies, and so on. Many feminists have begun to question the possibility of using any definition of 'women's experience' as normative, given that each woman has her own individual experiences which only she can articulate. If one cannot deduce any common threads among this vast diversity of women's experiences, the normative value of the category 'women's experience' becomes normative only for the individual who looks for a theological accounting of her particular experiences.

One's experiences influence the way one hears theological questions and answers and become part of the context from which one makes one's own formulations. One's experiences help shape one's commitments.

Within Christian feminist theology today one of the major challenges is the relation of the particular to the general or universal. If the particularity of women's experiences, and all other experiences, is the bottom line, how shall we talk to one another about the intersection, if any, of our experiences? The way we have usu-

An A to Z of Feminist Theology

ally named 'women's experience' names 'experience' as that which is already reflected upon; experience is only experience insofar as it is articulated in language. I would argue that experience is prelinguistic, yet seeks articulation in language. If this is so, then we may be able to find in the prelinguistic commonalities that, by the time they are articulated in language, have become diversely characterized. This would include, in my view, experience of the ultimate, which Christians, given their own religious inheritance, articulate as experience of God. It would also give a basis for threads of commonality in diversely articulated oppressions.

If a theology is to be both Christian and feminist, one that seeks to be more than just one individual's theology, it must find ways to accommodate the diversity of women's experiences while at the same time finding ways to talk about what it perceives to be commonalities that would link together all Christian feminist theologies.

Further reading: Chopp 1987; Ruether 1983; Young 1990.

FEMALE / FEMININE / FEMINIST
Dorothea McEwan

FEMALE—a woman or girl; female / male—the biological division of the species, in which female is designation the sex which can bear offspring or produce eggs.

Feminine—characteristic of, peculiar or appropriate to women or the female sex (used interchangeably with 'female' originally); womanly, womanish, effeminate, unmanly; now usage of 'femininity' narrowed down to 'idealized female servitude' (Mary Daly, *Wickedary*, 1988); feminine / masculine—characterizations of behaviour along gender lines, limiting the type of behaviour that is viewed as accepted for the sexes to a role-play, to a formula of behaviour.

Feminist—of or pertaining to feminism or the advocacy of women's equality and rights; advocating feminism, women's rights, the movement for the advancement and emancipation of women; in contradistinction to feminine, feminist centres its concern on women.

See also *The New Shorter Oxford English Dictionary*, 1993

FEMINISM AND POSTMODERNISM
Philippa Berry

MUCH RECENT feminist theory, and especially that influenced by the ideas of French feminism, has absorbed a set of concerns which can broadly be termed postmodern. The usefulness as well as the precise meaning of the concept of 'postmodernism' has been much debated; for example, some critics have asserted that we continue to inhabit a broadly 'modern' epoch. They have also questioned the assertion by postmodernists that the 'modern' values of rationality and scepticism, which have been dominant in Western culture and society at least since the Enlightenment, and arguably from the end of the Renaissance, are now facing an insoluble crisis. But however much some intellectuals may resist it, the widespread cultural impact of that intellectual movement which can loosely be described as postmodernism is unquestionable. What it is engendering is a new style of thinking which is much indebted to some of the most radical strands of continental philosophy as well as to Freudian psychoanalysis, and especially to the thought of Friedrich Nietzsche, Martin Heidegger, Jacques Lacan and Jacques Derrida. The radical critique by postmodernism of some of the fundamental tenets of recent thought—and especially its interest in exploring that which is 'other' to the rational subject of the modern era—has much relevance to the concerns of feminism, since the identity which postmodernism is busily deconstructing is agreed by all to be a model of identity based on male stereotypes. It is above all for this reason that many feminists expect the future development of feminist theory to be intimately entangled with that of postmodernism. But what have only recently begun to be assessed are the implications of this dialogue between feminism and postmodernism for feminist attitudes towards ideas of the sacred or numinous.

Many of its exponents have assumed that, like those which inform so much modern thought, the assumptions behind postmodern thinking are predominantly secular, even nihilistic. Nihilistic themes can certainly be found in postmodernism, and are often traceable to the work of Nietzsche, or to the works of some of his twentieth-century disciples, such as Georges Bataille. But even where such themes occur, they are curiously combined with an intense interest in states of ecstasy, or in the annulling of individual identity, and this often assumes a mystical dimension, especially when combined with postmodernism's quasi-apocalyptic concept of 'the end of history'. Indeed, in its pursuit of a sceptical method which deconstructs the assumptions of modern or rational styles of thinking (above all, by showing the mutability of what was believed to be the thinker's transparent and reliable instrument—language), postmodernism has been thought by some to provide a curious parallel to the negative theology of the Middle Ages; it has been observed, for example, that Heidegger knew the works of Meister Eckhart, as well as those of some Eastern mystics. Yet it is important to note that alongside its persistent questioning of the binarism of much Western thinking, postmodernism (following thinkers like Nietzsche and Freud) often places particular emphasis upon matter and the body, seemingly in order to correct the disembodied character of much modern thinking. At the same time, however, several postmodernists stress the need to transform ideas of the bounded and separate body, which demarcates the limits of identity, by figuratively emptying it; Luce Irigaray has figured the body of the future as an 'envelope', while Gilles Deleuze has referred, even more cryptically, to 'the body without organs'. Certainly the postmodern body seems to be curiously open to the motions of what could be termed 'spirit'; what appears particularly to intrigue those postmodernists who explore aspects of the sacred are forms of bodily rapture: Jacques Lacan devoted a famous essay, 'Encore', to an analysis of Bernini's statue of St Theresa in ecstasy.

In 'Encore', Lacan linked the ecstasy of the mystic with what he referred to as the unspeakable *jouissance* or bliss of woman, whose mysterious 'difference' or unknowable nature (at least within the framework of modern thought) has been a recurring theme of postmodernism. The influence of Lacan's essay may account in part for the interest of a number of postmodern thinkers in the female mystic: not only the feminists Julia Kristeva and Luce Irigaray, but also Jacques Derrida and Michel de Certeau have all referred, briefly or at length, to such figures. But to the Jewish thinker Emmanuel Levinas, who through his dialogue with Heidegger has also had a considerable impact on this intellectual movement, can be attributed the increasing recognition by postmodernists that the 'other' which has been repressed within modern thought is a category which is not just uncanny, but possibly even numinous. Levinas declared that 'What remains ever exterior to thought is thought in the idea of infinity'. As does Lacan's essay, Levinas's work places woman, as well as what he calls 'the infinite', on the side of the 'other' in relation to man. Derrida expressed a similar idea when he wrote in *Spurs/Eperans* (echoing Nietzsche): 'That which will not be pinned down by truth is, in truth, feminine'.

It therefore seems that postmodernism may be able to provide an important stimulus, not just to feminist theory, but also to the emergence within that theory of a new feminist spirituality. Certainly feminism can find in postmodernism some intriguing hints about the possible importance of woman in articulating new models of identity, and new paradigms of knowing, within which the dimension of the sacred would have an important place. But if the intellectual revolution initiated by postmodernism is to be taken seriously, then it seems that it also requires us to explore a new relationship to the sacred or numinous: one which, as Luce Irigaray has put it, is 'without maps'. Only by following this wayless way towards 'the divine', Irigaray contends, will both woman and man achieve the as yet unrealized perfection of their different subjectivities, and finally be able to meet one another on equal terms.

Further reading: Berry and Wernick (eds.) 1992; Conley 1992; de Certeau 1986; Irigaray 1993; Lacan 1982; Levin 1988.

FEMINIST SPIRITUALITY
Jean W. Waldron

THE WORD 'spirituality', though widely used, is surrounded by much terminological confusion. It has meant different things to different people in different ages, and the definitions of the word are legion. Spirituality is not just an idea or a concept, it is also a praxis which resonates with longings for the eternal, wholeness, peace and joy. It has been a subject of perennial human concern, and it is closely related to faith and is a lived experience. The word 'spirituality', as it is now understood, had its roots in the Jewish tradition of God's abiding presence, and a personal spirituality centred on recollection and attentiveness. The word was originally a Christian term, derived from the Pauline use of *pneumatikos*, that is, 'spiritual', to describe whatever was under the influence of the spirit of God. It now has a pluralism and universalism.

The New Dictionary of Catholic Spirituality states that spirituality

> might be defined as the experience of striving to integrate one's life in terms of self-transcendence towards the ultimate value one perceives.

Contemporary writers speak more of spirituality as lived experience, and 'an exploration of

FEMINIST SPIRITUALITY

what is involved in becoming human'. Walter Principe has described spirituality, in his article 'Towards Defining Spirituality' in *Studies in Religion* (1983), as

The way in which a person understands and lives within his or her historical context that aspect of his or her religion, philosophy, or ethic that is viewed as the loftiest, the noblest, the most calculated to lead to the fullness of the ideal or perfection being sought.

This appears to be a good broad inclusivist definition. Lisa Isherwood and Dorothea McEwan define spirituality in the glossary of their book *Introducing Feminist Theology* neatly and simply as 'Imagining wholeness' (Isherwood and McEwan 1993: 149). Mary Hunt believes that spirituality is part of an intentional, accountable process of 'Making choices about the quality of life for oneself, and one's community' (Hunt 1992: 105). She is wary about using the term 'spirituality', as it has come to mean almost anything, and therefore nothing. She mentions how people have even talked about the 'spirituality of popcorn' or the 'spirituality of gardening'.

Feminism is about the task of establishing the unity and inter-relatedness of all creation. Feminists of diverse persuasions are united in their common attempt to undo the far-reaching and devastating effects which patriarchal separation and division have had on our world. Where patriarchy tends to see differences as deficiency, feminism strives to be open to the richness and structural ways of relating that will ensure equal participation and opportunities for all people. The experience of being marginalized was, and is, formative in Christian feminist spirituality. Feminist spirituality struggles to free itself from fixed ideologies in favour of the authentic freedom of individuals and groups to be faithful to their own experiences.

In the Bible, even allowing for all its poetry and mythology, the belief firmly exists that God created male and female as two distinct persons, whatever else we may believe about the implications of this division of humanity into two different sexes. The two sexes are biologically apparent to us as having different morphological features. Different attitudes and theories resulting from this difference have existed throughout history, and feminism and feminist spirituality are obviously affected by these attitudes and opinions. In the ancient concepts of anthropology, much depended on the elements and humours. Men and women together formed the perfect human being and the elements were divided between them, with men being predominantly air and fire and women earth and water. Air and fire made for critical intellect, while earth signified fruitfulness, and water was a spiritual principle which opened women to visions and dreams. The expectation that women's spirituality would take the distinctive form of this type of experience led to an acceptance that paranormal experiences were normal for women, right until the fifteenth and sixteenth centuries. The early fathers of the church, with their dualistic notions, had also firmly differentiated male and female. For them the male was theomorphic, and associated with mind and spirit, while the woman was incomplete in herself, and associated with the 'carnal' and bodiliness. When women are discussed in historical literature, they are usually considered to be *different* from men, but as to why and how, the opinions are legion, and there is no apparent agreement, except for the fact that some sort of sexism is implicitly present.

Feminist spirituality, although having some distinctive features, is full of diversity, and the views about the influence of gender on spirituality are equally diverse. However, the one common view is that the patriarchal, male view of the female has been damaging, distorting, and dismembering, while differences have been accentuated so that male superiority may be asserted.

The differences seem adequately dealt with by Elisabeth Schüssler Fiorenza, who, writing in *A Discipleship of Equals*, does not reduce all women to a homogenous commonality, but upholds that women act as individuals, rather than representatives of their gender. She writes that talent, influence and opportunity are more the determining factors. Mary Daly, writing in *The Church and the Second Sex*, states with seeming accuracy that

> man's knowledge of man is constantly evolving. As to whether one is born or becomes man or woman, dogmatic assertions about an unchanging feminine essence do not find

anything like general acceptance among those who follow developments in modern philosophy and in the social sciences and psychology. In fact our awareness of the profound and subtle effects of conditioning upon the human personality is constantly increasing (Daly 1968: 71).

We now realize that differentiating too clearly between men and women can distort reality and create many painful and unnecessary caricatures. There are many spiritualities and there are many models of understanding the concept of spirituality embodied in particular forms, shaped by particular cultural matrices and religious traditions. Similarly in feminism there is no single feminist spirituality, just as there is no single feminist theology.

Traditionally, much of Christian spirituality has been linked to the sacraments, and grounded in ascetic and monastic practices. The earlier ages, on the whole, emphasized divine reality, transcendence and the soul's objective spiritual journey to the Other. Today's spirituality has more emphasis on the subjective side of experience, on inwardness, immanence, and the discovery of the true spiritual self. From being rooted in Christian tradition, spirituality has now become a kind of universal word for the search for direction and meaning. In the past spirituality has often been based on strong dualistic notions and there has a strong emphasis on renunciation and asceticism, and often many discrete anti-feminist and sexist orientations. Recent spirituality is much more holistic, and works in and through all human realities rather than apart from them. It calls for transformation, not just of the individual person, but also, because of the inter-connectedness of peoples, the transformation of communities. Feminist spirituality permeates the personal and the political. It seeks to animate action, as well as thoughts and emotions, as it attempts to respond to the aspirations of the suffering, marginalized, and oppressed peoples of the globe.

Feminists who argue that their spiritual experiences are conditioned from the outset by patriarchal conceptualizations of ultimate value and by sex-role differentiation in the practice of religion, have been aided by the recent work of Steven Katz. For a long time Rudolf Otto's ideas, expressed in *The Idea of the Holy* (1923), had been generally accepted, but Katz has significantly challenged his theories. Otto had declared that experience of the 'other', the numinous experience, is unconditioned and aconceptual, and is not influenced, as is believed in feminist spirituality, by the images encountered and the lived experience of the individual.

Otto writes as a dualist, and claims that there is a fundamental opposition between the flesh and the spirit, and that 'man' must recognize that 'he' is only a 'creature' if 'he' is to become holy. The person must be

> submerged and overwhelmed by its own nothingness in contrast to that which is supreme above all creatures.

This is obviously a statement that is particularly disturbing for women, who frequently feel themselves to be profaned and counting for nothing. Melissa Raphael writes that, for the feminist,

> her woman's embodied finitude is holy in that it belongs to the intramundane process of divine creativity. Consequently, feminist spirituality experiences female embodiment and its connections with other natural forms as the primary source of empowerment and hence sacrality (Raphael 1994: 519).

Raphael states that in feminist religious experience the medium is inseparable from what is experienced, and that the divine presence is mediated by mundane things. She believes, as do many others, that in fact,

> it is in and through finite things that we may apprehend the incarnate presence of the holy in all creation.

Feminists have always celebrated 'embodiment', and have lamented the distortion of body–mind dualism, which has been created by patriarchy. There is a basic connection between body–mind dualism and the assumption that people are most able to develop their spirituality when they are most detached and disengaged from the body and from body-mediated sensuality. We know and value the world through our ability to touch, hear and see. We need to perceive in order to conceive. Perception is dependent on our senses and feelings. Feminists believe that failure to live deeply with our body, our feelings and our perceptions means that we lose our connectedness and our ability to relate. In feminist spirituality, this connectedness and relatedness

An A to Z of Feminist Theology

FEMINIST SPIRITUALITY

has always been valued, and this is a point of differentiation from the male, whose tendency is to emphasize detachment. The centrality of relationship is found in much feminist thought and writing, and is obviously influential on feminist spirituality. Feminists celebrate that relationality is at the heart of all things, and that recognizing sensuality is fundamental to the work and power of love, on which so much of our spirituality depends.

The feminist theologian, Carter Heyward, has written on how far traditional Christian theism has wandered from the central concern with relationality that was so central to Jesus' ministry, and how the God that has emerged in patristic Christianity has been made so devoid of relationship. There has generally been a male tendency which has favoured self-reliance and autonomy as virtues and represented transcendence as unrelatedness and the 'holy other'. This idea feminist spirituality would oppose in its envisaging of a spirituality of mutual loving and relationship. Isabel Carter Heyward writes that

> [I]f God loves us, the human-divine relation is reciprocal, dynamic and of benefit to both parties... No lover is completely autonomous, wholly untouched, finally unmoved by the loved one... A love needs relation—if for no other reason, in order to love... I have wanted to help loosen the grip we have allowed a false 'God' to hold on us in order that we might be better able to experience God in-carnate as friend and lover (Heyward 1982: 6-7).

Carter Heyward shares in the feminist spirituality which does not believe in a god who loves in a remote immaterial way.

Spirituality is grounded in everyday life, and in our time the daily experience of women is being made more public. The rediscovery of women's voices is valuable because it affirms women in their spiritual and theological exploring, and emphasizes that the Christian tradition contains women's stories as well as those of men. For Christian feminists, their feminism is deeply rooted in gospel values, and they stress the God who unites, who is in relationship with his people, and who suffers with them. Dorothee Sölle expressed something of this when she writes that

> [W]e do not honour God because of God's power over us, we immerse ourselves in God, in God's love... Our relationship with God is not one of obedience but of unity, where we are not subject to the commands of some remote being that demands sacrifice and the relinquishing of self, but rather where we are asked to become one with all of life (Sölle 1984: 102).

In feminist spirituality, the concepts of the Almighty, remoteness, sacrifice, redemption and sin are not central as they are in patriarchal understanding. The emphasis is on the God who seeks, who suffers, and who, in his love, wishes unity and relationship with his creation. In their struggle against patriarchal concepts, feminists face a great deal of opposition and suspicion when they remain within the mainline Christian churches. There has been much suffering and rejection and, in a special way, the spirituality of feminists has had to be steeped in the Gospel practice of love, forgiveness and reconciliation, as they attempt to avoid bitterness and bigotry in themselves against those who persecute them. Feminist spirituality questions the prevalent metaphor of the spirit life as a 'journey', with its implicit notion of linear progression and stages, with the goal being all-important. It tends to see the spiritual life as a shared struggle, and salvation as the overcoming of separation. It is a process, and that process is involved in relationships. Male traditional spirituality has been suspicious of experience and has favoured instead the role of reason. Feminist spirituality believes that reason alone is inadequate, and that experience is also needed.

The mother and housewife can achieve transformation in the same way as the celibate monk. Instead of denying the flesh, and regarding sex and women as temptation, feminist scholars in the field of spirituality see the flesh as a way of relating to, serving and celebrating oneself and others. They do not believe that we are just on earth for some goal we may reach in our future relationship with God, but that we are here to relate, to weave and spin creative webs and, in our interactions and relationships, to find the God and the Godding of ourselves now, in our present situations and experiences. There is a common emphasis on experience, but some feminists have also made the point that experience alone is not the ultimate goal, and that if spirituality is the process of coming into rela-

An A to Z of Feminist Theology

tionships with reality, then we must also consider the reality of our experience. Emotional experiences contribute to our spirituality only by being understood as components of the life that gives rise to them. Experience can become meaningful only by being reflected upon. In spirituality, of whatever type, there always needs to be some element of a conscious, deliberate transformation of the self, in order to bring it into a closer relationship with reality. As Carol Ochs says in 'Women and Spirituality' (Ochs 1983: 10):

> Reality is that which is larger than our experiences and our consciousness. It enables our consciousness to grow, expand, and be transformed Spirituality is not merely a way of knowing, but also a way of being and doing.

Feminist spirituality is as varied as the personal lives of feminists, although there are distinctive general characteristics.

One of the distinctive features of feminist spirituality is its attention to interconnections, and a rootedness in the real day-to-day questions which are part of life for all embodied beings. It is a spirituality whose ideal of mutuality resists all forms of oppression, not only that of women, and seeks, in its action, to redress the imbalances not only of sexism, but of racism, culture and class. Feminist spirituality, like most liberation spirituality, seeks to permeate the political as well as the personal realms, and to animate action as one of its responses to a God whom it believes to be loving and just. It is a spirituality which has the vision of transformation towards a relating society, where there is mutuality, acceptance and justice for all. The mutuality is not just between people and people, but with creation and the earth, with feminists such as Sallie McFague having a spirituality which is deeply ecological, seeing the universe as part of God's body with a Mother–Lover concern for its good.

Feminists such as Carol Christ have also developed a spirituality with a deep ecological awareness, as well as connectedness to the goddess movement. Historical evidence has been difficult to establish, but they are describing an alternative 'God-language' metaphor which attempts to project an alternative model of spirituality. A radical form of goddess religion is found in Wicca. It is a revitalization of a nature and pagan religion, with its own specific type of spirituality, where the members come together in 'covens' or non-hierarchical support and worship communities, and have sometimes been labelled witches. This movement has seen considerable growth in recent years amongst some feminists seeking an alternative spirituality. It is another thread in the complex web.

Feminist spirituality permeates the personal and political; it is deeply incarnational; it seeks to animate our actions, thoughts and imagination, so that it can work for the transformation of ourselves and our world. It seeks to replace dualism with mutuality, and to give value to difference and diversity, and is acutely sensitive to the negative effects of dualistic thinking in any form. It seeks to reclaim female power, beginning with the likeness of women in the divine, the rehabilitation of the bodily as the locus of the divine and the right which women have to participate in their culture and religion. It is a spirituality which seeks to transform and respond to the hopes, loves, aspirations and agonies of our divided world.

FEMINIST THEOLOGY IN THE THIRD WORLD
Ursula King

FEMINIST THEOLOGY is a cross-cultural, globally interdependent phenomenon. It is important to take note of the many voices of women in the Third World. Out of their experience of struggle and suffering they are articulating a theology for working towards the transformation of church and society.

Given recent political changes, the term 'Third World' has become increasingly problematic, but it is retained here because it is used by many women themselves, not least by the Women's Commission of the Ecumenical Association of Third World Theologians (EATWOT). However, the so-called 'Third World' is not restricted to clearly demarcated geographical regions but has fluid boundaries, so that 'feminist theology in the Third World' refers not only to women doing theology in Asia, Africa or Latin America, but also to women minorities, especially women of colour, living on the margin of societies of great wealth such as those of

FT IN THE THIRD WORLD

the USA, South Africa, Israel, Japan, New Zealand, Australia and the Pacific.

History and Current Developments

Whether in the First or Third World, feminist theology would not have come into existence without women's access to theological education. Many women theologians from the Third World initially received their training in either the USA or Europe, sometimes with the encouragement and help of the World Council of Churches in Geneva. The importance of such training is evident from the fact that in several countries of the Third World women have formed associations of 'theologically trained women'. Although not all women thus trained describe themselves as 'feminists', once theologically trained and empowered, women are doing theology at many different levels, at grassroots level in their parishes and communities, through informal networks as well as consultations, meetings, conferences, official teaching positions and publications. Pioneering work was done in Asia (Marianne Katoppo, Indonesia, published *Compassionate and Free: An Asian Woman's Theology* in 1979; the Christian Conference in Asia established its Women's Desk in 1980–81; Revd Sun Ai Lee Park, Korea, founded the journal *In God's Image*, published regularly since December 1982).

The most decisive global development, however, was the networking among the women theologians of EATWOT (founded in 1976) which eventually, in 1983, resulted in setting up a distinct Women's Commission. The EATWOT women theologians from different continents worked out a programme of study and analysis which was systematically pursued through regional and national consultations, leading in turn to three separate continental conferences in Latin America, Asia and Africa (1985–86). Following these, an intercontinental conference was held in Mexico (December 1986). Selected papers and the final statement from each continental conference, together with the final document from the intercontinental conference, were published in *With Passion and Compassion: Third World Women Doing Theology* (Fabella and Oduyoye [eds.] 1988). The theological journey of the EATWOT women has been charted in detail by Virginia Fabella in *Beyond Bonding* (1993). This includes stories of representative African (Mercy Amba Oduyoye; Teresa Okure), Latin American (María Clara Bingemer; Elsa Tamez) and Asian (Mary John Mananzan; Aruna Gnanadason; Kwok Pui-lan; Sun Ai Lee Park) women theologians. A further development was represented by the EATWOT December 1994 conference in Costa Rica, at which women theologians from the Third World dialogued with women theologians from the First World.

More detailed information on Asian women's theology can be found in Chung 1991. For selected papers from Latin American women see Tamez (ed.) 1989 and for African women theologians see Oduyoye and Kanyoro (eds.) 1992. Women's theological voices can now also be heard from such widely different regions as Southern Africa, China and the Pacific. Important too are the developments of womanist theology, the *mujerista* theology of Hispanic women in the USA, and the theology of Asian-American women.

Methodology and Themes

Like all feminist theology, that from the Third World is experientially based, leading from action to reflection back to action. Women voice their experiences through stories and case-studies which then lead to analysis and critical reflection. The experiential and experimental quality of this theology is vibrantly felt in language and style, expressed in stories, poems, prayers, art work and new liturgies. At the local level, women express themselves in their own languages. But it is part of the global context of interdependence that much of the communication among EATWOT women, and most of the dissemination of feminist theology from the Third World, occurs primarily through the medium of English or Spanish, associated for many with the painful memory of colonialism and tainted by the exploitation of international capitalism.

Each continent provides a specific context for doing theology. In Latin America theological

An A to Z of Feminist Theology

work is focused on the class struggle and the theme of liberation, in Africa it is centred on the problem of indigenization and inculturation, and in Asia the challenge of religious pluralism and of Asian spirituality are central to the debate. Asian women have gone furthest in exploring interfaith dialogue through meeting with women of different faiths. From 1983 onwards the EATWOT Women's Commission, which works ecumenically by bringing together women from different Christian churches, planned and promoted work in the following areas: (1) the analysis of women's oppression in society and church; (2) the social analysis of each respective country, involving economic, political and socio-religious factors; (3) theological reflection bearing first on a hermeneutical analysis of the Bible, complemented by other sources such as myths, folklore, legends and indigenous religions, and then followed by further reflections on theological themes and their implications for women. The suggested themes were God-talk, Christology, mariology, pneumatology and emerging forms of spirituality.

Common to feminist theologians from the Third World are the experiences of oppression, suffering and struggle, but also the sharing of hope, of a new consciousness and vision, of daring to dream, of empowerment and liberation which may lead to new forms of community and a renewed church. Women doing theology in the Third World are feeling empowered by their vision of liberation and hope to envisage the transformation of their world. Women's theology from the Third World is, as Chung Hyun Kyung has said (1991), above all a theology which is woman-affirming, life-affirming and cosmos-affirming.

Further reading: King (ed.) 1994.

FLOURISHING
Grace Jantzen

'FLOURISHING' IS a significant biblical concept, which has, however, received much less attention than has 'salvation' in Christian theology in Western modernity. From a feminist perspective, it can be seen that the imbalance of attention is not innocent. It is therefore important to consider how things would be different if, instead of (or in addition to) a theology of salvation, we were to develop a theology of flourishing.

The word 'flourish' is etymologically linked with flowers, with blossoming. It is related to the Middle English *florir* and the Latin *florēre*, which means 'to flower': perhaps it is not insignificant that the noun in Latin is in the feminine. As a noun form, a 'flourish' is the mass of flowers on a fruit tree, or the bloom of luxuriant, verdant growth. In the more common verb form, to flourish is to blossom, to thrive, to throw out leaves and shoots, growing vigorously and luxuriantly. In the human sphere it denotes abundance, overflowing with vigour and energy and productiveness, prosperity, success and good health. 'Salvation', on the other hand, is a term which denotes rescue. One is saved *from* something: from drowning, from calamity, from loss. To be saved means to be delivered from a situation which was problematic or even intolerable; there is a sense of crisis and of rescue from danger which is wholly absent from the notion of flourishing.

Moreover, the concepts of flourishing and salvation respectively imply a different source or impetus. Salvation normally implies rescue by someone; there is a *saviour*. By contrast, flourishing occurs from an inner dynamic of growth, with no need for interference from the outside. A plant left to itself in appropriate conditions will of its own nature grow and flower and bear fruit; in normal circumstances the idea of rescue would be inappropriate. Although such flourishing of course draws upon external sources as a plant draws on the nutrients of the earth and air and water, this sort of continuing interdependence within the natural order is of an utterly different kind than the desperate need of someone in crisis for an external saviour or rescuer.

The choice of the language of salvation rather than the language of flourishing in Christian theology both denotes and reinforces a particular view of humanity. If we think in terms of salvation, then the human situation is a negative one, out of which we need to be delivered. In Christian theology, this obviously links with the idea of a divine saviour, and hence with Christology and with the doctrine of the incarnation and the trinity. But how would we char-

FLOURISHING

acterize the human situation in all its diversity if we used instead the model of flourishing? We could then see human beings as having natural inner capacity and dynamic, able to draw on inner resources and interconnection with one another, and potential to develop into great fruitfulness. Whereas with the metaphor of salvation God is seen as the Saviour who intervenes from outside the calamitous situation to bring about a rescue, the metaphor of flourishing would lead instead to an idea of the divine source and ground, the one in whom we are 'rooted and grounded in love', in whom we 'live and move and have our being', the vine of whom we are the branches and can bring forth much fruit. The biblical references are deliberate: they show again that there is ample scriptural warrant for developing a theology of flourishing, of growth and fruition from an inner creative and healthy dynamic, rather than a theology which begins from the premise that the human condition is a negative condition or crisis from which we must be rescued by an external saviour. Of course, the concept of the divine would then also necessarily be much less deistic: God would not be thought of as a being external to the world, but rather its source and wellspring; Jesus would not be envisaged as the heroic saviour entering human history from outside, but rather one who manifests what it may mean to live fully and naturally in the creative justice of God.

This would also entail a radical rethinking of the underlying assumptions about gender. If the female continues to be linked with nature, then contrary to tradition, the female must be linked with goodness, with the natural ability to flourish. Alternatively, if the male continues to be linked with goodness, then the male must now be linked with nature rather than with spirit or culture, that which stands over against nature, since it is from within nature, rather than from some external 'spiritual' source, that flourishing occurs. Or, even more radically, the whole millennia-old linkage of the male with spirit and goodness and the female with nature and sinfulness could be disrupted altogether. Whereas the model of salvation coheres unproblematically with a patriarchal structuring of society, a whole new theology of gender relations would be prompted by a theology modelled instead on flourishing.

Another highly significant aspect of the salvation model is that salvation is individualistic. A particular individual can be saved, singled out for rescue, though all others around her or him perish. Such individualism would be impossible in a theology built upon the model of flourishing rather than upon the model of salvation. The idea that one could flourish by oneself alone can get no purchase. Many of the biblical references to flourishing refer explicitly to the flourishing of the nation or community; indeed, the anthropology of atomistic individuals would be abhorrent to the mentality of the biblical prophets. In the sayings of Jesus, such as that of the vine and the branches, it is again implied that there are many branches, in relation with one another as well as with the vine. The model of flourishing is one which assumes the interconnectedness of people, and indeed of the ecosystem.

However, one of the questions which demands attention if one is thinking in terms of flourishing is the question of *who* flourishes, and at whose expense? In a world in which the North devours the labour of the South, with a huge flow of cash and goods from the poor to the rich, it is obvious that at least in economic terms it is possible for some groups to flourish off the backs of others, though their humanity may be stunted by it. However, ecologists are tireless in reminding us of the interconnectedness of the ecosystem, the dependence of each form of life on all the others in the biosphere. Though Darwin, drawing the language of competitiveness from the capitalist economics of his time, spoke in terms of a 'survival of the fittest', even a moderate understanding of the interdependence of plant and animal life makes obvious how misplaced such language is as an overall account of their adaptation and flourishing. The metaphor of flourishing carries with it an idea of connectedness which contrasts with the individualism of the metaphor of salvation. In the former, the question 'who benefits and who loses?' is insistent and demands to be addressed: who is labouring and suffering in order that I may flourish? In the latter, it can get no purchase: unless one had the idea that only a certain number of people could be saved, the question of who was damned because of my salvation would not arise. A theology of flourishing, therefore, lends itself readily to a politicized theology of

An A to Z of Feminist Theology

justice and protest; while a theology of salvation easily becomes introverted and depoliticized—which of course means that it supports the status quo.

According to a dualist conception of salvation, it is the soul which must be saved, while 'the flesh'—too often equated with the body and particularly with sexuality—must be mortified, put to death, as the enemy of the soul. The concept of flourishing is one which involves thriving, luxuriant growth, obvious and exuberant good health: all of these are rooted in bodily well-being, including both physical health and adequate material provision. Sick people, starving people, people whose existence is miserable because they lack the necessities of physical and psychological well-being cannot be said to be flourishing: the biblical writer connects flourishing with abundance of grain and wine. Of course it is sometimes possible that a person who falls ill can nevertheless flourish in mind or spirit for a time, just as a person kept in solitary confinement can sometimes rise above it and flourish inwardly; but these are occasions for wonder, for amazement, exceptions to our normal expectations. They should not therefore be seen as counter-examples to the idea that flourishing involves connectedness, adequate physical and psychological rootedness to support the blossoming and fruitfulness which grows out of that nourishing ground. A theology built on the model of flourishing, therefore, would be unable to ignore the physical and material realities of people, their bodiliness and their physical and psychological well-being, in the way that a theology built on the model of salvation of souls has sometimes done. While it is possible to be 'saved' while leaving everything else as it is, this is by no means the case with flourishing. Since flourishing involves the physical and communal realities of a person's life, a theology of flourishing could not content itself with looking piously to an after-life where present injustices will be abolished, while doing nothing in the struggle for their abolition here and now. For this reason a theology of flourishing would not be able to avoid confrontation with issues of domination, whether in terms of poverty, class, race, sex, or any other form of injustice; since these are the things which prevent people and communities from flourishing.

For spirituality, too, there are implications. From what I have said above, it might seem as though the model of flourishing would lead one to emphasize only the public and the political at the expense of the private and inner life. Closer attention to the metaphor, however, shows that that would not be the case. A plant which flourishes does so from its own inner life, 'rooted and grounded' in its source. If that inner life is gone, the plant withers and dries up, no matter how good its external circumstances. What is different from the model of salvation, however, is that the inner and the outer are not separable: there is no flourishing 'soul' of the plant while its 'body' withers in intolerable material conditions. A theology built on the model of flourishing is one whose spirituality is holistic, rather than the privatized, subjectivized spirituality so characteristic of contemporary Christianity.

FRENCH FEMINISM
Philippa Berry

JULIA KRISTEVA, Luce Irigaray and Hélène Cixous, three of the most notable feminists to write in French during the last two decades, have often used images and themes borrowed from religion in order to address some of the central questions of feminist theory. For example, the figure of the angel has been used on several occasions by Irigaray and Cixous, while both Irigaray and Kristeva have shown much interest in the figure of the female mystic. They have done this in spite of the secular attitudes which still dominate much academic feminist theory; indeed, it is because of the secular focus of many of their readers that the interest of these three thinkers in religion and spirituality has until recently been relatively overlooked. But the disinclination of many critics to identify and explore this aspect of their work can also be attributed to the unusual use of such motifs by these thinkers. For like other contemporary thinkers writing in French who have been influenced by the techniques of *bricolage* (the juxtaposition of diverse images and ideas) popularized by the anthropological theories of Claude Lévi-Strauss, these women have uprooted religious images and emblems from their traditional contexts. By transplanting them into a very different discursive field they are effectively

An A to Z of Feminist Theology

FRENCH FEMINISM

redefining the meaning of such motifs, often in a highly personal way. Yet this apparently eclectic relationship to the discourses of religion is fully consistent with the non-orthodoxy of these women's thought, and with their use of feminism to question dogmatic styles of thinking. To this extent, all three might be termed heretical thinkers, that is, thinkers outside the traditional formulae; indeed, Kristeva proposes a punning redefinition of heresy as 'her-ethics' at the end of her essay 'Stabat Mater' (1986), implying that there is an intimate relationship between the elaboration of a new style of heretical thinking and the search for a new feminist ethics.

The interest of Julia Kristeva in the traditions of Roman Catholicism has led some of her critics to conclude that she is herself a Catholic. Her now famous essay 'Stabat Mater' (much indebted to Marina Warner's *Alone of All Her Sex*) used an investigation of the cult of the Virgin Mary to explore the ecstasy of parturition, and in 'Motherhood according to Bellini' she analysed several paintings of the Virgin and Child by the Renaissance artist. Her interest in Mary is, however, closely related to her desire to elaborate, along psychoanalytic lines, a feminist account of the pre-oedipal developmental stage, in which the child is still dependent upon the mother. None the less, the two discourses, of psychoanalysis and spiritual experience, are accorded equal weight in these essays. In *Tales of Love*, however, a detailed investigation of the merits of Christian *agape*, which Kristeva considers to have lost its cultural centrality after the Middle Ages, leads her to the conclusion that it is the task of psychoanalysis to restore a comparable (if not identical) version of agapeic love in the modern world. Hence, while she does not see orthodox religion as having the answer to the problems of the twentieth century, she is clearly concerned to introduce a more spiritual awareness into psychoanalysis.

Luce Irigaray is more overtly mystical in her thinking than is Kristeva. At the centre of her first major work, *Speculum of the Other Woman* (published in French in 1974), she placed a chapter entitled 'La Mystérique', which established a punning relationship between the female mystic and hysteric. Since then, she has become increasingly emphatic in her assertion that woman's achievement of psychic balance, and the consequent establishment of equal relations between the sexes, will require the discovery of a new relationship to what she calls 'the divine'. In an echo of the medieval heresy of the Free Spirit (popularized in France in the late 1960s by Norman Cohn's *The Pursuit of the Millennium*), Irigaray also anticipates a third age of the Holy Spirit, which will be inaugurated by a marriage between the Spirit and the Bride. She asks in 'Divine Women': 'Could this be the period of the divine for, in, with, women?' It may be the frequent representation of the Holy Spirit as a dove that has led Irigaray to assert that women need to enter the 'envelope' of air and to become bird-like in their progress towards the reestablishment of a 'female divine'. Indeed, she has observed in *An Ethics of Sexual Difference* (1993) that women are closely related to angels, beings whom she sees as playing a vital role in the accomplishment of 'another parousia of the body'.

Hélène Cixous, who has privileged the novel and drama as vehicles for her feminist thought, has used motifs of flight on several occasions in her poetic and somewhat mystical reshaping of feminine identity. In *LA*, the narrator gradually discovers that she needs no trapeze to help her fly, since 'I am myself the trapeze and the trapezist'. Since *Vivre l'orange* (1978) angels have also been used by Cixous to refigure the I or *je* as *en-je* (in or towards I) or *enjeu* (in play, at stake). In this reformulation of the deconstructive concept of textual play, the female writer is intimately entangled with the non-human as angelic messenger, as a figure of communicating 'otherwise'.

In each of these writers, certain Christian motifs are given a new and feminist inflection. Above all, these images are 'differed' or redefined by these women's iconoclastic approach to all so-called 'truths'. It is worth noting, moreover, that these thinkers also draw upon themes and images from other faiths, scattering among their texts allusions to Buddhism, Confucianism, Judaism, Hindu yoga and the Greek mystery schools, as well as to astrology and Egyptian religion. In this reopening of the question of mystical experience, and of the human relationship to the divine, French feminism has implicitly challenged the secularism which dominates so much of twentieth-century thought.

An A to Z of Feminist Theology

FRIENDSHIP
Mary E. Hunt

FRIENDSHIP IS a rare topic in Christian theology. This is noteworthy in a tradition which features such dicta as 'Love your neighbors', 'Go and make friends in all nations', and other such friendly suggestions. Until feminist attention was drawn to it, friendship was generally buried within patriarchal moral theological treatments of relationships. In a patriarchal context, friendship was seen as a kind of ethical also-ran for marriage, what those who were never heterosexually partnered could hope to experience instead of so-called wedded bliss. Alternatively, friendship was spiritualized into some mythic sense of what persons attained with the divine, an asexual morass of feelings which was generally positive but unique to the God–human relationship. It was anything but the robust, sustaining relationship called friendship that so many people experience as central to personal well-being and communal enhancement.

Friendship is now understood from a feminist perspective as a normative adult relationship, a standard by which all relationships can be evaluated. This is a clear difference from the prevailing heterosexual norm in which all relationships were measured by how closely they approximated to heterosexual marriage, which itself was only available to a part of the whole community. Friendship, by contrast, can include heterosexual or homosexual marriage as a subset, but is in no way limited to it. That is, married people can be friends although under present social conditions not all friends can be married.

Unlike the marriage norm, friendship is a relationship which is not restricted to two people. Groups of friends are common. Friendship is possible for the range of relational constellations: women with women, men with men, women with men, adults with children, humans with animals, humans and animals with the earth, people with the divine. Not every relationship is a friendship, of course, but many friendships are passed over by more restrictive notions of the term which relegate friendship to something less important or mature than marriage, less serious or committed, something for children or young adults but not a real love relationship.

Friendship is a voluntary relationship which one chooses for oneself. Because of friendship's relational nature it is rare to talk about '*a* friend', and more common to talk about 'friends' in the plural. Friendship, theoretically, is open to everyone. Babies can be friends with their primary carers; elderly people who are ill can kindle friendships in communities of people who accompany them in their dying. People report being friends with animals. Family members develop friendships among themselves which transcend blood or adoption lines.

Friendship as a norm rather than as an exception levels the ethical playing field so that all relationships can be measured by the same criteria. Rather than giving heterosexual marriage a certain privileged place and measuring everything else against it, thus implicitly assuring that no other relationship can ever measure up, friendship as a norm simplifies the ethical discussion and makes it more just. What distinguishes friendship from other forms of relationship is the intention to enhance the well-being of a friend and to improve the quality of life in one's community in the process. Every friend is not necessarily conscious of these motivations, and the many losses or breakups of friendships refute them. But in fact this is what friendship means in its most positive, admittedly idealistic, sense.

In the history of Christian theology virtually all of the relatively few treatments of friendship are predicated on an Aristotelian framework. This places increasing weight on fewer and fewer friendships of greater intensity in a hierarchical model. According to this model, and typical of the epoch of Aristotle, only men could achieve the pinnacle of 'right relation' with one another, as in the case of a man with his best male friend. Further, a man could only have very few such friends in a lifetime. This resulted in a kind of relational pyramid, with acquaintances along the base line, closer friends in the middle, and a very few, usually one, perhaps two, men at the top.

The theo-ethical reflections which are predicated on this model are all based on quantitative ethics: how many friends, how long have they been friends, how deep is the commitment? Moreover, they are predicated on the experience

An A to Z of Feminist Theology

of men as friends with men, leaving aside entirely the content and dynamics of women's relationships with women, and women's relationships with men except as they are derived from the male model. This 'worked' theologically as long as marriage held sway, and as long as it was assumed that male experience could be taken as paradigmatic of human experience. But insofar as those assumptions have been rejected in feminist work, whole new possibilities have emerged, beginning with insights based on women's experiences. This means fundamental changes in Christian theological ethics, especially around sexuality, which have been rooted in the male-only model.

A feminist approach, by contrast, takes friendship as a qualitative experience rather than a quantitative one. Friendship, as I understand it, is the interaction of four components: love, power, sexuality and spirituality. Love is an orientation toward being more at one than separated; power is the ability to make choices; sexuality is embodied energy, and spirituality is attention to the quality of personal and communal life. Taken together, these four elements make up friendships, with every friendship distinguished by varying experiences of these dynamics. Theo-ethical judgments of friendships are predicated on whether the relationship is generative—whether it calls for or develops something beyond itself—as well as whether it is conducive of justice toward the persons involved and also towards the larger community of which it is a part.

Feminist theologians use friendship in at least three ways. Sallie McFague (1987) proposes Friend as a metaphor for the divine. Although her theology is still based on the Aristotelian model of friends, her suggestion is rich and evocative both because it connotes mutuality between humans and the divine and because it is an alternative to gender-based symbols and images. I am less enthusiastic about using friendship as a model for the divine because I am skeptical of any anthropomorphic images in that regard, but I see value in her insight.

Mary Daly (1984) focuses on Be-Friending as the process of developing a context in which women can be friends. This process radically reshapes a patriarchal context by inviting people to move toward new relational patterns. I agree that befriending and being befriended have far-reaching ramifications. But as a Euro-American woman living in the United States I note that the complex factors which ground experiences of friendship will result in culturally specific understandings of friendship which need to be recognized.

Based on my work on friendship (Hunt 1991), feminists are beginning to use friendship as the starting point for ethical reflection on relationships that differ from the heterosexual givens. I am wary of over-using the term, or presuming that everyone is interested in becoming friends, since choices and circumstances make that impossible. Experiences of friendship differ; however, many women report a plurality of friends in a lifetime rather than the tight pyramid of patriarchy. Many describe a wide range of relations in which they incorporate love, power, sexuality and spirituality in an infinite number of combinations. In short, the distinctions between friends and lovers, between relatives and friends, even between friends and enemies seem far more fluid than the patriarchal model permits.

For example, one can look at a long-term lesbian relationship and a long-term heterosexual marriage on an equal ethical footing, arguing that both are instances of committed friends in covenantal relationships which enhance the common good. An even better example would be three or four friends who live together or get together regularly. That a family which is widely scattered and gets together only for weddings and funerals would have ethical priority is simply counter-intuitive. Such family members would do well to become friends.

The problem with friendship as typically understood in a patriarchal context is that it has been so privatized and individualized as to seem personal rather than political. Feminist theologians have claimed that friendship is one of the most political relationships possible, wherein people make decisions because of their friends that have far-reaching implications. This is obvious in the case of same-sex friends who become lovers. The price is high in societies in which lesbian, gay, bisexual and transgendered friendships are not taken for granted on an equal footing with heterosexual ones. But it is equally the case when people befriend their animals, keeping them safe from violence or privation, acts which enhance the well-being of the whole of creation by safeguarding certain species. In a feminist construction, friendship is that quality of relationship that invites, virtually demands, risk-taking, both in terms of interpersonal intimacy and in terms of social action. Friends can be the oddest combinations of people, crossing race, class, age, gender and other boundaries. It is precisely because of friendship and not necessarily ideology that such differences are not transcended but attended to with care so that the power differences are handled in a just way.

It is frequently because of friends that people actually get involved in the rough and tumble of social change. Many social movements have been started by friends. For example, Jane Addams, social work pioneer who started the Hull House in Chicago, credited friends with sparking her work. The US-founded Catholic religious order known as the Sisters of Loretto was originally called 'The Little Society of the Friends of Mary under the Cross of Jesus', a title which emphasizes their roots in a nascent friendship model.

Far from being a private affair, friendships are public relationships which have consequences and implications far beyond the persons involved. One such set of implications has to do with what societies would look like if friendships and not marriage and/or blood ties held sway. Issues like inheritance, hospital visiting, legitimacy of children, mores around sexual relations and the like would be quite different. For instance, one's spouse or blood relatives would not automatically inherit one's property. Laws could be crafted so that everyone would designate (subject to change, of course) an heir upon reaching the age of majority, one way of decentering marriage as the norm.

The category 'single person' would be all but useless since virtually no one is without some form of friendship. Categories based on marital status would be replaced. Ethical discussions of pre-marital sex, for instance, would be refocused on the quality of the whole relationship of which sexual expression between friends is but a part. The illusion of societies held together by families would be shattered; with the divorce rate approaching 50 per cent in the United States and 35 per cent in the United Kingdom, this myth needs to be left aside. Otherwise, Christian theology and ethics will continue to be predicated on an outmoded social model, which will render them useless in cultures which are increasingly varied in their relational patterns.

Such changes are why the friendship norm has been slow to be accepted in mainline Christian circles, indeed why its revolutionary potential for social transformation is intuited and often rejected. Nonetheless, friendship continues to be, even in its most patriarchal form, one of the most satisfying, enduring relational experiences many people have wherein fidelity and generativity hold sway.

In the twenty-first century it is likely that friendship will become increasingly central to Christian theology. As it becomes the normative adult relationship, it will be the basis for the reformulation of sexual ethics and the development of communities in which justice-seeking is central and friendship valued in a wide range of expressions.

Further reading: Raymond 1986.

GAELIC WOMEN'S SPIRITUALITY
Noragh Jones

THE MAIN source material for Gaelic women's spirituality is the *Carmina Gadelica*, the printed version of the oral prayers, healing incantations and folk tales collected in the second half of the nineteenth century by Alexander Carmichael as he travelled among the Gaelic-speaking crofting communities in the Highlands and Western Isles of Scotland. The forms of Celtic Christianity he found there had their roots in the Isle of Iona, where Columba founded his monastery in the sixth century as a base for converting the people from Druidical paganism to Christianity. Due to the remoteness of their lives the Gaels retained a folk religion which infused into Christianity elements of their heritage.

The Gaels, aware of the natural world around them, respected human and elemental creation. They celebrated the turning of the seasons, reciting special prayers to greet the sun and the new moon, and holding domestic and community feasts on saints' days or on quarter days which marked the year's cycle. Personal expression lay at the heart of their spirituality, so every day they took responsibility for their own spiritual practices, giving voice to their hopes and fears and marking the daily events in their lives out loud in moving prayers and invocations to the powers that be.

The woman of the house as she banked down the household fire every night and as she revived the fire every morning would invoke protection and blessing on her household, for the fire was a reminder of the flame of life and of the need to rekindle basic energies and maintain warmth in ourselves and towards our family and neighbours.

There were prayers and blessings for every task in ordinary everyday life, from the milking to the churning, through every stage of wool working from spinning to the finishing of the cloth, and for sitting down around the table for family meals. For finishing the lengths of homespun material, neighbour women would gather round a trestle table and sing their waulking songs as they stretched and beat the cloth into shape. As the web emerged in good shape with the nap rising, three leading women would take it in turns to bless the cloth, turning sun-wise in a circle while holding the web and saying: 'I give a turn, sun-wise, in the name of the Father, the Son, the Holy Spirit'. Sometimes the finished cloth was passed round all the women at the table, again sun-wise, and each would give her own well-wishing turn and bless the cloth and whoever would be wearing it. But the waulking songs were not all solemn and serious, for it was an occasion for young women to sing about their boyfriends and to satirize girls who had tried to steal their lovers, or lovers who had abandoned them for the sake of material riches.

Gaelic women had their own women's celebration of a new-born child, the baptism of the knee-woman (midwife) which took place before any formal church baptism, to keep the infant safe from harm and from being spirited away by the mischievous fairy powers that lurked in hillock and stream and cave. The first drop of water on the baby's forehead was for wisdom, the second for peace, and the third for purity. When the knee-woman had finished the baptism she handed the baby to one of the aid women for the first bathing, and all the women present would sing an incantation, the Rune of the Nine Graces, over him or her.

St Brigid's help was invoked at a birth, for the fifth-century Irish saint had been preceded by a pagan goddess Brigid who had presided over the fertility of crops and flocks and humans, and pagan and Christian lore became inextricably mingled over the centuries of oral tradition.

Healing combined a blend of good spiritual disposition with sound knowledge of the properties of plants. Some of the healing plants were considered to be blessed by their association with the Christian story, which the Gaels always reset in their own temperate crofting villages and not in the desert lands of Palestine. They said that Christ had used a bramble stick to drive his ass on the ride into Jerusalem, and to drive the money changers from the temple, so the bramble was a blessed plant with great healing powers. They infused the leaves for a medicinal tea, and used the fruit for syrups and jellies to soothe winter coughs and sore throats, as well as extracting dye for their cloth from the roots.

An A to Z of Feminist Theology

Research into Gaelic spirituality has shown that a holistic way of life, a sense of community, an awareness of the natural world, and a hospitable disposition towards other human beings are central elements. Gaelic spirituality involves the celebration of the ordinary everyday things in life.

Further reading: Carmichael (ed.) 1992; De Waal 1991; Jones 1994.

GENDER
Elaine Graham

'GENDER' DENOTES the nature of our experience as women and men, female and male, feminine and masculine: the origins and attributions of these categories, and their implications for all aspects of individual and corporate life. Within the human and social sciences, analysis of gender is treated as an essential aspect of a broader analysis of the social order and human behaviour. Such theories of gender have three chief preoccupations:

1. The origins, formation and acquisition of individual gender identity and personality traits. This area is often associated with research into 'sex differences', which seeks to identify empirically the respective qualities of masculinity and femininity and their significance in constituting an individual's sense of self.

2. Theories of gender relations: patterns of power, norms and roles, the cultural representation of women and men, customs, legislation and the sexual division of labour; how material opportunities and rewards are distributed between women and men; differentials of power and influence according to gender.

3. The deeper structures of our culture, and how gender helps to organize our ideas not just about women and men, but about nature and knowledge, public and private, rationality and science. The fundamental metaphors of our very cultural life and social order are imbued with representations of gender: the binary pair masculine/feminine is associated with culture/nature, reason/emotion, mind/body, and so on. However, these do not represent innate bipolarities, but reflect the ideologies of patriarchal privilege. It is questionable therefore whether the terms 'masculine' and 'feminine' are complementary features. Rather, they are artefacts of a cultural and symbolic order which defines 'the feminine' as secondary, derivative and inferior.

Contemporary gender theorists are aware of the importance of considering the roles of women and men in the light of other categories of power and difference. Thus the dynamics of race and class, and the manner in which they intersect with gender relations, inform much of the critical study of gender. Similarly, questions of gender identity, relations and representation are closely related to, but not synonymous with, matters of sexuality, sexual orientation and sexual behaviour.

Three Characteristics of Gender Studies

Critical enquiry into theories of gender acquisition and development, gender relations and representation exhibits three dominant characteristics.

Interdisciplinary Enquiry

Critical studies of gender are now clearly established within a broad range of academic disciplines, including anthropology, psychology, biological sciences, sociology and social theory, history, philosophy and cultural studies. However, there is also a substantial body of material which seeks an integrated and multi-disciplinary analysis of gender. Recent examples include James Doyle and Michele Paludi's *Sex and Gender: The Human Experience* (1991), an overview of research perspectives and issues; Robert Connell's *Gender and Power* (1987), focusing particularly on social theory; Cynthia Fuchs Epstein's *Deceptive Distinctions* (1988), concentrating on the biological, sociological and psychological spheres; and Deborah Rhode's collection, *Theoretical Perspectives on Sexual Difference* (1990), which ranges between anthropology, biology, postmodern theory, history, ethics and legal studies. Indeed, such works may themselves be part of an inter-disciplinary genre which can be traced to such earlier works as Viola Klein's *The Feminine Character* (1946; reissued 1989), and Simone de Beauvoir's 'feminist classic', *The Second Sex* (1949).

This very heterogeneity of theories of gender suggests that gender relations must necessarily be

An A to Z of Feminist Theology

GENDER

analysed as the product of many different dimensions and levels of human behaviour; from the realm of individual subjectivity, through relationships of *cathexis* (intimacy) and kinship, to the structural organization and institutions of the social order, and the historical, symbolic and philosophical foundations of any given culture. In addition, it is apparent that critical analysis of gender consistently challenges notions of a 'unicausal' or reductionist model. Rather, it would appear that the origins of gender relations and gender identity are complex and multi-dimensional. Only an interdisciplinary perspective can adequately reflect this.

The Influence of Feminism

Much of the interest in gender as a category of human identity and social relations has been prompted by concern on the part of feminists to render women's lives and experiences more visible. This has involved critical attention to the ways in which 'patriarchal' society excludes and subordinates women; but also the grounds upon which a specifically 'feminist' theory and practice might be articulated, especially in terms of an appeal to 'women's experience' as both a critical and reconstructive resource. However, feminist theory is not monochrome. Most commentators identify several distinct schools or perspectives within feminism, reflecting a diversity of analyses and practical strategies.

Postmodernism

Theorists of gender have turned increasingly to 'postmodern' strategies and analyses for critical tools to guide their enquiries. Like gender theory, postmodern perspectives render problematic the central issues of selfhood, social order and power, and the authority of knowledge, reason and truth. Postmodernism has aroused strong opinion, not least over what are seen by many as its nihilist and relativist tendencies, occasioned by the collapse of modernist conventions of aesthetic value and moral truth. Yet its supporters hail its effects in liberating thought and culture from a rigid conformity to scientific objectivity and the binary oppositional categories used to evaluate truth, beauty and reason. Many commentators have indeed characterized feminism as one form of postmodernism. Both movements function to challenge conventions concerning the constitution of human nature, the grounds of reliable knowledge and the foundations of social relations, language and culture—which are also the perennial themes of gender theory (Flax 1990).

Emergent Perspectives on Gender

A comprehensive engagement with theories of gender therefore reveals some important insights, and challenges some traditional views. First, it is clear that gender is a fundamental form of social organization. Gender is but one manifestation of human social relations; it is not an ontological state, nor an intrinsic property of the individual. Theories about gender identity, gender relations and gender representations are therefore theories about the formation of human culture; being a gendered person is about inhabiting a particular culture. Such social relations—and thus gender as a form of social relations—are generated and maintained by human *practice*, symbolic and material.

Similarly, there is a move away from treating the categories of 'women' and 'men' as self-evident, rooted in separate ontological spheres, tied in to a series of cultural dualisms, such as nature/culture, private/public and emotion/reason. Instead, it is claimed that these ontological dichotomies—for which gender difference has appeared to be an integral organizing metaphor—are themselves the products of a gendered system of thought, which reflects a wider 'gender regime' of power and social relations.

Early accounts of 'sex' and 'gender', springing from the work of Robert Stoller in the late 1960s, posited the 'natural' categories of biological sex difference as foundational categories over which gender as a 'cultural' artefact is mapped (Oakley 1972). Such analysis was associated with studies of the acquisition of so-called 'sex roles' and the socialization into 'feminine' or 'masculine' qualities and behaviour. Both analyses have been of enormous value in fuelling feminist criticisms of earlier forms of biological determinism, and have allowed the-

An A to Z of Feminist Theology

orists to challenge the maxim that 'anatomy is destiny'. However, there is increasing dissatisfaction with such an 'additive' analysis of gender, because it poses an implicitly dualistic relationship between nature and culture, and body and mind. It presents gender as totally psychological or sociological, but denies the extent to which human identity and gender relations actually rest upon the appropriation and representation of morphological and biological experience.

Thus, critical theorists of gender argue that biological difference cannot be denied, that embodiment is an integral part of human experience, and that the realms of procreation, parturition and early mother–child relations do need to be considered within an adequate theory of gender. Feminists have been particularly wary of reassessing the role of biology or bodily difference for fear of collapsing into essentialism, but it is necessary to confront such aspects and construct theories of gender which account for embodied experience without, in Simone de Beauvoir's words, 'enclosing us in our differences' (Simons and Benjamin 1979).

Clearly, therefore, one of the key areas upon which debate about gender is located is a shift from what Connell (1987) terms 'categoricalism' (within both anti-feminism and radical feminism) towards a view of gender as a dialectical process, involving the material transformation of 'nature' into an integrated system of gender relations. Tracing the origins of gender *difference* thus becomes a question of how a variety of social practices and symbolic exchanges creates a human culture that is always already gendered. Difference is a social, not a self-evident, ontological or essentialist category.

A view of human personhood as gendered, therefore, understands it as a process of entering and inhabiting a gendered culture; as simultaneously being the creators, and creatures, of gender relations. Such a gendered culture is forged from the practices and conventions of science, work, technology, religion, reproduction and child-rearing, work, sexuality, power, symbolic exchange and language. Critical analyses of what it means to be a gendered person therefore have to focus upon human practices as the force which generates gender identity, representation and difference.

Implications for Theology

Feminist theology over the past twenty years has encouraged debates and policies for the greater participation and recognition of women in church life, as well as promoting a far wider agenda of justice-making. It has generated a greater sensitivity to the question of inclusive language, raised questions about the nature of God and encouraged research into the contemporary influence of a historical tradition largely shaped by conditions of patriarchy. However, underlying notions of gender identity and formation in such debates are largely unexamined. Therefore, the precise substance of 'feminine' and 'masculine' qualities—for example, in terms of the nature of the Divine and its relation to humanity—are seldom questioned. Similarly, there are hidden assumptions about the origins of gendered experience—innate versus socially constructed, the significance of embodiment—in appeals to the category of 'women's experience' as it fuels the critiques and reconstructions of feminist theology and spirituality.

Finally, an understanding of human personhood as gendered may have implications for theological language. When Christians use gendered terms for the Divine, they are deploying concepts derived from human experience. Gendered terms for God are thus—like all religious language—metaphors and models, not essential or ontological characteristics.

Feminist theology must therefore address itself critically to the presence of gender categories within theological concepts and practices, and the contribution of theology towards enforcing existing gender stereotypes. However, practical feminist strategies directed towards forms of pastoral care, worship, formation and direction, social action and preaching, might in turn foster relationships, values and symbols which enable a more 'gender-inclusive' community to be created (Graham 1995).

Further reading: Tong 1989.

GNOSTICISM
Estelle White

GNOSTICISM is a religious movement which, in its Christian form, flourished in the second century CE. It was suppressed by orthodoxy and virtually disappeared by the eighth century. There were many gnostic sects but certain beliefs were held in common. Salvation came by gnosis, esoteric knowledge given by a revealer figure. The creator of the visible universe, usually identified with the God of Israel, was not the true God. Matter was seen as evil compared to spirit and originated because of a pre-cosmic fall of a divine emanation. In some systems the latter was a female figure, Sophia.

Until halfway through this century most information about gnosticism came from the heresiologists. Then in 1945–46 a large quantity of gnostic documents were discovered at Nag Hammadi in Upper Egypt and these have produced vital information on gnostic thought and teaching (Filoramo 1991). These documents have been translated into English under the title *The Nag Hammadi Library in English* (Robinson [ed.] 1988; henceforth given as NHL).

There is a great deal of female imagery in gnostic writing and for a student of the role of women in early Christianity this imagery and its implications are vital, for it should be remembered that many of the gnostic sects regarded their adherents as the true Christians.

Although the culture of the time was androcentric, the god of the gnostics was portrayed in many of the documents as androgynous. In the long recension of the *Apocryphon of John* there is a female figure in the divine triad, 'I am the one who is [with you] always. I [am the Father], I am the Mother, I am the Son' (2.13-15 in NHL: 105, see also 4.27–5.11 in NHL: 107). The Father, Mother, Son motif is also found in the *Thought of Norea* (27.11-20 in NHL: 446). In the *Trimorphic Protennoia* there are both female and androgynous images of the divine (NHL: 513-22) and the Holy Spirit is perceived as female in the *Gospel of Philip* (55.20-30 in NHL: 143).

Valentinus, a prominent gnostic teacher (fl. 150 CE) suggests that God is a dyad, male and female (Irenaeus, *Adv. Haer.* 1.11.1). Irenaeus writes of another gnostic, Marcus, who, when celebrating the eucharist, invokes Charis (Grace, a female figure), with a prayer (*Adv. Haer.* 1.13.2).

Other examples of the androgynous god are given in ch. 4 of Filoramo's *History of Gnosticism*. In the same book (pp. 107-10) there is a brief description of the *Poimandres*, the first treatise in the *Corpus Hermeticum*, a pagan gnostic work (see Jonas 1958: ch. 7; Bentley 1987: 449-59 for translations). It should be noted that characters in the gnostic myths are often of indeterminate sex (Pétrement 1991: 124).

The role of Eve is sometimes seen in a different light from that given by patriarchal interpretations of Genesis 1–3. Instead of being the temptress she is depicted as a lifegiver and instructor (*Origin of the World* 115.31–116.8 in NHL: 182) and in the *Hypostasis of the Archons* she outwits the forces of evil (89.11–91.1 in NHL: 164. See also Pagels 1988: 412-23).

The image of Mary Magdalene in the gnostic writings also contradicts the conventional and disparaging view of her character given by some Church Fathers, a view which persists to the present day. She is often portrayed by the gnostics as a strong woman, a leader. Apart from the Saviour, in the *Pistis Sophia* she is the main person, often questioning Jesus and answering his most difficult questions. In the *Gospel of Mary* she is the principal speaker (NHL: 524-27) and is seen in confrontation with the apostle Peter. She is called the companion of Jesus in the *Gospel of Philip* (59.5-10 in NHL: 145) and the author describes how Jesus loved her more than the other disciples and often kissed her on the mouth (63.33–64.12). This hint of eroticism may 'indicate claims to mystical communion' (Pagels 1982: 47). For further analysis of the role of Mary Magdalene in the *Gospel of Philip* see Buckley 1988 and Rudolph 1988: 211-38).

Little is known of the structure and practices of gnostic groups but from the sparse sources it is clear that gnosticism attracted women, probably because the idea of the female aspect of the godhead was appealing and women could identify with heroines like Mary Magdalene and Norea (*Hypostasis of the Archons* in NHL: 161-69). There is the possibility, too, that the ascetic lifestyle practised by most sects provided an escape from marriage and childbearing.

An A to Z of Feminist Theology

Accusations that some sects rejected asceticism and indulged in libertine sexual behaviour were levelled by heresiologists. Scholars are divided about the accuracy of these reports (Goehring 1988).

The leadership of some women gnostics is acknowledged. Irenaeus names one woman, Marcellina, who first brought the teachings of a gnostic sect to Rome (*Adv. Haer.* 1.25.6) and Tertullian inveighs against gnostic women who teach, argue, exorcise, heal and baptize (*De Praescr.* 41.2-6; see Pagels 1982: 80-81).

Nevertheless, it must be said that not all portrayals of the female in the gnostic documents are positive. Sophia is seen as the cause of the creation of matter and evil, yet even here there is ambivalence, for she is also sometimes portrayed as a positive figure (Irenaeus, *Adv. Haer.* 1.30.6; 1.30.10; see also *Hypostasis of the Archons* 94.21–95.7 in NHL: 167-68).

The power of female sexuality is sometimes perceived to be something to be avoided at all costs (*Zostrianos* 130.20–131.14; *Dialogue of the Saviour* 144.15-23; the *Book of Thomas the Contender* 144.8-10, in NHL: 430, 254, 206). Logion 114 of the *Gospel of Thomas* in NHL: 138 states that 'every woman who will make herself male will enter the kingdom of heaven'. In the *Exegesis on the Soul* (NHL: 192-98) the soul has a female nature. On falling into the world she becomes a prostitute and is eventually saved by a male. These negative images should be seen as part of the link with asceticism and encratism (which was practised by members of several early Christian sects) found in a considerable number of writings—some gnostic, others not—of the late second and third centuries CE.

The question of gender in the gnostic literature is complex. While there are some assumptions that the male is superior to the female, these being a reflection of social experience, there are more than enough positive images of the female to offer a different picture.

Further reading: King (ed.) 1988.

GODDESS
Jules Cashford

AT SOME times and in some places—particularly, it seems, at the beginning of the world's religions—the image of a goddess has been primary, and the image of a god has been secondary, or absent. At other times and in other places, most particularly in the last two thousand years, the image of a god has been primary, and the image of a goddess has been secondary or absent.

With these precautions in mind, it remains true to archaeological fact that the earliest images of divinity in the Palaeolithic age were sculpted in the form of a woman. Yet these were not women in the literal sense of the females of the human race, but women whose capacity to give birth was rendered symbolic of the mystery of the birth of the universe itself. A 'goddess' is then an image of the creative force conceived as the mother who gives birth to all things as her children. The goddess of Laussel, for example, whose pregnant womb rose above the rock shelter overlooking the valley of Laussel in the Dordogne around 20,000 BCE, is one of the first images of the divine to be discovered. Carved out of the limestone rock, 17 inches long, she holds in one hand the curved horn of the bison in the shape of the crescent moon, notched with fourteen lines for the waxing phase of the moon; with the other hand she points to her swelling belly, so drawing a relation between heaven and earth, between what is above and what is below. The implication of her positioning at the peak of the fruitful landscape is that this is She Who, or That Which, gave birth to all that could be seen, and, metaphorically, to all that could be imagined, even the universe itself in all its bewildering fecundity.

Many such images have been found from the Palaeolithic age, over a hundred figurines from France to Siberia, often close to the entrances of caves. One was the goddess of Lespugue near the Pyrenees, who lay forgotten for millennia in a muddy ditch. Carved from mammoth ivory, five and a half inches high, this little statue has a body wholly focused on the act of giving birth: large breasts fall towards her belly; the ten lunar months of human gestation are incised on her buttocks; and her legs taper to a point without feet as though she were made to be held in the hand or pressed into the earth for ritual. It would seem, from these and many other figures, that for those whom we might call the children of the race, the first image of life was of a moth-

GODDESS

er. We still retain this idea poetically in the term 'Mother Nature'.

What is the unique characteristic of the divine mystery imagined as female? The image of the mother, in contrast to the Judaeo-Christian image of the father, remains eternally immanent in her creation. Father gods are characteristically imagined as transcendent to their creation, creating the world from outside or beyond it through art or craft: either through the word, as Ptah in Egypt, Enlil in Mesopotamia and Yahweh-Elohim in Genesis, or as a potter throwing the world egg on the potter's wheel, another image of the Egyptian god Ptah. Mother goddesses are imagined giving birth from their body to creation as their child, who is therefore of the same substance as their creator and able to participate directly in that original divinity. There is no radical separation of the created from the creator, no ontological gap into which the inevitable questions of the created can be turned against the questioners. The notion of 'original sin' is not one found in the hymns and stories of a goddess religion; in the Mesopotamian *Gilgamesh*, the earliest written story, the hero's quest for immortality teaches him simply a tragic vision: that eternal life is not human destiny. The other major, and related, difference between goddess and god religions lies in their vision of Earth. Earth, Nature, indeed the whole universe, as the 'body of the goddess', is seen as inherently alive and animate, that is, ensouled. What we do not find is that opposition between spirit and nature that is characteristic of god religions generally, and in which nature is seen as chaotic or 'fallen', and so in need of ordering by a superior spiritual principle. On the contrary, within the goddess religions, Nature is felt to be a 'Thou'—and often an overwhelming Thou—but never an 'It'.

This can be seen in the relatively recent discoveries of the Neolithic age (c. 7000–3500 BCE), defined as the beginning of agriculture. Now images of the goddess are extended to include the mystery of the growth, death and rebirth of vegetation. In an area called 'Old Europe' by the archaeologist Marija Gimbutas (1982), statues of pregnant goddesses were found. These were often seated on the throne of earth, and were decorated with seeds, plants, fields and raindrops. Goddesses also took the form of birds and serpents, as well as animals, bees, butterflies and fish. Gods began to appear, often sculpted in consort with a goddess, and sometimes carrying a sickle over the right shoulder. The man who cuts down the corn may here have become the god who ordains that the corn be cut down, or be himself an image of the corn in its necessary phases of death and rebirth. The male image also took the form of the bull, the ram and the stag. In seventh-millennium Anatolia, temples decorated with bulls' horns show a goddess giving birth to a bull, a dual goddess, and a vulture goddess who devours the dead, bringing them back into the cycle of life.

In the Bronze Age (c. 3500–1250 BCE), with the invention of writing, the visions and practice of the many goddess religions can be deciphered. All over the Near East, there appeared a virgin mother goddess of many names (virgin in the original symbolic sense of self-generating): she was called Inanna-Ishtar in Mesopotamia, Nut, Hathor and Isis in Egypt, and later, in the Iron Age (c. 1250 BCE), Demeter and Aphrodite in Greece, Cybele in Anatolia and Rome. The stories have a common lunar pattern of birth, fullness, loss and rebirth, evocative both of the waxing and waning cycles of the moon, and of life in time on earth for all created beings: plants, animals and humans alike.

In the earliest myth called 'The Descent of Inanna', about 2500 BCE, the Sumerian goddess Inanna, Queen of Heaven and Earth, leaves the Upper World and goes down into the Nether World to visit her sister Ereshkigal, Queen of the Underworld. Inanna must progressively shed her bright apparel at the seven gates to the underworld, as does the waning moon in the last seven days before the dark. Three days and three nights Inanna hangs as a naked corpse in the underworld, like the moon in the dark when all her light is gone, and then (having made provision for her rescue before she went), she slowly gathers her luminous coverings and ascends upwards, as the new moon at the beginning of the new cycle. But the laws of the underworld must be fulfilled, and Inanna's consort, Dumuzi, has to die in her place. Yet he is permitted to share his time in the underworld with his sister, and may live for half this year in the Upper World of Light.

An A to Z of Feminist Theology

GODDESS

This myth was the model for many explorations of the mystery of death and rebirth in nature which suggested analogies for the destiny and purpose of human life as part of nature. The Egyptian goddess Isis is separated from her brother-husband Osiris in death, revives him, loses him again and brings him back to a life that must be lived in the underworld. The Greek Demeter, goddess of the harvest, loses her daughter Persephone through the rape by Hades, god of the underworld. In her rage she turns the whole earth barren, like perpetual winter. Zeus, king of the gods, allows Persephone, whose name means both 'sprout' and 'she who shines in the dark', to return to her mother as the seed to the new plant, but because she had tasted food in death (the seeds of the pomegranate which Hades had slipped her), she must stay a third of the year in the darkness below. Spring was celebrated as the reunion of mother and daughter, the 'two goddesses as one', as they were known at the rites of Eleusis, held yearly in Greece, where the culminating moment was the holding up, by the officiating priest, of an ear of corn.

These ways of understanding life were, as is now well known, contemporary with the birth and teachings of Christ, and it would be unlikely if Christian teaching had not absorbed something of their wisdom, or at least their symbolism: 'Except a corn of wheat fall into the ground and die, it abideth alone; but if it die, it bringeth forth much fruit' (Jn 12.24). A common heritage was recognized at the time by St Jerome, who translated the Holy Scriptures into Latin, as he witnessed the rituals of Venus (the Roman name for the Greek Aphrodite) and her consort Adonis, who also 'died' for three days before he rose again, and whose name meant 'lord'.

But the goddess tradition entered Christianity directly through the figure of the Virgin Mary, who inherited, in image, symbol and legend—though not in doctrinal status—many of the attributes, powers and names of the mother goddesses of the Western world: Mystical Rose, Star of the Sea, Gate of Heaven, Seat of Wisdom, Refuge, Consolation and Queen of Peace. In the Christian Scriptures, Mary, the mother of Jesus, is simply a woman who 'found favour with God' (Lk. 1.18). Yet over the last two thousand years her status has risen in a way that would be difficult to explain without an appreciation of the earlier goddess tradition; or, more precisely, what that tradition implies, the need in many people to imagine divinity in a feminine dimension. In 431 CE, at a council in Ephesus, Mary was proclaimed not just 'Christ-bearer' but also 'God-bearer', *theotokos*. In 451 CE she was proclaimed *aeiparthenos*, 'Ever-Virgin' (in its literal not symbolic sense), and in 600 CE the Feast of the Dormition, or Falling Asleep, was celebrated, removing Mary still further from the human condition. In 1854 the Catholic Church declared the doctrine of the Immaculate Conception of Mary in addition to its doctrine of the virgin birth of Jesus; in 1950, in response to a petition signed by eight million people, Pope Pius XII declared the Assumption of the Virgin, where Mary was 'taken up body and soul into the glory of heaven'; and in 1954 Mary became 'Queen of Heaven'.

It is tempting to say of Mary, following the image rather than its interpretation, 'Queen of Heaven, like many another goddess before her', though, significantly, in our age of desacralized nature, not Queen of Earth. But in official doctrine, of course, Mary is by no means a goddess: she is only the mediator between heaven and earth, between the divine and human realms. Where God is owed *latria*, adoration, and the saints *dulia*, veneration, Mary may receive *hyperdulia*, superior veneration: she is more than fully human but less than fully divine. Yet it is possible that the vitality of the cult of the Virgin Mary in Catholic countries may point to a deeper yearning to redress the balance between the male and female images in the human psyche as they are expressed in the images of the divine.

The essence of the goddess tradition is to focus and inspire a vision of life as an organic, living and sacred whole, where all things participate in the divinity of the source. It may, however, justly be claimed that this vision of life is not unique to the goddess religions but is one to which all religions aspire, especially in their mystical aspects. Take, for instance, the words of Jesus in the gnostic *Gospel of Thomas*, Logion 77:

> Jesus said: 'Cleave a (piece of) wood, I am there;
> lift up the stone and you will find Me there'.

Further reading: Baring and Cashford 1993; Begg 1985; Campbell 1976; Warner 1985.

An A to Z of Feminist Theology

GODDING
Carter Heyward

'GODDING', FROM the verb 'to god', is a term used in feminist liberation theology. Evangelical feminist theologian Virginia Ramey Mollenkott writes, 'human responsibility, in its deepest and fullest dimension, entails *godding*, an embodiment or incarnation of God's love in human flesh, with the goal of cocreating with God a just and loving human society' (1988: 2). In *The Redemption of God: A Theology of Mutual Relation* (1982) I build on the suggestion of radical feminist philosopher Mary Daly (1973) that God may be best understood as a verb. 'In Jesus, we see that the human–divine relation is so intimate…and so immediate…that Jesus [chooses] to do God's activity, or to god, in the world' (Heyward 1982: 39). 'Co-creators, we god in love, a common awareness that no one of us is alone, and that in the relation between subject and subject, there is power' (p. 153).

In both Daly's work and my own, the formulation of the verb 'to god' is partially derived from Paul Tillich's theology of being: God is the spiritual basis, or ground, of our existence. But there are differences between Daly and myself. For Daly, patriarchal and feminist spiritualities are essentially oppositional, whereas for me, 'godding' is a more dialogical, less oppositional, relational process in which God is the essence of relational power, not merely its source.

Godding is a mutual process of co-creating right-relation in which all participants—including the relational power and process—are being affected and are changing. There is no unchanging deity in or beyond the universe, either patriarchal or feminist, although men have created just such a god, untouched and unmoved, in their own image and this fabricated god/father forms the basis of patriarchal religion.

Our capacity to god is the only creative, liberating response to the 'patriarchal logic' of traditional Christianity (Heyward 1993). Godding, we ourselves become agents of transformation in the world and church and, together, bear up the hope of the world. For Daly who, in attempting to break decisively from Christianity, does not actually employ the term 'to god' or 'godding' in her work, the only hope for women is to leave the church and patriarchal spirituality and, in one another's company, to build an Otherworld. The differences between Mollenkott's, Daly's and my own relationships to the church may be illuminated by differences in how we understand our sacred power to god. For Daly, it is essentially the power of women to separate themselves from the church in order to become who they are as women-defined women. For Mollenkott and myself, it is the power of women to struggle, sometimes apart from men, sometimes with men, for mutual relation in and out of the church. All of us understand this to be a power that liberates women.

GRACE
Anne Murphy

IT IS easier to experience grace than to define it. We have all had our moments of grace: hearing the 'Have mercy' aria from Bach's St Matthew Passion, witnessing the miracle of a birth, experiencing the transfigurative grace of sexual love, weeping tears of forgiveness and healing. We can begin to understand what God's gift may mean because we have experienced totally unexpected, unearned and uncalculated graced moments. These are moments of disclosure of presence which we cannot cling to or 'possess', but only receive with open heart and with gratitude.

Theologically grace refers to the unconditional, comprehensive and empowering love of God for all creation. It touches the positive and negative aspects of existence. In the first place it refers to the original blessings, all the God-given resources of life, creativity and inventiveness. But, paradoxically, grace is also given to us within our mortality and vulnerability. We are born with the potential for life but also with the certainty of death. We experience our mortality and finitude as well as our capacity to damage and to be damaged by others. God's presence comes to us in response to our longing for salvation from sin and death. We experience grace as forgiveness and as a foretaste of resurrection or final victory over death. Within the Christian tradition God's original and redemptive purposes for humankind are seen as embodied in the life, death and resurrection of Jesus Christ. God's offer of grace has become the Word made flesh, who dwells among us. It is present in the world through the power of God's Spirit.

God's graciousness makes us 'grace-ful'. The old English word suggests suppleness, ease and beauty of bodily movement, of being creatively at home in the body, and in the world. Yet the classical theologies of grace usually have not given primacy to its incarnational, embodied aspects. Throughout most of Christian tradition the distinctive features of human existence were said to lie in the rationality and self-awareness of human beings, while the body was regarded as the 'lower part' to be controlled and carefully guarded. Classical theology preferred an abstract and analytical approach which made distinctions between grace and nature, supernatural and natural, spirit and body, sacred and profane. In all these dualistic pairs the first or higher was associated with male, the lower with female qualities. Medieval and Early Modern theology also developed the notion of grace as restricted or scarce. At its narrowest it declared 'No salvation outside the church', or the Christian dispensation. Even with Christianity a drastic doctrine of double predestination further restricted the number who would finally be with God for all eternity.

Modern and contemporary theology prefers a synthetic, dynamic and experiential approach to an understanding of grace (cf. Henri de Lubac, Karl Rahner, Edward Schillebeeckx). There is a strong interest in how God works within human subjectivity, and in the dynamic of human development as a psychological, moral and religious process. The old dualistic divisions have given way to a more personalist, holistic and integrated approach. God's offer of saving grace is focused in, but not restricted to, those who belong to the Christian faith. It is a universal offer made to all human beings born into a 'graced world', with the possibility of growth and development at each stage of life (Rahner). There is a sense in which 'All is grace' (Bernanos), and yet God's own life is infinitely and qualitatively other than its reception and expression in our human lives. Most significantly grace is seen as God's offer of love—in relationship, constantly in process, capable of being deepened, yet vulnerable and at risk. In the end it is difficult to distinguish the experience of grace from the experience of love.

The related strands of liberation theology and feminist theology are in the process of articulating their own experience and language of grace. Liberation theology has stressed the social and political nature of grace: the love of God must extend beyond our selves and families, to the poor and the marginalized and the outcast. We have to recognize our solidarity in sin to experience our solidarity in grace. God's liberating grace, the realization of God's kingdom of justice and peace, is not just for the after-life, but for this life. Women and men, made in God's image, are called to live lives of human dignity and worth, not of poverty and hopelessness. Where this does not happen, sin is present, and liberative grace is needed. This grace is not merely intellectual assent, or passively experienced, but *performative*. Liberation theology shares with feminist theology a sense of prophetic urgency to collaborate in the transformation of society and attitudes. Both hope to identify and eliminate negative forces which diminish or destroy human 'livingness' and to bring unity where there has been fragmentation and isolation. This is the grace of social and political holiness.

A feminist theology of grace recalls the Christian tradition to its incarnational and embodied beginnings. Because of God's word in Gen. 1.31, all creation is good. It is doubly so because of God's becoming human within it. A theology of grace is related to an understanding of sin, or lack of wholeness in creation. Christian feminism focuses on three basic relationships which have been damaged or diminished by sin: human beings with each other (male/female), with the earth they inhabit, and with the life-giving Spirit of God. A renewed theology of grace seeks to restore those elements which have been trivialized, exploited or forgotten: women, earth and Holy Spirit (Johnson 1993). It is recognized that the exploitation of the resources of the earth (ecological sin) is closely related to the exploitation and marginalization of women (sexism) and a neglect of the notion of God's presence as immanent, life-giving Spirit. To heal each of these relationships is indeed to 'renew the face of the earth'.

The roots of sin in each of these areas lie in a hierarchical way of seeing reality in terms of who is superior/dominant, and who is inferior/subordinate. God is seen as 'above' creation,

GRACE

spirit 'above' body or matter, man 'above' woman, human beings 'above' non-human creation. As God is 'pure Spirit', those higher up the scale are presumed to be nearer God, because more 'spiritual'. Hierarchical language is also the language of power, significance and worth. Perfection is seen as climbing up a ladder, or overcoming the enemy in warfare. God was imaged as the all-mighty, the powerful one.

The language of hierarchical dualism has focused on the human to the disparagement of the non-human in creation. Traditionally we have seen ourselves as rational beings at the apex or crown of creation, entitled to dominion over what was 'below' us. More recently we have moved from a theology of dominion or lordship to one of stewardship over creation with a duty to care and preserve it. But even this change in attitude is not enough, for we actually depend for our continued existence on that which we steward. We are not *above* the earth, but *within* it; we need air, light, water and food to live. We depend upon ecosystems for our survival. In a very real sense the earth is our body, and the way in which it works must be respected, not abused. Human persons must take responsibility for ecological sin: for damaging, plundering and wasting the sources of our communal life. We can restore the lost harmony of our relationship with the earth by respecting its richness and diversity, and by seeing ourselves as part of the great web of life, linked in interdependence. This is a humbling and liberative experience of grace. But we must be wary of thinking that we can now live an unproblematic and innocent relationship with creation or the sensual world.

The language of hierarchical dualism has assumed that man is by nature superior to woman because he is more rational and more spiritual. The connection of women with bodiliness, and bodiliness with sin, has linked women with the profane, the 'merely natural' and the unholy. Women and nature have often been dismissed, trivialized or exploited in similar ways. It is therefore important for women to reclaim grace precisely as embodied grace, and to celebrate those aspects of bodiliness which have traditionally been covered with shame and silence: sexuality, menstruation, childbirth, breast-feeding. Feelings of shame or guilt often need to be articulated and brought out into the open before they can be healed. The recognition of sexism as sinful and damaging to both men and women makes possible the grace of mutuality or interrelatedness. This goes much further than attempts at equality, complementarity, or romanticism. Mutuality recognizes difference, and is clear-sighted about areas of possible conflict. But 'the other' is no longer a threat or an enemy but a source of my becoming myself.

The language of hierarchical dualism has tended to speak to God as transcendent and 'other', above and distinct from Creation. It has neglected the language of God's immanence within creation, sustaining and renewing it. It has spoken of the Father and the Son, but found it difficult to imagine the Spirit of the 'loving connectedness of all things' (Nicholas of Cusa). A renewed doctrine of the triune God as a community of persons, living in reciprocity and mutuality, should provide a sustaining image of grace as participation in divine life. A renewed understanding of the Spirit of God, immanent in creation, could be a source of healing divisions between man and woman, human and non-human creation. It could reveal the nature of grace as loving and relational connectedness.

Finally, a feminist theology of grace would include dance, music and ritual as participative and inclusive ways of experiencing and understanding grace. Down the ages artists have been inspired by the classical image of the 'three graces', or three young women, whose beauty and coordinated movement flows into the dance or rhythm of life (cf. Botticelli, La Primavera). The theologian Karl Barth had a deep sense of God as the 'one who loves in freedom'. He drew inspiration from the music of Mozart because it communicated an experience of creative, yet ordered, freedom. Music and dance are much neglected images of grace as a spontaneous, dynamic and unearned gift. They are also neglected images of at-one-ment, the harmony (rather than traditional divisions) of body and mind, earth and heaven, immanence and transcendence. Recent developments in music and dance therapy have enabled mentally and physically handicapped people to 'relax into' and experience the grace of their 'fragmented' minds and awkward bodies. Often they can respond to rhythm and movement, but are normally excluded by our more cerebral ways of knowing.

Our communal celebration of the Eucharist should reflect more faithfully such participative grace.

'Tomorrow shall be my dancing day / I would my true love did so chance / to see the legend of my play / to call my true love to my dance /.' The medieval carol images grace as God's call to participate in the dance of life. A feminist theology of grace retrieves and deepens this image. For this we, women and men, give thanks (*eucharistia*) and acknowledge the source of our joy and gratitude.

For example: Haight 1979; Ormerod 1992; Spretnak 1991.

GREENHAM COMMON WOMEN'S PEACE CAMP
Linda Hurcombe

IN SEPTEMBER 1981 forty women and four men bearing a banner proclaiming *Women for Life on Earth* marched 110 miles from Cardiff to RAF Greenham Common in Berkshire to protest the build-up of armaments for a first strike nuclear war and, in particular, the siting of 96 Cruise missiles. When the media and Ministry of Defence ignored their presence and their petition, the group agreed to chain themselves to the base's fence and remain there until the then Minister of Defence, John Nott, accepted an invitation to a television debate over the issue. The protesters were told they could stay as long as they liked. The chains were discarded, and thus began Greenham Common Women's Peace Camp.

Amidst considerable acrimony it was decided in the early days to forbid men from living at the camp, although it was made clear that male backup support would be welcome. The women insisted that the decision had less to do with rejecting men than *including* women. This resolution proved to be the most important and continually contentious determinant in the direction the camp took over ensuing months and years.

During the 1980s Greenham Common emerged as a focus for peace and spirituality issues in Britain and indeed the world over, a means of facing and protesting the possibility of global annihilation. The gates of the base's nine-mile perimeter fence were named after colours of the rainbow. Women's non-violent direct actions, sometimes involving tens of thousands of people, varied from linking arms to 'embrace the base' and decorating the fence with mementos of family and children, to an Easter action during which women dressed in furry animal costumes and climbed over the fence to distribute Easter eggs to soldiers and police. A Halloween Action produced the cutting down, by thousands of women armed with boltcutters, of more than half the base's perimeter fence. Women danced on the missile silos on a New Year's dawn and regularly cut through fences and razor wire to occupy or 'decorate' the base. Films and songs were produced. These actions inspired and redefined both traditional forms of non-violent direct action and women's role in the political and spiritual crises dominating the twentieth century. On a theological level the peace camp prompted a crucial debate over the value of martyrdom as a tool of redemption.

Dr Rosalie Bertell, international expert on low-level radiation and member of the Order of Grey Nuns, believed that the women were responding to the recognition of a kind of 'species death' grief process (1985). She based her opinion on the work of Elizabeth Kubler Ross, who saw the grieving process in four stages: denial, rage, partial acceptance, and finally, full acceptance and an attempt to take responsibility for the problem.

The Greenham years also opened opportunities to reconnect women's theological offerings with the wider women's movement. The Peace Camp welcomed all peace perspectives, at major actions designating certain gates 'religious' in order to provide women of all faiths with a place to pray and meditate. Christian women organized a regular twelve-hour dawn-to-dusk liturgy which strengthened participants and provided night watch for the permanent campers.

In the early 1990s Cruise missiles were removed from the base, and Greenham Common gradually reverted to its traditional role as a nature reserve and 'Site of Special Scientific Interest'. There was talk of turning the missile silos into mushroom factories. Conventional wisdom concluded that the base's closure reflected the end of the Cold War, the fall of the Berlin Wall and the 'opening up' of Eastern Europe. Whether the women's camp will come to be seen as a crucial influence in this outcome is a matter for the history books.

Further reading: Cambridge Women's Peace Collective 1984; Dowell and Williams 1994; Jones (ed.) 1983; Thompson (ed.) 1983; Tither (ed.) 1994.

GUILT
Anne Murphy

THE ADMISSION of guilt and the relief of remorse are only given to us by self-knowledge and are related to the possibility of forgiveness and healing. Authentic, justified or rational guilt is an awareness of having done something harmful, wrong or damaging to the 'livingness' of others (Barter 1993). In this sense guilt is as necessary as pain—a warning that something is wrong and needs to be put right. Without a capacity for guilt, there could be no sense of responsibility in personal relationships. A person who acts from good will may do something which has harmful consequences. This person will be responsible, but not culpable or blameworthy. Guilt feelings are directly related to culpability and may be entwined with self-reproach, anxiety, remorse, and loss of self-esteem. Such feelings can be resolved if insight into behaviour flows into appropriate action—admission, repentance, seeking forgiveness, and some way of making amends.

But there are two main problems with our feelings of guilt. In our immaturity, we often deny, hide or are unable to handle feelings of authentic or justified guilt. Secondly, in our brokenness and woundedness, we are often burdened with a sense of inauthentic, neurotic or so called 'imaginary' guilt. These distinctions are not clear to the one who experiences guilt, which is never 'imaginary' to the sufferer. This article will focus on women's experience of guilt in our Western, Christian/post-Christian culture. I am, however, aware that women will experience guilt and its related emotions in different ways within other cultures and religions, and that there is much variation even within a single culture.

Our inability to admit authentic guilt, or to be relieved of the burden of inauthentic guilt, has its root in infancy and childhood. Many people suffer greatly from the tyranny of the 'super-ego'—that voice of authority within us, formed by internalizing the demands and expectations of authority figures outside and 'above' us. It is important as the first shaper of standards of behaviour, but often lingers on into adulthood as an unhealthy influence. The developing infant or child has to test the world around it. It will feel 'good' if its actions are approved and acceptable; it will feel 'bad' or guilty if they are displeasing or punishable. Infants who are not touched or held in physical closeness later suffer impaired development because they have not been assured that their world is basically reliable and trustworthy. If a child experiences acute physical abuse, extreme lack of affection, or the loss of a prime carer, feelings may be so traumatic as to be unbearable, and are repressed below the level of consciousness. Alice Miller has described this most clearly in her book *Banished Knowledge* (1991).

In Jungian rather than Freudian terms, the mature adult has later to come to know and befriend the 'shadow-self'—all that we have repressed, rejected or found unacceptable in ourselves, and have been unable to face. What is significant for feminist theology is that the construction of both the 'super-ego' and the 'shadow-self' is gender-related. In childhood those 'above us' communicate differing expectations to their daughters and sons (Gilligan 1982). They do so from within the broader parameters of what is expected of women and men in a patriarchal society. In spite of many social changes in Western cultures, women's psychologies still reflect what has been absorbed while growing up: that women are somehow less valued, less important and have fewer opportunities than their male counterparts. A boy achieves self-identity by separation and independence from the mother figure, and develops morally through notions of justice and fair play. A girl will do so by remaining connected with her mother, identifying with the role model provided by her. She develops morally via an ethic of care and responsibility. She learns quite early on that her own needs must take second place to those of others; if she attends to them she feels 'guilty'.

An A to Z of Feminist Theology

GUILT

Because relational connectedness is at the core of her identity, a woman feels 'bad' and culpable when relationships break up or are at risk. In later life women frequently 'blame' themselves for the break-up of marriage, or 'failure' in bringing up children. If a woman works outside the home, and has children or an invalid husband, she often suffers the guilt of divided loyalties. If someone she loves dies, she may easily blame herself for not 'having done more' to prevent it. Women accept guilt and answer for it because an ethic of care and responsibility is built into their being and understanding. Women will often accept self-destroying and imprisoning patterns of life, rather than betray or go against these deep emotions. A battered and abused woman often finds it impossible to break away from her partner. It may be fear for the safety of her children rather than for her own safety that finally forces her to leave.

If a woman has a persistent feeling that she does not measure up to the person she ought to be, it is possible that her feelings of guilt will be compounded by a sense of shame. In theory the distinction between guilt and shame is very clear: we feel guilty for what *we have done or not done*; we feel shame for what *we are*. I feel guilty because I have lied or cheated; I feel ashamed because I am the kind of person who can do such things. But in practice guilt can merge into shame very easily. We often feel shame at the thought of a hidden secret coming to light. It can also be a public 'disgrace', which humiliates us. Feelings of guilt and shame are about our very selves, our self-esteem. They tell us we are unworthy, unacceptable, inadequate, inferior, flawed. Acute loss of self-esteem may lead to depression and a sense of hopelessness. Though it may be triggered off by an authentic, even traumatic experience in adult human living, acute loss of self-esteem is related more usually to lack of love or acceptance in early life. If children feel they can never earn the approval of parents, however hard they try, it can permanently damage their self-image. If they grow up in an atmosphere of fear of punishment, and can only survive by pleasing parents for the wrong reasons, it can leave them permanently scarred with a sense of guilt, unworthiness and even self-hate. For girls this is compounded by the 'fact of having been born a woman', and therefore being already undervalued by the system.

Both Freud and Jung recognized that a consciousness of guilt is a cultural as well as an individual phenomenon. Jean Delumeau (1990) argues that our Western culture is a culture of guilt and has traced its emergence through a period from the thirteenth to the eighteenth century. When ideas of individual conscience and moral responsibility developed in Europe this deeply affected the discourse and pastoral practice of all Christian denominations. Preachers used an excessive rhetoric of 'culpability', inflating the elements of sin over pardon and forgiveness. Their ultimate weapons were the judgment of the all-seeing eye of God and the fear of eternal damnation. The practices of private confession or public admonition were used to enforce strict codes of discipline, which had social as well as religious consequences. Religious observance was related to religious dependency and total obedience to an existing order.

Within this religious culture women were seen as morally weak, a source of possible 'temptation' to men and so in need of special 'control'. Civil and ecclesiastical law regarded women as 'minors', incapable of fully adult decision making or of acting in their own best interests. A rhetoric of 'contempt for this world' devalued human sexuality, procreation and the processes of menstruation and childbirth. So women suffered from a double burden of guilt and shame: first for sharing the fallen human condition, secondly for being born into its weaker half. For this women needed to be 'twice redeemed' and religious customs such as 'churching' or segregation in church re-inforced a sense of their separateness and unworthiness.

We need to examine the particular damage done to women's self-image within Christian traditions. Churches of all persuasions have been the authorities on sin and wrongdoing, and have often claimed to offer the only means of forgiveness and purification. God, seen as male, was the ultimate authority figure, watching even our innermost thoughts. God's authority was mediated through an all-male clerical structure on which women depended for the ministry of word and sacrament, especially that of forgiveness. All Christians, but especially women, were

GUILT

expected to live from an 'ethic of obedience' to lawful authority. Conformity was 'good'; rebellion was 'bad'. Dissension was heretical. The destiny of a 'good woman' lay in her vocation as wife and mother, roles which reflected the 'natural order' ordained by God.

But a deeper Christian tradition has spoken of the liberating move from law to gospel, or from an ethic of obedience and conformity to an ethic of creativity and responsive love. In the process of maturation and individuation the voice of the super-ego, and the demands of the ego, must give way to the voice of the true conscience of the deepest self. This is the individual voice of a person's own first-hand experience, rather than the handed-down conscience of the expectations of others. It does not operate in isolated independence; as human beings we continue to live in relatedness; we share and evaluate our ideas and experiences with others round us, and not only with those in authority 'above us'. Where we do accept traditional norms, it is because we have consciously chosen them and made them our own.

Feminist theology is particularly attentive to gender-specific experiences which shape the authentic self. Traditional theologies of sin and guilt, grace and salvation, were formulated by men, in relation to their own experiences, taken to be 'normative'. The traditional fall/redemption theology has identified pride as the prime sin. In a society where women have not usually held positions of power, pride (or an inflated sense of self) has not been characteristic of women. Rather they have lacked a sense of self and often taken refuge in submission, self-effacement and passivity. Feminist theologians have identified specifically female tendencies to sin in our culture: triviality, distractibility, dependence on others for one's own self-definition, sentimentality, gossipy sociability and the like. Often the meek wife has found it easier to defer to her husband's wishes, to enter a conspiracy of silence over domestic sexual abuse, to be a martyr to the wishes of others, to avoid making independent decisions. Often women have been successful in the art of 'learned helplessness', or the 'I can do nothing' syndrome. For these 'deadly sins' a woman may not experience guilt and may actually 'feel good'. But the damage done both to herself and others is incalculable. At the heart of the Christian mystery she may identify with Christ the victim, rather than accepting the healing forgiveness of the risen Lord.

A woman can be released from the burden of guilt by being put in touch with the creative, life-giving sources of her being, and by affirming the dignity and worth of what has formerly been devalued. The burden of genuine, authentic guilt may be heavy to bear and hard to cope with: negligence leading to a fatal accident, betrayal of a friend, actions which harm those we love most. Such guilt is best coped with by a person who has made some progress in self-knowledge, and learned to act from a mature conscience, rather than the voice of outside authority. Genuine guilt can move to repentance and forgiveness when it is not compounded by the burdens of 'inauthentic' guilt. In discerning either, we need the help of friends and loving relationships, who will in the words of Nelle Morton 'hear us into speech' honestly and openly, and accept us for what we really are, unconditionally and without judgment. We especially need them to help us overcome the deepest problem—not being able to forgive ourselves. To know oneself as guilty (a sinner), but forgiven, is to experience joy, release, happiness, and a sense of future. As Julian of Norwich wrote, it is to experience the goodness of a God who has looked on us 'with pity, not with blame' and who wishes us to 'rejoice in the fullness of love rather than sorrow over frequent failures'.

Finally, release from personal guilt may free us to develop broader concepts of collective responsibility and guilt for the ways in which our society or church has damaged others. Liberation theology in particular has developed the notion of social and structural sin, and so of responsibility for the poverty and inequalities of our world. Feminist theology must move beyond a tendency to speak of women as if they were the 'innocents of history'. Women are not merely the innocent victims of male use and abuse of power. Women must accept moral responsibility for ways in which they have made the system work for them, and so perpetuated its injustices. Such a confession of guilt can flow over into the transformative action which enables the creation of a better society and a better world.

Further reading: Kelly 1992; Vergote 1988.

HEALING
Geertje Bouwes

ETYMOLOGICALLY, THE word 'healing' means 'making whole'—(re)making whole people, animals, society and even Earth itself. Feminists within the various churches and those outside who are concerned with spirituality have emphasized the need for healing. The Confederation of Healing Organizations speaks of 'the beneficial effect which healers are believed to have on patients when, motivated by their own beliefs and following their normal practices, they administer healing through contact by hands or, at a distance by thought or prayer'. Healing is also described as the transforming of paraphysical energies. Healers themselves often speak about working with subtle energies.

Healing in the Bible and the Ancient Near East

In the Hebrew Scriptures God is the one who heals. He heals people from misfortune and illness. Being healed is seen as the restoration of the right relationship between God and humanity, which in turn secures a person's position in society. Sarah is given a son in her old age; Rachel tries to achieve fertility by modelling herself on Bilhah, practising (what could be called) sympathetic magic. She does not succeed and it is God who opens her womb. Hannah (1 Samuel) relies on prayer, confides in Samuel and offers her still unconceived child to temple service.

In the Christian Scriptures, Jesus' ministry is described in the Gospels as one of preaching and healing. In his time recovery from illness was thought to be brought about by a specific healing act, a prayer, or the forgiveness of sins, and sometimes by medical help. Being healed or having recovered from certain illnesses required the pronouncement of being clean by a priest. Such a pronouncement was the sign of readmittance to the community of God's people. Among the stories of Jesus' healing powers are seven that involve women.

The Gospel writers tell the story of the woman who broke a jar with expensive oil to anoint Jesus' body. Mark has her anointing his head, Luke his feet. While anointing the head could be a proclaiming of coming glory, anointing the feet is an act of caring for somebody who is tired, sick or dying (Lk. 7.46; Mk 14.3-11; Mt. 26.6-16; Jn 12.1-8). Both actions are acts transmitting healing power. At that time anointing with oil was a common healing practice in the Eastern Mediterranean countries. However, the disciples disapproved of the woman's action, thereby foreshadowing the negative attitude of the church throughout history to women engaged in healing.

Mark's Gospel also relates how the women set out to perform the last act of sharing healing attention for Jesus when they went to lay out his body (an action which is still performed by women today). But they found the tomb empty. In the story God has acted and Jesus no longer needs the caring hands and the oils of the women for his body.

In Acts various feats of healing performed by the apostles are mentioned. No women are named, but this does not mean that there were none. Priscilla and Thecla among Paul's co-apostles are likely to have healed as well as preached.

The ancient Egyptians worshipped Isis as goddess of healing. Priestesses of Isis performed healing rituals. Queen Hathseput (1503–1482 BCE) was the founder of three medical schools in Egypt.

Panacea and Hygeia, Aesculapius's daughters, are two of many Greek women healers. They and their mother Epion are believed to have practised around the ninth century BCE.

Philo, a Jew living in Alexandria in the last century BCE and the first century CE, described two separate communities of *theraputae* (healers), one of women and one of men. Both communities were engaged in the healing of those who were ill in body or spirit. Jerome wrote about Fabiola, who in the fourth century established places where the sick could be cared for.

Women and Healing throughout History

In some of the twelfth-century literature, an important role is played by females with healing power. This power can be used to hurt as well as

HEALING

to heal, but the healing function in general is given greater emphasis. In *Tristan and Isolde*, both the younger Isolde and her mother are sorceresses, who can heal. In the Arthurian legends, some of which can be dated back to the sixth century, Morgan and other healing women play an important role.

Hildegard of Bingen (1098–1189), leader of the Benedictine nuns at Disibodenberg and abbess of Rupertsberg, gives excellent advice on how to regain health and stay healthy and shows considerable knowledge of female ailments and childbirth. She wrote two medical works, *Physica* and *Causae et curae*. Hildegard recommends baths, light food and massage, describes how to reposition a foetus which gets stuck in its passage through the birth canal and how to sew tears in the vaginal wall with silk thread. She was known as a healer, an exorcist and what we nowadays call a psychotherapist. She had no academic training in medicine, but gained a vast knowledge of healing plants and other local remedies. Some of her potions have very exotic recipes, involving the use of ostriches, vultures or leopards. Others contain ordinary everyday ingredients and have proved to be very efficacious when used today by the nuns of Rupertsberg. Her recommendations for the use of certain metals and precious stones nowadays find an equivalent in certain modern-day practices of healing and alternative health care.

Trotula, a thirteenth-century physician, wrote *De passionibus mulieris (Concerning the Disorder of Women)*, also known as *De passionibus mulierum curandarum*. She is the best known of the academically educated women healers of the Middle Ages. She explains the writings of Galen and Hippocrates and gives practical conclusions following her own observations. She taught at Salerno, Europe's first and foremost medical school.

Many women in the Middle Ages practised midwifery and herbalism, skills passed on from mother to daughter, or between other female relations, and not subjected to trade regulations. Under the guild system of trades and crafts in the twelfth and thirteenth centuries women in towns and cities carried on their husbands' businesses in widowhood, and daughters succeeded fathers and exercised their profession as *femme sole*. Women were registered as apothecaries and surgeons.

Trials were held against women who overstepped the boundaries of their profession as laid down by the guilds or the universities and other authorities. Women were prosecuted for not using the proper methods or obeying the right authorities in their attempts to heal others of sickness, or to help women in childbirth.

One such woman is Jacoba Felicie de Almania, who in 1312 was accused by the university-trained masters of medicine of practising medicine without training and thus endangering the lives of her patients. The University of Paris had opened a medical school in 1240. As was the case in the trial of Dr Wendy Savage more than 700 years later, three of Jacoba's patients attested to her skill and honesty. Jacoba's medicines, her purges, herbal drinks and special bandages were effective. She not only prescribed, but stayed and watched and nursed the patient herself.

Jacoba argued that women must be permitted to practise medicine because a woman would only reveal the secrets of her illness to another woman, never to a man; that would be too shameful. But without a university degree and without a classical education, which involved logic, rhetoric and grammar, Jacoba was found guilty of malpractice and excommunicated by the church.

Julian of Norwich, the anchoress who was born around 1342 and who wrote down her visions, healed many who came to the window of her anchorhold.

In sixteenth-century Scotland the words for 'witch' and 'wise woman' were interchangeable. The wise women were healers, herbalists, midwives and surgeons. They were sometimes called blessing witches. The word 'wise' is etymologically related to the word 'wit'; they are both derived from *witan*, which still has equivalents in other European languages and means 'to know', in the sense of having knowledge of or being familiar with something. (Russell relates 'witch' to 'wicht', a small child or person [Russell 1980]. I am not so sure about this etymology.) Kramer and Sprenger, in their notorious book *Malleus Maleficarum (The Witches' Hammer*, 1448) stated: 'No man does more harm to the Catholic Church than midwifes'. They went on to claim:

An A to Z of Feminist Theology

HEALING

'It were a thousand times better for the land if all witches, but especially the blessing witch, might suffer death' (cited in Ehrenreich and English 1974: 13). It is clear that women's ability to heal was one of the factors that led to the witch-hunts and the widespread destruction of women, their communities and their knowledge by the church authorities.

The first known major work on obstetrics was written in France by Louise Bourgeois (1563–1636). At the age of 24, after having given birth to three children, she gave up lace-making and apprenticed herself to a midwife. She started practising in 1593 and became midwife to the queen of France in 1601. Her book *Several Observations on Sterility, Miscarriage, Fertility, Childbirth and Illnesses of Women and Newborn Infants* was translated into German and Dutch and plagiarized in English. Bourgeois meant the book to be an aid to midwives, but its contents soon became appropriated by the medical schools.

Until the Reformation monasteries and convents had the facilities to care for those who were poor and sick. With the Reformation, the rapid growth of towns and the rise of the universities and their monopoly on knowledge, many traditional ways of healing became gradually unacceptable and were finally outlawed. By the end of the eighteenth century almost all those who were engaged in a healing occupation involving medicine or surgery were university educated. Only midwifery remained officially in the realm of women, until the 1860s when training in obstetrics became a required part of training in medicine.

Women were regarded as being unskilled, because of their presumed inability to understand and practise scientific ways of dealing with illness. Forceps and other medical tools were developed to enable men to do what women had done with their hands in previous times. The daily care of the sick poor in hospitals was regarded as a low-status occupation.

Florence Nightingale is usually referred to as the founder of modern nursing. In 1857 she became the first person to establish a secular school of hospital nursing. The Anglican Sisters of St John the Divine, founded as a nursing community in 1848, were in charge of nursing and the nursing schools at King's College and Charing Cross Hospital in London until 1885 and 1888 respectively.

Mary Seacole (1805–1881), who practised as a physician and a surgeon in Kingston, Jamaica, came to London to offer her services as a nurse to the War Office. Her offer was refused so she decided to go to the Crimea as a sutler woman. With the assistance of a Scottish cousin, Mr Day, she furnished herself with ample provisions and met up with Florence Nightingale in Balaclava. Mary Seacole set up the British Hotel in Scutari: a messroom, store, dispensary and hospital. She went out to the battlefields to tend the wounded and the dying and was the first woman to enter and the first person to bring provisions to Sebastapol after the eighteen-month siege was over.

Dr 'James Barry' (1795–1866) pretended to be a man and qualified at Edinburgh University in 1812. She gained extensive experience in surgical treatment of wounds and in tropical medicine as a Regimental Surgeon serving in the Caribbean. The War Office rejected her request to be sent to the Crimea and she was sent instead to Corfu. Her secret was not revealed until after her death.

Elizabeth Blackwell (1821–1910), Elisabeth Garrett-Anderson (1837–1910) and Sophia Jex Blake (1840–1912) braved hostility and opposition in the USA, England, France and Ireland in order to become academically qualified and licensed practitioners of medicine. They also set up places of learning and places of care for other women.

Healing and Spirituality

The church throughout the centuries has believed in the healing power of the laying on of hands. Sadly, the enormous power of healing that could be conveyed in this manner is often lost, because those who practise it are not always aware that they themselves have to be open channels to convey this power.

Nearly all those who practice healing believe in a spiritual power, a source of energy outside themselves on which they draw. They use their ability to concentrate and to channel this energy, which many believe exists all around us, and direct this towards the person who wants to

HEALING

receive healing. A healer might not know what her or his client needs, but she or he simply asks for the person to be given what is missing. An important aspect of the gift of healing is the ability to convey to the person who is suffering awareness of, and trust in, the possibility of being healed. The ability to heal is similar to musical or artistic talent in that, while it may be seen as a gift, it is an ability that can be developed.

Healers learn from other healers in one-to-one relationships or in small groups. The learning is experiential rather than based on books. Healers may come from a wide variety of religious and spiritual backgrounds,.

Lucy Goodison, in her book *Moving Heaven and Earth* (1990), mentions different symbols which can be used to understand life processes in people. She uses fantasies and exercises as tools for healing.

At New York University a course in healing as part of an MA or PhD degree in nursing was pioneered by Dolores Krieger, who learned what she knew from Dora Kunz, in the late 1970s. She called the procedure 'therapeutic human field interaction', the actual activity performed 'therapeutic touch' (see Krieger 1986). Dolores Krieger teaches her students how to become centred and how to feel the energy field around the body of a person being healed. When people are ill or in pain this field often has blockages or distortions in it. Dolores Krieger teaches her students how to use their hands to unruffle these blockages. She describes how the process of learning to heal starts with learning to tolerate oneself and others, to be followed by acceptance, and after that, in helping to allow the healing process.

Many women in the UK have set up centres for healing. Dorothy Kerrin founded Burrswood, in a beautiful house in Surrey, where those who need healing can go for rest, prayer, the laying on of hands, counselling and therapy.

Penny Brohn founded the Bristol Cancer Help Centre after her own healing of breast cancer. When the disease recurred in her other breast she learned to accept it and live with it as part of herself. Many people have found healing in the Centre.

Cicely Saunders founded St Christopher's Hospice in South London, where extensive palliative care for terminally ill cancer patients has been developed. Patients receiving hospice care often experience healing in that they feel more whole and more themselves than they have ever before in their lives. This experience of healing happens in a sharing between patients and staff. Patients have an active role in deciding on the treatment they receive, and it is accepted that being healed can mean dying. Technology is important, but secondary to human relationships. (For instance, recent research into the efficiency of modern birthing technology has actually produced evidence that it is not the technology but the presence of a companion which shortens a woman's labour.)

Healing and Contemporary Medicine

Since the beginnings of the contemporary Western medical tradition in the late nineteenth century, doctors (usually male) have taken the role formerly ascribed to God: they have been seen as the givers or withholders of healing. Since doctors and health authorities have the power to decide whether infertile couples will be given the opportunity of modern treatments such as IVF, they may also be seen as holding the power of fertility.

Disease, pain and death are unacceptable or problematic notions for contemporary Western society, and much medical effort is put into combating illness, eradicating pain and postponing death. However, the practices and methods of modern-day medicine may in themselves create, or prolong, distress and suffering. The emphasis is increasingly on technology, rather than on patient–carer contact, often to the point of making the patient feel entirely negated. Patients are not always in accord with decisions made about them or treatment administered to them, nor are they always kept informed or asked for their consent.

There is a gender hierarchy in contemporary medicine, such that the majority of those in senior positions—doctors and consultants—are male, while the majority of nurses, with lower status and lower pay, are female. Although nurses spend more time at patients' bedsides than doctors and thus may have more direct knowledge and experience of the patients, they are

An A to Z of Feminist Theology

expected and often legally obliged to submit to the doctor's authority in matters of patient care and prescription of medicines.

In contrast to the approaches of contemporary Western medicine, healing is about wholeness, aiming to heal the split between mind and body and other such divisions within the person. It is about the acceptance and transformation of pain and distress. For this approach to healing modern Western society and its medical science have lacked the language and the symbolism.

However, healing is beginning to be recognized and accepted within medical practice, albeit in a limited way. The British Medical Association accepts the potential validity of healing as an element of recovery from illness; a patient can request to be attended by a healer, and a doctor can refer a patient to such a person. One Devonshire general practice, for instance, has a healer on its regular team, to whom patients with chronic conditions may be referred. The Royal Veterinary Society also allows the practice of healing on animals.

Healing is concerned with much more than curing disease, and needs to be given more importance in healthcare and in everyday life. The acceptance and sharing of pain and sorrow can lead to change and transformation, both in individuals and in communities.

Further reading: Anderson and Zinsser, 1989; Brooke 1993; Bowie and Davies 1990; Courtenay 1991.

HELL
Lisa Isherwood

AUGUSTINE OF HIPPO mused that the sweetness of being in heaven would be increased by viewing the suffering of those in hell. This may seem very unbecoming in a Christian saint and Father of the Church, but it is, in my opinion, a logical outcome of the patriarchal mindset when applied to Christian doctrine. It is a mindset that is best illustrated by the dualism of Greek metaphysics; it splits the world between the material and the spiritual and thereby creates a hierarchy that is reflected in all areas of life. That which is above is more perfect and therefore worthier than that which is beneath it in the hierarchy.

Monotheistic religion lends itself to patriarchy since if there is only one God there can only be one way that is right, one moral way to live one's life. The essence of the moral life within this model is to reflect the creator as closely as possible. The guidelines for doing this are laid down by an almighty monologue. Within the Judeo-Christian tradition one such monologue was said to have taken place on Mount Sinai where the Law was given. This was to be followed by all those wishing to be pleasing to God; there was no discussion about it, it was a given. Abstract laws were seen as holding sway in the everyday lives of the people.

In the Hebrew Scriptures we see that those who did not follow these 'givens' suffered consequences in their own lives which often carried over for generations; the various captivities of the people of Israel were attributed to their failure to keep the Law. Although there were doctrines at that time regarding what happened to people after death it is quite plain that punishment for transgressions would be handed out in this life to oneself and possibly to one's descendants. There was no doctrine of original sin in the religion of that time; the events that occurred in Eden were not seen as eternally damaging but rather as a learning experience and one that signalled progress. There is a Jewish understanding that one 'cannot make omelettes without cracking eggs', and so while the transgressing duo, Adam and Eve, were punished in this world the eternal significance that Christians have ascribed to their actions is entirely missing.

Christianity, under the influence of Greek dualism, took this event far more seriously and believed that only the death of God's son could atone for it. There was also a shift in emphasis from communal suffering for sin to individual suffering, and it was placed in another dimension apart from the earthly one. A linear ethical understanding developed in which one was either pleasing to God, in which case one moved upwards, or one was displeasing, in which case one moved downwards, to hell. Hell, with all its attendant discomforts, became the place to which a loving and just God sent those who did not keep the rules.

But where did such an understanding come from? It is my contention that it sprang straight from a psychological make-up exhibited mostly by men, and not from the divine. As male theologians have developed Christian theology we are given a dysfunctional part of male developmental psychology in the guise of holy doctrine!

I would like to back this claim with the research of Piaget, Lever and Chodorow. Piaget found that girls and boys have different approaches to play and the rules involved. He observed both sexes at play and found that boys follow rules rather rigidly while girls are far more pragmatic and easily reconciled to innovations. Lever followed up this research and found that boys will continue to obey rules even if others in the group are hurt by it. Girls on the other hand would rather stop the game than alienate one another. This means that girls and boys have very different experiences of life by the rules and with mixing and modifying the rules by the time they reach adolescence. Nancy Chodorow also found that young babies have very different experiences of life depending on their sex and that this deeply affects their idea of relationship and therefore moral judgments. Boys realize very early in their lives that they have to separate from their primary carer in order to establish their own male identity while girls realize that all it will take is time for them to become full adults; no separation is needed for them as they are like their primary carer who in our society is usually female. This experience makes boys see separation and distinct lines between things as necessary for ego identity, that is for a sense of self and self-worth; girls do not have this experience and so feel quite secure with sameness and with new innovations. When applied to moral development this means that men tend to develop an understanding that objectivity and rule-following constitute a moral life, while women tend to believe that maintaining relationships and adapting the rules to meet the needs of others are the height of moral virtue. The very distinct early experiences of boys and girls play a significant role in the adult view of what is good and what is bad. They also play a role in the concept of what happens to people who obey the rules and those who do not. As Piaget and Lever found when observing play, boys can alienate others from the game, even those who are supposed to be their friends, if they feel the rules have been breached; girls do not do this, but rather change the rules in order to maintain the relationship. It is easy to see how those same little boys when grown into Fathers of the Church can conceive of a place like hell where people, even their friends, go when they do not keep the rules.

The discipline of feminist theology aims to change this traditional theological understanding. As a liberation theology it is concerned with the justice that is, or is not, lived in this world; that is important in and of itself, not in order to gain some divine reward. Hell for feminist theology does not lie in another dimension as a punishment for those who have not kept the rules; rather it lies in the here and now when people live unjust and alienating lives. The patterns that are set up are not unlike those in Hebrew Scripture, in that they may continue from one generation to the next, but in a practical way; the West continues the exploitation of the Third World because the fathers in capitalism breed sons of capitalism; people die from cancer because nuclear waste has a long life far beyond that of those who gave it birth. Patriarchy tolerates this because it has its own rules which are kept no matter who gets hurt; the little boys continue to play and to refuse to reflect on another way of doing things. Feminist theology does not need a place to punish the transgressor but rather a process to show people that we are connected and that mutual cooperation is the key to our survival, on this earth rather than in some other dimension.

The elaborate system of threats culminating in an endless life in torment, as propounded by sermons and catechisms, is the ultimate stick with which to coerce obedience in the here and now. It is a doctrine which does not allow for moral growth beyond an infantile understanding of punishment. It has also fed the imagination of artists down the ages: medieval scenes of devils plucking and pinching, of sinners undergoing thirst and hunger and extremes in temperature are just a few of the torments that people have allowed themselves to imagine. Theologians have endlessly discussed all kinds of matters relating to this place of pain, including its temperature. In short, the construction of the doctrine of hell has crippled the development of the mind. It has also been a handy tool, as have sexism and racism, for alienating the 'others'—in this case those who do not follow one's own way of life.

Further reading: Grey 1989; Heyward 1982.

HERESY
Lisa Isherwood

THE WORD 'HERESY' comes from the Greek *haerens*, meaning 'an act of free choice'. This meaning is far removed from the understanding that has more popularly been applied to the word. The history of Christianity is littered with examples of the hounding of heretics which led either to their deaths or to banishment. These were the people who chose to believe something that was not sanctioned by the institutional church. It is important to make it clear that the church is indeed divided between the *people* of the church, and the institutional church, which is the hierarchy. It is the latter who have historically prescribed doctrine and have therefore also set the penalties for deviation from that 'norm'. They have also, for the most part, been the writers of history and so those who have been described as heretics have either been written out of history or represented in it through the eyes of their detractors.

It is easy to interpret church history as if it were a journey guided by the Spirit and moving from darkness to the Absolute Truth. Reflections on the life of Jesus led to debate about his nature and mission, after the debate the champions of truth laid it before the people, while those who believed falsely were cast out as heretics—or so the story goes! This is a comfortable telling of the tale but a false one, whose only purpose is to give power to those who tell it. This story encourages us to see the church as the guardian of Absolute Truth and therefore as safe and powerful. Heretics are in this view unholy people who are trying to pervert the course of holy history.

There has not always been this emphasis on orthodoxy within the church. In the early centuries ideas grew and had support that were later seen as heretical; equally, some ideas that were not given much credence became at a later date accepted doctrine. Two such examples are Arianism and Patripassianism: the former was at one time seen as quite orthodox and later declared heretical, while the latter was for centuries viewed as heretical and has since grown in acceptance.

There are those who would see this as quite logical, because they view the nature of Jesus as so complex that it is bound to lead to changing opinions in the early years of the church. It can, however, be argued that this definition and redefinition of doctrine had as much to do with the wish of the church hierarchy to be accepted as the state religion by the Roman Empire as with the revelation of divine and absolute truth. In the early fourth century, under the Emperor Constantine, that wish became a reality. That meant that the church also reassessed its role and began to understand itself in a more legalistic light; it was now a state religion and there could now be legislation where once there was charism and prophesy. Tolerance of free spirits was rapidly diminished and the church, instead of influencing the state, became influenced by it, wishing to exercise power over people rather than to empower them. The church held this power for over a thousand years and it was helped to do so by the concept of heresy, which enabled it to do away with those who challenged what was said.

The notion of heresy has moved, then, from the idea of acting with free choice into the realm of absolutes and power-over. Far from keeping the message of Jesus 'pure', it has turned it into a tool for the state and for those who thrive on power. It has, over the years, made Christianity a religion of orthodoxy rather than orthopraxis. We have tended to forget that creeds and codes of belief are nothing more than people's reflections on their personal experience. When there is a hierarchy in place that personal experience may be tinged by more than a small amount of self-interest. Further, what comes to be accepted as the faith of the church is only the reflections of those who are in positions of authority within that church. The experience of a few has been placed before the many as absolute doctrine, while deviation from that limited perspective is named as heretical.

If we acknowledge that we can only begin from personal experience in mattters of religion then we have to realize that we can no longer make universal claims. This means that those who define heresy lose their power to control. Heresy is a concept that has held people in fear or religious infancy; reflection on theological matters has been left to the hierarchy for fear of the consequences or in the mistaken belief that once one is told what to believe one only has to believe it in order for the kingdom of God to reign. The church hierarchy may constitute a 'kingdom', but one feels that it has little to do with the message of Jesus.

The reinstatement of this concept to its original meaning could once more present us with the radical message that was declared nearly two thousand years ago. People should be encouraged to make free choices in matters of theology and to trust their own experience of the divine which move them to justice and liberation.

Further reading: Armstrong 1993; Kelly 1958.

HERMENEUTICS FROM A FEMINIST PERSPECTIVE
Melissa Raphael

MARY DALY'S opinion that a depatriarchalized Bible might be no more substantial than an 'interesting pamphlet' is not shared by Christian feminism. Indeed, feminist biblical hermeneutics (or principles of textual interpretation) do not assume that the Bible can, in any straightforward sense, be depatriarchalized. Christian feminists fully acknowledge how the various biblical authors (usually) bear compliant witness to the way in which women's fate is at the disposal of husbands, fathers and brothers. Often feminist interpreters have *themselves* wanted to preface the Bible with the warning that it could be dangerous to women's health! As Elizabeth Cady Stanton recognized when she and her team compiled *The Women's Bible* (1895 and 1898), the Bible is written not merely by human authors but by male authors and has been interpreted and translated by male scholars who have rarely questioned the status of the Bible as the highest authority for the sanctification of the status quo.

The texts cannot, then, be simply depatriarchalized, however much they might be demythologized. Although the biblical texts are diverse and each text must be taken on its own merits, ideologies of social domination inform and burden the entire Bible's language, narratives and the history of its interpretation. But the Bible is not dismissed on this account. Feminist hermeneuticists allow for ambivalence. Theirs is the subtle, dialectical task of hearing those silenced voices within the texts which subvert, negate or bear witness against the narratives and their traditional interpretations to the story of divine presence in human life. As Mary Ann Tolbert has said, one must 'defeat the Bible as patriarchal authority by using the Bible as liberator'.

Feminism is not alone in its political interpretation of texts, and the works of H.G. Gadamer and J. Habermas have been helpful to feminism here. Gadamer has shown that all understanding of texts is new understanding: interpreters bring their own situation to the text, thereby creating a historically self-aware dialogue with tradition. Habermas, a critical social theorist, also analyses the social context of interpretation and proposes what now seems almost self-evident to the postmodern academy: that hermeneutics are neither value-free nor objective.

Feminism recognizes that taking patriarchy for granted *is* a political position, but in the past the powerful (male) reader controlled the meaning of the text by a fiction of political disinterest, claiming that the single intention of the first-century author—whose values were assumed to be identical to his own—could simply be read off from the text with sufficiently rigorous scholarship.

A feminist hermeneutic makes no pretence of offering an apolitical exegesis with a feminist perspective offered as an optional concluding flourish. However, feminist interpretation should not be understood as entirely postmodern. Its readings are guided by its own absolute ethical values; it believes that the text has a message to reclaim from its 'patriarchal captivity', and it has faith in the grand narrative of creation's final emancipation from patriarchy.

Women's past and present experience of oppression and liberation, silence and speech, structures all feminist hermeneutics. Nonetheless, Christian feminist scholars working in different but related disciplines propose

An A to Z of Feminist Theology

distinct and sometimes contesting methodologies. Two of the most important of these have come from Elisabeth Schüssler Fiorenza and Rosemary Radford Ruether.

Ruether and other feminist liberation theologians read the Bible from the perspective of the oppressed; not just women, but the 'dominated victims of society'. The critical theological principle Ruether brings to the text is the affirmation and promotion of the full humanity of women. Whatever does not affirm the full humanity of women is counted non-redemptive: sinful, idolatrous and implying the devaluation and exploitation of all categories of being 'other' to the male elite. Ruether finds a correlation between this feminist critical principle and the prophetic-messianic tradition in which the Bible critiques itself and, in doing so, renews its proclamation of liberation. In creating a new 'canon within a canon' of authoritative texts pointing to alternative, just social orderings, feminism and the Bible can work in tandem to destabilize (rather than sanctify) the status quo. The critique of sexism is implied in the prophetic refusal to sanctify domination and exploitation. As such, despite the prevalence of their misogynistic imagery and religious chauvinism, the prophets still speak to the present. Similarly, Ruether traces evidence in the Christian Scriptures that the good news of justice and liberation has not been wholly erased but can still be appropriated by women in new communities of critical consciousness for the 'mending of all creation'.

It is arguable that Ruether has taken her prophetic principle from a contemporary political ethic which is not intrinsic to the Bible or its period and which is not generally characteristic of biblical material—which may, in any case, be structurally unable to yield any one message. However, her selection may be justifiable on ethical and methodological grounds: texts have always been mediated through theological and ideological confessions. Perhaps more harmful to Ruether's (and all Christian feminists') method has been Daphne Hampson's contention that the 'medium is the message'. That is, the sexist language and imagery of the prophetic texts might, at the subconscious level, continue to damage women's religious imagination and self-esteem.

Elisabeth Schüssler Fiorenza looks to no other principle than that of the concrete life experience of women. She offers a hermeneutic which starts with suspicion of the patriarchal nature of the text and moves to remembrance, proclamation and actualization in the lives of those living 'the option for our women-selves'. She locates God's primary revelation and grace within 'women-church', a movement whose goal is the liberation of female Christian self-affirmation and power, rather than in the words of the biblical text itself. The text offers stories that can be reclaimed by feminist historical research as the legacy and heritage of women-church, providing women with a Christian identity and an open-ended historical prototype for new experiences of transformation. Her hermeneutic is self-authenticating, submitting to no extra-feminist ideological or academic norms. Schüssler Fiorenza's method of 'critical evaluation' means that all texts are evaluated on grounds of their legitimization of or resistance to patriarchal oppression. Whereas other feminist theologians, such as Ruether and Letty Russell, might evaluate a text according to its correlation with a particular canon of prophetic texts, Schüssler Fiorenza's measure is whether it is paradigmatic of women struggling for liberation (see 1984; [ed.] 1994).

However, Schüssler Fiorenza's method has not gone unchallenged. In *Theology and Feminism* (1990) Daphne Hampson questions how late twentieth-century women might *actually* be empowered by their heritage. She argues that the gap of time and consciousness between the biblical foremothers and ourselves cannot be bridged because our problems and options are radically different from theirs. Moreover, if the early Christian mindset is, as Schüssler Fiorenza admits, androcentric, then Hampson cannot see why that community would be inspirational unless one were already a Christian with a large investment in redeeming the authority of the Bible. Christian feminist readings of the Bible might make the texts more palatable to other Christian feminists, but do not, according to Hampson, address the central issue as to whether feminism and Christianity are compatible in the first place. For Hampson a reformist feminist reading 'fails to challenge the notion that they are scripture and not just ancient literature. At

HERMENEUTICS

worst it tends to substitute a belief that, in the case of the Bible, all we can do is interpret, we cannot dismiss' (1990: 105).

Rebecca Chopp, in her book *The Power to Speak* (1989), expands upon Schüssler Fiorenza's notion of Scripture as historical prototype open to its own transformation. Chopp's theology of proclamation proclaims God's Word in and through the many voices of Scripture. Dialogue with the texts is achieved through a hermeneutics of marginality which reads them in terms of their 'credible claims of freedom', their promise of emancipatory transformation. According to Chopp feminists read the Bible from the margins of the social and symbolic order and the margins of Christianity, but in this space receive the words of the Bible as words of plenitude and freedom. From the margins, Chopp's hermeneutic asks 'where and how God is testified to among the others of history, as well as where and how God is expressed as condoning the oppression, the silencing, and the abuse of women' (1989: 43). Hers is an active 'restless' dialogue with the text—a 'pushing, shoving and playing with the texts'. In celebrating women's difference, embodiment, mutuality, pain, pleasure and anticipation she urges feminists to use the text rather than simply examine it. Here reading a text is an experience of transformation in itself since God, the Word, the perfectly open sign, is incarnate in words, moving as the Spirit between the Scriptures, the community and the world. The sanctity of the Scriptures resides, then, in the way in which Christians speak through them to sanctify the world, offering 'the visions, attitudes, images, narratives and poetry to restore the world to transforming grace' (1989: 45).

Where Schüssler Fiorenza may have been influenced by her Catholicism to find a continuing authority in the history of the Christian tradition, women in the Protestant tradition might be expected to focus upon the biblical word. French literary theory, and that of Roland Barthes in particular, has enabled women to reclaim the Bible as a text. A text is its conceptualization—a reading. Just as a musician reads a musical score in her or his own way, giving the otherwise meaningless notes her or his own rendition, so, too, the reader creates the text as a meaningful whole.

Phyllis Trible, a Southern Baptist, uses literary (rhetorical) criticism to criticize the patriarchal tradition and also to affirm the salvific intention of biblical faith (1978; 1984). Her method is to re-tell stories *in memoriam* of the terrorization of women, which call patriarchy to repentance and inspire women to solidarity with the suffering and bravery of their foresisters. But she also uses the text to suggest positive countercultural translations and interpretations. Religious feminists might feel ambivalent about her results. While she can be accused of enabling conservative, evangelical feminists to 'make the best of' misogyny at its most gruesome, she does not accept the traditional reading of the Bible which reaffirms negative impressions of women in the Bible. (It is, after all, ironic that post-Christian feminism ends up reinforcing fundamentalism's largely negative view of women in the Bible.)

Christian feminism might also be inspired by the way in which Alicia Ostriker—the Jewish feminist literary critic who has turned her attention to the Hebrew Bible—has shown that hermeneutics can be an erotic art. She prefers to delight in the texts rather than to 'evaluate' them: 'Reader, my case is like yours, perhaps. Perhaps yours is like mine. A case of (some kind of) love' (1989: 543). The Latin word for 'text' can also mean 'tissue'. In *Feminist Revision and the Bible* (1993) Ostriker's hermeneutic of desire penetrates (*sic*) the tissue of the text with mystical love, drawing on Blake's intuition that somehow 'the inside is vaster than the outside. That's why I want to move from what I experience as the surface of a text to the inside of it. Whatever that means! (1993: 118). When patriarchal readings close off the experience of women, they destroy the very textuality, the tissue of the text— its almost biological capacity to self-revise. It is in that capacity to self-revise that Ostriker locates the authority of the Bible; otherwise it has no more intrinsic authority than other works of ancient literature. Women make the Bible sacred to themselves by making it say what they want it to say. Women exact a blessing from the text by their transgressive readings of what has degraded them (1993: 31).

It is clear that feminist hermeneutics refuse to apologize for the Bible in the way that post-Christian feminism accuses them of doing. Instead, the texts are reclaimed through a

An A to Z of Feminist Theology

dynamic fusion of feminist scholarship with theopolitical vision and praxis. Despite their differences, Christian feminist hermeneuticists are united on several counts. Whether beginning with theology, literary criticism, historical-critical reconstruction—or indeed a mixture of these—Christian feminism refuses to be defeated by the androcentrism of the biblical texts. As Letty Russell has said, feminist biblical hermeneuticists do not compete with one another but each enjoy authority as members of the community of new hearing, and in their common advocacy for women as 'the oppressed of every oppressed group'.

Together, the various hermeneutics reclaim those biblical images and metaphors which challenge the monopoly of masculinist language on the theological imagination, the ancient heritage of Christian feminism, the testimonies to the resilience of the foresisters, and the prototypes in which to situate contemporary women's discipleship. It is for these reasons that the Bible continues to have authority for (not over) women. Its authority is non-coercive; it is not the literal dictated word of God. The authority of the Bible arises out of its inspiration to feminist praxis: that grace event in which women are empowered to liberate themselves from patriarchal naming to act as subjects of their own history and proclaim the good news of liberation from patriarchy. The texts will live on for as long as they can liberate God's presence in the lives of women.

Further reading: Yarbro Collins 1985.

HILDEGARD OF BINGEN (1098–1179)
June Boyce-Tillman

HILDEGARD WAS born in the Nahe Valley in Germany, the tenth child in the family of a merchant. As a child oblate at eight she was sent to live with Jutta, an anchoress attached to the Abbey of St Disibode. A remarkable, visionary child, she kept silent about her insights until the age of forty when a powerful vision empowered her to speak out. From then on she preached and wrote freely. Consulted by the Emperor Barbarossa and found to be authentic by a papal commission, she incurred the wrath of local bishops by her outspoken attacks on the corruption of the church. Failing to get land from the monks on which to expand her community, she left Disibodenberg with her advisor, the monk Volmar, for Bingen where she founded her own community. For them she wrote much liturgical music in the style of her time but with her own distinctive idiom. This includes a morality play with music entitled *Ordo Virtutum*. Members of her community painted a series of illuminations based on her visions. She wrote over ten books on a variety of subjects including theology and medicine in which she expressed her belief in the basic goodness of the cosmos and saw sin as any broken relationship within this, including damage to the natural world.

Music brought Hildegard must closely in tune with heaven and in *Ordo Virtutum* it is the earth-bound devil who speaks, while the Soul progressing through life with the help of the Powers sings. Her style, though rooted in the plainchant traditions of her day, is exuberant, with clear examples of word-painting in a close relationship between text and melody. Her pieces range from relatively short antiphons to long hymns and a Kyrie. Towards the end of her life she collected all her musical works together in a sequence that reflected her theology—Father and Son, Mother and Son, the Holy Spirit, the Angels, the Saints. Later editors reordered it, placing Mary in the more conventional place at the head of the Saints. Hildegard's devotion to Mary inspired some of her most beautiful pieces, in which Mary is linked with the figure of Wisdom who features prominently in Hildegard's writing and her visions. Also central to her theology was the creative Spirit who guided all her artistic endeavour. She coined the word 'viriditas', meaning 'greening power', which encompassed her belief that creativity is the clearest manifestation of the Divine Spirit.

Further reading: Bowie and Davies 1990; Fox 1985; Hart and Bishop 1990; Newman 1988; Page 1982; Strehlow and Hertzka 1988; Uhlein 1983.

HYMNS AND HYMN WRITING
Janet Wootton

Hymns have played a fundamental part in the formation of popular theology, particularly in the free churches, where they are known and loved, and it is easy to underestimate the influence they have had.

The earliest Christian hymns are recorded in the Bible, and it is clear that singing formed an important element of worship from the beginning. The liturgies in use in the orthodox churches contain material from as early as the third century. Three great female figures are celebrated in these early hymns: Mary, the mother of God (*theotokos*), the wonder of whose virginity is sung; wisdom (*sophia*); and the heavenly city.

The Latin hymnody of the Middle Ages also venerated Mary. Latin hymns tended to be attributed, sometimes wrongly, to the great figures of the day, often with stories about the miraculous origin of the words. However, many hymns originated in the ordinary life of religious houses, written by anonymous monks or nuns. A celebrated hymn writer of the twelfth century was Hildegard of Bingen.

Hymn writing in English was at first no more than versification of the Psalms, thought to be the only fit words for Christian worship. From the beginning, women hymn writers have been prominent and successful, and their contribution has been largely undervalued.

Isaac Watts was known as the 'father of hymnody', and his works have undoubtedly been hugely influential. His contemporary, Anne Dutton (c. 1689–1756), wrote 61 'Hymns on Various Subjects'. Anne Steele (1717–78), under the pseudonym of Theodosia, wrote three volumes of hymns, which were used as a basis for a Baptist hymn book to supplement Watts.

Anne Barbauld (1743–1825) was a Unitarian writer, not only of hymns but also of political satire, which she wrote under several pseudonyms. Her hymns form a mainstay of early Unitarian collections, together with later writers, Helena Maria Williams, Sarah Flower Adams, the writer of 'Nearer my God to thee', and Harriet Martineau, an ardent feminist and campaigner. In America, Harriet Beecher Stowe and Julia Ward Howe's hymn writing arose from lives spent campaigning for human rights, including women's suffrage and women's rights.

The nineteenth century saw an explosion of hymn writing, to meet the needs of the great revival movements, and a renewed emphasis on human rights. The Salvation Army produced many powerful women preachers and leaders, many of whom wrote songs for home and foreign mission fields. Aunt and niece Charlotte and Emily Elliott, the elder woman a lifelong invalid, and the younger a tireless worker in the Mildmay Mission, both wrote from the evangelical wing of the Anglican Church.

In America, great revivalist women preachers arose, among them Phoebe Palmer Knapp, composer of the hymn tune Assurance. But the most prolific of American evangelical hymn writers was the blind Fanny Crosby, who is said to have written over 8000 hymns, many of which are well loved to this day.

This was a time of religious controversy, and hymn writing was one weapon in the theological armoury. Catherine Winkworth translated many German hymns of the Reformation in a deliberate attempt to render this tradition available to English congregations. The evangelical tradition produced Christina Rosetti and Katherine Hankey, while the Oxford Movement gave rise to the credal writings of Cecil Frances Alexander.

At the same time, a great deal of material for children was written by women, and for a long time this was thought to be their natural sphere. Alexander's hymns were written in deliberately simple language, to make the statements of the creed understandable to children.

Almost without exception, hymn writing well into the twentieth century used non-inclusive language. Even those writers who were feminists did not, for some reason, allow their radical thinking to enter their hymnody. Thus imagery of God was always male or neutral (as in 'Rock'), and humans were described as sons of God and brothers or brethren. Many hymns which were were otherwise radical in outlook talked of the brotherhood of man.

Even the modernizing tendency of the 1950s and the folk hymns of the 1960s largely failed to

An A to Z of Feminist Theology

address gender inclusiveness. The explosion of evangelical writing in the 1970s and 1980s perpetuates the use of exclusive language and imagery, with writers such as Betty Pulkingham and Mimi Farrer in America.

However, there is a growing movement to explore the experience of women in the language of hymnody. Some denominational hymnbooks published recently have acknowledged the issue. The Methodist and ecumenical *Hymns and Psalms* has made some attempt at inclusive language for human beings. The United Reformed Church *Rejoice and Sing* takes the principle much further, but is still cautious about female imagery for God. Only *Hymns for Living*, from the Unitarian tradition, really explores the possibilities of inclusive language. Many modern American books are also more open.

Material published for the World Council of Churches Decade for the Churches in Solidarity with Women (1988–98) included much exploratory writing. Hymns about the motherhood of God picked up scriptural and other language of birth-giving, nourishing and enfolding love. The Hebrew and Celtic concept of the Spirit as female was revived. New hymns were written about women in Scripture and in history, telling the stories which have been so long untold, and enabling women to celebrate their solidarity with their sisters.

Not all writers of feminist hymnody are women. Brian Wren, in particular, has written a number of feminist hymns and has studied the impact of female imagery. But many new women writers are entering this field with great enthusiasm, and congregations are learning to enjoy inclusive language and theology. Janet Morley has written hymns as well as a great deal of liturgical material. Jan Berry, Judith Driver and Ruth Thomas come out of very different traditions, and are representative of many more.

In 1993 *Reflecting Praise* was published, a book of 82 hymns which sought to capture the range of women's and feminist hymn writing (Boyce-Tillman and Wootton 1993). The book tapped a rich vein of writing, which will continue to inform the worship of the churches and challenge patriarchal theology right at the congregational level, as people find themselves singing feminist and inclusive theology.

An A to Z of Feminist Theology

IDOLATRY
Sarah Jane Boss

JEWISH, CHRISTIAN and Islamic monotheists consider the worship of any God but their own idolatrous (from the Greek *eidol*, 'image', and *latria*, 'worship'). Monotheism consists in the belief that there is only one God, and that God alone is worthy of worship. It is therefore forbidden to offer worship to anything or anyone apart from the one true God. By extension, idolatry is the love of anything instead of, or in preference to, God.

The Christian understanding of idolatry is tied to the doctrine of creation. God created all things out of nothing, and worship is due only to the eternal and infinite Creator, and not to temporal and finite creatures. This is why the Hebrew Scriptures forbid the making of graven images.

Some scholars have argued that Hebrew monotheism was developed by the prophets of the eighth and seventh centuries BCE, as they tried to account for Israel's changing fortunes while remaining faithful to the ancestral God of the Hebrews (Nicholson 1986: 191-217). Whether or not this is accurate, the biblical evidence suggests that at least some sections of Israelite society had practised exclusive devotion to YHWH, the Lord, from long before this time (Zeitlin 1984).

Throughout the Hebrew Scriptures, idolatry is associated with the oppression of the poor, while the worship of the Lord must be manifested in social justice.

The suppression of idolatry by both the Israelite prophets and Christian missionaries has included the elimination of both male and female objects of veneration. Hosea decried the practice of worshipping the masculine Baal (Hos. 9.10), and Jeremiah expressed anger at the women who baked cakes to the Queen of Heaven (Jer. 7.18). Paul and Barnabas tried to resist being identified with the gods Hermes and Zeus (Acts 14.8-18), while the metal-workers of Ephesus apparently protested that they would lose their livelihoods if Christianity turned people's devotion away from Artemis of the Ephesians (Acts 19.24-28).

The claim that God transcends all finite, created beings means that God cannot be said to be of one particular gender. This has had ambivalent consequences for the practice of monotheistic devotion. In cultures in which the male is taken to be normative, a genderless personal being is automatically referred to in masculine terms. If what it is to be a 'person' is to have male characteristics, then a God who transcends gender is talked about as masculine (Hannaford 1989). Thus, within a culture of male domination, even the most rigorous *via negativa* is likely to lead to an understanding of God which is coloured by masculinity.

On the other hand, the very ideal of a limitless God who is not confined by gender makes possible a critique of masculine language and imagery in theology and worship. The use of exclusively masculine symbols for God is itself idolatrous, since it represents the ultimate object of devotion as a being who is confined within the bounds of the created order.

Within Christianity, this tendency is especially marked, because of the claim that a male human being, Jesus, was God incarnate.

Waves of iconoclasm within the church have periodically abolished images of both male and female saints, on the grounds that these were idols. This has often left worshippers with only the starkly masculine language that is customarily used for the Deity. Nevertheless, some of the iconoclastic movements, such as Quakers, have accorded women greater authority than have the image-users whom they oppose (Trevett 1991).

Feminist theology looks at idolatry from another angle. It accuses patriarchal theology of directing the worshipping gaze outwards towards the transcendent God who in his male manifestation is a false god. The true God could never be that far removed from creation and is indeed involved in the process of creating a just and mutual society.

A feminist theological critique of patriarchal theology is that it disempowers individuals by leaving no space for the godding of one another and the cosmos. The transcendent, omnipotent and salvific god is a concept that encourages idolatry.

IMMACULATE CONCEPTION
Sarah Jane Boss

THE DOCTRINE of the Immaculate Conception holds that the Virgin Mary was conceived without original sin. It was made a dogma of the Roman Catholic Church in the encyclical *Ineffabilis Deus* (8th December 1854; see O'Carroll 1982: 179-84).

The feast of Mary's conception may have been celebrated in the West as early as the eighth century (Clayton 1990: 40-41). However, it was opposed by those who believed that an ordinary human conception was necessarily sinful. In standard Christian teaching, one consequence of Adam and Eve's 'fall' from grace is that humanity now suffers from a universal state of sinfulness known as 'original sin'. According to St Augustine, this is individually transmitted to each person through the act of being conceived. Hence, some theologians argued, Mary's conception must also have been sinful, and was no cause for rejoicing.

The supporters of the feast of Mary's conception therefore had to find a way of freeing the conception from the accusation of sinfulness. This was done in the twelfth century by the English monk, Eadmer of Canterbury. Eadmer implicitly rejected Augustine's understanding of original sin. Rather than seeing it as a condition of individual inheritance, Eadmer saw original sin as a condition of society at large. He compared Mary to a chestnut which, although it grows up surrounded by thorns, is not damaged by them. Further, he argued that since Mary had been made 'mistress' and 'empress' of all that exists, it is unlikely that God would deny her any privilege (Thurston and Slater [eds.] 1904).

Throughout the Middle Ages, the view of Mary as unaffected by sin, and therefore as immaculately conceived, grew out of the understanding of the inherent goodness of God's creation and its capacity for redemption. The opponents of the doctrine tended to emphasize the fallenness of the world and the severity of human sinfulness (see Miegge 1955).

In the modern period, however, the doctrine has been given a different emphasis. It has been seen predominantly as a symbol of moral purity, especially as this relates to women and to sexual matters (see for example Warner 1978: 253-54). Furthermore, the modern iconography of the Immaculate Conception typically represents Mary in an attitude of submissiveness (for example, in Velasquez's painting *The Virgin of the Immaculate Conception*). In practice, a doctrine which formerly indicated the potential goodness of the whole creation now tends to signify the exceptional purity and humility of a single woman.

However, even at the present time, the Immaculate Conception is susceptible to a variety of interpretations. Andrea Dahlberg, in her studies of pilgrimages to Lourdes, argues that many pilgrims regard Mary's freedom from sin as being analogous to the freedom from bodily suffering which they themselves are seeking (Dahlberg 1987; 1991). The Immaculate Conception thus becomes a sign of hope for healing.

Some contemporary feminist theologians have taken up medieval motifs in their interpretation of the doctrine. The Immaculate Conception means that Mary is in the state of natural goodness which signifies 'the capacity within created nature for perfection' (Ruether 1979: 56). The doctrine anticipates 'the final glorification...of creation' (Ruether 1979: 57) which will be reflected in a just and mutually empowering society.

IMMANENCE
Lisa Isherwood

IMMANENCE, OR the notion that God dwells in creation, has been played down by Christian theology. The Incarnation, or taking of flesh by God in the person of Jesus, should have emphasized the immanent nature of the divine. However, the manner in which the Incarnation occurred has lent itself to emphasis on the transcendent, since God 'sent down' his son and placed him by artificial means in the body of a virgin. The natural order was therefore disrupted and God drew close to creation in a very unnatural way. This gives the impression that the world as we know it cannot be the bearer of the divine. It would be wrong to suggest that Christian theology has not placed some

An A to Z of Feminist Theology

emphasis on the immanence of God, and indeed it has been a frequent theme in the writings of the mystics; the weight of emphasis has, however, been on the transcendent.

Feminist theology wishes to rethink the idea of immanence and place it centrally in the weaving of theology. By rejecting the material–spiritual dualism of Greek metaphysics feminist theology is declaring that God cannot be experienced as separate from creation. God is part of the evolutionary process of the created order and cannot stand apart from it. This has direct consequences for many areas of theology. For example, Christology can be reimaged from seeing the Christ descending to viewing the Christ growing up from the divinizing process of communities and the individuals within them. Ethics can no longer be seen as 'sent down' but once again have to be experienced as growing out of the creative immanence that exists between people. Redemption is likewise viewed in a different manner as something that comes from the fabric of life and not as something sent down to those who are pleasing to the transcendent deity. Placing the emphasis on divine immanence also requires the construction of a new relationship between humanity and the rest of the created order; since the latter conveys the divine as much as the former, the understanding of redemption has to be extended to the whole of the created order.

Further reading: Allchin 1988; Freeman 1993; Whitehead 1978.

INCLUSIVE LANGUAGE
Ianthe Pratt

IN A narrow sense, 'inclusive language' is language that openly includes women; more broadly, the term covers non-verbal forms of language and symbol, or verbal language and symbol, or verbal language that includes any marginalized group.

Language is a tool of communication but it is not neutral. It is the means by which human beings have classified and ordered the world and is a way of understanding reality. If the rules and symbolic order that underlie our language system are invalid, our understanding is distorted. One such rule that has exercised a very destructive influence is that of seeing the male as the norm, the standard from which woman is a deviation, a subordinate being.

The sort of language we use shapes our perceptions. Although secular society has been struggling to put the principle of equality into effect, in the religious sphere the patriarchal mindset lingers on tenaciously, particularly because the Scriptures were written in the context of a male-centred society.

However, over the last two decades there has been a growing realization of the need for language in worship and church documents that does not exclude women—this means rejecting the use of male pronouns and adjectives, terms like 'sons' and 'brothers' for both sexes, and 'men' and 'man' in a generic sense.

The USA and Canada have been pioneers in the English speaking world in pressing for rethinking about languge, both on the biblical and liturgical front. The United Church of Canada's publication, 'Bad Language in Church', was seminal, as has been the biblical research of scholars such as Phyllis Trible (1978), Rosemary Radford Ruether (1983) and Sallie McFague (1983).

The Roman Catholic International Commission for English in the Liturgy (ICEL) produced in 1980 a suggested revision of the eucharistic prayers, emphasizing that 'language is a powerful tool of communication' and must therefore be used with precision, since it affects the way people perceive themselves and others. It pointed out, as is borne out by linguistic research, that 'man' and 'men' are increasingly understood in a non-generic sense and that this leads to much ambiguity.

This ICEL document also indicated the harmful effects of many biblical passages which reflect the culture of the time in which they were written and so relegate women to inferior positions. Also highlighted were mistranslations whereby 'man' is often used to translate words that mean 'human' and similar distortions.

Both the Church of England in its 1988 report *Making Woman Visible* and the 1992 British Methodist Church report *Inclusive Language and Imagery* about God explore the issues of inclusive language and recommend change to a certain extent. The Methodist report goes further in that it also deals with the ways we speak about or to God, which use almost exclusively male imagery. The report suggests that such imagery should be continued but needs to be balanced by the use of female imagery drawn from Scripture, which has been much neglected.

This is the same conclusion as that of Janet Morley, whose book *All Desires Known* (1992) is an outstanding collection of new inclusive prayers. She writes of the difficulty of finding new words for existing prayers, and believes that the way forward is 'to write new texts in vigorous language, which also respects and inhabits ancient worship forms, evocative biblical imagery, and familiar cadences and rhythms' (Morley 1992: xi). She cites the psalms and Christian mysticism as rich sources of imagery.

The use by Jesus of 'father' imagery is often used by the opponents of change. Education is needed so that people not only look at what the concept 'father' means, but at the ways in which it has distorted the thinking of Christians: because we speak of God in terms of 'Father' and 'He', most people envisage a God who is male, whereas the theologians of all the major churches would agree that God has no gender. Not only is the image male, but, according to Brian Wren (1989), it represents a flawed ideas of maleness which stresses power, domination and aggression. However, according to the tradition, we see the Father through Jesus, who shows very different characteristics.

Where Christ's relation to his 'Father' is concerned, Rosemary Radford Ruether has pointed out that his use of the intimate and affectionate term 'Abba' affirms a primary relationship with God based on love and trust that transforms the patriarchal concept of fatherhood into a more maternal and nurturing role. The early Jesus movement used the concept of God as Abba to liberate the community from dominant–subordinate relationships—unfortunately this did not last, and much of the language we now use in worship reinforces partriarchal images.

The feminist theologians who have spearheaded the movement towards inclusive language have emphasized that what is said of God is by way of analogy and metaphor and is not reality itself. One answer to the 'father' problem seems to be not to do away with this image but to bring in the idea of the mothering God, as is notably done by Jim Cotter in his 'Prayer at Night' (Cotter 1988: 42):

> Eternal Spirit,
> Life Giver, Pain-Bearer, Love-Maker,
> Source of all that is and that shall be,
> Father and Mother of us all,
> Loving God, in whom is heaven.

People are fearful of change and there is a tendency to see translations of Scripture as sacrosanct, even where mistranslation can be proved. ICEL, in their third report, recommend that the words of the Creed should read 'and was made human', not 'man', arguing that it is Christ's humanity rather than his maleness that is important.

Understanding the value of inclusive language has led to wider interpretations and to an outburst of creativity in women's and mixed-sex groups which seek to find new ways of expressing their own needs and their relationship to God. Informal worship is becoming greatly enriched through being able to respond to the Spirit, rather than having to keep to the rules, language and thought forms of the past.

Further reading: Association for Inclusive Language 1990; Spender 1980.

INTERFAITH DIALOGUE
Alison Williams

INTERFAITH DIALOGUE is the practice of encounter and discussion between world faiths in order to achieve a greater understanding of the faiths, to find common points and to understand the theological differences. Some see the end of interfaith dialogue as interfaith worship

It is primarily a process, and although it may have goals, practitioners would consider the process worthwhile even if the ends were not achieved. The process occurs on various levels. There is the dialogue of life which involves people meeting in everyday experience—at the school gate, in the high street—and reflects people's attitude to each other. This is grassroots dialogue. Dialogue also occurs when issues bring people together and a relationship is created.

INTERFAITH DIALOGUE

The third level is theological, when meetings to discuss doctrine are set up in a community, or people share spirituality.

The 'Faiths and Fellowship' conference in 1936 held by the World Congress of Faiths was a starting point for interfaith dialogue. Since then the World Council of Churches has supported this work. Interfaith dialogue is one aspect of the links between world faiths which include interchurch dialogue and the involvement of the churches and world faiths in social action. Believers of all faiths live *in* the world and their concerns for people become part of the dialogue process. However, differences of social concern and culture are a part of the process of dialogue, and at times a hindrance to it; but in order for real dialogue to take place they cannot be ignored.

Interfaith dialogue presupposes starting from a position of equality—a partnership. The classic christocentric position, based on the uniqueness of Christ, is not a position (some theologians argue) that the person engaged in dialogue can easily defend and still be engaged in dialogue; nevertheless, it is generally held by most in the field that true dialogue can best take place between people holding firm positions in their own faiths. Dialogue presupposes the possibility of change—but this change must come out of strength not weakness.

Although in Britain we live in a multi-faith society, and people generally want peaceful co-existence between the faiths, the barriers between religions are great. Not only do we have to contend with ignorance and racism but the attempts to allow Christianity to dominate in our schools raise questions about the need for and acceptance of interfaith dialogue. Many clergy within Christianity are suspicious of the process, fearing that it is ultimately leading to an artificial world religion. Others are simply uninterested.

In evangelical Christianity, the 'exclusivist' position may dominate. According to this view, all non-Christian religions are blind and lost in their unbelief. Possibly, they are even works of Satan to keep people in darkness. In the extreme forms of this view, nothing can be learned spiritually from other faiths. A slightly less extreme form may allow that there is a purpose in world faiths in that they promote conscience, but they are totally inadequate for salvation, since their messengers were in error. However, it may be allowed that good Muslims, for instance, may find their way to Christ if they are given the gospel—their hearts being first prepared by their own faith.

An 'inclusivist' view would hold that while Christ is supreme and unique as Son of God, God's activity is not confined to Jesus Christ. This view will focus on the pervading Spirit of God who is not tied to the church but active generally in God's creation. Other religions have a role in pointing people to Christ. This view was held by Panniker, who spoke of the 'unknown Christ of Hinduism'; and Karl Rahner also spoke of the 'anonymous Christian'.

A pluralist view will maintain that different religions show different facets of the nature of God. The best-known proponent of this view is John Hick, who proposed a 'Copernican revolution' in world faiths: instead of Christ and Christianity being at the top of a pyramid, with world faiths stretching below (the monotheistic religions nearer to the summit, the 'idol-worshipping' religions further away), all faiths circle the Godhead, but none is more valuable than another in offering insights into that Godhead. The idea that no one revelation is complete is indicated even in Christianity through the concept of eschatological fulfilment. Within Judaism and Islam there is still the fulfilment image through the Prophet to come, even if he is a previous prophet, as with the Imams. The Christian faith may be spoken of as a true revelation but it may not reveal the totality of God. In an extreme form this view would reject any attempt to compare religions, holding that all religions are entirely distinct and not to be measured against each other—especially not against a Christian 'norm', which smacks of religious imperialism. The pluralist position is supported by those who point to the disruptive influence of aggressive religion on communities through the centuries. The pluralist argues that there is a need for greater understanding to avoid this conflict.

One's view of the place of Christianity in relation to world faiths will clearly affect how one views interfaith dialogue. Exclusivists may feel

An A to Z of Feminist Theology

that the purpose of contact with other people is conversion, and therefore a process of dialogue which leaves open the possibility of both sides being open to change would be seen as a waste of time. The danger of a pluralist view is that it does not take any positions on issues, and so the dialogue becomes merely an agreement session with everyone being nice. Nothing of worth is addressed.

The main issue from a Christian point of view is that of deity. Christocentricity, and the idea that in Christ is the fullness of God, are challenged by Muslim and Sikh assertions of further revelation—in the former case, a revelation transmitted without error which corrects the errors of the Bible and the misunderstandings of the inheritors of Jesus' message. Not only are Christians being challenged about the role and place of Jesus Christ, but the authority of the Bible is being challenged as well—on a different level from the challenge of biblical criticism. The place of imagery and art in religions is also an issue: images in a Buddhist mandala and stained glass images of the crucified Christ offend Muslims and Jews, and even some groups within Christianity. Goddess concepts within Hinduism go against mainstream Protestant Christian thought. How can such differences lead to a meeting of minds, let alone communal worship?

Such issues of theology may be out of touch with grassroots interfaith dialogue where links are being built at community level. People on all sides who are committed to interfaith dialogue see it as a way of building community cooperation, combatting racism and ignorance. The 'enemy' is not the partners in spirituality but secularism, in a society where believers in general are in the minority. Those who are people of faith are drawn closer. This may also occur at a very practical level, where buildings may be shared, or interfaith workers may be appointed. These are sensitive areas—for instance, the decoration of buildings must offend none; but they are the matter for grassroots dialogue rather than the nuances of theology. Projects like this bring people of faith together.

However, for many members of a faith the conflict between interfaith dialogue and the command to convert is also a practical issue. The Incarnation implies superiority, and it was this sense of uniqueness and worth that led to the great missionary movements of the last century. The fear among some evangelicals may be that belief in tolerance and liberalism has led some Christians to 'sell out' their faith and ignore the command of Jesus in Mt. 28.20 to 'go and make disciples of all nations'.

Another practical issue is the role of women in dialogue. It is in this area that culture and theology are intertwined and the issues are not just of belief, but also participation. More cultural and theological freedom may be given to women in one religious tradition than in another; restrictions may be placed on women which, if followed literally by orthodox and fundamentalist groups, operate to prevent women from talking in public or with men. Dialogue founders if the participants disagree about who can conduct it, and its validity is questioned if a gender is not allowed to participate. Others would argue, however, that any form of dialogue is a beginning and is valid.

Interfaith dialogue encourages re-examination of the tenets of faith—seeing them through the other's eyes. Therefore, it raises the possibility of assimilation through such contact, and this may be unwelcome to members of all faith communities. Interfaith dialogue may even be viewed as a form of subtle espionage to convert the young or to make them challenge and question the tenets of their own culture or religion. From the point of view of an already threatened minority faith community interfaith dialogue can be viewed as yet another attempt—in the guise of friendship—to undermine that community, or even as a new form of missionary movement.

Christianity has central beliefs, as do all the world faiths, and at the outset those interested in participating in interfaith dialogue need to be clear in their own minds about what is vital, central and primary for their belief and worldview. The secondary issues may have to be surrendered for the process to move forward. Participants have to be clear about what they want to emphasize in their own faith without making crude judgments about what is true or false, so that they do not get caught up in issues that are not really that important.

Part of the process of beginning interfaith dia-

INTERFAITH DIALOGUE

logue, then, involves addressing the questions of who participates, and for what purpose? Those wishing to further the process may need to be prepared to work with whatever situation they find. It may not be a perfect beginning, but it could be the start. Others might argue that the conditions have to be acceptable at the outset, and that anything less would legitimize a role or position which would be unacceptable (for example, restrictions on gender participation).

The main emphasis in current material on interfaith dialogue is on adults in community coming together for dialogue. However, this does not recognize the work taking place in schools in Religious Education departments, and through multi-cultural programmes of study. Many schools, in urban areas particularly, do have a community already formed in which dialogue can take place; and in rural areas the advisory team will provide speakers, or contacts to the nearest faith communities for visits. The 1988 Education Act has a (controversial) emphasis on Christianity in RE syllabi, and there are currently discussions going on in local Standing Advisory Committees for Religious Education (SACREs) about how to interpret this legislation. However, Religious Education in schools is one of the places where, at least, the preparation for dialogue is taking place, through the study of world faiths alongside Christianity. They are generally taught in a open and sympathetic way by most teachers, with the emphasis being no longer on comparative religion, but more on understanding the differences and being able both to appreciate them and evaluate them. Pupils are also encouraged to explore the social and cultural issues which arise in a multi-faith Britain. Women are key players in this area, not just because of the gender imbalance in the teaching staff, but also because many of the members of faith communities who are able to visit schools may also be women. Those who are interested in furthering the process of interfaith dialogue may do well to start in the schools and extend the work done there into the adult community. Educational issues are issues which mobilize all sections of the community.

The benefits of interfaith dialogue may seem to be obvious—in the strengthening of community ties and greater understanding of culture and beliefs. Communities can also work together on social issues. Of course, this can occur without the dialogue, but communities which dialogue may develop deeper bonds which could be mobilized in times of difficulty, such as outbreaks of racist violence. The experience of spirituality may also be deepened through interfaith worship, including pilgrimages and vigils.

The problems, theological and practical, are many and important. People have to believe in the process, just as much as they do in their faith. Relevance is a key obstacle to beginning the process of dialogue. Some simply do not see the relevance of hearing about beliefs and discussing ideas with those of a different faith when there is so much other work to do. Interfaith worship is also questioned on the grounds that all those who take part may have very different (and 'wrong') interpretations of the experience, or be praying to a concept of a deity that others would find unacceptable (or who may not be 'there'!). The worship act may be simply an expression of the lowest common denominator, and so not satisfactory as a worship experience for all those taking part, the only value being that 'we did it together'. It depends on the context whether this is enough of a reason to justify it.

Another obstacle could be fear. This fear may be of conversion, and so the loss of something previously held dear—a cherished belief that gives comfort, or a way of life; as interfaith dialogue is still in its early years, it is not clear what the long-term impact is going to be on any of the world faiths involved in the dialogue. This uncertainty is risky and fearful for many. We ought also to recognize that religions are generally structured on a power system and those who have invested in this system may be reluctant (consciously or subconsciously) to engage in dialogue because they feel that it could lessen their power. If women are generally less concerned with power structure than relationships, then the gradual entrance of women into the hierarchy of the Church of England, as in other denominations of Christianity, could move communities further in the direction of dialogue. Whether this could hinder or help the gender issues between faiths is unclear as yet.

For many women in Christianity, interfaith dialogue is a way of participating in theology. Other routes may be denied—or hi-jacked by

An A to Z of Feminist Theology

men. The process challenges established forms of hierarchy, and it focuses on the value of relationships. Many women are better listeners than many men, and they may not be generally so competitive. Men focus on doctrine, while women focus on shared experience. Christian feminists may see in interfaith dialogue the possibility of doing theology in a way that is different from the male-dominated system already in existence. Its focus on encounter and relationships provides a setting which women may value more than men. They find a justification for this approach in the encounter of Jesus with the woman from Samaria in John 4. Jesus initially establishes a relationship of trust with the woman through a focus on his need for water, and then uses this to enter into a dialogue over her theological presuppositions. Freedom of choice has always been the 'official' position of Christianity (although people have been threatened with God's revenge if they did not convert), but interfaith dialogue provides an emphasis on encounter without pressure to convert that is attractive.

Many women view their role in society through conditioned eyes. Women in particular have been excluded from active roles in Christianity unless they are prepared to deny themselves (especially in relation to sexuality); women acting in the 'male' role in religion have been the exception rather than the rule. Interfaith dialogue presents a practical way of doing theology and one that has a useful purpose in our multi-faith society. Dialogue is certainly less aggressive than the old missionary approach of contact with world faiths, and is to be done here, in this situation, and so does not require a change of life to participate in it. Women are being encouraged by this to resist the conditioning and to explore their own faith and to take an active role through contact with other faiths.

Further reading: Arai and Ariarajah 1989; D'Costa 1986; Hooker and Lamb 1986; Knitter 1985; Church of England General Synod 1986; World Council of Churches 1990.

INVISIBILITY
Janet Martin Soskice

INVISIBILITY AND voicelessness are terms common to feminist and liberation theology, indicating the condition of those whose presence or opinion has no real influence on the decision-making structures which affect their lives. Voicelessness, for instance, does not mean simply that these individuals or groups are not consulted (although in many cases they may not be), but suggests more strongly that even when they are consulted, their opinions, desires and needs are not heard. Many Christian feminists will recognize this pattern from church life, where a clergyman will dismiss suggestions that women do not have a proper voice in the church by insisting that he spends all his time with the women of the parish, that they talk all the time, and that he knows exactly what they think.

Voicelessness shades into invisibility when matters affecting women, or some other subordinate group, are not even named by the dominant culture. For instance, Christian ethics texts may be replete with topics of concern to the men who wrote them (murder, masturbation, embezzlement) but say nothing at all of domestic violence or pornography. It takes time within the academy for women's issues, and women's texts, to become 'canonical'.

One of the most damaging forms of invisibility is the naming of certain matters as 'just women's problems'; for instance, while proper toilets or canteens are legitimate concerns of the trade union and management, workplace creches are 'just women's problems'. The double hurdle for 'invisible' groups is that in some cases they do not only need to make a dominant culture change its mind on a particular issue, but also to make the dominant culture see a particular issue as an issue at all.

Further reading: Ardener 1978 (for an anthropological account of the 'muting' of woman); Gilligan 1982; Okin 1989; Soskice 1993.

JUSTICE
Maureen McBride

Legal and Social Justice

WESTERN CULTURES have been influenced both by Greek philosophical traditions and by the Bible in their concerns for justice. But what people perceive to be involved in justice varies, even within modern Western traditions. In the narrower legal sense, justice is applied through the administration of law and conceptualized and theorized through jurisdiction. But a sense of justice extends beyond the forensic and expresses principles of just conduct and social equity within humn community generally, and indeed between human communities and the animal and natural world.

Social justice, then, extends beyond the narrower scope of legal right and legislative code, embracing the sphere of interpersonal face-to-face relationships as well as the public spheres of political and economic structures. It is concerned with how society is organized, how wealth, power, privilege, rights and responsibilities are distributed at every level of social interaction. Here, being 'just' means creating a society in which the relationships and structures at all levels are not distorted by inequalities of privilege, power or wealth. In the view of some people, it extends beyond human society and includes right relationships with the land, sea and air, and all the species and creatures that inhabit them.

Examples of social injustice therefore can be found in the existence of endemic poverty alongside conspicuous wealth; in the powerful nations and institutions exercising a politics of exclusion; in the systematic application of state military apparatus in economically poor countries to suppress dissent and repress peoples' movements for liberation and transformation; in the displacement and disempowerment of indigenous peoples as their sacred ancestral lands are ravaged by rapacious logging and mining concessionists and avaricious landgrabbers; in the denial of the rights of workers and peasants to organize; in the oppression and discrimination, violence and abuse endured by women and children; in the lack of clean water, sanitation and access to basic health care and education experienced by millions of urban poor people in megacities and squatter areas throughout the world.

Justice in the Bible

'Justice' (Hebrew, *mishpat*) is a central biblical word, frequently linked with 'righteousness' (or integrity), though the terms are often used in generalized ways: to 'know' God is to 'do justice' (Jer. 7.8-10), and the Psalms speak of God 'loving the person of justice and righteousness' (Pss. 11.7; 37.38; 45.8). But how the various biblical narratives, law-codes and exhortations understand justice varies, and they all differ in some respects from the notions of justice in our modern societies.

The law codes (found in Exodus, Deuteronomy and Leviticus) place beliefs about God's justice, mercy and graciousness at the centre of their rhetoric, and teach that the believing community who have received God's gifts should imitate his practice in their community relations. The metaphor of God as Father and Israelites as sons (rarely are daughters mentioned but women, children and strangers within the land are included in the community) is used to suggest that these sons should be like their Father. So, loyalty to God, conceived in personal terms, is paramount, rather than abstract principles. In Leviticus 19, for example, justice within the community is set in the context of holiness—'You shall be holy because I am holy'—and set alongside examples and summaries: you shall love your neighbour as yourself, and you shall love the stranger as yourself. The summaries suggest that the prohibitions and commands are examples which could be multiplied. Thus, while there are individual laws which prescribe redress for injured humans (including slaves), these books contain many exhortations to generosity and love, which encompass the kinds of behaviour that could not be enforced by a law-court.

The prophets are generally uncompromising in their attack on those who exploit and abuse the poor, the widowed, the orphan and the stranger. They denounce the injustice perpetrated by judges, kings, and the wealthy, in their oppression of the poor. However, it is not clear whether this critique arose from Israelite legal tradition or practice, or from a widely-accepted ethic, such as may be reflected in the wisdom literature of the Bible, which is far from being legislative.

In the wisdom literature (Greek, *sophia*, Hebrew, *hokmah*), there appears the personification of wisdom and justice. The favourite loci of her actions and instructions are at the centres of social activity: at the city gates; among the chattering throng of vendors and buyers at the marketplaces and cross-roads; at banquets where the young, the poor, the simple and the uneducated (Proverbs 9.4) find ripe and rich food, wisdom (justice), and understanding (Sir. 15.3), to nourish and 'inebriate' them (Sir. 1.14-15). Wisdom is represented as having been present when God founded the universe (Prov. 8), and thus as providing its moral order. Justice, then, according to the wisdom literature of the Old Testament, is part of the order of creation, and of the will of the creator. But it is taught not in the law-courts but by parents (see for example, Prov. 4.1-9), emphasizing that this is something to be assimilated at an early age as part of social and religious education.

Universal and National Justice

Nevertheless, the biblical ethic of justice is not always universal. In Exodus, for example, God's justice relates to an enslaved, marginalized, suffering people in concrete acts of deliverance from oppression (Exod. 3.7-8); elsewhere God protects and defends the most vulnerable and exploited in society (Deut. 15.7). But it is the chosen people of Israel who are in view. The Bible's perception of human relations to God as personal, a matter of loyalty, explains the focus on just and merciful social relations *within* the community (in the Old Testament and Acts). The Jewish laws and exhortations are for Jews with this commitment, not for outsiders. So, behaviour towards fellow Jews and strangers within the land is distinguished from behaviour towards outsiders as, for example, in the matter of lending at interest or war (see also Acts in relation to matters of community support for the poor and widowed). Outsiders are understood to serve other gods, and Israel is forbidden such service, which is portrayed as the disloyalty of sons, or, more frequently, the adultery of a wife. (This applies also to Christians. See for example 1 Cor. 8–10.) By the New Testament period, however, more abstract conceptions of God, as transcendent, invisible and incorruptible, that were borrowed from Greek philosophy, led to the conception of idolatry as a failure to recognize God's transcendence. This perception was further developed at the end of the Middle Ages by the Jewish philosopher Maimonides and the Christian philosopher Aquinas—both, in fact, influenced by reading Aristotle. Naturally, this led to more abstract concepts of social justice. But all these writings, like the Bible, still insist that ethics is theological ethics, not an autonomous system. They treat piety towards God as the essential prerequisite for an ethical life.

Justice in Contemporary Debate

Most contemporary Western writings, treat ethics as autonomous, and are not interested in theological ethics. They assert or assume that justice, like all ethics, is a human endeavour, irrespective of people's religious beliefs. In increasingly pluralist societies, both Western legal systems and the teaching of ethics are secular. They try to encapsulate or explore what is required for all human individuals to live well. Modern societies are much more individualistic than ancient agricultural societies. Since the eighteenth century, this has involved attempts to specify human *rights*, and to set them out in constitutions and charters which governments are encouraged to sign. Also since the eighteenth century, limited notions of the equality of all individuals, for example, in law and in the possibility of voting in elections, have also had their effect. Abstract principles have taken the place of personal loyalty. We cannot deny that a great deal has been gained. Has anything been lost?

This changed perception has led to a questioning of some aspects of the biblical view of justice. Many narratives in the Jewish scriptures (Genesis–11 Chron) conceive God as saving his people so that they could establish a just society through victory in war (did the Canaanites get justice?). New Testament texts, which understand Jesus as God's Messiah and represent him as crucified by his enemies, never see war as a way of bringing about a more just society. New Testament texts never link justice and courage as

JUSTICE

the Greek traditions do—this kind of courage in battle is never mentioned. They seem to teach that violent persecution should never be met by violent retaliation, and encourage endurance, the kind of courage appropriate to such a lifestyle. After the conversion of Constantine, however, Christian churches (apart from Quakers and some other small groups) have taught that war, in some circumstances, is justified (the just war).

On the other hand, there is an element of social upheaval in the teaching of Jesus. The rules are reversed as suddenly, women, children, tax collectors, the illiterate and inarticulate, become the central images of the Kingdom of God. Poor people are not only raised up (Lk. 1.52), but they are given the dignity of being named, while the rich go unrecognized (cf. Lazarus and the Rich Man: Lk. 17.19-31); workers not only receive a just wage but are the beneficiaries of God's gratuitousness (Mt. 20.1-16). Wisdom's banquet is realized in the table-fellowship of Jesus where the invited become the alienated, and the unlikely and unexpected, are the locus of God's justice (Lk. 14.15-24).

Justice in Feminist Perspective

To 'do justice' in a feminist context, means to restore the dignity and uniqueness of the qualities of knowing, loving and relating to life. At the personal, interpersonal and institutional levels, it means addressing the issues that seriously affect women's lives: health; sexual autonomy; earning power; social and political status, and sense of self-worth. But it also means concern for other underprivileged groups: opposing racist and elitist attitudes that alienate people; supporting the struggles of indigenous peoples to reclaim their ancestral lands, their cultural heritage, and their history. It can lead to the challenging of powerful elites to relinquish their thirst for wealth, power and exploitation of people and the world's resources, challenging attitudes and behaviour that diminish others, and being open to learn other ways of being, living, acting, worshipping and celebrating. For many feminists it means especially reverencing the mother earth and her fruits—the mountains, forests, lakes, plains, deserts and seas; it means the active desire for peace and freedom from nuclear proliferation, and committing oneself to a radical activity of love, to a way of being in the world that deepens relationships, embodies and extends community, and passes on the gift of life.

Perhaps perfect justice cannot ever be realized. But without a strong commitment to it by individuals and groups, injustice will always flourish, especially where power accumulates. The Christian vision is of an end to the powers of oppression and exploitation, when all those suffering will have their rights restored as equal children of God and a new human community of justice and peace will be born. However, while the Bible offers final justice as an act of God, it does not relieve humans of the responsibility of striving for that justice.

KINGDOM
Jenny Dines

FOR MANY feminists, 'kingdom' language is problematic. Used of God, it is pervasive in both the Old Testament (the notion of the kingship of YHWH) and the New Testament ('the kingdom [i.e. rule] of God/Heaven', chiefly in the Synoptic Gospels, and drawing on both Old Testament and contemporary eschatological ideas). It is symbolic, not literal; a particularly powerful 'root' metaphor, that is, a symbol that inhabits the imagination, and goes on generating multiple images. In the Old Testament it reflects the ancient Near Eastern ideology of kingship expressed in both historical and mythological texts; in the latter, various gods achieved sovereignty by fighting the chaos-monster, or death, and then by creating and controlling the cosmos, or aspects of it, often with the help of a goddess. In the New Testament, there are also influences from the Hellenistic and Roman worlds.

The Old Testament's monotheistic version left little room for female participation, although it contains some historical queens (mainly demonized; Jezebel, 1 Kgs 21; Athaliah, 2 Kgs 10, 11). But Yhwh's goddess-consort is barely glimpsed; in any case, the queen-goddesses were made in the male warrior image, so 'queenship' is not helpful as an extension of the metaphor. The New Testament has few explicit statements linking women with Jesus' startling proclamation of the kingdom. The most striking is Mt. 21.31, about tax-collectors and prostitutes entering the kingdom first. The evidence of the Gospels as a whole makes it clear that women received the benefits of the kingdom in their encounters with Jesus (for instance in healings, one of the signs of its existence). But women seldom feature in the parables, which is disturbing, since these reveal *par excellence* what 'the kingdom of heaven is like'. Mark's parables have no female characters at all. Mt. 13.33 (= Lk. 13.20) describes the woman making fantastic quantities of bread, and Lk. 15.8 has the vignette of the woman searching for her lost coin. Mt. 25.1-13 tells the story of the ten bridesmaids, and Lk. 18.1-8 that of the justice-seeking widow. The impact of these parables should not blind us to their rarity.

The problem is not simply one of inadequate representation; it goes much deeper, into the nature of the kingdom image itself. First, the imagery is explicitly patriarchal. In the New Testament, it is linked with God imaged as father (for example in the Lord's Prayer), and so reinforces male supremacy with its implications. Secondly, the underlying mythology contains violent aspects: lordship over creation is an act of domination (less obvious in Gen. 1–2, but see for example Isa. 27.1, Ps. 74.12-17 for the fight with the chaos-dragon). In the historical mode, God is portrayed as the Divine Warrior, prominent in Israel's story (for example in the exodus from Egypt and the conquest of Canaan). Thirdly, the imagery is dualistic: God is 'outside' and 'above' creation, interventionalist rather than part of the process. Fourthly, although 'king' is only one of the ways in which God is symbolized in the Bible, it has become perhaps the most dominant of them, boosted by the traditional substitution of LORD (*adonai, kyrios*) for YHWH, which is not in itself a 'king' word. Finally, as a symbol which has lost much of its social immediacy, it risks widening the gap between what we assent to in religious terms and what we believe about the actual workings of the cosmos.

There are various responses to these problems. One is to stress acceptable elements within the tradition and to lay down definitions of what 'kingdom' really means. For instance, the Gospels, for all their use of the imagery of warlike monarchical power, constantly subvert their own language, with pictures of a kingdom which turns convention upside down, where children come first, servants are friends, women share men's privileges (Lk. 10.39; Mk 14.3), the master does the dirty work (Jn 13.5), and the king dies a dishonourable death. The Old Testament also contains benign features: caring for the weak, delivering the oppressed, judging impartially, creating 'shalom', are all part of what kingship, human and divine, involves (Pss. 72; 89); hence 'the kingdom' has been an important element in liberation theology (though its ambivalence is now being recognized). The partial democratization of the kingship idea in post-monarchic Israel also offers possibilities: for example, Matthew Fox stresses the importance of the royal stewardship given to all humans in Gen. 1.28 ('image of God' is kingship language). Also positive is the paradise myth, reworked by

An A to Z of Feminist Theology

KINGDOM

the prophets as a vision of a 'peaceable kingdom' (Isa. 11.6-9, but cf. v. 4; Hos. 2.18-23, but cf. vv. 2-13!). The problem remains that this state of 'shalom' is achieved only after powerful intervention by Israel's conquering king, who defeats Israel's enemies and brings them into subservience (Isa. 60.10-12). The 'pacific' texts only work when separated from their wider contexts.

Another strategy is to extend the range of symbols so that the kingdom image, retained because of its venerable place in Christian faith and worship, is more relativized than at present. In particular, female images of God, many of which are already found in Scripture, are upgraded. Other feminine symbols are introduced: for instance, Kathleen Fischer uses images of nets, webs and circles in the context of spiritual direction. Brian Wren urges the liturgical use of a wide variety of strong images which can complement and even contradict each other (chaos is needed as well as order!), and so dislodge the tyranny of the prevailing 'Kingafap' ('King-God-Almighty-Father-Protector') favourite.

The most radical proposal is to abandon 'kingdom' as the central organizing Christian symbol (as do, for instance, Dorothee Sölle, Sallie McFague and Jürgen Moltmann), in favour of another. Of the various suggestions (including 'trinity' and 'shalom'), 'body' (McFague) could perhaps have sufficient psychological and imaginative power to replace 'kingdom' as the primary symbol for divine–human–cosmic relationships. The results would be far-reaching: meanings change when metaphors are changed (Wren). But when a venerable archetypal symbol is also fundamentally flawed, it may have to be relinquished. We are still seeking our new images, and this will take time. Ivone Gebara counsels 'a certain atheism from overly precise images', while the 'Copernican Revolution in our culture and theology' gets underway 'with historical consequences that are not yet foreseeable'.

Further reading: Eaton 1990; Gebara 1994; Hooker 1990; McFague 1987; Perrin 1976; Wren 1989.

LAW
Catherine Norris

FEMINIST THEORY, anticipating fundamental social change after the elimination of gender hierarchies, holds no place for any system of 'norms of action for the community set by legitimate authority for the appropriation of values by the community' (Orsy 1992: 37-38) and would find every word of this definition contentious. Neither does it concern itself with the rule-making inherent in a male view of society, nor the arguing about ingenious ways of rule-breaking that are such high-energy activities in the patriarchal tradition (Gilligan 1982).

Feminist theology, having rejected the transcendent male God operating from off the planet as law-giver and judge, ruler of his own creation and interpreter of his own scheme of justice (with its necessary corollary, mercy), has also disposed of the traditional imitation of this schema in which a God-delegated authority imposes its values on the community it purports to serve, and makes itself responsible for punishing those who are 'disobedient'. Feminism prefers to focus on relationality and, when making suggestions about behavioural choices, requires them to be made on the basis of personal responsibility, taking into account individual experience, with respect for personal and community relations and an appreciation of accountability.

Any specifically Christian notion of law has to be aware of centuries of ecclesiological tradition based on the Catholic Rock or Fortress model, with its tendency to universalize local pastoral decisions and to subject them to theological back-formation with a view to the stability of the institution. It is instructive to see how non-conformist churches using different models have seen the need for less rigidly binding rules, though all have some, and even the Society of Friends acknowledge some guidelines for members on points of discipline.

Womanchurches as they evolve will doubtless also find themselves having to take decisions affecting their members and their relations with other bodies: here feminist organization theory can offer its expertise on the process of non-hierarchical decision-making, using the experience of many non-competitive power-sharing women's organizations in which time is taken to hear many points of view, and consensus, on grounds understood and accepted by all participants, is the aim. This would seem to be in line with the best of Christian theory and practice, and would render the very concept of 'law' unnecessary (Iannello 1992).

LESBIAN PERSPECTIVES IN FEMINIST THEOLOGY
Elizabeth Stuart

'FEMINISM IS the theory, lesbianism is the practice' was a popular slogan in the feminist movement of the 1960s and 1970s. However, neither the secular feminist movement nor the Christian feminist movement has been immune from homophobia (fear of lesbians and gay men) and in Britain and Europe the number of self-identified lesbians producing works of Christian theology remains small. In the United States a number of women have offered exciting and challenging theological reflections grounded in their experience as lesbians. Among these women are Carter Heyward (1982; 1984; 1989), Mary Hunt (1991) and Beverly Wildung Harrison (1985).

The web of power relationships which feminists name 'patriarchy' is buttressed by the discourse of heterosexism, the belief that men and women were created to become 'one flesh' and reproduce and that no other sexual relationship is 'natural'. Janice Raymond talks about 'heterorelations' as 'the wide range of affective, social, political and economic relations that are ordained between men and women *by men*' (1986: 7; my emphasis). Christian theology has articulated and sanctified heterosexism as it has patriarchy. The very existence of women who have intimate sexual relations with women shakes the foundations upon which patriarchy is built. Lesbians are living proof that heterosexuality is not as 'natural' or universal as its proponents claim. They expose the lie that men and women need to be in a sexual relationship with each other to be fulfilled and whole, and they demonstrate that sex is not primarily about

LESBIAN PERSPECTIVES

reproduction but about passion, delight, mutuality and justice. The rampant homophobia that exists in almost every part of our society is recognition of how dangerous lesbians and gay men are to the structures of patriarchy. Fear, discrimination, ignorance and violence conspire to make these men and women invisible.

Feminist theology has just begun to get to grips with the debate between essentialist and social constructionist understandings of sexuality, a debate which has been going on in feminist and gay studies and other branches of the social sciences for years. Social constructionists argue that the concept of a homosexual person, a person with a distinct, intrinsic sexual orientation towards members of the same sex, is an invention of nineteenth-century Western scientific society. This challenge to the essentialist view, although it has its weaknesses, actually confirms the experience of many women that our sexual identities and relational choices are fluid and capable of change. Once again we have to reclaim our bodies and experiences from medicine, psychology and tolerant liberals who accept us because we 'cannot help being the way we are' and claim the freedom to choose to whom we relate sexually.

Rarely is the transformative, relational power of God more clearly in evidence than in the process of 'coming out', when a woman names herself as a lesbian, because 'making a statement about ourselves in this way can mean that we cease to be victims of our cultural inheritance and condition and start to become survivors of it' (Willis 1987: 109). In naming ourselves in this way we affirm that our bodies, our sexuality, our relationships are at the centre of our lives. It is also a request for affirmation from others, a statement that we need the love of others in order to be ourselves. Coming out is an acted parable of the triumph of erotic power over the webs of patriarchal power. Whenever a woman publicly names herself as lesbian she causes disease wherever she goes.

Lesbian relationships, although certainly not immune from the abuse of power, take place in a space beyond the boundaries of patriarchy and heterosexism, although still within its shadow. In that space the relational dimension of sexual love is most clearly evident and the transformative potential of the heady but fragile mixture of passion, desire, friendship and vulnerability in relationships between people of equal status becomes obvious. Even beyond patriarchy, justice has to be created—we have to learn to hold tensions in balance.

> Sexual orgasm can be literally a high point, a climax in our capacity to know, ecstatically for a moment, the coming together of self and other; sexuality and other dimensions of our lives; a desire for control and an equally strong desire to let go; a sense of self and other as both revealed and concealed; the simultaneity of clarity and confusion about who we are; and tension between the immediacy of vitality and pleasure and a pervasive awareness, even in moments of erotic ecstasy, that the basis of our connection is the ongoing movement—that is, the friendship—that brings us into this excitement and releases us into the rest of our lives, including the rest of this particular relationship. There is remarkable erotic power in these tensions. To stretch and pull with one another is to come more and more into our erotic possibilities, into a fullness of ourselves in mutual relation, in which the Sacred is being born among us (Heyward 1989: 33-34).

It is Heyward who has done more than any other feminist theologian to claim God as the source of relational power. 'For in the beginning is the relation and in the relation is the power that creates the world, through us, and with us, and by us, you and I, you and we, and none of us alone' (Heyward 1982: 162). It is our experience of right relationships, of mutuality, justice and passion in our personal relationships, which fuels our work for salvation—for right relationship—in the world around us. 'With you, I begin to see that the hungry can eat again, the children can play again, the women can rage and stand again... And "I love you" means "Let the revolution begin!" ' (Heyward 1982: 9). The denial of interconnectedness is sin. Where right relationship does not exist God is absent.

In describing her experience of a lesbian relationship, the poet Adrienne Rich wrote 'we're out in a country that has no language' (1984). Lesbian feminists have had to seek for a language that expresses the nature and quality of their relationships, and the language they have claimed is the language of friendship. Mary

An A to Z of Feminist Theology

Hunt and Elizabeth Stuart, in their analysis of the experience of women's friendship (1995), for so long dismissed and trivialized by men, found that the qualities that emerge in many friendships between women are qualities found in many lesbian relationships. These qualities include mutuality, non-exclusivity (in the sense of rejecting a closed-off coupledom in preference to a desire to be part of a network of friends), flexibility in being willing to abandon patriarchal role-models, an honest recognition of the dynamics of sexuality in their relationships, and being 'other-directed', in that they point beyond themselves to something bigger, which some might name as divine. For relationships to be just they require attention, creativity and community. The recognition that erotic power is present in all friendships blurs the distinction between women who do not give sexual expression to their relationship and women who do. Thus friendship becomes the first model of relationship which is fully inclusive; it can be used to describe a variety of differently expressed relationships which share similar qualities. It becomes the vision of what things will be like in a post-patriarchal age, while at the same time being the means to build that new age. The inclusive nature of friendship offers a new model for understanding what it means to be human. No one would be objectified or rejected as being 'other' than us. A 'mine' mentality would be replaced by an 'our' mentality. Flexibility and other-directedness would allow us to reject the human-centredness of our thought and allow us to enter into a different relationship with the planet and non-human life. A habit of honesty would protect us from being swept up in dangerous ideologies. Hunt recognizes that not all women are equal and that unequal power relationships between different groups of women need to be recognized. Until equality is reached the demands for justice are paramount. Hunt suggests that women's friendship offers us an exciting new basis on which to do theology. Like Sallie McFague she explores the metaphor of God as 'friend', or better, 'friends':

> 'Friends,' when used to speak of the divine, conjures up far more than parent or sibling, though it can include both of them. It announces relationship without having to say 'we'. It connotes co-responsibility, mutual influence and commitment on both sides of the divine–human equation. It is a voluntary relationship entered into with intention and maintained with love. It has an enduring quality that takes friends over time and into history. It is fierce and tender all at once and without explanation (1991: 168).

'Friends' is also a helpful model of God when we reflect on prayer. Friends do speak words of comfort and affection to each other, they turn to each other in moments of need and they do sometimes fail each other. In McFague's view God is attentive in cooperating in the building up of justice and community and forever waiting for that cooperation to happen. God does not dominate or threaten, nor is she passive or distanced. God is generative: erotic power, pulsing through creation, forever bringing to birth new relationships. This God is always standing with the marginalized and oppressed, exposing the barriers to community while at the same time embodying it herself in her bountiful embrace of all.

Beverly Harrison has attempted to develop a framework for the development of a feminist ethic. She argues that it needs to ground its analysis in *doing;* we have to recognize that we have the power through our acts to create or destroy. We build each other into persons through our actions towards one another. The most urgent task that our world faces is the building of community. We have the power to accomplish it. We must also recognize that all our knowledge, including our moral knowledge, is embodied knowledge, it is mediated through our bodies. Feeling 'is the basic bodily ingredient that mediates our connectedness to the world. All power, including intellectual power, is rooted in feeling' (1985: 3-21). If we lose our power to feel we cannot be effective moral agents, we have lost our rationality. Harrison suggests that the moral crisis of our day may owe much to the fact that people do not really live in their bodies and have therefore lost their sense of interconnectedness. She is convinced that Christian feminists need to reclaim anger from the bin of sin to which it has been consigned by the tradition. Anger is vital because it is an embodied signal that all is not well in our relationship. It is anger that spurs us to action. The most important part of the framework is the recognition of the centrality of relationship.

LESBIAN PERSPECTIVES - LIBERATION

No survey of the contribution of lesbians to feminist theology would be complete without reference to Mary Daly. Daly stands as an inspirational force behind much Christian feminist theology even though she now proudly stands outside the Christian tradition. She describes a lesbian as 'a Woman-Loving woman; a woman who broken the Terrible Taboo against Women-Touching women on all levels. Woman-identified woman: one who has rejected false loyalties to men in every sphere' (1984: 250-51). Charlotte Bunch has also argued that the term 'lesbian' should be used in this broader sense of any woman who centres herself, her energies and her political, social and economic concern around women.

One of the future tasks of Christian feminist theology must be to engage in reflection on the growing body of feminist critical theory which focuses on the lesbian and which is raising challenging notions of gender, sexuality and the body. The works of Judith Butler (1990), Luce Irigaray, Monique Wittig and Julia Kristeva cry out for theological reflection.

LIBERATION
Lisa Isherwood

LIBERATION IS a word that is used when we become aware of oppression; those who are the oppressors rarely speak of liberation! For it to be a meaningful word we need to imagine that another reality can exist, one in which there is no need for oppression. If we are to develop a theology of liberation we have to assume that God also wants us to live in a free and liberating way. This assumption needs to be extended to this life, rather than seeing the great liberation as occurring only in death. The churches, however, have often been content to ignore oppression; indeed it is not too strong to suggest that they have been part of the oppression of many people. They have justified this by saying that reward and liberation from suffering would be found in the next world.

Liberation theology argues that people have the ability to transcend their present oppressive situations and therefore need the concrete circumstances in which to bring this about: that is, they need to be dealt with in a just way.

Therefore liberation theologians reject the common assumptions about the state of the world: they do not see it as intrinsically evil or as something to be escaped in order to find holiness. They see evil as socially constructed and therefore deconstructable in this life. Equally they see the Incarnation as signalling that salvation and human history are linked; the one comes in and through the other. This leads to a change in focus regarding theological questions. Traditional theology begins by looking at God, while liberation theology begins by looking at the situations of people's lives and asking where, if at all, God and justice are to be found in these situations.

Liberation theology understands itself as a dialogue between tradition and Scripture on the one hand and the everyday lives of people on the other. It encourages us to do theology by being involved with the world and not by contemplating some abstract realm. It therefore calls us to task, since we can no longer see injustice as something that we did not contribute to and as something that will be overcome in the next life. We are held accountable for the way things are.

The Latin American liberation theologians are now beginning to realize that when they spoke in this way and encouraged the inclusion of the marginalized they did not mean women! This task has been taken up by feminist theologians, who use some of the methods of liberation theology in order to view the world and reconstruct reality from the margins. There is the same strong emphasis on theology being made by those at the grassroots level. This has meant that liberation theology now has many branches as each group is finding a voice for itself. Oppression comes in many different shapes but the underlying methods of liberation theology have enabled people to realize that they all spring from the same roots. As such we are able to share many of our insights and methods of dealing with the problems.

Liberation means fundamentally the same thing for most people although how that is enacted in their lives will differ. It means that they have a sense of worth, they have dignity, equality and the acknowledgment that their distinctive identities are valued by the community. For a black South African this will have a distinctive flavour as it will for a Western woman in the business world. In order to bring this into being oppression has to be understood; it works on different levels and has to be dealt with at those levels.

Oppression usually works on the levels of economics, law, institutions and individual consciousness. All these have to be addressed if oppression is really to be overcome. The economics of oppression revolve around making the oppressed dependent and therefore making sure that work, wealth and land are unequally distributed. Barring people from certain forms of work is one strategy used here. This can be backed up by laws and institutions that regulate on behalf of the favoured; apartheid laws, lower pay for women and so on fall into this category. Consciousness of oppression is a difficult area to deal with because it is so ingrained that many of the injustices we see can be accepted as the way nature is. The oppressor and the oppressed create pictures of themselves and the other that can reinforce the injustice. Women have believed themselves to be emotionally weak and intellectually inferior because the institutions have colluded to make it appear so; how can women be famous scientists if they have no scientific education or composers if access to musical training is denied them? When women suffer emotional stress because of the frustration of being denied access to their culture, they may accept the patriarchal view that they are emotionally weak. There is a tension in the oppressed that is often relieved by believing the negative stories about themselves; this tension arises if they trust their experience of themselves and realize that they are not all that their oppressors would have them be. This is sometimes expressed in art or music and once again it is this culture that is usually suppressed by the dominant group. An important step to liberation is to reclaim those cultures that have been lost or suppressed by the oppressors.

Those working for liberation will begin at different points of the oppression spectrum. It is rare that all aspects are dealt with at one time. However, it is necessary to see that they all play their part in the oppression and that they all need to be rooted out if liberation is really to shine through. There may nonetheless be an order of priorities; so, for example, it was important that women should have sought the vote before beginning to question the whole political system. Equally, it is important that women be ordained even though they may now go on to question the whole nature of priesthood and ask whether it is necessary at all. Liberation has many aspects to it and is a process that begins with trusting our own experience and then acting upon it.

Further reading: Boff 1980; Daly 1973; Hyun Kyung 1990; Isasi-Diaz and Tarango 1992; Isherwood and McEwan 1993.

LOVE
Julie Clague

THE VASTNESS of this topic precludes any comprehensive or systematic treatment of issues. The scope of this discussion will therefore be confined to a number of points which arise from the following two assumptions: that an exhaustive elaboration of the meaning of love is not possible; and that love is fundamentally concerned with humans relating to their environment—particularly at an interpersonal level.

Love and Language

The elusive quality of the word 'love' lies in epistemological limitations. The variety of ways in which humans 'know' about love are subject to virtually insurmountable problems of interpretation.

First, there is the subjective experience of love by the person and the extent to which she or he understands or is able to analyse the experience. Humans encounter a large number of loving relationships of different types between birth and death: with parents, family, friends and lovers. The word 'love' makes no distinction between these. Furthermore, from birth to death these loving relationships are in process, never the same, always changing. Likewise, knowledge or understanding of these relationships is constantly evolving, always partial and always subjective, requiring reappraisal and reinterpretation.

Secondly, there is the difficulty of describing this subjective experience. Consider linguistic issues: discussion of love basically involves an attempt to express the inexpressible (as does language about the divine). Devices such as

LOVE

metaphors and similes are often employed in order to describe abstract ideas such as love ('My love is like a red red rose'). However, this can have the effect of limiting rather than expanding our understanding of the term.

More important from the feminist perspective is the gender bias which exists in language and literature (and other forms of representation such as fine art). The world of love has been described by males. Women have constantly been represented as objects of love. They have become encased—like museum exhibits—in a male construction, as though reality is on display. The ways in which women have been portrayed in (male) texts are not just inaccurate distortions. This would mean that language was simply a carrier of misinformation which could be corrected at a later date. Language works at a far deeper level in human life and culture, playing an important part in the development of self-identity. Language, images and representations comprise a symbolic order which shapes who we are. The role of language and symbol in the formation of human subjectivity has become an important focus for feminist theorists such as Julia Kristeva and Luce Irigaray.

Since objectification of women has denied them the knowledge of who they are, an important task for feminists involves the demolition of the male constructions and a rewriting of women's subjective experiences of love, thereby providing the foundations for a proper sense of female subjectivity. Without a sense of self there can be no transition to the autonomous state which enables liberation from patriarchy.

In short, human attempts to make the uncommunicable realm of love accessible through the use of language and symbol are inadequate. This is not only because these are limited tools of expression, but because the tools have become weapons in the hands of men.

Love, Relationships and Sexuality

It is uncontentious to assert that the meaning of love, to a large degree, can be found in human relationships. Nevertheless, despite the primacy of love in Christian tradition, and despite plentiful images of loving relationships within Christianity, there has often been a tendency to disembody love from human relating. The negative attitude to sexuality which has pervaded much of the tradition is largely responsible.

Christianity has wanted to control love, to castrate it and make it safe by removing the sexual dimension. In the twentieth century this is illustrated in Anders Nygren's polarization of *agape* and *eros*. Christian mistrust of human sexuality has often been accompanied by a disturbing misogyny. It is particularly ironic that marriage—the institution which Christianity sees as the ideal and normative context for loving relationships—has been a source of oppression to women.

Freud's insight that sexuality permeates every sphere of human living is now widely acknowledged. Much contemporary theology attempts to reintegrate Christian understanding of love and sexuality. It is commonplace to hear sex described as a language of love. This inevitably leads to questions of the relationship between types of sexuality and love. For instance, if female and male sexualities differ, and if gay and lesbian sexualities differ from heterosexuality, how might this affect the way in which love is understood and expressed in these forms of relating?

Self-Sacrificing Love

Christianity has always upheld the witness of self-sacrifice and martyrdom in light of Jesus's self-sacrificing love for humanity. Many Christians have therefore suffered for their faith or for some important moral principle. Portrayals of female sacrificial love can, however, reinforce Christian pedestalization of 'woman' as either virgin or martyr.

Women often make sacrifices for the sake of those dear to them and seek the good of others before themselves. This arises especially in family relations. For instance, some wives have given up their identity and future aspirations in favour of their husbands' success.

This presents problems for Christian feminists, for it is possible that the notion of self-sacrifice has contributed to, or been used as a justification for, the continued exploitation and mistreatment of women in society. Female self-sacrifice is learnt behaviour, which patriarchal society inculcates and expects, and which can be dam-

An A to Z of Feminist Theology

aging to women by perpetuating patriarchy. However, unselfish love may sometimes act as a witness against the patriarchal system, enabling societal transformation by indicating an alternative way of relating.

Further reading: Fuchs 1983; Kristeva 1983; Nelson 1978; Nelson and Longfellow (eds.) 1994.

LUST
Julie Clague

LUST IS defined by patriarchal theologians as an immoderate desire. It frequently refers to sexual desire, but also denotes any excessive or intensive love for items such as money, success and power which the person greedily covets.

The Hebrew and Christian Testaments are unanimous in condemning lust. Christian tradition has identified lust as one of the seven deadly sins. It is clear that lust can lead to negative consequences. For instance, one possible consequence of excessive and self-seeking sexual desire is the use and abuse of pornographic material, which feminists almost unanimously abhor.

Sexual lust tends to objectify persons and reduce them to the status of possession. This is dehumanizing because the desire is frequently based on outward appearances rather than on the whole person.

Most societies have maintained that sexual lust requires control since it does not respect the societal boundaries marking out appropriate objects of desire. Inappropriate objects of desire might include persons married to someone else, persons of the same sex, close relatives, and those who are under the legal age of consent. While Christianity would endorse these prescriptions, it would also argue that desire of this nature is a distorted use of human sexuality and is incompatible with human desire for God.

This raises the issue of the extent to which human institutions such as marriage and the family are essentially incompatible with the experience of human sexuality. Christian marriage and family life, rather than the ideal context for sexual relationships, would therefore be a mutual, contractual compromise.

Throughout the Christian centuries some theologians have been suspicious of all sexual desire, but it is now more common for Christians to make a connection between sexual desire and human desire for God, and to trace this connection in the writings of some of the Christian mystics.

Further, it is now acknowledged that the repression of desires can be harmful and damaging, just as the inappropriate expression of desire is harmful. Repression of desires in the lives of religious—particularly religious celibates—has led to many destroyed lives. This is yet one more illustration of how Christianity is in dire need of a humanizing theology of sexuality.

Feminist theology does not fear lust in the same way that patriarchy does. It acknowledges its place in human nature and sees its potential for divinization, as with all human qualities. It is an energizing force which if expressed in mutuality releases erotic power—a power that has the potential to change patriarchal society. Feminist theology encourages the joyful and mutual expression of lust through sexual relationships.

Further reading: Countryman 1988; Daly 1984; Foucault 1984; Fuchs 1983.

MACHO - MARRIAGE AS SACRAMENT

MACHO / MASCULINE / MASCULINIST
Dorothea McEwan

MACHO (Mexican, Spanish): male, masculine, an assertively vigorous man, tough guy. Machismo is the quality of being macho, the cluster of male traits related to virility, pride, honour. The essence of machismo 'requires emphasis of gender difference and constant reinforcing of traditional roles' (*International Reports* 1981: 11). It is individualistic, a self-perception, a conditioned mode of thought finding approval in society's perception. 'Very closely associated with potency and virility, it will affect birth control decisions within and outside marriage. Paternity (illegitimate and legitimate) is a source of pride, a symbol of power, a target of respect but seldom of responsibility' (*International Reports* 1981: 11).

Masculine (of a person or animal): the male characteristic of men, virile, manly, vigorous, powerful, strong.

Masculinist: an advocate of the rights of man, of or pertaining to the advocacy of the rights of man, characterized by or designating attitudes, values etc. held to be typical of men.

MARRIAGE AS SACRAMENT
Susan Dowell

THE TEACHING of marriage as sacrament originates in the Pauline Epistles and is most fully developed in Eph. 5.22-23. The description of marriage as a 'mystery, concerning Christ and his church' (v. 32) has been incorporated into the wedding service of most Christian churches. It is by raising marriage from a civil contract to a 'mystical'—and therefore indissoluble—union that Christianity is generally perceived to have had the greatest impact on society.

This aspect of Christian thought has also, therefore, attracted widespread critical scrutiny. Enlightenment thinkers such as John Stuart Mill (in his *Subjection of Women* [1869]) argued that the church's 'mystification' of marriage had obscured its social and political reality. More recently, feminists have stressed the sexist imbalance in the Pauline picture (see Eph. 5.22-24). Paul's own stated reference for celibacy supports the generally held suspicion that Christianity is fundamentally biased against sexual relations in general and women in particular.

A more favourable interpretation can be argued on the basis of other Pauline teachings, such as 1 Cor. 6.16-20; 8.4, 14, which suggest a more egalitarian view of marriage and a view more affirming of sexuality. It is also important to look at the biblical texts in their wider cultural and historical context.

While Christianity has undoubtedly served to absolutize monogamy as a social and ethical norm (see 1 Cor. 7.39-40; Mt. 5.32; 19.9; Mk 10.11-12; Lk. 16.18 [LXX]), the concept did not originate with Christianity. It had developed as a norm in biblical culture (replacing the tribal polygamy practised by the early patriarchs) and in the surrounding pagan cultures. Counsels to sexual fidelity appear as a consistent theme in both biblical and extra-biblical writings from the fifth century BCE onwards. These writings also affirm the ideal of love within marriage. Jewish monotheism went on to develop a theological metaphor around this idea; in the Hebrew Bible the relationship between God and his chosen people is imaged as faithful union of spouses.

The later, Christian idea of marriage as sacrament can thus be seen as adding a christological layer to this older metaphor. However, it is important to note that the sacramentality of marriage is not taught in the Gospels; Jesus did no more than affirm the precept of fidelity between husband and wife, their becoming as 'one flesh'; and the church has always understood marriage as deriving not from faith in Christ but from nature and society. We may see Jesus' and Paul's affirmations of marital fidelity as attempts to counter the non-egalitarian sexual mores of the dominant Graeco-Roman culture.

While many feminist theologians concede certain progressive elements in biblical teaching, they would dispute the claim that Christian teaching on marriage has, historically, had positive consequences for women. The rise of asceticism within Christian culture effectively precluded further affirmation of either the emotional or sacramental significance of mar-

An A to Z of Feminist Theology

riage. Of the three purposes of marriage officially taught by the church—procreation, 'remedy against fornication' and the 'mutual society, help and comfort' of spouses—the emphasis remained firmly on the first two, from the Patristic era through to the late Middle Ages. Conjugal sex was thought to be at best a compromise with the desires of the flesh, redeemable only by its procreative purpose. Throughout the feudal period dynastic marriages were made and dissolved with ease; this system reduced wives and daughters to sexual objects valuable only for their reproductive capacities. It was not until the thirteenth century that concerted attempts were made to being marriage under the church's control and to require its public blessing in church.

A number of developments in religious and secular thought combined to raise the spiritual and social status of marriage in the late Renaissance period. Marital sex came to be seen as valuable in itself, even without the desire for children. The demise of monasticism in the Reformed churches gave a new importance to the Christian home as a site of holiness. The emphasis on romantic love in the late Middle Ages, though it had no immediate effect on the practice of arranged marriage, did much to discredit a system which took no regard of the wishes and affections of the couple themselves.

The Western church now accepts freedom of choice as integral to marriage. Feminist theologians and ethicists, while welcoming this development, believe that it should be extended to other aspects of married life; for example, no woman should be expected to forfeit her right to a full public or professional life on marriage.

The official teaching of the Church of England and the Roman Catholic Church has always been that the two people getting married administer the sacrament to themselves, with the priest present only to accord them the blessing of the church. The sacrament itself consists in the couple's sexual union—hence the validity of non-consummation as ground for the annulment of a marriage. In this sense a civil marriage is just as much a true marriage as one celebrated in church. However, since the sixteenth century the Roman Catholic Church has ruled that for a marriage to be valid it must take place before a priest. This ruling has been used to invalidate many 'mixed' marriages which may not have taken place before a Catholic priest. The question of the indissolubility of marriage remains a difficult one for all denominations. Protestantism has, however, tended towards greater flexibility on issues of divorce and remarriage, on the grounds that entrapment in marital misery is inconsistent with an understanding of marriage as a holy or honourable estate.

Further reading: West 1990; Dowell 1990.

MARTYRDOM
Maureen A. Tilley

THOSE WHO suffer death as a testimony to their faith are called martyrs. Literally, 'martyr' means *witness* (to the Faith) (Rev. 17.6). Christianity finds the roots for the concept first in heroes of the Bible, such as the unnamed mother and her sons in the book of Maccabees (2 Macc. 6.1–7.42) and the deacon Stephen (Acts 6.8–8.1), and secondly in philosophers, like Socrates, who died for their beliefs. In traditional theology, the value of martyrdom rests in fidelity to Christ and imitation of his death (Rev. 1.5).

Women as Historical Martyrs

Martyrdoms in antiquity often resulted from mob violence, as in the case of Stephen. However, during the third century, Roman officials engaged in organized, legalized persecution. Sometimes they required Christian officials to hand over the Scriptures to be burned or they ordered clergy—and sometimes laity—to sacrifice to Roman divinities or suffer penalties ranging from fines to execution. These circumstances would seem to limit opportunities for women to become martyrs, if one accepts traditional representation of women in antiquity. If they were docile and rarely engaged in activities outside the home, how could they be objects of mob violence? If they were not counted as clergy, how could they be harassed under the statutes aimed at bishops and priests? Finally, if the *paterfamilias* were the arbiter of family piety and owner of property, how could women be called on to sacrifice or suffer penalties? Their fathers, husbands or guardians would bear the brunt of the laws.

Yet we do know that women were tortured

MARTYRDOM

and martyred during the period of earliest Christianity. In the early second century Pliny the Younger (*Ep.* 10.96-97) gives evidence of women's leadership in his report of the interrogation of a deaconess in the community at Bithynia (northern Turkey) about the rituals and moral conduct of Christians. Blandina in Lyons (177 CE) and Perpetua in Carthage (203 CE) were the de facto leaders of imprisoned Christians. Girls as young as twelve presented their own preliminary defences, as stories of Maxima, Donatilla and Secunda of Carthage (303 CE) and Crispina of Thagora (304 CE) imply. Many Christian women were married to non-Christians and were thus subject to double jeopardy as their Christianity was disruptive to both the state and the family. In earliest Christianity the vocation to martyrdom was the most highly-prized state in life, even more than status as ordained clergy.

With the legalization of Christianity under Constantine (312 CE), martyrdom declined, but whenever religion became politicized, there were martyrs. In the fourth century some died for their refusal to be reconciled with Constantinian Christianity, for example, Donatists in Roman North Africa (Algeria and Tunisia) and Melitians in Egypt. Later others also suffered for their doctrinal stands: there were Catholic and Protestant martyrs of the Reformation, such as Margaret Clitherow in England and Anne Dubourg in France. Missionaries and their converts were martyred for their faith when the introduction of the customs or flag of a conquering nation was accompanied by the introduction of particular forms of Christianity—see for example, Boniface in Frisia c. 750 and Jesuits in Canada in the 1600s. Sometimes Christians were persecuted and executed when Christianity seemed a threat to the religious or political system of a missionized area, for instance missionaries and their converts in Japan in 1596–98 and American church women in El Salvador in 1980. Often the emphasis in the stories of women and men who have been martyred is on their active opposition to evil oppressors.

Women in Hagiography

From New Testament times onwards Christians have written accounts of the martyrs' deaths to inspire one another. Critical questions about this sort of hagiography have included the historicity of the accounts versus their conformity to literary conventions. Do martyrs always lecture their torturers as they suffer their torments? Were martyrs always virgins? Were women martyrs routinely sexually assaulted? These literary conventions reveal the value put on testimony and virginity by Christianity as it developed. That value even transformed the historical facts. One example is the case of Perpetua and Felicity. Their passion story clearly portrays them as mothers. Perpetua has a young child and Felicity gives birth in prison. But by the Middle Ages virginity had eclipsed martyrdom as the valorized mode of being and from that time almost to the present they were commemorated liturgically with the Mass of Virgin-martyrs.

The Use of the Martyr Figure in Christian Patriarchy

Few women are venerated as martyrs without the title 'virgin'. The hagiographical focus on virginity and sexually-oriented tortures reflects the social position of women as 'other'. The female body is assaulted in ways that emphasize not only the domination of the politically powerful over the minority but also of men over women. Many women martyrs were sentenced to brothels. One of the charges against Joan of Arc was that, contrary to Bible teaching and in obedience to the voices she heard, she wore men's clothing on the battlefield. The preservation of the record of sexual oppression may indeed reflect the situation at the time the stories were originally recorded. However, the emphatic esteem for the long-suffering virgin-martyr as the best model for Christian women is a dangerous one: women must inevitably suffer, they should not actively oppose even the worst treatment of the systems which allow this suffering. Such a promotion of passivity in the face of evil and such a lack of respect for one's own person is central to a patriarchal understanding of martyrdom. The canonization of the virgin-martyr Maria Goretti is a case in point. Goretti was a twelve-year-old Italian peasant who died in 1902 as the result of an attempted rape by a neighbour. In her veneration little attention is given to the social situation which allowed and perhaps

An A to Z of Feminist Theology

encouraged her assailant to feel free to attack her. The sole model derived is one of chastity linked to heroic forgiveness. There is a vast difference between this view of martyrdom and that of the earliest martyrs, whose stories emphasize their intrepid resistance to a social and political system which attacked them for their adherence to Christ and their willingness to name their persecutors for what they were.

Further reading: Frend 1967; Miles 1989; Tilley 1991, 1995; Weiner and Weiner 1990.

MARY
Ann Loades

MARY THE MOTHER of Jesus remains a major focus of piety and theology in many different cultural contexts. In inter-church dialogue, which now includes women's voices, she is inevitably a subject of careful consideration as women search in Scripture and through tradition for possible paradigms to encourage them in their own life-journeys.

The most thorough critical evaluation of the biblical material relating to Mary is to be found in a work which was the fruit of joint Roman Catholic and Lutheran study in North America, Mary in the New Testament (Brown, Donfried, Fitzmyer and Reumann [eds.] 1978). The relationship between any historical event and the so-called infancy narratives of the Gospels is problematic, and not only because of the profound resonance of the narratives with Old Testament texts. What is clear is that the understanding of Christ which finds expression in Rom. 1.3-4 is that he is 'Son' of God from his conception, but this does not require a 'virginal' conception such as two Gospel narratives suggest. Nor does a virginal conception (a sign of the blessing of fertility) necessitate the belief that Mary remained 'virginal' during that pregnancy and Jesus' birth, nor that she remained a virgin forever so far as her relationship to Joseph was concerned. Some theologians find the belief in the virginal conception of Jesus to be at odds with the belief in the pre-existent Son of God to be found in other New Testament texts (for example Phil. 2.6-7 and Jn 1.1-18), though the Nicene creed and many hymns and carols seem to indicate that belief flourishes with such apparent incongruities.

The symbol of the virgin contains a range of meaning beyond that of a merely genital sexual state, however. The virginal conception of Jesus represents the capacity for new beginnings (closely related to the capacity for and the possibility of rapturous cooperation with God). Mary's virginity has also symbolized the priority of Christian discipleship over the claims of family and kin, in women's lives especially, for a virgin may remain autonomous, unexploitable and unexploited. Virginity has unfortunately in some contexts also represented female/feminine non-entity, passivity, the lack of a sense of self ('be it unto me according to thy will') and a stony asexuality.

When combined with the notion of motherhood (in the figure of the virgin–mother) the paradoxical weight of this symbol can represent all too obvious difficulties for women, since no real woman can live up to it. Thus although at first glance Mary may be a symbol of hope for women, she may serve to reinforce women's second-class status relative to men (insofar as men are regarded as normatively human), since the very ideal of Mary, mother and virgin, is an intolerable one.

The difficulties may have been exacerbated by the Roman Catholic dogmas of the Immaculate Conception (1854) and of the Assumption (1950), both of them with a long and contentious history. Here again there are areas of acute ecumenical disagreement to negotiate between Roman Catholics, Protestants and Orthodox Christians, focused on 'original sin' and on the understanding of papal authority, both the manner of its exercise and the extent of its dogmatic claims (see the important collection of articles in *The Month*, August–September 1989). The two dogmas are intimately connected, since one's view on the Immaculate Conception makes a difference as to whether one is to think of the end of Mary's life as 'Assumption' or, as in the Orthodox tradition, 'Dormition', the sleep of death (depending on the significance attributed to the latter). Again, however, women have found nourishment in these dogmas; for instance, in the belief that Mary embodies an unlimited yearning for life, rescued from humiliation, alive in God, full of affection and power, closely connected to people's immediate and vital needs, the sign of the

An A to Z of Feminist Theology

possibility of a transformed world and much more (see Gebara and Bingemer 1989).

The symbolic meanings of Mary are rich and varied. She may be seen as the first of the redeemed; Mother of the Church; revolution; growth in understanding of the divine purpose; identification with Christ's suffering and with the suffering of all those who lose their children; witness of the resurrection of the 'flesh of her flesh, bone of her bone'; the immanence and living presence of God (Gerard Manley Hopkins's 'Wild air, world mothering air'); as well as submission, humility, subordination, incapacity for independent action and so on. She may be a route towards envisaging the divine in gender-inclusive ways, and to the association of the female with the mystery of God.

There have been some interesting papal statements about Mary in the latter part of the twentieth century. *Marialis Cultus* (To Honour Mary) of 1974 is particularly generous in its suggestions that the church is by no means bound to particular expressions of the cult of any particular epoch, let alone to particular anthropological traditions associated with the Christian churches. In this document, Mary is taken into dialogue with God, as a woman of courageous choice, proclaiming God's vindication of those who need it, surviving poverty, flight, exile and so on. *Redemptoris Mater* (Mother of the Redeemer) of 1987 merits careful scrutiny and assessment in the light of the earlier statement, especially for the way in which its gender constructions interlock with the present papal position on the ordination of women to the priesthood.

Further reading: Storkey 1989; Warner 1976.

MARY MAGDALENE
Lisa Isherwood

MARY MAGDALENE is a very significant figure in feminist theology because she shows how the reality of women's lives can be moulded to fit the dominant myth. She has been misrepresented under patriarchy, as have countless other women. Mary is first referred to by name in Mark 15 where she is one of the women standing by the cross. These women are those who have followed Jesus and 'ministered unto him' (Mk 15.41). This phrase has recently been seen in a new light: where previously it was taken to refer to traditionally 'female' roles such as preparing food, it is now seen as referring more widely to all the activities of the Jesus community, including preaching. There is no evidence in the texts that Jesus regarded these women as in any way different from his male followers. What does mark them out is that while the other disciples ran from Jesus' death, the women stayed with him.

Not only did Mary witness the death of Jesus, but according to John she was the sole witness of the resurrection. She calls Jesus 'Rabboni', which is an exalted title, and thereby signals that she understands the implications of what she has witnessed. She is showing that a new reality is born. It would not be too extreme to suggest that she is witnessing to the true nature of church and empowered community, a vision that has been lost under patriarchy. She was the first recipient of an apostolic commission, but this has been forgotten.

What has been emphasized instead is Jesus' healing of Mary, the casting out of seven devils. There has been much speculation as to what this means, but it has been assumed that Mary was guilty of sexual sin and that this casting out was an act of forgiveness. No such assumption is made when Jesus casts devils out of men! It is likely that Mary suffered from some kind of psychological disorder, but the sexual label has stuck. This may be because her second name, Magdalene, signified that she was from a prosperous fishing village on the northwest bank of the lake of Galilee which was known for its riotous and permissive way of life. It may also be simply because she was a woman, and therefore, in the eyes of the Church Fathers, inherently sexually sinful. In constructing this image of Mary they have transformed the beloved friend of Jesus and first apostle into the repentant whore who dwells in every woman. Mary Magdalene is a lesson to us all as we struggle with patriarchy; she needs reclaiming so that we may recover something of the dignity of all women.

Further reading: Carmody 1992; Haskins 1994; Newsom and Ringe (eds.).

MATRIARCHY
Susan Smith

THERE ARE two significantly different interpretations of matriarchy. First, and more commonly, matriarchy is defined as a social system whereby women dominate men. However, some feminist historians argue that matriarchy, defined as 'the mirror image of patriarchy', never existed, although they do presume that matriarchy was the normative social system in Old Europe (7000–3500 BCE). But rather than seeing matriarchy as the female counterpart of an oppressive patriarchy, they endow matriarchy with qualities they recognize as significant in their own struggle against patriarchy. Matriarchy as an ideological construct is defined by harmony, connectedness and mutuality.

Feminist explanations, some ideologically motivated, are numerous as to how patriarchy came to replace matriarchy in Old Europe and the Near East. Certitude about the reasons for the disappearance of matriarchy is not possible but archaeological evidence does suggest that a more harmonious way of life flourished until scarcity of resources led to warfare between different groups of people. Such ecologically and socially-driven military adventures favoured the development of patriarchy, and the subsequent domination of women.

These socio-economic changes were paralleled in the theological world by the appearance of male gods—Ares and Mars in the Greek and Roman pantheons respectively, and the monotheistic Yahweh of the Hebrew world. Patriarchal religions believed that such gods, more appropriate to a militaristic culture, intervened on the behalf of their believers in their struggle for land. The emergence of patriarchal religions restricted women's roles to what best served the needs of a patriarchal society.

Some contemporary feminists are revisioning ancient matriarchy as both a social system and a bearer of religion that celebrates humanity's relationship with the natural world. They hypothesize that the Eden story and 'Golden Age' story of Greek mythology describe a pre-patriarchal age of non-domination and inclusion. Ecofeminists point to the contemporary value of ancient symbols for an ecologically devastated world. They argue that patriarchy, a system of domination, legitimated man's exploitation of nature.

Such idyllic reconstructions may be regarded somewhat sceptically, since there is insufficient historical or archaeological evidence to support such revisioning. But feminists argue that these mythological reconstructions of a pre-patriarchal era in which women were honoured can energize contemporary women in their struggle against patriarchy. Therefore, at the theological level, Christian feminists are retrieving female or feminine images of the divine in the Jewish and Christian Scriptures. Some suggest that perhaps these images have their genesis in the ancient goddess religions. Post-Christian feminists are reviving what Caroline Merchant (1980) calls the 'Old Religion', a type of nature religion or pantheism which emphasizes humanity's connectedness with nature.

Mainstream religions tend to be critical of such emerging religious trends. Feminists ask if the critics are ideologically driven, recognizing the challenge that matriarchal religion could be to traditional patriarchal religions. Post-Christian feminists would argue that a monotheistic male-god religion has been used to marginalize women socially and theologically, and therefore women have to look elsewhere for salvation. Contemporary feminist interpretations of matriarchy emphasize its connectedness and ecocentric ethic. This is believed to be helpful in empowering women, in encouraging an ecological sensitivity, and in meeting women's felt needs for a spirituality that nurtures and nourishes them.

Further reading: Gimbutas 1982, 1989; Lerner 1986; Ruether 1992.

MEDICAL ETHICS
Grace Jantzen

THE HIPPOCRATIC Oath, dating from about the fourth century bce, has for millennia enshrined the principles of ethics in medicine. Although there are continuing conflicts about just what these principles should be and how they should be expressed in medical practice, there is wide agreement that medical research and clinical practice should be subject to ethical

MEDICAL ETHICS

guidance. In all Western countries medical practitioners, whether doctors, nurses, researchers, or technicians, are bound by professional codes of practice as well as by civil and criminal law to abide by standards of conduct framed according to ethical principles. Hospitals and research facilities regularly have ethics committees which adjudicate particular cases or research protocols; and where new issues emerge with the advancement of technology, as with *in vitro* fertilization or genetic engineering, national or international committees of enquiry are often set up to investigate the ethical implications and make recommendations for public policy. Theologians and church people are usually represented on such committees, so that Christian values are taken into account.

It might therefore seem that although some specific issues such as abortion and euthanasia are still hotly contested, the overall commitment of medical practitioners is beyond dispute. However, feminists who have been probing various aspects of medical theory and practice have raised serious ethical concerns. These concerns fall into two main categories. In the first, the standard ethical principles are accepted, but there are allegations that they are being applied unevenly, such that women are treated differently from men, people of colour differently from white people, poor people differently from wealthy people (especially in countries such as the UK and USA where private medical insurance is available to the affluent). The second sort of feminist concern is more radical. This is that the whole framework of medical research and practice, including the ethical principles themselves, is masculinist to the core. Not only are people at the top of the medical hierarchy predominantly male (whereas in former times medical care was in the hands of wise women and midwives), but the practices and even the moral framework on which the practices rest are inherently patriarchal.

Principles of Traditional Medical Ethics

Many ethicists try to derive their ethical principles from overarching ethical theories (called 'metaethics') which in turn find a place within their particular philosophical stance. One broad type of ethical theory is known as 'consequentialism', which holds that the rightness or wrongness of an action can be decided in terms of its consequences: will it bring about health and happiness, or will it cause suffering and harm? Utilitarianism, the theory that the morally right act is the one which brings about the greatest amount of good for the greatest number of people, is one popular variety of consequentialism. By contrast, ethical theories known as 'deontological' argue that some things are intrinsically right or wrong no matter what their consequences. For example, a deontologist might hold that murder is always wrong, even if the intended victim is a Hitler whose death would have good consequences for a vast number of people. It is easy to see that consequentialists and deontologists could have fundamentally different views about the morality of such medical practices as abortion or euthanasia. Consequentialists would argue that such practices could sometimes be right if they maximized happiness or minimized suffering; whereas deontologists might argue that human persons are of intrinsic value and their lives should always be preserved no matter what the suffering or other consequences. (Many deontologists would of course go on to say that we then have a moral duty to try to help the people who are suffering).

Consequentialists and deontologists have been arguing with each other for centuries, and in the meantime it has been necessary to develop more specific rules and principles of medical ethics. Many ethicists would agree that whatever overarching metaethical theory is adopted, the following principles (which are enshrined in professional codes of practice and in law in many countries) constitute an essential framework for medical ethics.

The Principle of Nonmaleficence

This principle is often seen as the most fundamental in the Hippocratic tradition, coming from the maxim 'Above all, do no harm'. Medical research and practice is duty bound not to be the cause of increasing injury or suffering, though of course this does not mean that doctors may never hurt or injure patients in their efforts to cure them—say, in setting a fractured bone, or in surgery. What it does mean is that

An A to Z of Feminist Theology

medical personnel are not to use their skills against the well-being of patients: deliberately poisoning them with drugs, for instance, or using patients contrary to their own interests for experimental purposes. The principle of nonmaleficence prohibits medical intervention if it will cause harm or suffering to the patient unless that suffering is considered a necessary means of curing the patient or alleviating her or his pain in the longer term. It also prohibits *negligence*, that is, failure to take adequate care in a situation where such failure harms the patient: for example, failure to remove swabs or surgical instruments from inside a patient's body. Negligence which causes actual harm can render a physician liable to a charge of *malpractice*.

The Principle of Beneficence

As it is usually understood, the principle of nonmaleficence goes beyond the concept of avoiding harm and becomes a positive commitment to try to prevent harm and develop methods and practices whose outcome is likely to be beneficial. The principle of beneficence encapsulates this positive effort to bring about good, whether that is preventing or curing an illness, alleviating suffering, or allowing a person to die with dignity. Although there are limits to the extent that medical personnel are required actively to bring about good to people (especially if people resist), it is completely accepted that the purpose of medicine is to bring about beneficial results. For example, once vaccinations against smallpox became available, it became the moral duty of the public health system to provide such vaccination services, though if some people absolutely refused, it would not be the physician's job to force them to be vaccinated. Again, physicians are not obligated under the principle of beneficence to donate their own kidneys to patients who are in need of them; they are, however, obligated to use their professional skills to the best of their ability on the patients' behalf.

Respect for Autonomy

Over against the principles of nonmaleficence and beneficence, and sometimes in tension with them, is the principle of *autonomy*, literally 'self-rule'. This principle enshrines the patients' right to make decisions about their own health care and the right of freedom to choose what happens to their bodies. A physician is morally bound to obtain the consent of the patient for any course of treatment, as well as for surgery: failure to meet this obligation may render a surgeon liable to a charge of assault. Furthermore, the principle of autonomy requires that the consent for treatment must not be given in ignorance of what is likely to happen and what risks are involved; in other words, it must be *informed* consent. Some jurisdictions go further, and require not only that patients give their consent to any specific course of treatment, but also that they are told about any possible alternatives, with their attendant risks and benefits, and are allowed to make an informed *choice* among the possibilities. The principle of respect for autonomy also lays upon medical personnel the duty of *confidentiality*. As in the case of the other principles, there are situations where this principle does not apply: for example, a surgeon can perform emergency operations on unconscious victims of accidents who cannot give consent, or on infants or mentally handicapped adults with the consent of their next of kin.

Justice

There are many different concepts of justice and its practical applications in medical ethics; but at the bottom of most of them is the requirement that people in need of medical care should be treated equally. That is, they should be treated strictly on the basis of their need, not on the basis of their sex, skin colour, age, wealth, or mental competence. A mentally handicapped person who breaks a leg has a right to the same standard of medical care that a politician would receive.

The principle of justice is a principle within which issues of economics and issues of ethics intersect. In a situation of limited resources, how should decisions be made about how those resources should be allocated? If some people do not get even a decent minimum of basic health care, is it right that others, perhaps the more wealthy, should have access to extremely expensive medical technology? Should very premature babies, chronically ill or elderly patients be given continuing costly treatment at vast public expense? The answers one gives to these questions are a fair indication of what concept of justice one holds.

An A to Z of Feminist Theology

MEDICAL ETHICS

Protection of the Vulnerable

Although this principle is essentially contained within the principles already listed, it is so important in medical ethics that it is worth spelling out separately. Vulnerability is related to an imbalance of power; and the principle of protection of the vulnerable means that those who are less powerful or who could be exploited in some way are entitled to special protection. Children and the elderly are obvious examples. In relation to medical care, however, vulnerability is a feature of the transactions between the physician and virtually any patient, not only those we readily think of as vulnerable members of society. Any patient who is ill, perhaps in pain and fearful, is very much at the mercy of the doctor, whose skills and position place her or him in a situation of power relative to the patient. The principle of protection of the vulnerable requires that this power not be abused, that the trust which the patient places in the doctor or nurse be met with sympathy and skill, never with exploitation or manipulation.

Problems with the Principles

Although the principles discussed above are very important for medical ethics, it is obvious that they do not provide a solution for all moral problems. Quite apart from the concerns which have been raised from a feminist perspective, which will be considered later, a wide range of problems arise about the application of these principles to actual cases. These problems may emerge *within* any particular principle, or in a tension *between* principles.

Problems that arise within principles often have to do with what are the appropriate *limits* of the principle: we have already noted some of these. For example, with regard to the principle of nonmaleficence a particularly pressing moral dilemma for doctors, patients and their families is the question of when it is right to let someone die, or even to administer a drug which would relieve extreme suffering but which would hasten death. The more sophisticated medical technology becomes, the more it is necessary to confront this problem: at what point is it right to switch the machines off? Or again, with reference to the principle of respect for autonomy, is it sometimes right for a physician to override the stated choice of a patient when the physician has good reason to believe that the patient is making a bad decision—say, refusing a needed blood transfusion, or refusing to eat?

Problems that arise in tensions *between* principles often involve having to decide which principle should have priority. For example, if a man diagnosed to have syphilis declines to notify his sexual partner(s) so that they could receive necessary treatment, which takes priority, the duty of confidentiality to the man, or the duty to protect his vulnerable partner(s)? Or again, which takes priority: the principle of beneficence, whereby an infertile couple are assisted to have a child using highly sophisticated technology, or the principle of justice whereby resources are spent on basic medical care for existing children around the world rather than on bringing more children into it? Standard textbooks in medical ethics discuss issues as though medical problems and resources had national boundaries, and rarely ask what moral obligations arise because of the international inequalities of needs, resources and facilities. Yet as the trafficking in human organs or the AIDS epidemic makes obvious, the idea that any country need concern itself only with its internal health problems and policies is one of the greatest ethical and prudential follies imaginable.

Feminist Concerns with Practice

One of the most significant books in relation to medical practice in the past twenty-five years is the large manual *Our Bodies, Ourselves* (Phillips and Rakusen [eds.] 1989), first published jointly in the USA and the UK in 1973 and with repeated subsequent editions. This book was developed by women increasingly concerned that in spite of official affirmation of the fundamental principles of medical ethics, the medical system practised something other than it preached in its treatment of women. Doctors were infantilizing women and not respecting women's autonomy or women's health choices; and women were too often colluding with this paternalistic attitude, treating the doctor like a god in a white coat whose word could not be questioned. *Our Bodies, Ourselves* was written to

An A to Z of Feminist Theology

help women realize that we are responsible for our own bodies and our own health choices, and we do not need to be passive and unquestioning. In extended sections on sexuality, fertility, childbearing, menopause, and health problems specific to women such as breast cancer or uterine disease, this book presents clear factual information, including information about alternative perspectives and treatment possibilities. It thereby empowers women to make informed choices and to enter into medical situations less as passive victims and more as intelligent and responsible adults.

Feminist writers have made great progress in investigating areas of misfit between standard principles of medical ethics and actual practice, particularly in the treatment of women. Not surprisingly, the misfits most frequently discussed have been in the areas of *discrimination* against women, contravening the principle of justice, and of *paternalism*, contravening respect for autonomy. Often, the ethical problems within the medical context reflect and reinforce unjust or patriarchal attitudes and situations within the wider society.

A blatant example occurs in the area of mental health. From the Victorian period onwards, far more women than men have been diagnosed as suffering from mental disorders, especially depression and hysteria ('hysteria' literally means 'wandering womb'). Far more have been admitted to mental hospitals. And overwhelmingly more women than men have regular prescriptions of sedatives and 'tranquillizing' drugs. The explanation of this disproportion involves more than one factor. First, many medical personnel (like society as a whole, including women) are predisposed to think of women as less mentally stable than men: women are stereotyped as emotional or sensitive while men are rational. Secondly, many women do have to cope with enormous psychological stresses, often combining motherhood with paid work (or having to choose between them), dealing with sexism in society and often at home and in the workplace, and subject to the low self-esteem which is a product of internalized sexism. Thirdly, whereas in Western societies men are more likely to deal with stresses by becoming aggressive and violent, women are socialized to turn their aggression inward into depression or self-destruction. Clearly, this cannot all be blamed on the medical system; equally clearly, medical practice too often colludes with and reinforces sexist stereotypes and injustices.

Another example is the area of fertility, pregnancy and childbirth. All of these are normal and healthy aspects of women's lives; yet since about 1850 they have increasingly been treated as 'medical conditions' and taken into the hands of medical professionals. Whereas formerly women who were pregnant might have consulted a midwife, who would also assist at the birth, far more women now give birth in hospitals, and it would be virtually unthinkable for a pregnant woman in a Western country not to have ongoing medical supervision. Moreover, vastly more hospital births are now by Caesarean section; and medical technology such as foetal monitoring and ultrasound equipment can replace the woman as the focus of attention. While all these techniques can sometimes be beneficial or even necessary, the statistics of infant and mother morbidity and mortality have not been improved in proportion to the increase of medicalization. (Cleanliness and sterilization of equipment is much more closely related to health outcomes than is hospitalization.) At the same time, many women find their autonomy eroded, as they are expected to be compliant with hospital routines and mechanical monitoring, which may be more for the convenience and interest of medical staff than for the patient's welfare. Thus the wonder of giving birth can be replaced by a feeling of alienation from one's own body and even from the newborn infant.

Feminists have also become aware of the ways in which medical research and even the language of medical textbooks is often skewed against women. It is hardly credible, for instance, to suppose that if as many men suffered from monthly discomfort as there are women who have menstrual problems, there would not have been a massive research effort to try to alleviate the symptoms. Again, medical textbooks refer to menstrual blood as 'waste' or as a result of 'failed' or 'thwarted' fertilization—terms which would hardly be used for male ejaculate. Descriptions of fertilization often characterize the egg as passively waiting for the active sperm swimming valiantly up the reproductive canal and finally piercing the egg: more recent research suggests that actually the egg sends out tentacles which select and draw the sperm into union with it.

Feminist Concerns with the Ethical Framework

In addition to their critique of particular medical practices and attitudes, feminists have also begun a critique of the whole framework of Western ethics, including medical ethics, and have begun to develop an alternative ethical stance often called an 'ethic of care'. Traditional ethics is usually based on 'rights': in medical ethics, the right to informed choice, the right to a fair share of resources, and so on. Underlying such a rights-based ethic is an idea of human beings as isolated individuals in competitive and even adversarial relationships with one another as each strives for her or his rights. A particularly unhelpful instance of this kind of rights-based conceptualization in medical ethics occurs in the debate about abortion, which is often characterized in terms of a conflict between the rights of the foetus and the rights of the pregnant woman.

Feminists have been pointing out that this view of human personhood as isolated individuals is typically masculinist and is mistaken. Women who gestate and give birth to children, or who spend a significant amount of our lives nurturing and caring for others, know from our own experience that people are interconnected with one another, and that human well-being is increased not by aggressive competition but by fostering mutual care and connection. An ethic of care based on that principle holds that moral reasoning is not primarily about arbitrating between conflicting rights. Rather, moral wisdom and sensitivity consist, in the first instance, in focusing on the ways in which our interests are often interdependent, and in trying to find creative solutions that remove or reduce conflict. Thus for example medical commitment to the empowerment of women by access to information and building up confidence to take responsibility for our health care choices would reduce the conflict between a woman's right to autonomy and her right of beneficence (which otherwise becomes paternalistic).

Much work remains to be done in developing the ethic of care and in applying it to medical ethics. It is important not to take the ethic of care as implying that rights can be disregarded: its aim is not to undermine human rights but to replace adversarial attitudes and relationships with a celebration of connection in diversity. Nor is it the intent to lumber women with doing all the caring in the community. Rather, an ethic of care is built on the insights of women, the traditional care-givers, and is an attempt to translate those hard-won insights into public policy and medical practice.

Further reading: Beauchamp and Childress 1989; Holmes and Purdy (eds.) 1992; Martin 1989; Ussher 1991.

MENSTRUATION AND LAWS OF PURITY
Melissa Raphael

THE PERCEPTION of blood as the most powerful and dangerous of all substances is common to most religions of the world; so much so that it is possible to speculate that patriarchy itself developed at least in part as a response to men's fear of the mystery of women's menstruation and their subsequent need to control women's power to nourish and bring forth new life. At any rate, as Deut. 12.23 puts it, 'the blood is the life', so any control over the emission of blood that laws of purity attempt to establish gives a measure of quasi-divine control over life. In *Purity and Danger* (1966) Mary Douglas argues that the perception of menstrual blood as dirty is closely related to fears about dirt in general. Dirt or impurity is feared as 'matter out of place' and so threatens the cosmic and social order. Pollution beliefs, of which those concerning menstruation are perhaps the most conspicuous, seem to function as instruments of power relationships in religion and hence society. Ruling groups can define what is clean and therefore acceptable to God and men. Dirt is unacceptable to the divine presence and, socially, becomes a mark of poor bodily and moral self-control. Rules of purification therefore legitimate the supposedly benign power of the dominant ideology to protect society from the danger of its own impurity. It is not surprising, then, that purification beliefs are not only vehicles of misogyny: racism and classism are likewise characterized by a belief that the Other is less hygienic and less rational than the ruling class.

MENSTRUATION

The Christian concept of ritual purity derives largely from the Jewish priestly codes of Lev. 12.1-5 and 15.19-30 in which menstruation and childbirth were deemed to make a woman unclean or impure for specified lengths of time. In attempting to be fit to come into the presence of God, the Jewish people were required to be holy, that is, separated from the contagion of the profane, of which contact with blood was a key source. In removing a woman from the divine presence to protect those spaces and objects which were particularly associated with the divine will and presence, these laws limited a woman's participation in religious ritual and circumscribed her relationship with her husband. The emission of seminal fluids made men temporarily impure as well but for a far shorter duration and obviously posed no obstacle to priesthood or, later, the rabbinate. These codes have been elaborated and remain in place in modern orthodox Judaism. The rise of Jewish fundamentalism has ensured that the laws of female purity have assumed a new centrality. Conservative apologists often argue that women's blood is not repulsive to the divine presence but that, on the contrary, women are taboo at those times when they have come too close to the divine life force.

So while it is possible to interpret the laws of purity as maps of male reverence for women, the taboos against menstruation and childbirth—the defining characteristics of femaleness—have been perhaps the most profound cause of women's exclusion from the altar and of a long-internalized sense that female physiology has a negative charge which precludes intimacy with God. It is this forced separation from the divine presence that leaves women susceptible to the charge of evil-doing. The European witchcraze probably owes something to the idea that women's menstruation gave the moon—rather than men—control over their bodies and that postmenopausal women retained their magical life-giving blood inside their bodies, thus giving them occult or pagan wisdom and power.

At every stage of a woman's life—menarche, 'defloration', childbirth and the onset of menopause—there is a flow of blood. Women's lives come to symbolize what is natural and therefore outside the systems of morality and reason which characterize civilization. A part of the patriarchal desire to control nature by assuming the power of life and death has been represented in the control of women's bodies through laws of purity and pollution. Blood is an awesome substance whose uncontrollable flow represents the power of life. It has been argued that women's possession of this chaotic power poses at least a threat to the patriarchal aspiration to control the created order. The cultic regulation of such a power by laws of purity and pollution, by the institution of patriarchal marriage, and by the sanctification of virginity has brought the sacrality of female embodiment—its power to give life—under male control.

Consequently many feminists would argue that the labelling of female blood as profane corresponds to a dramatic fall in the socio-religious status of women, when, under monotheism, menstruation was to be perceived as a debilitating 'curse'; a punishment for Eve's primal disobedience. Patriarchal monotheism, while limiting the power of menstrual blood by law, also seems to have appropriated that power by imitating its flow. The practice of male circumcision, the blood spilt by Jesus' crucifixion for the eternal life of humankind, the sacramental nourishment of the eucharist which imitates the nourishing blood that the womb gives to the child, and the ritual of baptism in which a man gives a child a second birth which cleanses it from the blood of the womb, can all be interpreted as the patriarchal appropriation of the power of women's 'menstrual magic'. Indeed, among others, Rosemary Ruether (1992) has suggested that the whole function of patriarchal religion is to usurp and marginalize the mysteries of female creativity.

However, on the surface it would appear that Israelite laws of purity and pollution play no part in modern Christian life. The ancient superstitions of the Church Fathers (such as the belief recorded by Isidore of Seville that menstrual blood inhibited the germination of fruits, soured wine, corroded bronze and iron, and made dogs rabid) belong to the pre-modern world view which will no longer be taken seriously in a church which has now largely accepted the scientific reasoning which gives patriarchy more effective control over nature than any law of purity could do. It was, after all, in the ancient patristic period that virgins achieved a measure of equality with men by fasting to stop menstru-

An A to Z of Feminist Theology

MENSTRUATION

ation. The ruling of the thirteenth-century Synod of Würzburg that no one should go near a menstruant now appears outdated, and menstruating women have not been forbidden to take communion in the Western church since the late seventeenth century.

More importantly, Jesus appears to have violated the menstrual taboo in the story found in all three of the Synoptic Gospels in which he heals a woman who has been unclean for twelve years through continuous haemorrhaging. Instead of condemning her for touching him and making him unclean, he praises her faith in his healing power (Mk 5.24-34; Mt. 9.18-26; Lk. 8.40-56.) In Jn 4.1-42 Jesus makes himself unclean by taking a drink from a Samaritan woman despite the prevalent Jewish belief that Samaritan women were menstruants from birth. Moreover, according to John, Jesus first revealed his messiahship to this unclean woman. For the first three centuries after Jesus' death, the belief that his redemptive death had abolished any distinction between the clean and the unclean was one of the most significant marks of the new covenant with God.

While few Christians today would admit to believing that female blood is a malign source of corruption, the historical and symbolic role of these laws continues to have a psychological and political impact on the life of the church. Laws of purity were inherited by Christianity and have been perpetuated in many denominations in concepts of priesthood taken from the Hebrew tradition and celibacy and hierarchical philosophies of Being from the Greek tradition. Here the efficacy of the sacraments depends on the celibacy of the priesthood; that is, the purification brought about by the male priests' separation from women. The doctrine of the Virgin Birth also protects Christ from the impurity of the blood of loss of virginity and birth.

Women continue to internalize the message of their impurity, particularly as voiced in the arguments of those who seek to bar women from ordination by implying that female physiology disqualifies women from properly imaging Christ. Catholic, Orthodox and some Protestant traditions would still claim that women officiating at the altar would pollute it and desecrate the sacred rituals. In many Catholic churches all women, including nuns, are kept outside the altar rail if they are called upon to fulfil roles such as altar server or lector in the absence of any man to perform the task.

A Christian adaptation of the purification rite of Lev. 12.2-4 was common until the 1960s in the ritual of 'churching' a woman who had given birth. Churching can be interpreted as a restoration of the preeminence of male sacrality. Men had traditionally been excluded from the magical, messy event of childbirth and the sorority it entailed. But forty days after giving birth (hence the word 'quarantine') churching defused the power of female sacrality by its reintegration into the male sacred order. The churching liturgy thus represents a subjugation of femaleness whose chaotic sexuality threatens the ideals of disembodied rationality and spirituality upheld in patriarchal Christian communities.

In the secular realm the advertising of 'female hygiene' products still conveys the message of female impurity. The presentation of these products plays upon women's supposed anxieties and shame by promising 'protection' and by wrapping the products in ever more layers of prettily decorated plastic. Among others, Shuttle and Redgrove (1978) and Weideger (1978) provide ample evidence that menstrual taboos persist in modern culture. However, Sophie Laws, a secular radical feminist, rejects the theory that society is still governed by any supernatural dictates on purity. She prefers to understand menstruation as governed by what she calls 'etiquette': a system of rules in which women may not draw men's attention to their menstruation (1990). Nonetheless, there seems to bee no reason why religious laws of purity have not informed such rules of etiquette.

The view of Robert Briffault and Erich Neumann (among others) that it was women and not men who invented the menstrual prohibition in order to enjoy the freedom from male sexual advances that self-segregation entails has been taken up in some quarters, notably by Elizabeth Gould Davis in *The First Sex* (1971). Clearly, these hypotheses cannot be proved. Nonetheless, whether these ideas are historically verifiable or not, some women are inspired by the idea of a time when the female 'transformation mysteries' were venerated as a function of venerating the Earth as Mother. The very exis-

An A to Z of Feminist Theology

tence of any blood taboo is held to express a primary intuition of the sacredness of female embodiment and the care needed to ensure its precious health. Although this intuition has been distorted by the patriarchal will to power and the replacement of cyclic with linear models of history, many feminists (particularly Jewish feminists and witches) are reclaiming the rituals surrounding their own menstruation and the celebration of the new moon. The celebration of a daughter's menarche has become an awesome and joyful rite of passage.

In sum, the laws of purity and pollution have had a key role to play in the construction of female difference. Under patriarchy, female impurity is inalienable from female physiology and has become a badge of Otherness. At the very least it underpins a conservative theological anthropology of the complementarity of the sexes which most feminists recognize as the source of women's marginalization and oppression. Recently, however, the feminist spirituality movement (especially in its postbiblical groupings) has reclaimed menstruation and childbirth as the focus of women's self-affirmation and celebration of essential female difference. Menstrual blood symbolizes the gift of life in opposition to the patriarchal power to control, exploit and destroy. For Christian women, the dualistic exclusions instituted by laws of ritual purity also contradict the egalitarian universalism of the Christian gospel of salvation.

Further reading: Grahn 1982; Joseph (ed.) 1990.

METHODOLOGY
Lisa Isherwood

MARY DALY warned feminist theology about the 'tyranny of methodolatry' (1986: 11), by which she meant that if one follows a method slavishly it becomes counter-productive. This is because methods by their nature will only allow certain questions to be asked; they are limiting, and they cannot always expand sufficiently to deal with all the data one is presented with. Bearing in mind this caution, what then are the methods employed by feminist theology?

The most basic and generally agreed upon method is to take the experience of women seriously and to place it at the centre of creating theology and reflecting upon already-created theology. Taking experience as a norm for creating theology is not a new departure; people have always reflected upon their world and their experiences and placed them within a theological framework. Using *women's* experience in this way is indeed new and dynamic, since our experience has been largely overlooked or pushed into male understandings of how things are; the parts that did not fit have been for the most part disregarded as faulty logic or delusion. In the West the main reason for this has been the effect of Greek thought on our understanding of ourselves. In that scheme men were viewed as rational and logical while women were seen as emotional and earthy, not capable of philosophical reasoning and too prone to passion to be able to create and sustain a world-view. The churches also reflected this understanding; women's experience was not seen as valid for theological reflection.

There have been two major theological shifts which have enabled the development of feminist theological method. These are the acceptance of both process thought and liberation theology as valid forms of theological reflection. The former insists upon the interpenetrative nature of the world. The world is not one of dualities but of relationships; therefore the highest form of thinking is not objective reason but empathetic feeling. We are all part of the process of cosmic evolution and this is evident in many areas of life and many life experiences. Everything is moving, changing and evolving and it is this process which is the reality and truth of life. There can be no searching for absolutes and ultimate truths, since nothing is beyond the process and all is revealed within it. As humans we cannot stand back from this if we are to understand how life is, and God could never conceive of being removed from the process; God is within it, in the process of becoming, along with the rest of reality.

Two things become clear if we accept this understanding; first, that while things may be new they too can carry this cosmic continuity; and secondly, that the decisions that we make have a major impact on the eternal reality. There is no external force which will eventually put it all right for us; that force is in the process and is

An A to Z of Feminist Theology

METHODOLOGY

affected by it. Once decisions are made nothing can be the same.

Process thought values our own experience because this is the way that we relate to the world, and therefore to the process. From there we can begin to make certain generalizations about the nature of the world. These of course may also change. Since our knowledge is limited, we would be wise to compare our knowing with that of others in the hope of developing a broader picture.

In this scheme God is not an 'unmoved mover' as Aquinas would have us believe, nor is he 'ultimately real' or the terrifying judge of many traditions. This God is the one who makes all things new (Rev. 21.5) and who leads, through his involvement in the process, to a greater picture of beauty and goodness.

Process thought is very valuable for feminist theology because it places experience as the central tenet in religious knowing; this is quite different from the received tradition of Christianity, which assumes that there are certain 'givens' and that we merely have to assent to them. The notion of the world as still in process also relieves women in the Christian tradition of the guilt heaped on them because of the events in Eden. In this tradition woman is seen as having reduced the world from a state of grace to one of sin in one swift action. The world is seen as having become an innately evil place in need of redemption as a result of those actions. According to process thought this is not correct, since the world has never yet been perfect; it is not in decline, it is ever in pursuit of greater beauty and goodness. God is not outside as judge but inside urging on the process. The notion of punishment must therefore be dispensed with. Further, process thought speaks of the relation of all things. Mutuality in relation is the centre of all ethical and theological thinking for feminist theology. The founders of process thought also used imagination as a method. Using imagination to push further into the realms of interrelatedness has become part of feminist method too. Even if many feminist theologians would no longer speak of 'process thought' they are nonetheless using some of its methods.

Another major theological leap in this century has been in the area of liberation theology. Until the 1960s the prevailing view in the Roman Catholic church was that the world could not be changed by political means. Theologians such as Rahner and de Lubac began to suggest that people had great potential to transcend themselves and that therefore their living conditions should aid this process rather than hindering it. Moltmann and Metz suggested that the world is basically a place of grace and so everyone should strive to eliminate injustice. In 1968 in Columbia the Roman Catholic bishops openly challenged the situation of poverty and injustice in their countries, since they realized that the questions posed about God came from the situations of people's lives and they had to be taken seriously. They were grappling with the question of how to tell people who are suffering that God loves them, and to tell them this in a way that seemed real. They were rejecting the idea that the world is evil and that the best thing to do is to withdraw from it. Liberation theologians began looking for ways to change the world, not just to condemn it as unredeemed. They found their impetus for this in the Hebrew Scriptures, which told the readers that God is acting in history. They also pointed to the incarnation as a further example of how God exists in the very fabric of the created order. Salvation became an event in history.

There are two aspects of liberation method that are important for our present feminist theology: these are universality and preference. The former acknowledges the universal love of God, while the latter makes us realize that we are not able to deal with all the problems in the world and so encourages us to be committed to that area that is closest to our own experience. It is there that we should strive for justice. Liberation theology asserts that if the church is to be Good News then it has to be accessible to all, particularly the marginalized. The church is understood as the people in it and this of course means that there has to be an abolition of hierarchical power. Liberation theology grew out of the tension arising from a dialogue between Scripture and tradition on the one hand and the concrete experiences of people on the other. It sees evil as concrete, not just an abstract concept, and therefore understands that the way to overcome it is through concrete action.

The methods of liberation theology have

An A to Z of Feminist Theology

extended into black and feminist theology, and have encouraged women to work for justice for women both within and outside the church. Liberation theology also emphasizes the base community as a worshipping group. This has enabled the growth within feminist theological circles of women-churches, groups of justice-seeking friends who meet to find support. These groups are determined to create a discipleship of equals which is woman-identified. This is aimed at making people true religious agents in the world, encouraging them to take their own experience seriously and act upon it (Hunt 1991: 160-61).

Liberation theology, which sees liberation as being lived out in history, has not only encouraged women to take their present experience seriously, but has also encouraged them to recover their history, both religious and secular. Women are certainly absent from much religious literature and where we are present we are not always seen in a positive light: we are either victims of abuse or we are perpetrators of some evil deed. This has led to a theological hermeneutic of suspicion, so named by Elisabeth Schüssler Fiorenza, who says that we have to treat the Scriptures with suspicion and always look behind the texts which have redacted out women's stories in order to find out where the women were and what they were doing.

The fundamental uniting asset in feminist method is the belief in taking women's experience seriously. This has enabled women to value themselves and their own experiences as normative in a world that reacts in exactly the opposite way. Women are bringing to light a new reality through their eyes. This, of course, carries with it fundamental questioning of the notion of authority. Authority no longer lies outside but is found in lived experience; it cannot be imposed. Women have spent so many centuries being dictated to by outside agencies that we may feel that it is impossible to come to the stage at which we can act on our own experience and instincts. It will not be easy but that does not mean that it is impossible.

Networking is important in feminist method because it is one safeguard against the whole process becoming self-indulgent. Through networks we are reminded of the concerns and actions of others in such a way that we will not cause damage to the realities of others by the limits of our own insights. There are as many types of networking as there are people involved in it, but each helps to root theology in the here-and-now experience of women. Networks therefore provide the material from which and with which theology will be created by women together.

For some feminist theologians, such as Mary Daly and Daphne Hampson, this networking and using our experience now overrides a desire to reclaim our Christian heritage. They declare that it is too patriarchal to be redeemed. Women have been totally erased from the pages of Christian history and nothing justifies the effort of reclaiming them. For Daly there is no point in concerning oneself with that kind of careful and painstaking historiographical recovery. We simply have to build a new community here from scratch. Others, such as Schüssler Fiorenza, are not willing to abandon what they see as a potential source of power for women. Schüssler Fiorenza views our religious history as our property and not something we should relinquish easily. To do so would be to award a victory to the oppressors (Schüssler Fiorenza 1983: xix).

Some scholars think that as women our best approach is to seek other sources for our spirituality, such as Goddess history. However, Schüssler Fiorenza believes that we have to consider the sources we have in a different light. This means that we must employ a different method, one that allows for the content of the Scripture to be extricated from its patriarchal casing. Each text has to be tested for its liberating potential for women in both the historical and contemporary contexts. Of course, such an approach means that the Scriptures are no longer viewed as revealed and final but rather as tools to open up the present reality of the divine by reflecting on some past events. According to Schüssler Fiorenza the Bible is only one aspect of creating theology, but it is not one that she is willing to abandon entirely. She shows in *In Memory of Her* (1983) that if we look at texts with women and the issues of women in mind we will be surprised at what we can find.

Schüssler Fiorenza has four basic hermeneutical approaches to Scripture. The first is suspicion, which means that the androcentrism of a text is assumed; proclamation examines how the text can be used today; remembrance attempts to find where the women are and what they are doing; creative actualization allows women to enter the text through imagination and to create greater wholes from the fragments that are available. Schüssler Fiorenza decides on the appropriateness of a method by asking if it relates to the struggle of the oppressed.

Rosemary Ruether declares that the important requirement of any methodology is that it promote the full humanity of women (1983). She acknowledges that any methodology will be limited, since we can only do theology from our own context and we cannot claim that context for everyone. Ruether's own context is Western, Christian and middle class. It is from this context that her method will arise, and this will shape the questions she asks. However, Ruether speaks of an eclectic approach, meaning that one can use other sources to promote the full humanity of women. This means that feminist theology takes place between traditions and does not feel bound by traditional Christian limits. Ruether focuses on even those trends seen as heretical in order to find more positive pictures for women. She is not suggesting, however, that all the problems will be solved if traditional thought is replaced by the non-traditional kind.

Ruether bases her understanding of the Bible on the prophetic-messianic core. Where it reflects this kind of liberation, it is authoritative for feminist theology, otherwise it is not. This means that the side of the marginalized and oppressed is taken, and corruption in systems, whether religious or secular, is exposed and criticized. The liberative authority of theological and biblical claims means that their universality has to be questioned; universality is rarely (if ever) liberating, since the experiences of our lives differ so dramatically. Because the experiences of women, half of humanity, have been excluded from theology for so long, it is hard to realize that women's views are not expressed in the Scriptures, and thus that these texts do not stand up to their claim of expressing universal experiences. We need a yardstick for assessing them, and the promotion of the full humanity of women is the one that Ruether uses.

There are a number of feminist methodologies but all value the experience of women. We must realize that this can never give a uniform view, since we are all very different and experience the world in a variety of ways. The strength of feminism is that it is willing to live with that tension and indeed to find joy in the diversity. One could create very much tidier theology if one were willing to overlook the experience and reality of large numbers of people, but this would be methodolatry of the worst kind.

Further reading: Daly 1986; Hunt 1991; Ruether 1983; Schüssler Fiorenza 1983; Young 1990.

MILITARISM
Dorothea McEwan

MILITARISM IS the phenomenon of overemphasis on the military in society because of accelerated increase of military technology, defence systems, wars, technological industrial complexes and international systems of weapons research. It is the one-directional approach to solving problems, the comprehensive management of violence in the name of society. The belief in strength to defend one's nation and its values becomes the leading ideology so much so that militarism becomes the sole, overriding principle of ordering the affairs of society, enhancing conformity, ideological conservatism, moral authoritarianism, egotism. The military mind seems determined to contribute to a wide variety of social conflicts in a relatively destructive manner. As a development in which 'military perceptions of value and behaviour start to dissolve civilian attitudes and their bases in society' (von Bredow 1983: 9), militarism has shown itself as the root cause of many decisions with devastating effects. Militarism is a costly obsession, claiming that everything can be subsumed under the overriding need of the state or group to defend itself. 'It would be nice, if hospitals and schools had all the money they needed and the army had to hold jumble sales to buy guns', a message seen on a T-shirt, or the old 'guns vs butter' slogan show that people no longer believe that everything has to be sacrificed to service the danger of war.

Sexism and militarism are two phenomena linked irrevocably to each other like the two

An A to Z of Feminist Theology

sides of a coin, bonded by the will to dominate, the conviction of superiority and licence of recklessness towards the victim. Through the use of violence and victimization the two are related. The growing militarization of civil society blurs the borders between the military and the civilian spheres, but not between the private and the public spheres. On the contrary, it exaggerates beliefs in safety in the private sphere and danger in the public sphere. Whereas sexism tries to eliminate women, bar them and generally keep them in their 'place' and 'role', militarism tries to eliminate the 'enemies', control their movements, manpower, material resources. In justification of this one-dimensional, excluding approach we are confronted with some very unpleasant fantasies, which prove deep-seated because we have a system to contend with as well as individual assumptions, we labour under the double burden of group and individual prejudice. Our shared humanity and shared creation are overlooked, filtered out of the militaristic consciousness. Inclusiveness, equality in relationships and interactions become blocked, and exclusiveness, inequality and domination in relationships become the norm. Not justice, but retribution, not understanding, but vengeance dictate relationships.

Militarism draws on patriarchal authority, an assumption of leadership, conferred upon or arrogated, demands 'loyalty that arrests the evolution of individual consciousness and offers instead the ecstatic fulfilments of blind sectarian passion' (Naipaul 1986: 46). Institutional churches equally draw on patriarchal authority, based not so much on 'might is right', but on unquestioned obedience to the officeholders. When gods are interpreted, however, as 'tribal possessions', as strong leaders, even going into battle, meting out punishment and anger and fear, violence can easily be seen as necessary, can even assume redemptive qualities. In contradistinction, the Christian concept of God's equal love of everybody is a difficult concept, because it essentially means that the Christian God loves everybody, does not belong to one tribe exclusively or to one sex exclusively. It is true to say that in the history of Christianity this inclusivity has not always been pursued.

In World War One women were told that 'shells and machine guns are the principal munitions of the present war, but infants are the munitions of the future peace' (Emmeline Pethick-Lawrence; cited in Marshall 1987: 32). The concept behind this conviction and urging was that wars could be won (that is, conventional wars). The sophistication of modern weapons systems, however, based on computer reactions and interactions, the phenomenal increase on spending in the military research field, personnel and resources at the ready, and all the other modern manifestations of the machinery of war are based on the fantastic assumption that even nuclear wars can be won. Christians, looking at the Gospels to find the way to peace, cannot derive 'even indirect criteria which will lead to a consensus of opinion...concerning the concrete strategic details of the (necessary) steps that should be taken in the direction of unilateral disarmament' (Schillebeeckx 1985: 11).

This massive build-up of obsession is only possible by lies and demagoguery. The pronouncements of the military are couched in doublespeak, a codified and mystical language, anaesthetizing the public by using seemingly reasonable concepts and harmless phrases such as 'multiple overfulfillment of target', or 'We had to destroy the village in order to save it', a well-known military argument when the cure is to kill.

The old idea that war is an extension of politics by other means is no longer valid. A mindset which fosters a culture of violence thrives on the distinction between the 'strong' and the 'weak', the 'desirable' and the 'undesirable'. It filters out the common strand of humanity and reverts back to operate a dualism of values. Feminist theologies argue for an end to such practices, not only because they diminish the worth of the individual, but because they also threaten the survival of the planet.

Further reading: Sölle 1984.

MINISTRY: A HISTORICAL SURVEY
Janet Wootton

IT IS clear that women exercised a kind of ministry in the early churches. Some of the evidence has been suppressed by textual amend-

An A to Z of Feminist Theology

MINISTRY

ment, translation and interpretation.

No scriptural models of women's leadership survived into the Middle Ages. In effect, the only models offered to women were Eve and Mary: the impossible example of the virgin mother or the origin of evil and of temptation for men. Besides this, neo-Platonism taught that women represented the emotional side of the human character, which needed to be ruled by the masculine character of reason, and that women are inherently unreasonable and emotional.

Within the Catholic and Orthodox traditions, women could find a vocation in the celibate life of the religious community. Hildegard of Bingen and Julian of Norwich exercised great influence in their day.

Sects appeared throughout pre-Reformation Europe, denying the institutional hierarchy of the church, in many of which women were permitted leadership roles, a fact which above all others condemned such movements in the eyes of the ruling church.

The Reformed churches once again allowed clergy to marry. The theological understanding of the position of women changed. No longer was the celibate life regarded as perfection for men or for women. Women as well as men were educated, and many women used their position of power within the household to support Lutheran and Calvinist groups.

Despite the exploration of the role of deacon or deaconess, as a ministry of service, but without authority, for women, there was little opportunity for the formal recognition of their role in church life in the mainstream churches of the Reformation.

Within radical Protestantism, with the emphasis on freedom of conscience under the direction of the Holy Spirit, on the priesthood of all believers, and the shared authority of the local congregation, there was clearly more room theologically and ecclesiologically for women to exercise ministry.

In public worship, women were generally allowed to prophesy, but not to preach. However, it is clear that women in this tradition did exercise a preaching ministry, and often gained great acclaim. More often, women formed single sex groups, it being thought more proper for women to speak if there were no men under their ministry.

In one radical grouping only, women were given full equality with men in the exercise of their ministry. The Quakers did not ordain individuals to the ministry, but recognized the ministry of certain gifted people. Women were recognized alongside men as preachers and leaders of meetings for business and worship. Separate women's meetings were formed in 1672 and 1681. George Fox himself defended the right of women to full participation, and one of his first converts, Elizabeth Hooten, was a preacher, and a missionary to the West Indies and to America.

The late eighteenth century and the nineteenth century saw an awakening of spiritual experience, the revival of early dissenting denominations, and the formation of new ones. Here again, as rigid patterns of institution were swept away, women gained greater freedom to participate in leadership. Wesley appointed women as class leaders, and encouraged them to lead in prayer, and give their testimony. Further, he gave approval to Sarah Mallet, Mary Fletcher and other women for 'biblical exegesis and application'—in other words, public preaching. However, his first ministers in congregations were all men. In the other evangelical groups, women played a major part. The Free Will Baptists in New Hampshire had women evangelists and preachers as early as 1791.

Women were in the forefront of a growing movement for social reform, writing and even speaking in support. In the United States, Sarah and Angelina Grimké addressed 'promiscuous' (that is, mixed) audiences, and Lucretia Mott, a Quaker leader, with Elizabeth Cady Stanton asked to be received and seated with the male delegates to the World Anti-Slavery Convention in London. Instead, they were seated in a screened, separate section of the hall, and could listen, but take no part in the proceedings.

These two, with others, formed an organized movement for women's rights in New York in 1848, and, much later, in the 1880s, the Seneca Falls convention began to question the traditional interpretations of Scripture. *The Women's Bible* was published from 1895 to 1898.

In the growing evangelical movement, women

were active in education and mission. Women's missionary societies were formed, either independent of or as auxiliaries to the main societies. As well as missionary wives, single women began to enter missionary service, preaching and teaching, and exercising gifts and leadership which they were prevented from exercising at home.

As women worked alongside men in the field, attitudes to the skill and propriety of women's leadership began to change, and during the late nineteenth century, many denominations were raising the question of women's ordination to the ministry, and the opening of theological colleges to women.

The evangelist Charles Finney allowed women to witness and to pray before mixed groups. He was later the president of Oberlin College, the first in the United States to admit women, and from which came Antoinette Brown, the first woman to be ordained to the ministry of the congregational churches.

Within the Holiness movement, which, again, emphasized the power and authority bestowed by the Holy Spirit, women preachers were a major force. Phoebe Palmer travelled through the States, and to Great Britain and Canada as an evangelist and preacher. It was under her ministry that Catherine Booth and Frances Willard received their calling.

Frances Willard travelled with Dwight Moody, and was a preacher on social reform. She wrote supporting the ministry of women, and objected to the use of 'men' and 'brethren' as supposedly inclusive terms.

Catherine Booth was an outstanding revivalist preacher. Both she and her husband William were firm believers in equality for women in all spheres. Their own marriage was based on this principle, and the movement which they founded, the Salvation Army, has offered equal opportunities for women and men in every sphere of service from the beginning. Like Frances Willard, Catherine wrote in support of female ministry.

Also influenced by Phoebe Palmer was Amanda Berry Smith, a black washerwomen who became an effective and prominent Holiness preacher. Many of the Black Majority Churches have traditionally been open to the ministry of women preachers and leaders. Both the Church of the Nazarene and the Pilgrim Holiness Church guaranteed the right of women to preach, the former in its constitution of 1894.

By the turn of the century the question of women's full participation in ministry, including ordination in those churches which practised ordination, had been raised in most of the Free Churches. In the USA, the Wesleyan Methodists were ordaining women in the 1860s. A Women's Ministerial Conference was set up in 1882 as a network of support. By 1900 there were 40 ordained women in the American congregational churches, and by 1927 there were about 100.

In Britain, the Unitarian College in Manchester allowed women to attend lectures as early as 1875–76. Gertrude Von Petzold became the first woman to graduate from Manchester College, finishing as one of four students, the other three, of course, male. Though she had been 'told on all sides that there would be no prospect of finding a pulpit', she did receive a call to the Leicester Free Christian Church, where she ministered for just under two years before being removed by a vote of no confidence, due to her controversial style.

In 1909, a meeting of the General Purposes Committee of the Congregational Union recommended that women should be accepted for ordination if they completed the appropriate college training and received a valid call. At the same time, Maud Royden, an Anglican and member of the Council of Temple's Life and Liberty movement, was called to the pastoral ministry at the City Temple. This caused a furore in the Anglican Church, and she was forced to resign from the Council. The Bristol Baptist College agreed to admit women in 1918–19, though none were in fact admitted for many years.

Very few women trained during the period between the wars. The colleges were ambivalent about accepting women, and either ceased accepting for periods during this time, or, as Mansfield and New College did, refused them any financial support from endowments, on the grounds that the Trust Deeds referred to young men. Once trained, women often found it difficult to gain acceptance by congregations.

The Methodist Church in England and Wales voted to accept the ordination of women in

1972 and the Church of England made the historic decision on November 11th 1992, with the first priests being ordained in 1994. Other sections of the Anglican communion had ordained women much earlier. Florence Li Tim-Oi was made deacon in 1941, and was given charge of the Anglican congregation in the Portuguese colony of Macao. When a priest could no longer travel from Japanese-occupied territory to preside for her at the eucharist, the Bishop of Hong Kong asked her to meet him in Free China, where on January 25th 1944 he ordained her 'a priest in the Church of God'.

The Roman Catholic and Orthodox Churches do not currently ordain women, and many fundamentalist groups will not allow women to teach or preach or allow them positions of authority. A fundamentalist backlash in some churches is depriving women of advances already made.

The Society for the Ministry of Women in the Church and the International Association of Women Ministers are ecumenical societies for the support of women in ministry, and for the cause of women's ordination.

Further reading: Booth 1870; Edwards 1989; Herzel 1981; MacHaffie 1986; Russell 1974; Williams 1993.

MISOGYNY
Mary Ann Rossi

THE MISOGYNY, or hatred of women, that provokes and perpetuates the slaughter of millions of women yearly throughout the world is reviled by all thinking people. More subtle is the underlying assumption of women's inferiority to men; this assumption is the foundation of Christian doctrine on women. Although women were present and indeed were leaders among the disciples, apostles and ordained priests of the early Christian communities, they were gradually excluded from leadership by four canons in the fifth century CE (Raming 1976). Later the wives of priests and bishops were imprisoned in order to execute the new mandate of celibacy (Ranke-Heinemann 1990). In the seventh century the Council of Trullo passed more stringent canons that prohibited women even from responding to prayers or singing in church. They were also prohibited from celebrating the birth of their children (on the ground that Mary did not have a normal delivery). Instead new mothers were to be 'churched' or cleansed of the sullying of childbirth; until this purification was performed, the woman could not enter the church, even to attend her own child's baptism.

The most damaging and pervasive myth for women is the creation myth, the source of misogyny. This Christian story with its false moral message has hurt women inestimably. We must realize how far our internalization of God as male in the West has undermined our sense of women as also in the image of God. Our religion is our vision of the world, but if our vision is obscured by unethical realities, such as the abuse and assault of women, we must regroup in order to recover the central message of the early church: the egalitarian vision of women and men imaging God equally and working mutually for the improvement of our laws and our lives.

The Vatican in 1994 reconfirmed its refusal to ordain women priests in *Ordinatio Sacerdotalis*; this papal letter, aimed at the control and elimination of women from decision-making bodies of the church, is then called a matter which is not debatable. The misogyny of the Vatican is thus made ever more visible.

The deep-seated misogyny of the church has coloured the historiography of Christianity. The evidence of women leaders of early Christian communities has gradually been removed, omitted or obliterated. One example is the inscription of Leta the Priest, clearly referring to a woman ordained to Holy Orders and dedicated by her husband (*maritus*); the usual reading of *presbytera* in this inscription is 'wife of the priest', since this is the 'convention' used by the church historians to conform with their mindset that women were never priests (Otranto 1982). Other evidence is dismissed as coming from 'heretical communities', even when the community in question, such as Leta's Tropea, was in close communion with Rome.

The misogyny of the Church Fathers (such as Tertullian, who said of woman, 'You are the Devil's gateway') is again reflected in British church architecture of the twelfth century (Weir and Jerman 1986). The tradition of 'sheela-nagig' carvings of a woman exhibitionist was misused in an effort to vilify woman, the cause of the Fall of Man. Influential theologians (such as Aquinas and Gratian) conveyed the theme that woman is unclean, and whoever touches her is defiled. The works of such theologians, with their unbelievable misogyny, were the constant study of monks.

The most insidious inculcation of misogyny is Rome's holding up of models of women that mirror misogynistic teachings of the church. For example, the canonization of Maria Goretti, the young girl who died of wounds incurred while she was resisting rape, glorifies the victim for forgiving her murderer, who remained unrepentant. Now the Supreme Court of Pennsylvania has ruled that unless a woman shows physical signs of force, she has not been raped. According to this ruling, unless a woman endangers her life, she has not been assaulted. Misogyny in the law mirrors the misogyny of the church.

On April 24, 1994, the Vatican solemnly declared two women to be saints because they were 'models of Christian perfection'. Both were women who endured violence. Dr Gianna Beretta Molla, a twentieth-century pediatrician from Rome, had chosen not to have an abortion in a dangerous pregnancy. Had she done so to save her own life she would probably have been excommunicated by her church after a medical investigation to establish the severity of her disease. Because she did not have the abortion, she died at childbirth and left eight children motherless. The other woman lived more than a century earlier. Elisabetta Canori Mora of Italy had chosen to stay in an abusive marriage and was killed by her husband. These women's suffering was quoted by Pope John Paul II as reason for their elevation to the sainthood, 'to pay homage to all those courageous mothers who devote themselves unreservedly to their families and who suffer to bring their children into the world'. It is the mindset of the 'good Christian woman' to endure and suffer in silence, and her role model is St Augustine's mother Monica, who advised women who were battered (as she herself was) to endure in silence. The message of the Catholic church through two thousand years has been: women do not count; they are expendable; they must keep silence. The end of women's silence has marked the beginning of our road to full humanity and full personhood in the renewed church of our daughters and granddaughters.

Further reading: Daly 1978; Pagels 1988; Kissling 1994; *National Catholic Reporter* 1991.

MODELS OF GOD
Melissa Raphael

ALTHOUGH FEMINIST theology is an enthusiastic advocate of dance, sculpture and painting as properly theological media, words remain the central medium in which to communicate about God. But, like art, verbal images are historical, creative acts of the imagination: 'God' as a proper name refers to a personality whose character has been negotiated and contested over time. The concept of God is, then, in the permanent flux of its dialectical relationship with the history of culture.

Feminist theology is not alone in its recognition that concepts or models of God are historically relative, but few have coupled this idea with so comprehensive and radical a critique. Feminist theology argues that these models reflected injustice from the outset, and have, in their obsolescence, not merely ceased to inspire faith but have actually corroded it. Any wordpicture of God which is modelled on social structures of domination and then held up as a literal description of God is utterly rejected by Christian and Jewish feminism. Models of God as King, Lord and Father, as head of the patriarchal family, sanctify brutality: the triumphal imperialism that permits the exploitation of human labour and nature, and underpins escapist delusions that humanity will survive any protest an exhausted and poisoned nature might make. Christian and Jewish feminists prophetically resist such models of God:

> Such imaging of God should be juged for what it is—as idolatry, as the setting up of certain human figures as the privileged images and representations of God. To the extent that such political and ecclesiastical patriarchy incarnates unjust and oppressive relationships, such images of God become sanctions of evil (Ruether 1983: 66).

It is no longer controversial—in liberal theological circles at least—to say that men have projected their own image onto God. But in its vig-

MODELS OF GOD

orous prophetic engagement with culture feminist theology recognizes that such a projection (and its deconstruction) is a political as well as a religious act. After all, the power of naming is more than an opportunity for self-expression; it is the principal instrument by which to transform or re-create reality. Exclusively male models of God have sustained a political order which has deliberately alienated women from the powers of their own woman-being, silenced their witness, and excluded them from the workings of the salvific economy. Women have been hurt, in every sense of that word, by their exclusion from the process and product of theological imagining,

To some extent the mass media of the late twentieth century have already demystified and discredited many authority figures—particularly those of the royal family. Demystification has arisen in part from postmodern awareness of the construction of ideas by the ideological interests of the elite. The subsequent democratization of language has led to celebration of difference and plurality. The ascription of feudal power to God would now appear quaint were it not still put to such intimidating uses. But outside fundamentalism, the postmodern deconstruction of the white, male, imperialist worldview has helped to each woman to speak, in Rebecca Chopp's words, 'her self, her desires, her time and space, her hopes, her God'. The patriarchal centre is, she says, 'cracking, its fissures are widening, and in those fissures and cracks, discourses of emancipatory transformation may be formed' (Chopp 1989: 16).

Furthermore, ecological consciousness has provided new imaginative and practical opportunities for developing cooperative, organic models of God that can speak to the political and scientific, as well as religious, communities of the present age. Creation spirituality, ethics, some branches of science, and feminism have come together to affirm the connectedness of all things in the cosmos. Our models of God are not relevant in any of these respects if they are not open-ended: reflecting the holistic paradigm shift which understands how the life of creation is in its interdependent relationships, not in mechanistic, immutable laws. For these reasons, process models of God have often recommended themselves to feminist appropriation.

As a largely metaphorical endeavour, feminist theology shares with negative theology the insistence that, as Sallie McFague has put it, 'theology is mostly fiction' (1987): the elaboration of concepts from metaphors whose very nature proposes an 'is not' with the 'is' and which deny any identity with the essentially ineffable object of their assertions. This does not mean that metaphors are picked according to aesthetic preference. Some models are morally and spiritually preferable representations of the Christian gospel to a particular age. However, patriarchy has a vested interest in forgetting that its words about God are made from a number of metaphors. Consequently there is little that enrages conservative churchmen and churchwomen as much as the proposal and use of feminist models of God. In trying to understand the vilification of projects like *Women Included: A Book of Services and Prayers* (1991) one must ask what interests are threatened by inclusive language—let alone by the remodelling of our concepts of God.

If language is a means to political power, then patriarchy will guard it jealously. But when feminism makes language provisional it also makes power provisional. So its attempts to change language will be met with extreme hostility, often sublimated as derision. The revolutionary implications posed by feminist models of God cannot be overstated by their critics or their proponents. If God is not the omniscient, omnipotent ruler of his universe men cannot, as regents of the God-king, derive, absolutize and sanctify their own power structures from the hierarchies of the celestial sphere. Hence Mary Daly's only slightly overstated syllogism: 'If God is male, then the male is God'. If God's relation to the world can be modelled convincingly on, say, friendship, then patriarchal power structures are shown to be what they are: the arrogations and distortions of divine power to secure profit of many kinds from the exploitation of women, subject men, and nature. Patriarchy is also compelled to accept its own responsibility for history if the world is not and has not been under the command of an omnipotent divine will.

There is more at issue, then, than whether some feminist models of God are unbiblical (God is never referred to as 'Mother' in the Bible). Feminist models of God are routinely (and deliberately?) misrepresented. Few, if any, Christian feminists would want to say that God is a woman any more than God is a man. Female God-imagery is regarded by patriarchal theology as a pagan revival of the ancient mother goddesses that Judaism and Christianity have gone to great lengths to eradicate. But the fear of mother-models of God covers a misogyny which finds images of female embodiment and fertility offensive. This cannot be justified. Nor can the use of symbols which secure the rule of a male, transcendent deity over the subjugated, exploited 'female' earth.

However, critics might reasonably question whether simply believing that God-talk should be inclusive is a specifically *Christian* warrant for change. And there are fears that feminist models of God have circumvented the Christian history of revelation and proclamation to such a degree that they have crossed the line beyond which theology ceases to be Christian. Daphne Hampson, for example, while a feminist and sympathetic to McFague's work, suspects that it proposes a different (humanistic) religion (1990: 160). But this is a philosophical problem of definition not confined to feminist reformulations. In any case, feminist theology does not intend the literal application of any of its images of God, but borrows spiritually nourishing images and transforms their meaning and intention by setting them in a Christian context. In fact, feminist God-talk can represent heresy at its best: that is, as the challenge of the new that rouses the church and mainstream theology from its dogmatic slumbers.

Once feminist consciousness has been raised, services which use exclusively male images of God grate on the ears. Often women silently, or under their breath, fill in 'she' when they are supposed to say 'he'. There are many defiant women for whom calling God 'she' or 'Mother' instead of 'Father' is sufficient to change the quality of their worship and to vastly increase their self-esteem. It is also a courageous act, since women who do this can become very isolated in their communities.

Ultimately, however, feminist theology wants a more thoroughgoing conceptual and spiritual revolution than the substitution of one pronoun for another. Since feminist theology is more than a corrective to mainstream theology it seems important to avoid dressing the patriarchal God in a skirt. This would merely temper his aggressive excesses with the virtues of infinite kindness and patience that have characterized sentimental ideologies of femininity, defusing women's anger at injustice and rewarding their submission. As Mary Daly wrote in *Beyond God the Father* (1986), making God merely transsexual 'would be a trivialization of the deep problem of human becoming in women' (1986: 19). Of course, motherhood is and will remain an immensely rich resource for feminist theology. Female modes of being and doing must indeed be taken into the sphere of the holy as microcosmic of divine life. But feminist theology is also cautious of infantilizing humankind by an over-reliance on parental models of God, and of inadvertently projecting stereotypical images of femininity onto God.

The feminist academy has done much to retrieve the female components of patriarchal models of God. For example it has been pointed out that many of the words naming functions of the Hebrew God are of feminine gender: *Torah* (teaching), *hochmah* (wisdom), *shechinah* (presence), *rua'* (spirit) are some important instances. Similarly, it is important to know that biblical imagery for God is sometimes feminine; for example, Isaiah compares God to a woman in labour, and Jesus compares himself to a mother hen comforting Jerusalem like chicks under her wing. The (often heterodox) mystical traditions have also used feminine imagery: Julian of Norwich referred to God as mother as well as father, and to Jesus as mother, brother and saviour. But, again, not all feminists are willing to settle for a God with merely feminine *aspects*; with secondary characteristics that qualify but do not transform the patriarchal concept of God, nor develop our understanding of what it is to be a woman. Feminist theology may want to be more radical—that is, treating the roots of the patriarchal model of God rather than its branches. Such accommodations of femininity into the patriarchal model of God also mirror a long history of the assimilation of female sacral power into the power functions of the masculine God and of the repression and abuse of those sacral functions of womanhood that could not be customized by patriarchy.

MODELS OF GOD - MOTHERHOOD OF GOD

Women speak about God from the margins; from their experience of oppression (though when feminist theologians speak from the academy they are also speaking from the centre). While accepting that the biblical models of God reflect the patriarchal environment in which the Bible was written, Christian feminists like Rosemary Ruether can still find images there and elsewhere showing that God is the one who does not validate oppression but liberates us from it; images which can point us 'back to our authentic potential and forward to new redeemed possibilities'. In sustaining the unity of political-material reality with our spiritual personhood, God can be named as 'the *Shalom* of our being' (Ruether 1983: 69-70).

In sum, feminist theology wants to celebrate an inclusive multiplicity of images of God, including male images that are not predicated upon domination and those which make no reference to gender at all. In *Models of God: Theology for an Ecological, Nuclear Age* (1987), Sallie McFague supplements her model of God as mother with that of lover and friend—images which suggest human maturity, erotic pleasure and mutual responsibility. These models show how God can relate to the world as a personal agent but in a mode of non-hierarchical love. The intimate sense of God's presence suggests to McFague that the world can be imagined sacramentally as God's body. Here the immanent God is not pantheistically identical with the world but also transcends it, just as our consciousness transcends our bodies.

Feminist reconstructions of God are not easily reached. All of us have been intellectually and emotionally shaped and damaged by the patriarchal mindset. Many would identify with Celie's remark in Alice Walker's *The Color Purple* (1983): 'Us talk and talk bout God, but I'm still adrift. Trying to chase that old white man out of my head.' It may be that God is still awaiting woman-speech. As Rosemary Ruether suggests, 'we have no adequate name for the true God/ess, the "I am who I shall become". Intimations of Her / His name will appear as we emerge from false naming of God/ess modelled on patriarchal alienation' (1983: 71). If, as Catherine of Siena is reputed to have said, 'My real me is God', then feminist renaming of God must come not only from the academy but also from those numerous places where women are engaged in the struggles and joys of becoming.

MOTHERHOOD OF GOD
Noragh Jones

IN THE Old Testament mothering imagery is used to describe divine mercy and empowering compassion, and provides a vital balance to the fathering imagery of God as king, judge and patriarchal Lord. The main use of female images for God is in the Psalms and the prophetic literature, where it is used to express the relationship between God and his chosen people. When the people have turned away from him God says to them, 'Can a woman forget her sucking child, that she should not have compassion on the son of her womb? Yea, they may forget, but I will not forget thee' (Isa. 49.15). Israel's experience is unfolded in recurring images as a relationship with a maternal God who 'conceives and brings the people to birth, suckles and feeds them, comforts them as a mother, and provides clothes to cover their nakedness' (McFague 1987: 169). There has been reluctance among traditional male theologians to acknowledge female body imagery for the divine (Caird's *The Language and Imagery of the Bible* omits womb and breasts while including other body parts), but feminist theologians are working to rectify this imbalance. Phyllis Trible provides a profound commentary on the womb as a metaphor for God's compassion and his nurturance of the human being to full maturity:

> God conceives in the womb, God fashions in the womb; God judges in the womb; and God carries from the womb to gray hairs. From this uterine perspective then Yahweh molds life for individuals and for the nation Israel. Accordingly in biblical traditions an organ unique to the female becomes a vehicle pointing to the compassion of God (Trible 1978: 38).

In addition to the direct use of maternal imagery in the Old Testament, the Wisdom tradition brings maternal attributes to the divine. Wisdom is portrayed as the presence of God on earth, permeating all things with the spirit of God. Solomon takes Wisdom for his bride, but she also appears to have maternal attributes of an active and teaching kind, and to be mother in the sense of taking part in the original creation, coeval with God the Father (Prov. 8.23-26). In the New Testament the Wisdom or Sophia tradition surfaces again in the Logos, but now male symbolism is dominant in the figure of Jesus as God's presence on earth. Jesus is our teacher and saviour, revealer and reconciler of God to humanity, as Mother Wisdom had been in the Old Testament. Yet the early Church Fathers retained the Wisdom element in Jesus, and acknowledged the androgyny of Jesus as Wisdom by depicting him with maternal breasts flowing with the milk of Wisdom to give succour to human souls. Clement of Alexandria says that Christ 'is called Wisdom by the prophets…the teacher of all created things, the fellow counsellor of God who foreknows all things; and he who trains and perfects' (see Engelsman 1987: 143). But the Wisdom tradition in Christology was repressed when the Arian controversy was settled by rejecting the identification of Christ with Wisdom, and by turning down the hypostatic status of Wisdom in the Trinity and reassigning her attributes to God the Father.

The early Fathers also acknowledged the female in the divine (in spite of their condemnation of earthly females as the wicked daughters of Eve and the devil's gateway) by conceiving of the Holy Spirit as female, as the Womb of God (Clement of Alexandria) or as Mother, the eternal feminine in God (St Efrem).

A continuous if fragile tradition of imaging God as Mother threads its way through the Middle Ages, from its beginnings with the Alexandrine fathers, through the Cistercian revival of affectivity and a feminine/passive spirituality in the twelfth century, to the later medieval writers of spiritual treatises such as Richard Rolle, Mechtild von Hackeborn and the author of the Ancren Riwle. It culminates in the writings of Julian of Norwich, the anchorite of Norwich who received her divine revelations in May 1373 and spent many years working out her theology of Christ our Mother. But it should be remembered that imaging God as Mother was a popular devotion for the laity as well as a matter of theological meditation in the late Middle Ages, as surviving homilies and sermons indicate (see Colledge and Walsh [eds.] 1978: 151).

Julian's mothering imagery for the divine is threefold. Christ is Mother because he bears us to our spiritual birth. He is mother because he is present at our original creation. And thirdly it is through his Motherhood of Working that he persuades and guides us to our spiritual birth. Julian follows a long line of medieval theologians in seeing Christ as the Mother who labours to bring us to our spiritual birth. Anselm, in his *Oratio* 65, calls Christ's sufferings on the cross the labour pangs of our second birth in him as Mother; Richard Rolle sees Christ carrying us in his womb until we are born again spiritually; and the Carthusian prioress Marguerite of Oingt speaks of Christ as the Mother who laboured for more than thirty years and suffered the worst birth pangs of all on the hard bed of the cross to give birth to the whole world.

Julian's motherhood of redemption is a powerful reinstatement of the maternal in the divine, and gives us a different model of mothering from the usual one offered by the churches to women, where mothering is seen as private women's work, confined to the domestic situation, and self-sacrificing without empowerment. Julian's imagery of Christ our Mother suggests another kind of mothering model, which is more mature, creative and salvific. Christ's mothering is the ultimate creativity which unites our fragmented selves into wholeness. His Motherhood of Working involves directing our ways towards maturity while giving us space to make our own mistakes and learn in our own ways, to fall and yet have the loving protective attention of Christ our Mother always with us, ready to lift us up again when we are ready. The Revelations are significant in their exposition of Christ's divine mothering, and in the consequent revaluing of human everyday mothering which, however imperfect, reflects the divine mothering:

> To the property of motherhood belong nature, wisdom and knowledge, and this is God. For though it may be that our bodily bringing to birth is only little, humble and simple compared with our spiritual bringing to birth, still it is He Christ our Mother who does it in the creatures by whom it is done (Colledge and Walsh [eds.] 1978: ch. 60).

The suppression of Mother imagery for God in the post-medieval Christian tradition means that many twentieth-century Christians find the old imagery new and shocking, and resist Christian feminist efforts to include female images for God in liturgies and prayers. The excellent report on the Motherhood of God produced by the Church of Scotland Women's Guild in 1984 reminds us of this neglected 'theological and devotional inheritance from the Christian past', and points to the need for 'Christian women and men to understand and speak of God in ways which reflect more fully the female experience of life along with the male' (Church of Scotland Women's Guild 1984).

Reinstating motherhood in the divine image involves more than using inclusive language and revaluing mothering as a metaphor for creativity and nurturing care. Ecological feminist theologians emphasize the need to extend mothering to include our planet as well as the people who live on it, and socialist feminist theologians stress women's role in reforming the public world rather than being satisfied with private nurturing. New paths are opening up for women to extend their mothering work from private personal nurturing to include public ecological nurturing:

> We must become the gardeners and caretakers of our Eden, our beautiful, bountiful garden, not taming it and ruling it, let alone despoiling it...willing the existence of all species, and as a good housekeeper ordering the just distribution of the necessities of existence (McFague 1987: 120).

MOVEMENT FOR THE ORDINATION OF WOMEN
Caroline Davis

THE MOVEMENT for the Ordination of Women came into being on July 4th 1979 as a direct result of the General Synod of the Church of England refusing to remove the legal barriers to women's ordination in November 1978.

In 1978 a public declaration had been organized by Christian Action, signed by 100 prominent lay women and men, giving their support, which had been published before the Synod meeting. But the House of Clergy failed to pass the motion and it fell. So in 1979 a mixed group of people gathered to work out what to do next. They were women and men, lay and ordained; some had been campaigning for years, others were only just beginning. Christian Action provided an office and Margaret Webster, who lived very near, agreed to come in and out to see what was going on. Very soon it became obvious that this was inadequate and a proper office was offered at St Stephen's, Rochester Row church offices, which is where MOW remained.

There had been other organizations: the League for the Church Militant in the 1920s, the interdenominational Society for the Ministry of Women in the Church (one of the founders in 1929 being Maude Royden), the Anglican Group for the Ordination of Women, founded in 1930 following the statement from the bishops of the Lambeth Conference on the impossibility of women's ordination, Christian Parity and Christian Action working in the 1970s.

Soon groups were forming in every diocese in England. Newcastle had been the first, even before MOW was founded. Public meetings, regional meetings, diocesan meetings were held. A Central Council was formed which had representation on it from all over the country. The first Moderator of MOW was Stanley Booth-Clibborn, then Bishop of Manchester. Following him were Monica Furlong, Diana McClatchey and Cathy Milford. The first Secretary was Margaret Webster and her successors have been Margaret Orr Deas and Caroline Davis.

Right from the beginning MOW saw its work in three strands: prayer, education and witness. Prayer has been an integral part of everything MOW has done. Many dioceses have held vigils of prayer before ordinations, a novena of prayer has been written on two separate occasions before crucial Synod votes, experimental liturgies have been written and used. *Celebrating Women*, edited by Janet Morley and Hannah Ward, was published in 1986, and *All Desires Known*, collects, prayers, psalms and poems, edited by Janet Morley, in 1988. The demand for both books was so great that they had to be reprinted very quickly and were also published in other countries. Juliantide was introduced as a time when dioceses would hold services and meetings, particularly remembering Julian of Norwich.

Large services have been held: in 1984 in Westminster Abbey to celebrate the fortieth anniversary of Li Tim-Oi's priesting; in 1986 in Canterbury Cathedral as the centrepiece of an international weekend conference; in 1991 in Westminster Abbey with a dialogue between Dr Sarah Coakley and Bishop Richard Holloway instead of a sermon; in 1992 in Coventry Cathedral, again with a dialogue, this time between Bishop Rowan Williams and the Revd Cathy Milford, and, finally, in Ripon Cathedral in 1994. The celebrant at that last service of thanksgiving was the Moderator, Cathy Milford, who had been ordained to the priesthood two days before, and the preacher was Bishop Penny Jamieson, Bishop of Dunedin, New Zealand.

Education has gone on constantly. MOW have published many booklets and leaflets, giving the different theological arguments for women's ordination as well as viewpoints from the Free Churches and Roman Catholics. MOW was helped in the later years by an advertising agency, GGK, who gave their creative services for free and helped put out some very professional leaflets and advertisements.

A newsletter was printed right from the beginning and a magazine, *Chrysalis*, was started in 1986 under the editorship of Monica Furlong (and, later, Caroline Davis). Speakers at public meetings would always make sure that there was plenty of written material available for distribution. There was a literature group which planned all the publications and which met regularly.

Public witness was essential. Few members of the general public had started to think about women priests and the issue needed to be brought into the public arena. Prayer cards were handed out at ordinations. 'Irregular' Eucharists were held at which the celebrant would be a woman priest ordained overseas. Demonstrations happened, balloons and rockets were launched, people marched, appeared on television and radio, wrote articles in newspapers and magazines. Vigils were held outside Lambeth Palace; the last one leading up to the final vote lasted for four days and nights. At the Lambeth Conference of 1988, MOW was now allowed space on the university campus (unlike some other organizations), so it set up an exhibition place in the town.

Meanwhile, work had been continuing in the diocese and synods. In 1984, Southwark Diocesan Synod brought a motion to General Synod asking them to bring forward legislation for the ordination of women in the provinces of Canterbury and York. This was passed in all three Houses and so the process began which was to end in 1994. In July 1986, a Measure to allow women lawfully ordained abroad to exercise their priestly ministry in England was defeated in the House of Clergy after the voting rules had been changed at the last minute. This spurred some of the more radical members of MOW into a new initiative which culminated in the establishment of the St Hilda Community in 1987. This was a group which met every Sunday and which, to begin with, existed to offer Eucharistic hospitality to women ordained abroad. It soon became an autonomous group although many of its members were from MOW.

In 1987, women were admitted to Holy Orders as deacons. This had passed through General Synod and the Houses of Parliament the previous year and about 750 deaconesses were ordained deacon at services in every diocese in mainland England. Since then they have served with distinction in every form of ministry open to them and have been a crucial factor in the success of the campaign.

By now the Church of England was gearing itself up for the final haul. The legislation asked for in 1984 was starting to take shape. It was debated, amended and passed. Then, in its final form, it went on to the dioceses. MOW did an immense amount of work, providing speakers and disseminating information to those in the parishes and on the various synods, at deanery and diocesan level. 38 of the 44 dioceses voted in favour of it in both Houses of Clergy and Laity and it came back to General Synod for its final vote in November 1992. There it received the historic two-thirds majority in all three Houses.

MOW (rather like the Church of England) has always been a broad organization of people with widely different views. The membership has ranged from those who want the Church of England to stay the same as it has always been but with women in the ordained priesthood to those who see the ordination of women to the priesthood as nothing short of a complete revolution—and all the shades of opinion between the two. This has led to arguments within MOW over many of the actions taken. There were those who wanted no campaigning, just prayer, and at the other extreme there were those for whom campaigning was the raison d'être and who did not wholly welcome success.

MOW has always been funded by membership subscription. It could never be a charity, because its aims were seen to be 'political' by the Charity Commissioner. The opposition frequently claimed that MOW was funded by rich overseas churches, which was simply not true. The membership remained 95 per cent within England and probably 99 per cent Anglican. Probably MOW's greatest strength was that right from the beginning it was fully inclusive, involving women and men, lay and ordained. Over the years there must have been 12,000 or more people who joined MOW.

The time between November 1992 and the first ordinations in March 1994 was like living in limbo. While campaigning had to go on, for the Houses of Parliament had to pass the Measures in 1993, the attention was given by the press and media to those who could not accept what was happening. MOW was caught in a dilemma. It had achieved its objective—and yet women were still being treated in an abysmal fashion by the church. The Act of Synod was passed in 1993 which institutionalized special provisions for clergy, lay people and parishes opposed to women priests. 'Flying' bishops were appointed to provide pastoral care for these people, seemingly without thought as to what the church was saying about its attitude towards its women clergy.

But, in the end, nothing could take away the utter joy that lived with everyone in MOW from November 11th 1992 onwards. Following the first ordinations of women to the priesthood in Bristol on March 12th 1994, every mainland diocese in England held their own ordinations. The emotions experienced on seeing women, some of whom had been waiting for more than 50 years, ordained priest were indescribable. Some dioceses managed to ordain as many as 60 women in one service, others had to hold two, three, four or even five services. Even then only a token number of wellwishers were able to attend. By July 1994, over 1300 women priests had been ordained in the Church of England. It will never be the same again.

Further reading: Furlong 1991.

MUJERISTA THEOLOGY
Ada María Isasi-Díaz

TO NAME oneself is one of the most powerful acts any human person can perform. A name is not just a word by which one is identified. A name also provides the conceptual framework, the point of reference, the mental constructs that are used in thinking, understanding and relating to a person, an idea, a movement. It is with this in mind that a group of Latina (Hispanic) women who live in the United States of America and who are keenly aware of how sexism, heterosexism, ethnic prejudice and economic oppression subjugate them, started to use the term *mujerista* to refer to themselves and to use '*mujerista* theology' to refer to the explanations of their faith and its role in their struggle for liberation. (Note that we do *not* use the term *mujerismo*, since this could be taken to mean that we see our natural identity as grounded in being women, when in fact our identity as women is grounded in being human. See Rodríguez 1991: 11 n. 6).

A *mujerista* is someone who makes a preferential option for Latina women, for their struggle for liberation (and while the rest of this article refers more directly to *mujerista* Latina women, I intend here to make explicit that Latino men as well as men and women from other racial/ethnic groups can also opt to be *mujeristas*). Because the term *mujerista* was developed by Latina women theologians and pastoral agents the initial understandings of the term were from a religious perspective. At present the term is beginning to be used in other fields such as literature and history. It is also beginning to be used by community organizers working with Latinas at grassroots level. Its meaning, therefore, is being amplified without losing as its core the struggle for liberation of Latina women.

Mujeristas struggle to liberate themselves not as

individuals but as members of a Latina community. They work to build bridges among Latinas/Latinos while denouncing sectarianism and divisionary tactics. *Mujeristas* understand that their task is to gather the hopes and expectations of the people about justice and peace. Because Christianity, in particular the Latin American inculturation of Roman Catholicism, is an intrinsic part of Latino culture, *mujeristas* believe that in them, though not exclusively so, God chooses once again to vindicate the divine image and likeness of women made visible from the very beginning in the person of Eve. *Mujeristas* are called to gestate new women and new men—Latino people willing to work for the common good, knowing that such work requires the denunciation of all destructive sense of self-abnegation (see Zárate Macías n.d. Much of this description is based on the song composed and interpreted by Rosa Marta in response to several Latinas' insistence on the need for a song that would help to express who they are and would inspire them in the struggle. For the full text of her song in English and Spanish see Isasi-Díaz 1989: 560-62).

Mujerista theology, which includes both ethics and theology, is a liberative praxis: reflective action that has as its goal liberation. As a liberative praxis *mujerista* theology is a process of enablement for Latina women, insisting on the development of a strong sense of moral agency, and clarifying the importance and value of who they are, what they think, and what they do. Secondly, as a liberative praxis, *mujerista* theology seeks to impact mainstream theologies, the theologies which support what is normative in church and, to a large degree, in society.

Mujerista theology engages in this two-pronged liberative praxis first by working to enable Latinas to understand the many oppressive structures that almost completely determine their daily lives. It enables them to understand that the goal of their struggle should be not to participate in and to benefit from these structures but to change them radically. In theological and religious language this means that *mujerista* theology helps Latinas to discover and affirm the presence of God in the midst of their communities and the revelation of God in their daily lives. Latinas must come to understand the reality of structural sin and find ways of combating it because it effectively hides God's ongoing revelation from them and from society at large.

Secondly, *mujerista* theology insists on and aids Latinas in defining their preferred future: What will a radically different society look like? What will be its values and norms? In theological and religious language this means that *mujerista* theology enables Latinas to understand the centrality of eschatology in the life of every Christian. Latinas' preferred future breaks into the present oppression they suffer in many different ways. They must recognize those eschatological glimpses, rejoice in them, and struggle to make those glimpses become their whole horizon. Thirdly, *mujerista* theology enables Latinas to understand how much they have already bought into the prevailing systems in society—including the religious systems—thus internalizing their own oppression. *Mujerista* theology helps Latinas to see that radical structural change cannot happen unless radical change takes place in each and every one of them. In theological and religious language this means that *mujerista* theology assists Latinas in the process of conversion, helping them to see the reality of sin in their lives. Further, it enables them to understand that to resign themselves to what others tell them is their lot and to accept suffering and self-effacement are not necessarily virtuous.

Other important elements of *mujerista* theology are the following. First, the source of *mujerista* theology is the lived experience of Latinas, experience that they are conscious of and have reflected upon. Here *mujerista* theology follows St Anselm's understanding of theology as faith seeking intellect: it is the faith of Latinas, which historically has proven to be a resource in their struggles for liberation, that is at the heart of *mujerista* theology. This does not preclude church teaching and traditions, or biblical understandings. But neither does it preclude religious understandings and practices labelled 'popular religion', which are mainly a mixture of Roman Catholicism Amerindian and African religions (certain Pentecostal elements are also beginning to be integrated into Latino popular religion). In *mujerista* theology all of these religious-theological elements are looked at through the lens of Latinas' struggle for liberation. Secondly, *mujerista* theology is communal theology: the materials developed in this theology are gathered mostly during reflection sessions of groups of Latinas meeting for this purpose in different parts of the USA. Thirdly, *mujerista* theology benefits from feminist and Latin American liberationist understandings but adds two other elements: critique of oppressive elements in Latino culture as well as of the dominant culture in the USA, and denunciation of racism/ethnic prejudice. *Mujerista* theology has challenged Euro-American feminist theologians and Latin American liberation theologians for the lack of inclusion of these two key perspectives in their work.

The first publication dealing with *mujerista* theology—then called Hispanic Women's Liberation Theology—appeared in the USA in 1987 (Isasi-Díaz and Tarango 1993). Necessarily, then, because of its newness as well as the small number of Latina theologians at present, *mujerista* theology is but a small daughter born of the hope of Latina women for their liberation and the liberation of all peoples.

Further reading: Isasi-Díaz 1993; Isasi-Díaz *et al.* 1992.

MUTUALITY
Carter Heyward

MUTUALITY, in feminist liberation theology, is the basis of right-relation. It is a relational process in which all persons, or parties, are empowered, thereby experiencing themselves as able to survive, affect others creatively, and make a constructive difference in the world around them.

> Mutuality is sharing power in such a way that each participant in the relationship is called forth into becoming who she is—a whole person with integrity... Experientially, mutuality is a process, a relational movement. It is not a static place to be, because it grows with/in the relationship. As we are formed by mutuality, so too does the shape of our mutuality change as our lives-in-relation grow (Heyward 1989).

As a theological, ethical and pastoral concept, 'mutuality' emerged among Christian feminists in *The Redemption of God: A Theology of Mutual Relation* (Heyward 1982). This book draws upon the work of Jewish existentialist and social philosopher Martin Buber, especially his *I and Thou*, in which the concern is primarily social and theological, not psychological. Mutuality does not refer primarily to 'feelings', but rather to the connectedness at the heart of the universe. Whether we realize it or not, we are mutually interdependent, immediately and intimately connected. This mutuality is our ontology, our theological anthropology. It provides the vision for our justice-work and the basis for our health and well-being. Our 'power in relation', or our sacred/erotic power for making right, mutual, relation, is God (Heyward 1982, 1989).

Working often in relation to each other's work, many feminist theologians (Christians and others) have employed the concept of mutuality. Mary Grey (UK), Dorothee Sölle (Germany), Delores Williams, Ada Maria Isasi-Díaz, and Rita Nakashima Brock (USA), Chung Hyun Kyung (Korea), Kwok Pui-lan (Hong Kong), Virginia Fabella (Philippines), Mercy Amba Oduyoye (Ghana), and Ivona Gebara (Brazil) are among the Christian theologians for whom mutuality is important, to their understandings of God as well as to their social anthropologies. It is important to realize that feminist theologians have come to this understanding of mutuality via many different cultures, experiences and theological educations. They are not all students of the same theological tradition or teacher. Their lives as women, across cultures and religious backgrounds, have been their teachers about 'mutually empowering relation' and their 'power in mutual relation'.

Research associates at the Stone Center for Developmental Services and Studies, Wellesley College, Massachusetts, began in the early 1990s to develop a psychological theory of 'mutual empathy and empowerment' (Jordan *et al.* 1991). They suggested that only a mutually empowering relationship is 'growth-fostering'. As the director of the Stone Center's educational program, feminist psychiatrist Jean Baker Miller had characterized such a relationship as one in which five 'good things' happen:

> Each person feels a greater sense of 'zest' (vitality, energy). Each person feels more able to act and does act. Each person has a more accurate picture of her/himself and the other person(s). Each person feels a greater sense of worth. Each person feels more connected to the other person(s) and a

greater motivation for connections with other people beyond those in the specific relationship (Miller 1986: 3).

Continued collaboration between theologians and psychologists has shown that a 'mutual relationship' cannot exist in itself. Mutuality is relational *movement* and mutual relationships are not only not static but can be understood as *mutual*, only in relation to their larger social context. Differences also play a creative role in mutuality; recognizing and respecting cultural, racial, ethnic, class, sexual, religious and other differences among women is *basic* to any mutually empowering relational process among us.

Most feminist liberation theologians agree that, ethically and pastorally, mutuality is a slippery concept, hard to define in practice, yet essential to right-relation. In order to ascertain whether relationships are more or less mutual, a power analysis is often necessary: who, in the particular relational situation, has what kind of power (for example, economic, racial, sexual, physical, intellectual, emotional, charismatic, professional, intuitive)? Is the power being exercised as control, or is it being shared for the well-being of all? If the power is, for a time, controlling, such as that of parent over child, teacher over student, doctor over patient, one group or nation over another, is there an active commitment on the part of all parties to become increasingly mutual? In other words, is there a mutually empowering relational dynamic at work in the relationship, transforming it? If not, it is not a right-relationship.

In the 1990s, feminist liberation theologians have begun more explicitly to name the importance of the whole creation, not only its human members, in the sacred work of mutuality. US theologians Sallie McFague and Rosemary Radford Ruether have helped pave the way for more sustained theological and ethical attentiveness to a mutuality that might be genuinely ecological.

Further reading: Harrison 1985; Williams 1993.

NEW TESTAMENT WOMEN: AN OVERVIEW
Robert Evans

THE EARLIEST surviving Christian writings, the letters of Paul from the 50s, are as often addressed to women as to men, with greetings to and commendations of named women. For example, in Romans 16 Paul refers to Phoebe, 'deacon' and 'benefactor', Prisca who 'worked with [Paul] in Christ', Junia (who is often taken to be a man) 'prominent among the apostles', and Mary, Tryphaena, Tryphosa and Persis, 'workers in the Lord'. In Philippians he speaks of Euodia and Syntyche, who have 'struggled beside [Paul] in the work of the gospel'. However, it is arguable how often Paul has men rather than women in mind as the primary recipients of his words.

In Gal. 3.27-28 Paul cites what may have been the core of a pre-Pauline baptismal confession that for those in Christ 'there is neither Jew nor Greek, there is neither slave nor free, there is not male and female'. The phrase contains a reference to Gen. 1.27, and illustrates Paul's teaching on the new order in Christ which is a transformation of the order of creation: the third pairing confesses that patriarchal marriage and sexual relationships between male and female are no longer constitutive of the new community in Christ, of which women are members irrespective of their procreative capacities and of the social roles connected with them (Schüssler Fiorenza 1983: 211).

When Paul addresses the congregation(s) of Corinth on matters of marriage and women in worship, it is this radical transformation of world order that has informed his original teaching in Corinth; the Christians there quote back to him elements of his teaching overthrowing old order hierarchies: 'all of us possess knowledge', 'All things are lawful'. It is not that Paul in 1 Corinthians is imposing a Christian gender stratification on unruly pagans but that he and his correspondents are both working out the implications of his gospel of freedom. However, in practice Paul may be seen to compromise the radicalism of the new order teaching.

The reciprocal injunctions to marriage partners in 1 Cor. 7.2-5 are the outworkings of a new mutual freedom and accountability, though they are not matched by the injunctions to men only later in the chapter. More radically, it is directly counter to the social hierarchy and to the rights of the *paterfamilias* that Paul advises Christian women to remain free from marriage—and this would have produced conflicts for the Christian community in its interaction with society. The validity of—and in Paul's case preference for—the single state seems to have been one feature of Jesus' teaching and one with particular implications for women.

Paul's teaching on the manner in which women pray and prophesy in public worship in 1 Cor. 11.2-16 is based on the premise that in Christ women as well as men have the freedom and the authority to do this. His anxiety is that they should 'cover' their heads when they do so and his reasons are curious, deriving from Jewish exegesis of Gen. 1.27-28, which denies that woman reflects the 'glory' of God (Hooker 1963–64). It is possible that 'covering their heads' refers not to women's wearing veils but to their putting their hair up—they had probably been letting their hair down as a sign of their new, eschatological freedom. Even though Paul prescribes this difference for women and men in worship, he calls this covering of her head a woman's 'authority' (11.10)—though RSV and other translations render this 'authority' as 'veil', and thus allow for erroneous interpretations of this practice as one of subordination rather than of authority. Paul's several arguments for a woman's prophetic authority being marked out by a particular cultural practice were probably no more convincing then than now.

To be consonant with this teaching of women's authority, 1 Cor. 14.33-36 cannot mean that women (or even 'wives'; the Greek word is the same) were to be silent in all community worship; rather, there are circumstances not entirely detailed here in which married women were not to challenge their husbands during public worship, just as speakers in tongues, male or female, under some circumstances were to be silent (1 Cor. 14.28). That Paul resolves this with recourse to a social hierarchy distinct from the transformed order of Gal. 3.28 is a measure of his quietism ('Give no offence', 1 Cor. 10.32); the social status of women outside the commu-

An A to Z of Feminist Theology

nity seems to inhibit in his view the freedom Christian women could exercise inside it.

The less certainly Pauline letters Colossians and Ephesians feature 'household codes' (Col. 3.18–4.1; Eph. 5.21–6.9, cf. 1 Pet. 2.13–3.7) drawn with few alterations from contemporary Hellenist sources. The Graeco-Roman patriarchal pattern of marital relationships is thus adopted as part of a 'Christian' social ethic. The Ephesians code actually theologizes the social structures of domination.

The least certainly Pauline letters, the Pastorals, take the development into the gradual exclusion of women from ecclesial office and towards the patriarchialization of the whole church. The regularization of 'widows' in 1 Timothy 5 is in one sense a direct response to the Pauline teaching that a woman might remain non-married: if women making this choice were not supported as traditionally by husband or father, the community would have to make provision.

Such a reinterpretation of the baptismal vision of Gal. 3.28 is late—not before the last third of the first century—and in the New Testament is only in the post-Pauline tradition: it may have had little or no impact on the Jesus traditions in the communities of the Evangelists. After the period of writing of the New Testament, however, the insistence on equality and mutuality in Christian community is largely ignored.

The impact of Jesus' teaching on women and the roles that women took during his ministry are mediated through the Gospels, which record and interpret the sayings and events of the 30s CE. From the Gospel of Mark in the 60s to the Gospel of John at the end of the century, the Evangelists were writing for their communities and their narratives are likely to reveal the life and teaching of the women and men in these communities through the selection and redaction of material about Jesus.

The Gospel of Mark records the healing of a woman commended for her faith (5.24-34), a Gentile woman who argues with Jesus and gains a reversal of his refusal (7.24-30), a widow whose action Jesus commends as a example of offering and trust (12.41-44) and a woman who anoints Jesus' body 'beforehand for burial', of whom Jesus says, 'wherever the good news is proclaimed in the whole world, what she has done will be told in remembrance of her' (14.3-9)—the latter a prophecy perhaps yet to be fulfilled. The Twelve however are a male inner circle, who are taken aside by Jesus to be given private teaching in discipleship. In fact, the Gospel suggests that they are often fearful, faithless and lack understanding (e.g. 4.40, 6.42) and the foremost of them, Peter, publicly denies and curses Jesus (14.66-72)—so the model of good discipleship is not the monopoly of the twelve men, and it seems that their particular ministry was not constitutive for the ministry of the later church.

It is in the narratives of the passion and resurrection that the Gospel of Mark focuses especially on the women among the disciples. Three named woman, Mary Magdalene, Salome and Mary of Joses, with 'many other women' and no male disciples, are identified as the witnesses of Jesus' death; they had been Jesus' benefactors in Galilee and 'used to follow him' ('follow' is a key word in the early traditions of discipleship); two of these women are witnesses of his burial, and the three again witnesses of the empty tomb and the first to hear the message of the resurrection. The mention of their names in this repeated pattern is surely because they are known as the authenticating witness of these crucial traditions—standing out against the contemporary legal dismissal of the witness of women.

The redaction of Markan material in the Gospel of Matthew leads to a repetition of some of these features, but beyond this the Gospel shows a concern for the primacy of Peter in the establishment of a church order rather than an interest in the roles of women in discipleship. The ethos of the community of this Gospel seems to have been conservatively Jewish-Christian. Fascinatingly, however, the opening genealogy of Jesus includes five women, agents of God: Tamar, Rahab, Ruth, 'the wife of Uriah' and Mary—women moreover involved in 'irregular' sexual unions.

The Gospel of Luke shows a much greater interest in material concerning women. This is consonant with the Evangelist's understanding that the liberation of the poor and the oppressed is central to the ministry of Jesus and of his followers (4.16-19)—hence an increase in references to widows as a particularly disadvantaged

NEW TESTAMENT WOMEN

group of women. There is also an apparent structuring of the material so that male–female parallels appears in pairs of parables (e.g. 13.18-21, 15.4-10) and in other Lukan passages such as the prophecies of Simeon and Anna (2.25-38); and male–female contrasts in passages where the male character is shown to disadvantage, such as Simon the Pharisee against a woman 'who was a sinner' (7.36-50).

There is a concentration of this design and focus in the birth narratives. Luke's treatment of Mary, the mother of Jesus, is considerably more positive than that of Mark or Matthew, and she takes a central role in these narratives. In particular, she forms a striking contrast to the priest Zechariah—who is surpassed also by Elizabeth.

The book of Acts, by the same author, does not have the same design—which may suggest that source material, oral or written, featuring women was less plentiful from the time of the apostles than from the ministry of Jesus. However, the passages concerning named women reveal a variety of roles: Lydia and Mary the mother of John Mark as benefactors and hosts, Dorcas/Tabitha as a charitable woman, Philip's daughters as prophets and Prisc(ill)a as a teacher able to explain more accurately 'the Way of God' to a male evangelist.

The Fourth Evangelist characteristically focuses on individual, often named, characters, and of these there are women whose words and actions suggest that in the Johannine community women were not less honoured than men in discipleship. Through the word of the Samaritan woman, who stood and argued theology with Jesus, a village comes to faith in him (4.7-42). Peter's confession in Mt. 16.16 which led him being designated 'the rock' on which the church would be built appears in John on the lips of Martha (11.27). In 20.14, not Peter but Mary Magdalene is first to see the risen Jesus, and first to make the Easter proclamation—she is apostle to the apostles. The designation of the close disciples as 'the Twelve' largely yields in the Fourth Gospel to their being Jesus' 'own'; in chapter 10 his 'own' are said to know his voice and be called by their name—this is demonstrated by Mary Magdalene outside the tomb.

There may be a form of rebuttal of the primacy of Peter in this Gospel—the foremost among the disciples is here the 'disciple Jesus loved'. Peter is not treated derogatorily but there seems to be a primacy in this community, ideally at least, not of hierarchy but of discipleship characterized by being loved by Jesus—which means that the foremost status in the community was a category open to women as to men. In the Gospel, among those loved by Jesus in this way are the sisters Martha and Mary (11.5); and Mary, the mother of Jesus, is included in the community in a relationship with the Beloved Disciple (19.26-27).

A similar perspective is not explicit in the other, distinct but related, Johannine literature, the three epistles and Revelation. The probably symbolic 'elect lady' and her 'elect sister' of 2 John, and the female images and sexual language of Revelation—whoring and fornication as metaphors for idolatry and the symbolic understanding of Israel as bride of Yahweh—reflect gender models but their gendered meaning is not primary.

It is the later two of the four Gospels that give us the greater material and more positive perspectives of women in discipleship; this may reflect the characteristics of their Evangelists or their communities, but may also signal that if the place of women in the transformed order in Christ was to be maintained from its beginnings in the teaching and practice of Jesus, it needed towards the end of the first century to be restated and demonstrated—perhaps in the face of resistance. Certainly this material in the Gospel of John makes a stark contrast to the roughly contemporary teachings in the communities of 1 Tim. 2.12 and 2 Tim. 3.7.

The difference in teaching in different parts of the New Testament divides its commentators: there are those, such as Witherington (1990), who see the Christian order as *ab initio* one of patriarchalism modified in some partial way, a patriarchy of responsibilities rather than rights where the 'obligation' in the freedom/obligation tension is characterized by patriarchal inequalities; and there are those, such as Schüssler Fiorenza and myself, who observe a radicalism in equality and mutuality in the earliest Christian movement which underwent rapid modification and patriarchalization.

Further reading: Moltmann-Wendel 1982.

An A to Z of Feminist Theology

NORM
Pamela Dickey Young

IN THEOLOGY a norm is a specific criterion or set of criteria by which any given theological sources or formulations are judged to be adequate or inadequate for theology in general or for the type of theology being done. A norm for theology is different from and more restrictive than a source for theology. A source is any resource on which one might draw in the formulation of a theology. Sources can be widespread and may be widely divergent. But it is the norm or norms by which one decides whether any given source is fittingly used.

In a Christian feminist theology, then, the norm or norms would be the criterion or criteria by which the theology could be judged to be adequate both as a Christian theology and as a feminist theology. Norms might be stated either formally or materially. For instance, Scripture might be agreed on as a formal norm for Christian theology, but one would then have to explore the material content of such a norm, that is, in what ways one ought to appeal to Scripture as normative.

In Christian feminist theology there is general agreement that women's experience is normative. How to define women's experience, how to make material use of women's experience in judging theology, whether or not women's experience is the only norm or one norm among others, are matters that vary from one feminist theology to another. There is less agreement in Christian feminist theology about whether or how the Christian tradition or some criterion or criteria derived therefrom might be normative.

Some feminist theologians, including Elisabeth Schüssler Fiorenza (1984), suggest that the norm of Christian feminist theology is derived solely from women's struggles for liberation. Thus, whatever resources are used in theology are judged adequate or inadequate by their service in the liberation of women from patriarchal oppression. The tradition is judged in light of its potential for liberating women. There is no independent norm derived from within the Christian tradition.

Others would argue that for any theology to be a *Christian* theology it needs not only to use the Christian tradition as one source among others, but it needs to accept a norm derived from the Christian tradition. There are indeed feminist theologies that see no need and have no desire to be Christian theologies. What might set these feminist theologies apart from those that are feminist Christian theologies would seem to be some normative connection to Christian tradition on the part of the latter.

Theological reflection through the centuries has yielded a wide variety of both formal and material norms, appealing to one or both of some criterion or criteria derived from the historic Christian tradition and some criterion or criteria derived from the present situation.

Regardless of whether women's experience is seen as one norm among others or the sole norm for a Christian feminist theology, Christian feminist theologians agree that no Christian theology is adequate if it fails to allow norms derived from the present situation. Specifically, in the case of feminist theology, no adequate theology can fail to accept women as full human beings. Women's full humanity must be normative. No adequate theology maintains the superiority of men and the inferiority of women or promotes or sanctions conduct that subordinates women to men. For instance, any theology that sees the *imago dei* to reside only or fully in men, or only in the partnership of men and women, fails to recognize the full personhood of women and can, on feminist grounds, be judged inadequate. One can see how conduct might be said to follow from such teaching and become enshrined in ecclesial, social and political structures that perpetuate the dominance of men and the subordination of women. One can also see how unjust treatment of women might encourage theologies that theorize and perpetuate such conduct.

Within the bounds of virtually any norm or set of norms there is room for theological expansion from a variety of sources including the creative imagination of the author. Thus, although theological reflection might bind itself to certain norms, this need not constrain the feminist development of theological thought.

I would argue that an adequate feminist Christian theology needs to use two formal norms, a norm drawn from Christian tradition (the norm of appropriateness) and a norm drawn from the present situation (the norm of credibility). Credibility has several facets: intellectual credibility (does the proposed theology hold up to standards of contemporary rationality?); practical credibility (does the proposed theology serve the interests of the whole or only of a small group?); aesthetic credibility (does the proposed theology promote the fulness of existence in all its dimensions?). I would draw the material norm of appropriateness from the earliest witness to Jesus available in the Gospels, recognizing that all Gospel witness to Jesus is already a witness of faith. In terms of practical credibility, I would draw the material norm of Christian feminist theology from women's feminist experience of claiming the right to define themselves rather than letting themselves be defined by others.

If I, as a feminist, were to decide that Christianity was inherently patriarchal, that is, if no non-patriarchal interpretation of the earliest witness to Jesus was possible, I would be faced with the dilemma of choosing either Christianity or feminism and no Christian feminist theology would be possible. Some feminists have determined this to be the case. Thus the matter of norms is solved by deciding that no theology can be both feminist and Christian. Those feminists who do not see Christianity as inherently patriarchal continue to try to bring together their feminism and their Christianity in a way that does not compromise what is crucial to each and in a way that struggles with the normative claims of both even if, in the end, these normative claims are sorted out in a variety of ways.

Further reading: Ruether 1983; Russell 1987; Young 1990.

OLD TESTAMENT WOMEN: AN OVERVIEW

Jane Richardson Jensen

THE COLLECTION of writings recognized as the Old Testament by Christians and, in a different arrangement, as the Hebrew Bible by the Jewish community, is about a particular group of people (the Hebrews or Israelites). Yet at times, it speaks to the universal human condition, in relation to the consequences of certain actions (Jer. 10.23; Ezek. 28.2, 9), human nature (Gen. 6.5; 8.21; Num. 16.29) and God's relationship to humanity (Ps. 14.2; 33.13; 89.48).

The often-heard comment that the God of the Old Testament is a Judge and the God of the New Testament is Love overlooks the great love God repeatedly shows to the Hebrews (in the books of Genesis, Exodus, the Psalms, Daniel, Ezekiel and Hosea, to name but a few) and even, occasionally, to their enemies (Jonah). For many people the major concern with the Old Testament is the violence. From that perspective, it may not matter whether a battle was won by a man or a woman.

Since the writings came out of a patriarchal society, it is no surprise that the Old Testament focuses on male characters and masculine images of the deity. Much of the traditional scholarly work done on the Old Testament has also had a male-centred bias (Ellis 1976) or has been either idealistic or patronizing towards women (Deen 1955, valuable because it includes all the women of the Bible).

In the Old Testament, over 137 female characters are named. The number is not exact because some characters have the same name and determining a character's sex can be difficult at times. For instance, there are seven distinct characters named Maachah. Six are definitely women. But, despite these six other women called Maachah, the child of Abraham's brother, who is also named Maachah (Gen. 22.24), has been referred to as both a daughter and a son depending on the commentator's disposition.

Even people who are reasonably familiar with the Bible have probably not heard of many of the women mentioned there. The fact that many of the women's stories have either sexual or violent elements to them may prevent their being taught to children in their formative religious education. The unfamiliarity with biblical women and the dual standard which allows the sex and violence in men's stories, like David's and Solomon's, to be conveniently omitted indicate the traditional lack of interest in women and their place in the Bible (in either Testament).

Generally speaking, the female characters in the Old Testament can be grouped according to their familial roles—mothers, wives/co-wives, widows, daughters—or their function within society—queens, wise women (including craftswomen and mourners), poets, prophetesses, magicians (sorcerers, 'witches'), and prostitutes (Brenner 1985). There are also numerous nameless individual women, various groups of women, and personifications of abstract concepts as female (such as Wisdom). Recognized by some in the early church, but then largely ignored until recently, there are even a few female images of God (Mollenkott 1983).

The Old Testament characterization of a woman basically depends on two criteria: nationality (whether the woman is Hebrew or foreign) and faithfulness/obedience (whether she observes the Hebrew laws and customs regarding women). So a good Jewish woman like Esther who obeys her uncle Mordecai throughout the book named for her is praised, but not as much as Mordecai is (Est. 10). Sarah, who oppresses Hagar (Gen. 16), is still acceptable because she is Hebrew and meant to be the mother of Abraham's children. Similarly, the story of Ruth, from Moab, is recounted because she became David's grandmother (Ruth 4.17). But Ruth's marriage to Boaz was a consequence of her obeying her mother-in-law. Therefore obedience again plays a role in the Old Testament's evaluation of a woman. The earliest 'Hebrew' mother, Eve, was punished because she disobeyed either Adam or God (Gen. 3); the text is silent on which. Likewise the Sidonian princess, Jezebel, was renowned as a thoroughly evil foreign women. Her offence was violent opposition to the Hebrew God and his prophets (1 Kgs 16.31; 2 Kgs 9.30-37). Jezebel's fidelity to her own faith and culture counted against her.

Deborah (Judg. 4–5), Huldah (2 Kgs 22.14-20), the Queen of Sheba (1 Kgs 10.1; 2 Chron. 9.1),

An A to Z of Feminist Theology

OLD TESTAMENT WOMEN

and the Shunnamite (2 Kgs 4.8-37) are among the few women who act independently of a male family figure. But their actions are still related to males, namely Barak and Sisera, King Josiah's officials, King Solomon, and the prophet Elisha, respectively.

The patriarchal nature of the Bible is illustrated in several ways. First, the main characters are usually male. Even a story ostensibly about women, such as that of Genesis 16 (about Hagar and Sarah), begins and ends by focusing attention on the male, Abraham.

Secondly, women are generally secondary characters with very little character development. No female's character is as multi-faceted as David's, for example. The lack of space devoted to women makes it clear that they are simply not of interest except as adjuncts to men, usually as mothers, wives, daughters, or temptations to idolatry or sex. The dearth of information about women is telling. Why are there so many nameless women?

Finally, when a female and a male character have done the same thing, the female is treated much more harshly than the male. Aaron and Miriam both rebelled against Moses. While Aaron went unpunished, Miriam suffered leprosy and was banned from the village for a week. Abraham and Sarah both laughed in disbelief about Sarah's possible conception. Yet nothing was said to Abraham, while the angel rebuked Sarah.

Regardless of which language the Old Testament is read in, the above features are evident. Besides these marks of patriarchal influence, traditional English translations of the Old Testament (and New Testament) also reflect the male-centred bias of translators. An obvious example of androcentric translating is using 'Adam/man' for 'human/humanity' (see for instance Gen. 2.7; 6.5; Exod. 33.20; Deut. 4.32; 8.3; Mic. 6.8). Some of the subtitles supplied to introduce chapters are prime examples of androcentric editorial practices; for instance, the NIV's use of 'witch' in a subtitle before 1 Samuel 28 when the Hebrew has 'a woman who has a familiar spirit' (i.e., medium), or subtitles which ignore violence done to a woman (NIV: 'Dinah and the Shechemites', or 'David and Bathsheba' instead of 'the rape of Dinah/Bathsheba').

English grammar has led to the removal of feminine characteristics from the Divine because most parts of speech are not grammatically feminine or masculine. So, for instance, a word like 'spirit', which is grammatically feminine in the Hebrew, becomes sexless in translation. This in part enabled the feminine aspect of the Spirit of God in the Old Testament to be missed by the majority of readers. It was up to the scholars throughout the centuries who would have been aware of it to render their translations accordingly or, at least, to mention the matter in a footnote!

With regard to relationships between the sexes in the twentieth-century British Isles, male control of socio-religious institutions and language means that men influence women's perceptions of themselves, other women, and even their understanding of God and how people perceive God's attitude to women. Sometimes men even control conversations by their silence (Sattel 1983). If male dominance is still so pervasive after a century of work by feminists to change perceptions, patriarchal power was even stronger during the biblical era. This is not to say that a patriarchal system has always held sway throughout the whole of the ancient Near East. But certainly in the regions and times of the Old Testament (and New Testament), institutional and interpersonal relationships were based on patriarchal rule.

In view of the problems raised for women in reading a patriarchal document such as the Bible, it must be asked, 'How can a thinking, feeling woman approach the Bible?' (The whole Bible is referred to, because, despite Jesus' affirmation of women, patriarchal influence is apparent in the New Testament too.) There are a number of different possibilities:

1. To disregard the Bible altogether because it seems irrelevant to modern life;

2. To treat it as patriarchal propaganda;

3. To remember that the Bible was written in a context that was different from that of the twentieth-century West;

4. To provide new translations which are as inclusive as possible while giving an accurate understanding of the original text (see the NRSV;

An A to Z of Feminist Theology

5. To reinterpret as much as possible from a feminist perspective;

6. To hold translators more responsible for their word choices; or

7. To show the manifestation of the patriarchal failure: the prevalence of war, in the Bible and now, the continued oppression of so many people worldwide (even the way God chose for salvation—Jesus' crucifixion). Obviously Christianity cannot be blamed for all of the suffering because it has little, or no, influence in many parts of the world.

Disregarding the Bible or treating it as propaganda (choices 1 and 2) is unhelpful because many people in powerful positions regard it as authoritative. So patriarchal attitudes to women still affect their everyday lives. Attempting to consider the context which is culturally very different from the modern West (choice 3) helps the reader to understand the background of the text. But because, on the surface, the biblical era seems so remote, a contextual approach can indirectly lead some people to think that the text is simply meaningless to modern life (then choice 1 results).

The remaining four options have all been used in feminist scholarship. Prooftexting, studying and emphasizing biblical characters like Deborah or Ruth as role models were the methods of nineteenth-century feminists, such as Elizabeth Cady Stanton and Margaret Fuller. In addition to these methods, present-day techniques also include developing feminist critical principles which are based on the Bible (Collins [ed.] 1985: 4-5). In analysing patriarchal manifestations in modern society, feminist studies in religion are important because ancient and modern Church Fathers' interpretations of God, Scripture and the church have been instrumental in maintaining power-structured relationships.

A useful step in biblical scholarship has been recognizing that meaning is based on the possibilities the text offers as well as factors affecting the reader (see Bal [ed.] 1989: 11-24). This means that both the text and the reader are accountable for interpreting the message and acting on it. Readerly interpretations allow for unexpected insights, like that of St Ephrem the Syrian who saw Jephthah's daughter as a Christ figure.

In closing, the question that must be answered is, 'If the tradition and Scriptures which shape women's lives are so inherently patriarchal, is there any hope for affirming modern women when reading the Old Testament?' Some answer 'No', and opt out of Christianity altogether. Others say 'Yes, because women are part of humanity and the Old Testament tells us about the relationship between God and a group of people and that both sexes are created in the divine image.' Throughout the ages, the Bible has spoken to the human condition, although from a male perspective. In Gen. 16.13-14, a foreign woman, Hagar, calls the God of the Hebrews 'the God of Seeing, or Vision'. She is the only person in the Old Testament who actually names God, instead of simply calling on the name of the Lord. The centuries-long price of ignoring women's contributions to their communities has been inestimable.

OMNIPOTENCE
Lisa Isherwood

PATRIARCHAL THEOLOGY insists upon the omnipotence of God; indeed, this is one of the features that makes God an object of worship. We see examples of God's supposed omnipotence throughout Hebrew and Christian Scripture. He is the master who rules over all things and has the power to control all things; nothing happens unless it has been allowed by God. However, the presence of evil and suffering in the world causes a problem for believers who also wish to claim that God is compassionate. The suffering of the good was the theme of the book of Job. This problem is solved by traditionalists by speaking of justice, and at the same time of the virtue of suffering. While God is indeed all-powerful and can do anything he so wishes, he is also just and so he will let the wicked suffer. The righteous, however, suffer in order to increase their virtue, since (on this view) many noble lessons are learned by a person in distress.

This is a picture that troubles feminist theology, which cannot accept a God who acts in this manner; if he has the power to stop the horrors of this world then he should, and if he does not this suggests that the claims for his power have been exaggerated or that he is a very uncaring, almost despotic ruler.

An A to Z of Feminist Theology

As feminist theology is mindful of the research in process thought it sees another view as being both possible and desirable. Process thought suggests that God is within creation and it finds the notion that he could be the 'unmoved mover' of Aquinas to be beyond imagination. Feminist theology builds on this and suggests that God and the world are in process together; both the world and God are coming to fullness together. Rather than seeing the world as in decline from the time of Eden, feminist thinkers suggest that the world is seeking in all ways to become more complete. This urge within it is the God essence. The result of such thinking is to reduce the omnipotence of God, indeed to deny it altogether as an unethical doctrine. God is becoming with the world and so God also suffers with the world; the God of feminist theology cannot be so removed as to be untouched by suffering. Once we realize that God is not omnipotent then we begin to develop a more co-creative theology which is extremely positive for both the individual and the world. The omnipotence of God renders humanity powerless, while the vulnerability and limited power of God actually empowers the created order.

ORIGINAL SIN (1)
Ann Gilroy

THE DOCTRINE of original sin was first developed as a Christian teaching by Augustine of Hippo, who used the Genesis account of the Fall (Gen. 2–3) and Paul's letter (Rom. 5–7), in which the apostle wrestled with the question of why people find themselves unable to unite their will and being to do good even though they may know what this would be and desire it. Why do people find themselves at odds with each other and God? Paul concluded that we are divided between two opposite types of existence; sin and death, derived from the fallen Adam, and goodness and spiritual life, from Christ. Augustine built on Paul's anthropology of the fallen self that had lost the freedom to do what it willed, and on the notion of God's gift of transcendent grace through the saving work of Christ, which restored humanity's fallen state. His teaching became foundational for the doctrine of original sin.

According to Augustine, God created Adam and Eve in a state of original righteousness with their nature directed towards good and freedom of will. Because their wills were united to God's, the first couple did not sin and would not die. However, they lost this original capacity to choose good, free will and undying existence, when they chose sin and self-will over God's will. They brought sin into the world. After the Fall all humans inherited original sin from Adam and Eve, which meant that their acts were corrupted by self-will and there was nothing humanly possible they could do to change this. God, in the redemptive work of Jesus Christ, intervened and saved humanity from this state of alienation from relationship with God. Christ's grace transforms human beings' corrupted will and empowers them to do the good that they could not do on their own. Augustine thought that redeemed humanity was not just restored to the original state, but that, transformed by Christ, it surpassed the original state so that people could no longer die or sin.

The saving work of Christ was ritualized in the Christian community at baptism when the candidates were plunged into water and then dressed in new, white garments. They were not only initiated into the Christian mysteries but their original and personal sins were washed away and they were transformed in the grace of God.

Augustine's teaching, although influential in the Christian tradition, had problems in its interpretation of human free will and sexuality. Whereas Augustine taught that original sin was transmitted to humanity through the libido, or concupiscence, of parents' sexual activity when a new human being was conceived, later theologians rejected this because it distorted the relationships of human sexuality and marriage. Death came to be seen not so much as a punishment for sin that had to be escaped or overcome, but as integral to humanity in the temporal order. Christians hope that death is not their end but that God will resurrect them into eternal life. Original sin was never seen as more pervasive in humanity nor more universal than Christ's redemption of humanity.

Feminist theology expresses the relationships of women and men and God in different ways from the worldview of Augustine and later theologians, who thought of human beings as unchanging, static and the centre of the cosmos. A contemporary historicized and process-based perspective of humans and the universe shows that people are influenced by and constituted through the network of relationships within their particular contexts. Women and men live with the memory of distorted relationships that leave their legacy of damage on communities of people; for example, the poverty and degradation of an original people exploited through colonization; the grief of the former partners at the breakdown of an interpersonal relationship; the genocide of groups of people; the devastation of a town wrecked by floods caused largely by the prior defoliation of the land. Feminist theology acknowledges that women and men participate in contributing to such evil in the world but at the same time urges them to take responsibility to diminish evil by working at life-giving, right relationships in private and public areas of life. Feminist theology refuses polarities or dualisms between the sacred and secular realms and instead emphasizes that women and men belong to a complex, interconnected cosmos in which they participate.

Brock's account of original sin (1988), although inadequate in some respects, illustrates the interdependence of human relationships. Original sin, she holds, is psychological damage inflicted on children through adult parenting. This 'cosmic child abuse' is perpetuated by adults who have not been healed of the damage of their own childhood. Salvation, for Brock, is found within the 'Christa community', not in Jesus as an individual. The Christa community is a messianic community in whose relationships life-giving power is experienced. Redeeming action is placed in the hands of humans. Christa, the power of love at the heart of the community, is unleashed as healing within the community.

As well as constructing theologies, feminist theology has been very critical of the way the classical accounts of the Fall and original sin have been used against women. Børresen ([ed.] 1991) outlines the ways in which androcentric and literal exegeses of Genesis 2–3 in Christian teaching have been responsible for disproportionate blame and punishment for sin being mapped onto women compared to men. The notion that women, like men, were created in *imago Dei* has not always been affirmed in the practices or theologies of Christianity, and feminist theology challenges as sexist and immoral those teachings that deny the full humanity of women. Eve, the woman, has often been represented as the serpent's accomplice and blamed for tempting Adam, the man, to sin as if he was not equally responsible for the Fall. A false dualism developed identifying all women with Eve as weak, easily tempted to sin because their bleeding, lactating bodies identified them as physical and material, controlled by bodily passions rather than by rationality and the powers of the soul. Men identified with Adam as sinning through self-will and pride, but also with Christ, the saviour. They were seen as strong, rational and controlled in comparison with women. Male domination of women became legitimated through this dualistic view of humanity and the social system and structures of patriarchy are sustained by the false belief that women are less human than men.

The question of whether women's natures are as fully human as men's lingers like a poison in the Christian tradition. This sexism is expressed in such practices as women being told that they cannot signify Christ in the Christian community as leaders in worship, because their gender is different from Jesus'. There was never any doubt that the *imago Dei* in men made them capable of signifying Christ. Women were frequently denied pain relief in childbirth even when it was available, because the pain was seen as women's natural punishment. Women's attempts to express their spirituality in language that was different from men's were deliberately ignored or met with incredulity. They were frequently accused of heresy and witchcraft and many met grisly deaths. Women have been advised by religious people to accept abusive relationships as their participation in the will of God, instead of being supported to make changes in the relationships and to challenge the abuser to repentance. Such advice for women to endure meaningless suffering stems from the interpretation of the Fall that men were by nature to dominate over women.

In feminist theology original sin is not construed as a single past event tied to 'Adam and Eve' in a literal reading of the biblical story, but rather as sin, the breakdown of the relationship with God and with human beings that denies the human responsibility for participation in the salvation of the world. Feminist theology stresses relational, communitarian and pluralistic characteristics that call women and men to repentance and liberate women and men from sin, to reconciliation, freedom and life.

Further reading: Johnson 1993; Ruether 1993.

ORIGINAL SIN (2)
Dorothea McEwan

THE CONCEPT that a blessed state of obedience has been ruptured by an event, usually referred to as the Fall, which ushered sin into the world, is the construct of the writers of Scripture. According to them, original sin was visited upon all children of Adam and Eve by an all-powerful and all-loving God. To remedy this sentence, this same God, now called Father, is said to have sent his Son to reconstitute the primordial state of unquestioning obedience, a state of blissful existence amid plenty.

In a feminist understanding there are two major flaws to this theory. The first one is that the event of experimentation and enlightenment is interpreted as disobedience which requires punishment. Thus, this first act of disobedience marks the beginning of a long list of human shortcomings, such as pride, greed and lying, which contravene God's unconditional offer of love. The second flaw with this theory is that enlightenment is seen as a distancing between God and creation. Thus an act of willpower and speculative thinking, with which capacities humankind alone among the creatures is endowed, is called a sin, the origin of sin. The originator of this is woman, Eve, the consort of Adam. This interpretation is the origin not of sin, but of ascribing 'bad' behaviour to Eve, who stands then for woman, all women, as the bringer of sin.

The story of the Fall, constructed as disobedience to God and the display of primeval powers like pride and greed, has been instrumental in vilifying the 'daughters' of Eve, women, for having brought sin into the world. It required the counterbalancing story of 'salvation' through the Son of God/Son of Man to show how powerful, how all-loving and all-forgiving, God really is.

If there must be a concept which castigates behaviour as sinful, in which all of humanity is caught, a feminist reading of the texts suggests a different story: sin is violence done by human beings to each other, as exemplified by Cain's murder of Abel. Such violence constitutes a break in relationships which cannot be remedied. This fits the notion of 'sin' much better than the concept of experimentation, sharing and learning, which is the true meaning of Genesis 1–3. The use of the term 'fall' as evidence that Eve sinned, is a patriarchal interpretation (Isherwood and McEwan 1993: 40-41).

Radical feminist scholar Mary Daly (1984) suggests that within Christianity 'original sin' amounts simply to the fact of having been born female. The misogyny of church and society puts an intolerable burden on women, resulting in pathologically low self-esteem. Daly elaborates on the need to 'develop the Courage to Sin, burning away false guilt'. She turns the biblical fantasy on its head by stressing the importance of challenging the story and the guilt it loads onto women.

One example of the church's misogyny is the continued papal attitude that women are unfit for priestly service. The papal letter *On the Dignity of Women* of 1988 stated that women's role and place are 'equal' to those of men, but 'special'. Rosemary Radford Ruether, in her analysis of this construction (1991), discusses the switch which the church has taken before our very eyes in the teaching of creational anthropology and its Christology. The traditional view was that women were unequal and fundamentally inferior to men in nature, but in their baptism as Christians this disability was washed away, since in the language of Gal. 3.28, 'in Christ there is neither male nor female'. The modern view, however, can no longer talk of women's inequality in nature. Societal experiences simply do not justify such an interpretation any longer. In order to justify the continued exclusion of women from ministry, then, modern Catholic teaching accepts women as 'equal in nature', that is, in secular society, but claims that they are 'unequal in grace'. The creational image-of-God interpretation includes women, whereas the image-of-Christ interpretation, as put forward in the discussion on ministry, excludes women. This neat theological package is still the reason for women's exclusion from formal ministry in the Roman Catholic church.

The concept of 'original sin' and Eve's disobedience has played havoc with women's lives. A vital part of the feminist agenda is to expose and eradicate the patriarchal lust for vilifying women. We have to read 'behind' the Scriptures, to see what has been added and what has been left out. In Robin Lane Fox's words: 'The scriptures are not unerring; they are not the "word of God"; what we now read is sometimes only one textual version among earlier alternatives; its story may be demonstrably false (Joshua's conquests or Jesus's Nativity); it may ascribe sayings to people which they never said' (1992: 415). Fox tried to find what the authors might have meant and not what exegetes, critics and canonists now claim that Scriptures mean. 'To Christians, that present meaning may be ascribed to the Holy Spirit, promised...as a help in seeing what scriptures are saying. Others may wonder if the Spirit is indeed so holy when interpretations have often been so false, saddling us with original sin, the virgin birth, or the belief that bits of the Old Testament predict the New' (p. 416).

PAGANISM

PAGANISM
Vivianne Crowley

PAGANISM IS the name given to the pre-Christian religions and to other contemporary religions which do not worship a monotheistic male god. In Europe the Pagan religions are undergoing a revival and, with Christianity, Paganism is one of the two official state religions of Iceland.

In the West, Pagans worship mainly the Celtic, Norse-German, Roman or Greek deities. Some Pagans are polytheists and see the deities as separate entities; but most Pagans view the many forms in which the Divine has been worshipped as aspects of the One Divine Reality. All branches of Paganism have elements of pantheism. Pagans believe that the Divine is immanent in the universe and is akin to the Soul of Nature. However, the Divine is seen as transcendent as well as immanent and Pagans could more properly be defined as panentheists. Paganism does not claim a monopoly on religious truth. Human understanding is seen as evolving. Truth is revealed through meditation and contemplation.

How is Paganism Organized?

Many Pagans take an eclectic approach to their faith, preferring to use material from a number of sources to evolve their own spiritual practice. This can be termed generic Paganism. Within Paganism, however, there are distinct denominations or traditions. The most widely-practised are Druidry, based on the Celtic deities; Asatru or Odinism (sometimes called the Northern Tradition), based on the Norse Gods; and Wicca, which worships the Great Goddess and the Horned God.

Druidry and Asatru have a number of structured organizations with sub-groups. In Druidry these are called groves and in Asatru hearths. Wicca meets in small autonomous groups known as covens. There are also Pagan umbrella organizations such as the Pagan Federation, which act as information-giving bodies. However, people do not have to join one of these organizations or go through a particular ceremony to become Pagans.

Pagan Worship

Pagans mainly meet to worship in people's homes, outside in woods and fields or in rented halls. Many Pagans also keep an altar, shrine or devotional room in their own homes. Most Pagans celebrate a cycle of eight seasonal festivals: the four solar festivals marked by the equinoxes and solstices, and four Celtic festivals: Imbolc (Candlemas), Beltane (May Day), Lughnasadh (the old August bank holiday) and Samhain (All Souls). Some Pagans honour the seasonal festivals through complex ritual which includes a mystery play depicting the relevant part of the myth cycle. Others will simply sit and meditate or go outside to commune with Nature. There are in effect low and high church, field and temple Pagans.

Pagan Ethics

Respect for Nature, concern with ecological issues and the role of the Goddess and of women are distinctive features of Paganism. The Principles of Paganism as defined by the Pagan Federation are: love for and kinship with Nature; the Pagan Ethic: if it harms none, do what you will; and honoring both the female and male aspects of the Divine Reality (i.e. worship of both Goddess and God).

The Goddess

Pagans worship both Goddess and God but the Goddess receives greater emphasis in Paganism than in most religions. Even in Asatru, which has a more patriarchal group of deities than some Pagan traditions, the role of the Goddess and of the priestess, the *volva* or *seidkona*, is of growing importance.

There are also groups dedicated exclusively to the worship of the Goddess. The Fellowship of Isis, one of the largest, ordains both women and men as priestesses and priests of the Goddess. The Dianic movement, named in honour of the goddess Diana, is matriarchal. Many Dianic groups exclude men and see their tradition as a sisterhood, as 'wimmin's religion'. Other Dianic groups work with men, but see the role of men as less important than that of women. There are also groups of women who meet together on an informal basis and draw inspiration for their rites from a variety of sources.

An A to Z of Feminist Theology

PAGANISM

Women and Paganism

In its information pack, the Pagan Federation describes women's spirituality as an important part of the revival of Pagan religions in the Western world. Women are seen as having enriched Paganism with a powerful vision of the Goddess—the long-ignored feminine aspect of the Divine:

> Drawing upon the inspiration of the image of the Goddess, women explore their own feminine mysteries. For some women, this involves a denial of all things seen as patriarchal; for others it is a spiritual calling to throw off the conditioning chains of society's stereotypes of women. These women see themselves as reclaiming or creating a new understanding of what it is to be female. They seek to bring their discoveries to life in their own lives, sharing this new found knowledge by way of myth, song, dance and, where needed, political action (Pagan Federation 1992).

The women's movement has inspired many women to question and reject the religious forms which have been familiar since childhood and to turn away from the image of a patriarchal God to other spiritual paths. Women drawn to Paganism from the women's movement are often more politically aware than longer-standing Pagans. Many come from a background of radical campaigning and bring to their Paganism a political stance which is anti-materialist and pro-environmental.

Issues of power and control are of concern to Pagans. Many Pagans are individualists who reject the usurpation of control of the religious function by male priestly hierarchies. Where women have felt themselves oppressed by the structures of patriarchal society, they are eager not to emulate and reproduce those structures in their own religious movements. Within generic Paganism and women's Pagan traditions, groups are often eclectic and loosely-structured. Creativity and spontaneity are strongly encouraged, as is free emotional expression. The emphasis in these groups is on immanent power—power from within.

Pagans believe that religions which portray the Divine solely as masculine are damaging to women. The aim is that by worshipping the Goddess women internalize those qualities associated with the Goddess and learn to reject social and political philosophies and systems which oppress women. They learn to seek social roles through which they can function as whole human beings, realizing all and not just some of their inner qualities. Often ritual incorporates powerful self-affirmation and affirmation by others.

> I am Goddess and thou art Goddess,
> Within me and without me is She,
> eternal yet ever-becoming,
> and in all Womanhood we see Her face.

To Pagans, the Goddess is not passive but an active and energizing force. She is the Creatrix, the dynamism which activates the universe. She is the power which calls the power of the God to her and, in that movement, the process of creation begins. This energizing image of the female is important in Paganism, since it empowers women to be active rather than passive. Paganism offers a spiritual path in which women can honour the feminine aspect of the Divine and play a full role as priestesses and celebrants of the mysteries of the Goddess. In taking on the role of priestess, a woman demonstrates for herself her own inner power and, for other women, provides a much needed role of strong womanhood to which they can aspire. When she has experienced this sense of strength, she can move forward. There is a song which is often sung at Pagan gatherings:

> I am a strong woman,
> I am a story woman,
> I am a healer,
> My soul will never die.

The realization of inner strength benefits not only women's spiritual lives but also their functioning in Pagan society. Women are priestesses in the Pagan movement; they also take a leading role in teaching men and women Paganism and in organizing Pagan umbrella organizations such as the Pagan Federation. The Pagan Federation's structure is interesting in that its membership is comprised of almost equal numbers of men and women. In the 1980s, a democratically elected committee was established. Concern was expressed that, as is typical in parliamentary democracy, it would be mainly men who would stand and be elected. These fears were not borne out, with the main offices having been held by both women and men. Affirmative action has not been necessary to persuade women to stand for election, and voting (with members able to vote for two committee members each year) shows that most members tend to vote for one male and one female candidate. To this extent, therefore, the symbolic system of Goddess and God in balance seems to have manifested itself in outer political functioning. Through empowering women and contributing to the political debate, Paganism has provided one spiritual path for feminists.

Further reading: Aswynn 1988; Carr-Gomm 1991; Crowley 1996a, 1996b; Matthews (ed.) 1991; Pagan Federation 1992.

PASTORAL THEOLOGY
Elaine Graham

THE NOTION of 'pastoral care' may conjure up an image of predominantly individual and personal care, but the normative activities of pastoral care within the Christian tradition have always been considered as more diverse. Clebsch and Jaekle (1964) identify the tasks of healing, guiding, sustaining and reconciling, mediated through a variety of models of care. By the eighteenth century, the study of pastoral theology denoted the practical tasks of the ministry and mission of the church: personal care, Christian formation, spiritual direction, preaching, church administration and social action.

Contemporary pastoral theology has been influenced by Roman Catholic pastoral theology after Vatican II, in which the 'pastoral' is considered to denote the entire life and vocation of the whole people of God. Protestant pastoral theology has also been examining its identity, and especially its relationship to the new psychologies and secular therapies. These were extremely influential in the US, and to a lesser extent in Britain, from the early twentieth century, and arguably did much to correct the judgmental and moralistic excesses of an earlier era. However, there are moves now to recover the specifically theological and normative roots of Christian pastoral care, especially in the reappropriation of scriptural and ethical norms (see Browning 1991; Pattison 1993).

At such a time of significant reappraisal of the discipline, it is perhaps surprising that the influence of feminism was minimal until the late 1980s. However, the changing role of women within the churches highlights the significance of feminist issues for pastoral theology. In the practical relationships and models of personhood and vocation commended—however implicitly—through the pastoral activities of the church, Christians gain messages about ideal virtues, the nature of human destiny and even images of God. Gender relations are therefore forged in, and reinforced by, particular models of pastoral ministry. They have a critical impact on the treatment of women by the Christian church, whether pastoral practice ultimately serves to liberate women, or restricts them to stereotypical roles and aspirations.

Since its emergence as a discrete theological discipline in the middle of the eighteenth century, pastoral care literature—popular and academic—has tended to concentrate upon the qualities that characterize the good pastor. Pastoral *theology* has therefore been synonymous with writings on the activity and characteristics of the pastoral *agent*. For most of Christian history this also means that pastoral theology so understood has implicitly restricted itself to the study of the activities of male, ordained and professionally accredited persons. The needs of the 'client', or the dynamics and relationships within the Christian community as a whole, were obscured.

Furthermore, alternative models of pastoral agency—for example, pastoral care exercised by lay women—were ignored. The supposedly 'normative' pattern of Christian pastoral practice reflected the powerful and privileged status of the clergy; and the contributions and gifts of women as pastoral agents were extensively undervalued and unacknowledged. Women's unequal position in society has thus gone unchallenged by the churches because pastoral theology has been caught in a 'clerical paradigm' which implicitly disavows the expertise and vocation of lay people and women.

Thus, both in terms of women's contribution as pastoral carers and in establishing the parameters of pastoral need, pastoral theology has circumscribed the lives and ambitions of women through stereotypical role models and visions of selfhood and self-fulfilment. Exclusive concentration on the person and role of the (ordained, male) pastor results in a pastoral theology that neglects the needs of (female) lay people and reflects the value-assumptions of a male hierarchy in ruling on questions of legitimate pastoral need and how to address it; in short, a pastoral theology that is both sexist and clericalist.

Valerie Saiving's contention (1979) that the values informing Christian notions of sin and virtue contained a male bias provided a compelling thesis which did much to fuel the earliest insights of feminist theology. The standards of virtue by which the exemplary Christian life was judged ignored women's experiences and represented androcentric values. To elevate the ideals of service, self-abnegation and sacrifice may be an appropriate corrective to patriarchal values of power and domination; but such ideals merely confirm women's subordination and serve to veil the unequal and exploitative nature of gender relations. Her argument illustrates the extent to which many of the values informing Christian pastoral practice are subject to sexist distortion. Anne Borrowdale (1989) has developed this analysis, and illustrated how the Christian vocation to servanthood has become a licence for women's servility and submission.

Vital areas of pastoral need for women—questions of abortion, contraception, childcare, sexuality, violence and sexual abuse—have only begun to emerge as legitimate pastoral concerns or priorities since women have achieved greater visibility and entered positions of leadership in the churches. Thus, despite the historical exclusion of women from pastoral care and the pastoral theology tradition, examples of woman-centred pastoral care are beginning to emerge. They tend to be rooted in concrete examples of feminist praxis as women work to build more inclusive Christian communities focused upon new models of worship and liturgy, spiritual direction and therapy, and accounts of women's experiences throughout the 'life-cycle'.

Feminist Liturgies and 'Women-Church'

The debates over the ordination of women and the introduction of inclusive language in Christian worship have highlighted how the invisibility of women, their lack of representation in liturgical leadership, and the androcentric nature of metaphors for the Divine have served implicitly to exclude and deny the experiences and situations of women. This has pastoral implications: in its rituals and rites of passage, the church has failed to give sufficient recognition to specific events such as childbirth and menstruation, or concerns like violence against women, sexuality and body-image. As a result, these things are not given public or corporate attention, and implicitly rendered taboo or considered not 'holy' and therefore unworthy of liturgical expression.

The solution of many feminist liturgical communities, such as 'Women-Church' and Women in Theology, has been to generate new forms of liturgy and ritual which address women's lives and needs (see for instance Gray [ed.] 1988; Milhaven [ed.] 1991; Ruether 1985; Sears 1989; Stuart [ed.] 1992; B.G. Walker 1990). Pastorally, this offers fertile ground for strengthening women's self-esteem, by naming and affirming such personal experiences and offering rituals and metaphors of healing and reconciliation. Furthermore, by proclaiming these experiences as worthy of liturgical celebration, such groups offer such concerns to God and name the Divine as the source of unconditional love, healing, hope and redemption for women.

The Psychology of Women

Another resource for a renewed pastoral care for women has been feminist insights into the psychology of women, represented by the essays edited by Maxine Glaz and Jeanne Moessner (1991). Given the predominance of psychotherapeutic and psychologically-derived notions of human need, development, relationship and healing within the North American pastoral care tradition, the authors consider it essential to detect the androcentric bias and to articulate new norms, derived from the psychology of women.

Emergent themes include the embodied nature of human personality; the role of cultural archetypes (Earth Mother/Wise Woman) in forming notions of self, integrity and wholeness; the prominence of social factors and family dynamics in the incidence of depression and mental illness among women; consideration of therapeutic issues around abuse, violence, marriage, divorce, singleness, and lesbian lifestyles; and the influence of religious symbolism and images of God on women's psychological and spiritual development. Moessner and Glaz consider that such wisdom will provide a corrective to androcentric psychologies and offer new dynamics of growth and development and more authentic models of pastoral intervention.

Women Giving and Receiving Pastoral Care

A recent volume, *Life Cycles*, on women and pastoral care (Graham and Halsey [eds.] 1993), represents a gathering of narratives, poems and academic accounts of women giving and receiving pastoral care. Such a charting of women's experiences through the life-cycle emphasizes the specific, the discursive and the concrete as the starting point for a transformed pastoral theology. The essays portray women's lives as complex, circumvented by conflicting expectations and fraught with contradictions. Women's caring roles are not idealized, but are spoken from the standpoints of mothering, caring for elderly parents, being single, or lesbian, and of growing older. However, such personal experiences are seen as lived against a wider context of social and public policy, with regard to women in the caring professions, and women in receipt of diverse forms of social welfare provision.

Life-Cycles is therefore an anthology which stresses the diversity of care given and received by women: care administered in word and deed, and in the use of ritual and liturgy, embracing the needs of women and articulating new self-understandings. Much of this stresses the importance of informal, mutual care, and identifies women's solidarity and self-sufficiency often ignored by the 'experts'. Kathleen Fischer's work (1989) provides a similar model of spiritual direction drawing upon feminist principles of collaboration and mutuality.

The feminist maxim that 'the personal is political' is nowhere more true than when applied to Christian pastoral care. As the examples of women-centred pastoral care are making clear, women's personal circumstances and pastoral needs are not simply individual problems but cast light on the social causes of health and illness, the influence of cultural norms and the dynamics of family life on expectations of giving and receiving care, and the structural aspects of public policy and socio-economic change. Appropriate pastoral responses to the needs of women therefore move from models of amelioration or crisis management to promote a more proactive ministry, involving social change and political intervention (see Dale and Foster 1986; Pattison 1994; M. Walker 1990).

Such voices also serve as signs of a movement towards linking feminist pastoral praxis with a wider reconstruction of pastoral theology. The challenge of women to pastoral care does not simply require their inclusion in a tradition that remains otherwise unchanged. Instead, it is a programme for reconstituting the values and understandings which underpin Christian practice (Graham 1996). These are ultimately theological, because they are no less than ways of talking about and apprehending the divine presence at the heart of human care. This is a vision of a God who affirms human experience through the incarnation and who works to redeem the whole of creation by actions of self-giving love and vulnerability. The gospel imperative of the 'bias to the poor'—including women as a marginalized and oppressed group—thus involves practising pastoral strategies which deny the foreclosure and stereotyping of sexism, racism and other forms of discrimination, and celebrate and affirm the diversity, integrity and significance of women's experience. Such values are properly realized as rooted in communities of praxis which attempt to practise gender-inclusive pastoral care. A feminist pastoral theology will therefore aspire to the values and practices of empowerment, inclusion and justice at the heart of Christian ministry and vocation.

PATRIARCHY
Rosemary Radford Ruether

PATRIARCHY IS a key category of social analysis in feminist theology. Patriarchal societies are those in which the rule of the father is the basic principle of social organization of the family and of society as a whole. Patriarchal systems of society seem to have arisen first in nomadic herding groups. Agricultural societies took on the patriarchal order as they became socially stratified in early urban settlements. This seems to have taken place in the ancient Near East about the fifth millennium BCE.

As a developed legal, economic and social system, patriarchy gives the male head of family sovereign power over dependants in the household, the wife or wives, children and slaves. The patriarch is also owner of property passed through the paternal lineage: buildings, animals and land. An example of this system is found in Roman law, where these persons and things are defined as the domain (*familia*) of the *paterfamilias*.

In its classical form patriarchy was associated with a domestic economy in which the basic food and goods consumed by the society were produced in the household. Women, slaves and older children were the workforce for this system of production. Small independent farmers or artisans depended on the wife and children, with one or two apprentices, servants or other family members, for work. Large estates might have thousands of slaves toiling on the land and in the household.

In the large household the male children would be relieved of work to pursue education in preparation for their future careers. Daughters might still spin and weave, and the wife would function as household manager. Although the wife might acquire considerable secondary power through her role as manager of the household, women as a gender class remained restricted in education, access to property and in political roles and legal status.

Daughters were married young to cement alliances between patriarchal families. Women's education was generally limited to the elementary level, and their chief roles were to reproduce heirs for the husband's lineage and to care for the household. Legally they were defined as lacking citizenship status. They were excluded from the army, political assemblies, voting and public professions, such as the law. Wives and children, along with slaves, could be physically chastised and in some cases even sold, if they displeased the patriarch.

In the late nineteenth century a challenge to this patriarchal ordering of the family developed. By the first quarter of the twentieth century women had won citizen rights to vote, serve in political assemblies and hold property, as well as admission to higher education and professions in Western Europe and North America. However, women continued to be seen as responsible for domestic work and child care, effectively excluding them from the ability to compete with men in the public arena on an equal basis. The culture, particularly through religion, continues to reproduce the ideal of the dependent wife whose main work is in the home. Thus many of the patterns of patriarchy continue in the modern world, even though the legal basis for it has been partially dissolved.

Patriarchy has shaped the cultural symbolism of classical societies and their religious expressions. In the Jewish and Christian traditions this means that God is seen as an all-sovereign patriarchal male ruling over his household, the earth, and his *familia*, symbolized as sons or servants. The community, Israel, or the church is symbolized collectively as the wife of God or bride of Christ. Reality is divided between heaven and earth, the intellectual or spiritual and the material or bodily, the first seen as male and the second as female.

Thus patriarchal relations have structured both the social system and the cultural symbols about the nature of reality into a hierarchy of male over female, father over sons, master over slaves (servants). The major task of feminist theology is to identify and critique this patriarchal symbolic pattern of theology and change it into one of egalitarian mutual relations of women and men.

Further reading: Brown and Bohn 1989; Lerner 1986; Smart 1984.

PEACE MOVEMENT
Linda Hurcombe

THE CLOSING years of a century and millennium bring with them an atmosphere of stark critique and endless analysis. *Fin de siècle* predictions become commonplace, not least, in our own time, because the twentieth century has twinned virtuoso technology with ultimate brutality. In the six decades since World War II—deemed a time of peace in the Western world—more than 130 wars have been or still are being fought. More than six million children—the

PEACE MOVEMENT

most vulnerable and defenceless human beings—have been killed in wars; 20 million adults have been killed. Countless millions more have been maimed, bereaved, exiled or have died of hunger and disease in the aftermath of wars.

For decades a balance of terror, starting with the lethal bombs which decimated Hiroshima and Nagasaki, served as the official instrument of international peace negotiations. Yet miraculously the last years of the twentieth century have witnessed an end to the Cold War, the collapse of oppressive regimes in central and Eastern Europe, the dismantling of the Berlin Wall, and the possibility of a truly just and brave new world. A huge chunk of graffitied Wall stands outside the Imperial War Museum in London. Even the intractable hatreds of Israel and Ireland have begun to retreat as politicians and diplomats give ear to the notion that non-violent conflict resolution is preferable to continued terrorism. Some have suggested that nuclear weaponry deserves to win the Nobel Peace Prize. Others would contend that protestors against mutual assured destruction (MAD) have turned the tide.

The history of the church and war, summed up in the 'just war' tradition which dominated theological theories from the fifth century onward, largely removed the gospel imperative of non-violence from its centrality. The 'just war' tradition was only one formal system of dogma which turned Christian teaching on its head (few if any of the wars at the time of this writing would fulfill its conditions). This tradition permits Christians to act as citizen soldiers in a way that would have been unthinkable to earlier Christians. Arthur Koestler quoted one of the more chilling dicta in his masterpiece *Darkness at Noon*:

> When the existence of the Church is threatened, she is released from the commandments of morality. With unity as the end, the use of every means is sanctified, even cunning, treachery, violence, simony, prison, death. For all order is for the sake of the community, and the individual must be sacrificed to the common good (*De schismate libre III*).

History has tended to neglect women's experience of war, with the exceptions of the rare woman warrior, or women who sanctioned and buttressed war efforts. Women have also sometimes even welcomed violence as an unquestioned reality or token of regard. Traditionally, female protest against war has been silenced by the sheer horrors of war; on the whole they have been kept busy picking up the pieces. But there seems to have been a sea-change inspired in large part by the women's peace movement.

The women's peace movement has existed in one form or another from time immemorial. As defined by a patriarchal culture, women's efforts for peace have most often been identified with 'feminine' values which are considered to be a 'natural' female leaning toward nurturance and passivity. Therefore, history before and indeed well into the twentieth century saw women relegated to auxiliary or supportive roles under the guidance of male leaders (Mahatma Gandhi and Martin Luther King serve as eminent examples). However, a comprehensive account of the peace movement reveals that women have usually formed the majority, working most consistently, providing the greater impetus and transcending class barriers. In the twentieth century women decided to make war, or more precisely the renunciation of war, their business.

It is important to point out that the women's liberation movement did not invent either the women's peace movement or Christian feminism; from earliest days the peacemaking concerns of religious feminists spilled over and merged with secular concerns in virtually every area and were never contained by solely 'churchy' issues.

Modern feminism was preceded by a great wave of women's activity throughout the nineteenth and early twentieth centuries. The Religious Society of Friends formed a continuing focus and catalyst to the peace movement, constantly challenging the 'just war' tradition of mainstream Christianity. American theologian and suffragist Elizabeth Cady Stanton saw that the institution of womanhood and particularly of motherhood had been colonized for less than noble purposes through the centuries by the church. This institution, which idealizes the notions of nurturance, tenderness and caring, imprisons and privatizes the first commandment of love in clan and family chauvinism. Thus the institution of motherhood and by extension that of the family must be radically reappropriated in

An A to Z of Feminist Theology

order to release the creation and sustenance of life into the same realm of decision, struggle, surprise, imagination and conscious intelligence as any other difficult, but freely chosen, work.

The first wave of feminist activity centered mainly on the vote. After achieving the franchise women began to turn their energies to various struggles which they knew to be important; these included peace work. One powerhouse was the Women's International League for Peace and Freedom, formed in 1915 'to protest against war and to suggest steps which may lead to warfare becoming an impossibility', but it came after a period of relative silence about women's liberation.

Ordinary folk often saw women's stake in making peace from a biological perspective. Mrs Nesbit from Eccles put her views on peace at a Women's Co-operative Guild Congress in 1915:

> We women…can best ask for the preservation of life, because we give life. We know the price which we pay for life, and therefore, we place a high value on life. We ask that posterity shall not suffer the bereavements or the sorrow for the wounded, maimed and dying which we are suffering (cited in Wiltshire 1985).

She did not wish, she said, to mystify or glorify maternity, rather to assert that childbearing is bloody, hard work, which women can do and men cannot. One does not have to be a mother to see the logic of this statement.

In many respects it is this passionate engagement with peace movements which bridges the period from early twentieth-century feminism to the modern movement. Some in the movement saw the male as the implacable enemy of peace: the notion that women are naturally peaceful and nurturing and that men are hunter-gatherers who are aggressively protective of their territory gripped and continues to grip the imagination and fuel furious debate. Virginia Woolf laid responsibility at the feet of men: 'If you insist on fighting to protect me, or "our" country, let it be understood, soberly and rationally between us, that you are fighting to gratify a sex instinct which I cannot share; to procure benefits which I have not shared and probably will not share…' (1938). The anarchist Emma Goldman had previously spoken out against this kind of simplification: 'I resented my sex's placing every evil at the door of the male. I pointed out that if he were really as great a sinner as he was being painted by the ladies, women shared the responsibility with him'. The debate of gender and nature continues to simmer and occasionally has boiled over. Jill Tweedie bravely theorized about the flipside of the tarnished coin:

> In essence, women have the same proclivities as men towards good or evil. Nevertheless a large part of the female sex has been forced into the guardian role through history, if only because the strictures of society have weighed more heavily upon them and their opportunities for action have been much more limited (cited in Oldfield 1989).

A number of Christian feminists believed that the overarching problem is that the world languishes in the grip of a negative and lopsided 'masculine' principle. The theological expression of this phenomenon brought rich outpourings of new peace liturgies espousing *Sophia* or divine wisdom, a feminine principle so long neglected in Christianity.

Whether or not peace and ecological responsibility are 'feminine' values remains a moot point. Underlying all the differences between the present and the past is a fundamental perceptual shift—the mounting awareness that war may not be as we have been led to believe; in brief, war is not inevitable, but rather the by-product of a fundamentally imbalanced and anti-human way of organizing the way we perceive the world and act within it. Riane Eisler spoke unambiguously:

> what becomes evident is that the progressive modern social movements—such as republicanism, socialism, pacifism, abolitionism, and feminism, which began to emerge after the 18th century enlightenment—have definitely been moving us in a womanly direction. What further becomes evident is that to a far greater extent than is generally realised our future and perhaps the future of our planet hinges on the success or failure of feminism (1982: 38).

Rightly or wrongly, Eisler was forging connections between a war-torn world and the absence of women's thoughts from the processes of culture and history-making. She proposed that while women's history may have been hidden, their cultural importance is not thereby negated. In a fragile, nuclear age women's contribution to

PEACE MOVEMENT

history and theology might well be to teach the world to stay alive.

Nuclear weapons and their proliferation have inevitably made a solution to violence more urgent not least because in a nuclear age the old principles for which wars were fought will have no meaning, as E.P. Thompson succinctly observed:

> Those who have supported the policy of deterrence have done so in the confidence that this policy would prevent nuclear war from taking place. They have not contemplated the alternatives and have been able to avoid facing certain questions raised by that alternative. First: is nuclear war preferable to being overcome by an enemy? Are the deaths of 15 or 20 million people and the utter destruction of the country preferable to an occupation which might offer the possibility...of resurgence and recuperation? Second: are we prepared to endorse the use of such weapons against the innocent, the children and the aged of an 'enemy'? (cited in Dowell and Hurcombe 1987).

Countless women scholars and workers add their voices to newly reclaimed insights. At the moment of sharing the cup at the Last Supper Christ taught his disciples that God's way of suffering love was directly opposed to secular power and striving for cult survival or cult supremacy: 'The kings of the Gentiles exercise lordship over them; and those in authority over them are called benefactors. But not so with you; rather let the greatest among you become as the youngest, and the leader as one who serves' (Lk. 22.24-27). Others find comfort in the promise in Isa. 2.4: 'And they shall beat their swords into ploughshares, and their spears into pruning hooks; nation shall not lift up sword against nation, neither shall they learn war any more'.

Women in peace camps everywhere have developed models of civil disobedience which have led to fruitful debate over the value of martyrdom as a tool of redemption. Peace activities have fomented and redefined both the traditional forms of non-violent direct action and women's role in the political and spiritual crises of the twentieth century.

Today more and more women are taking positions of leadership and initiating independent action to bring about the cessation of war as a way of resolving conflict. In sharp contrast to the past when men controlled both the pen and the sword, claiming these tools as their virtually exclusive property, women have authored most forceful anti-war writings, such as Nobel Peace Prize winner Alva Myrdal's book *The Game of Disarmament* and Helen Caldicott's *Nuclear Madness*. The 1980s in particular saw a burgeoning of women-organized and partly or wholly Christian-based organizations: Christian CND, Women's Action for Nuclear Disarmament (WAND), Women for Life on Earth (WFLOE).

The peacemaking concerns of religious feminists continue to encompass not only 'churchy' issues (such as women's ordination and the transformation of sexist liturgies and patriarchal power structures), but also secular social concerns in virtually every area of life.

Shall the children of Sarah and Hagar learn to live together in peace? Women in the peace movement think they can, and for many such a hope is worth staking their lives on. Whether or not the violence of war is uniquely immoral, Christian women in the peace movement continue to press for the importance of the end of wars while at the same time being morally demanding of the methods of achieving them. Meanwhile the resources of faith will continue to inspire the imagination and build spiritual endowments which give strength to live with the now and the hoped for, in the radical vision of welfare, work and world peace which they hope to leave for their children in the twenty-first century, the third millennium.

Further reading: Bacon 1993; Cambridge Women's Peace Collective 1984; Dowell and Hurcombe 1987; Ingram and Patai (eds.) 1993; Marshall and Ogden 1987; McAllister 1988; Melichap 1993; Oldfield 1989; Wiltshire 1985. In England the most useful collections on women and the peace movement remain the Fawcett Library and the Library at Friends House, both located in London. In the United States a comprehensive collection exists at Swarthmore College, 500 College Avenue, Swarthmore, PA 19081-1397, USA.

POLLUTION LAWS IN JUDAISM
Sylvia Rothschild

THE LAWS of ritual purity and impurity originate in the context of the need to maintain the sanctity of the temple and its precincts. There is no value judgment expressed in Judaism about ritual impurity, merely the acceptance that for a variety of reasons both men and women will regularly find themselves to be in this state. The laws were therefore formulated in the Bible in an attempt to deal with this inevitable condition, and to allow the people to make themselves ritually pure *(tahor)* once again. A sin can only be said to have occurred when someone or something in a state of ritual impurity *(tamei)* is brought into contact with the sacred.

The laws which pertain to the *niddah* (the menstruous woman) are thus set within the general laws of ritual purity found in the book of Leviticus. Specifically, most of the laws of *niddah* are found within the context of *zav*, the person (male or female) from whom there is genital issue or discharge (Lev. 15.33). A woman who is in the state of *niddah* is in a state of ritual impurity. Anyone who touches her will become ritually impure until the evening; anything she lies or sits on becomes *tamei*. If anyone touches her bedding or anything on which she sits, they should wash their clothes and bathe themselves in water, and they will remain *tamei* until the evening. If a man sleeps with her while she is in a state of *niddah*, his ritual impurity lasts for seven days, and all his bedding, like hers, becomes *tamei*. The text then notes that a woman may become *zavah* by having a discharge of blood not at the time of her menses, or if her menses are prolonged for an unnatural amount of time. In this case the same rules apply: her bedding and so on becomes *tamei*, and all who touch her become *tamei*. They must wash themselves and their clothes, and will remain *tamei* until the evening. By biblical statute the woman will become clean *(tahor)* after her discharge, by counting off seven days from the end of the discharge. There is no mention in the biblical text about immersion in water, although this is later inferred. The prohibition against sexual intercourse with a woman in the state of *niddah* is given twice more (Lev. 18.19; 20.18), and the punishment of *karet* (being cut off from the community) for both man and woman is added in the final prohibition. This seems to come from a different strand of the tradition, and does not appear to be concerned solely with temple purity. Possibly it is more connected to an ancient cultic blood taboo, with menstrual blood signifying the absence of new life. Certainly when the second temple was destroyed in the year 70 CE, the relevance to daily life of the laws of purity and impurity lessened and the prohibition about sexual relations while in a state of *niddah* became the major focus for women. Study of the laws of purity continued after the fall of the second temple, and they can be found in detail in the Mishnah, *Seder Tohorot* (c. second century CE). However, only one area of ritual impurity and its correction continued to be commented upon after the mishnaic period: the treatise exploring *niddah* is the only one with a further rabbinic commentary *(gemara)* in *Seder Tohorot*, and from here are derived the laws of *Tacharat HaMishpacha* (family purity).

Rabbinic law developed the biblical system by expanding the seven days of *niddah* when a woman is set apart from her husband into a minimum of twelve days—a minimum of five days for the blood flow and a further seven 'white' days following the last day of the flow. Rabbinic law also added the requirement of *mikveh* (immersion in the ritual bath) before the woman may resume sexual relations with her husband.

Biblically it is clear that ritual impurity is transmitted by contact, and so the woman in *niddah* would be secluded so as to prevent any accidental transmission of the impurity. However, it is clear that in rabbinic rulings the *niddah* was able to function normally within the household and thus to pass on her state of ritual impurity. Rashi (Rabbi Shlomo Yitzhaki) stated that the laws which were predicated on the prevention of the transmission of impurity were no longer based on such a concept. They were observed in his time only to accentuate the special state of the *niddah*, and to support the separation from her husband, which prescription remained in force. Rashi's justification for this view is that the laws of purity and impurity are in suspension for all practical purposes, until the rebuilding of the temple.

An A to Z of Feminist Theology

Childbirth also renders a woman *niddah*. She counts the seven white days from the end of the blood flow, but before going to the *mikveh* there is a minimum of seven days in the case of her having had a male child, and fourteen in the case of a female child.

The laws concerning the *niddah* have been codified and can be found in the *Shulchan Aruch, Yoreh Deah*, 183-200. The word *niddah* is interesting. Older scholarship has assumed it to be derived from the root *ndd* (to depart, retreat, stray, flee), in such a way as to imply disgust (to abhor or to shun), and so denote a defiling impurity. It is, however, more likely to derive either from another meaning of the root *ndd* (to urinate, or a gathering up of waters), or from the root *ndh*, which has the meaning of putting away or excluding, but which also has a secondary meaning of moistness, and of 'befalling', as with rain or dew, leading to the idea of a life-enhancing gift. Derivation from this root would give a completely different theological slant, reaffirming the importance of the natural bodily functions of women, while at the same time fitting in with the biblical 'separating from others' at the particular time in the menstrual cycle.

Further reading: Biale 1984; Greenberg 1983; Plaut 1981.

PORNOGRAPHY
Lisa Isherwood

PATRIARCHY TRADITIONALLY likes to confine women to the private sphere, except for those women who are expected to display themselves for the gratification of men. Traditional Christianity disapproves of pornography because it emphasizes the desires of the flesh over those of the spirit; nakedness is viewed by the church as immodest and as leading others astray. Some secular feminism disapproves of pornography because it sees it as exploiting women. So where does feminist theology stand? It begins with the notion of erotic power, which is the innate and raw power that allows people to create mutual relations and to live radically, and from there examines what is meant by pornography. Feminist theology does not understand pornography to be about naked flesh or the portrayal of sexual activity; it is more concerned with the message that is given. Any material that shows empowering sex is not in the realm of pornography. What is viewed as pornographic is any material that shows an unequal power relation, any that is involved with domination and coercion. Sexuality is not celebrated in pornographic material but rather it is imprisoned and punished through objectivity and power. The pornographer becomes the censor who leaves out anything that is relational and erotic. Even those magazines that used to be considered 'soft' porn magazines are now more interested in violence and domination.

Feminist ethicists who put forward the notion of erotic power as the heart of ethics are saying that nothing awakens a sense of justice more than bodily sensation, because we live in our bodies and experience the world through them. Therefore the deadening and objectifying of the body is a form of blasphemy because it denies the ultimate source of our divine understanding. This is quite different from saying that the body is 'dirty'; it is actually saying that it is the source of our divinity and therefore needs to be empowered and not strangled. We seem to live in a society that worships sex but hates the female body. Pornography is a way of silencing the female body while using it through making it public property and therefore appearing to hear it. What is projected is fantasy, while real women and their needs are being overlooked. A fundamental source of their own experience is removed from women and they are told that the experience of others is more important. The objectification of women is seen in material ranging from 'page three girls' to sado-masochistic images and 'snuff movies'. Pornography actually chains and represses erotic power and for that reason concerns feminist research.

Pornography generates a great deal of money, and those who argue that the women involved are acting as free agents should examine where the money is going. In the case of hard-core material the vast majority of the £500 million a year generated does not go into the pockets of the women. The claim that these women are acting 'freely' also needs to be viewed in the light of the fact that a large number of the women and girls who are used in pornography have been abused as youngsters. Society exploits them even further instead of helping to heal their wounds.

There is growing concern that pornography leads to violence against women. The constant

An A to Z of Feminist Theology

exposure to harm being inflicted actually desensitizes the men who view it and they find it easier to inflict pain. Shere Hite (1994) has uncovered a worrying trend, reporting that a large percentage of men view sex as a weapon with which to keep women in their place. Sexual violence has been used as a weapon of war. It is unlikely that little boys are born with this idea and so we need seriously to question where it came from.

Pornography can be viewed as a sign of men's perceived helplessness, which would explain why it is on the increase at a time when women are asserting their independence. Pornography presents men with a world in which they feel more comfortable since they are in charge. If this is the case then feminist theology has a role to play in education for boys that helps them deal with their insecurities without having to resort to a world of violent fantasy that is often lived out; that way of living is demeaning to themselves and to women and is not a sign of a liberating environment.

Feminist theologians postulate that the erotic needs to be put back into our society. This will involve a change in the understanding of sexuality by the churches. The dualism of patriarchy has meant that the body is seen as inferior to the things of the spirit; this has meant that Christianity has never properly respected the body. Feminist theology wants to overcome this age-old dualism and so views the body as a vehicle for the divine. The body is central in the creation of theology because it is central to the way in which we experience both ourselves and the world.

Since feminist theology views the objectification of people as pornographic, this is a term that can be applied to patriarchal theological doctrine. This is a form of theologizing that actually makes both God and people into objects. God is seen as so far removed from the world that people cannot appreciate how God can exist. When feminist theologians look at pornography they are examining a whole system of objectifications that enslave the erotic power in people.

Further reading: Dworkin 1981; Griffin 1988; MacKinnon 1994; Russell (ed.) 1993.

POST-CHRISTIAN FEMINISM
Lisa Isherwood

WHEN FEMINISTS begin to reflect on Christian theology they do so by striking at its very heart. Feminism believes that the patriarchal worldview created by Christian theology is neither true nor moral. Feminism is challenging the patriarchal myths that are at the heart of religion and it is doing so because it sees them as damaging to women. Post-Christians argue that a revolution is needed in religion if we are to remain in any meaningful way 'religious'. Women are trying to express an understanding of God within a different thought structure. It is relatively easy to make laws that strive for the equality of women but it is more radical to try to show how the deeper structures that support those laws are in need of changing if the needs of women are to be met.

In the meeting of those needs we find a new understanding of what God means and what human relationships mean. This revolution in religion will affect human society on all levels because it will shatter the picture of reality which came out of a patriarchal world.

Post-Christian theology is still relatively young and so it has all the excitement and difficulties of a movement that is trying to look beyond the structures to new and liberating possibilities. In Britain Daphne Hampson is leading the post-Christian debate and her work (1990) clearly sets out the major difficulties that appear when feminism and Christianity stand face to face. The first problem arises with the claim of Christianity that Jesus was in some way unique. Christian history shows that the content of this claim differs from generation to generation, but that Jesus' uniqueness is always stressed. The most constant claim to uniqueness is of course the virgin birth. Feminism challenges this view because it implies a hierarchical division between spirit and matter that is abhorrent to feminist thought. Even those who do not perceive Jesus in the orthodox way have spoken of uniqueness. Post-Enlightenment thinkers have found something unique in Jesus. For example, Schleiermacher, writing in the nineteenth century thought that Jesus had a unique God-con-

POST CHRISTIAN FEMINISM

sciousness. Bultmann located Jesus' uniqueness in the resurrection. There are those who claim that Jesus had a unique moral teaching; this would be an incorrect claim, as modern scholarship has shown that much of Jesus' moral teaching was in no way unique. Certainly, according to Hampson, such a claim would not constitute a declaration of Christian faith. To be considered a Christian, Hampson (1990) thinks, one has to make more definite statements. She insists that Christians are those who not only proclaim the message *of* Jesus but also a message *about* Jesus. It is the post-Christian argument that this cannot be done; further, modern scholarship shows that this is the case.

The stance of uniqueness requires that history be viewed in a certain way. Hampson argues that the belief in the uniqueness of Jesus requires us always to return to a certain period in history to evaluate our actions. Those who criticize her think that she is viewing Christian history as static and unable to unfold. They also accuse her of thinking that the past has to be entirely disregarded and everything has to start from now. Rosemary Radford Ruether (1987) accuses Hampson of failing to realize that Christian history is orientated to the future and not the past. Hampson acknowledges that this is the case to some degree but that Christians never manage to make their vision a radical reality because they are always looking back. This can be seen, for example, in the debate over the ordination of women to the priesthood. There were many who debated from the position of what Jesus did and would do; Hampson claims that this is all irrelevant and what matters is that it is right and just to ordain women now, regardless of what may have occurrred in the past and in the life of one man.

Hampson suggests that Christianity's conception of its history is quite different from that of science, for example. In the history of science there are revolutionary discoveries and paradigm shifts, but these are not accorded the status of 'revelations' to humanity. Science, in common with other disciplines, acknowledges its tradition but is free to use what it wishes and to move on while discarding what is no longer useful.

Post-Christians claim that history, like nature, is interwoven into a whole. The kind of uniqueness of which Christians speak cannot therefore be possible—the kind of uniqueness which involves the breaking of the laws of nature, the moving of things outside their usual categories. Resurrection is an example of this; it has not been known for dead people to come back to life. Christianity does not fit the paradigms of knowledge that we have. It postulates a God who made all the rules but also breaks them at will; this is not only inconsistent, it is at times immoral.

If there can be no particular revelation in the past then there is no necessity to keep referring back to the past as a measure of what is acceptable in the present. Hampson and other post-Christians are clear that we have to find what is true and moral without referring to the past. This is not to suggest that the past will not influence us, but rather that we should be aware that we may need to rid ourselves of some of that past rather than venerating it. Post-Christians suggest that this means that we can therefore speak of god theology but not Christian theology.

Biblical texts cause great problems for post-Christians. It has been suggested that this is because post-Christians tend to read the texts in a fundamentalist, simplistic way. However, this fails to take into account the post-Christian argument that the Bible, however it is read, has no normative status. Even on a liberal reading the Christian Scriptures still cause problems for feminists because they are almost completely written by men and reflect issues of importance to men. The imagery and the language are harmful to women and no amount of reclaiming can undo the damage. Mary Daly (1986) thinks that it is not worth spending the amount of time that would be necessary to reclaim the texts and find the woman-space within them; for her they are so patriarchal that they are best left alone.

Hampson and other post-Christians believe that all that is available to use is the awareness of God; while people have tried to capture this throughout history, there is no one revelation that is the 'true' revelation. However, this does not mean that theology becomes a private affair, rather, it still has to be worked out in community. We experience God in community and so this is where theology has its roots. Post-

An A to Z of Feminist Theology

Christians argue that if we would be willing, as in other disciplines, to start with the present and only take from the past what is useful then there need be no problems for women. Hampson claims that many women are being dishonest in trying to be both feminist and Christian, which she views as impossible in the light of the fundamental differences in method.

Mary Daly's evolution of thought is intriguing. She coined the phrase 'post-Christian' in the 1970s and intended it to express her movement beyond the confines of Christianity. She argued that it was necessary for women to make this move since Christianity is irredeemably sexist and patriarchal. It was her belief that if one removed patriarchy from Christianity there would be nothing left at all. Daly clearly shows how destructive patriarchy is for the universe and its inhabitants.

Her position in the 1990s has changed; she no longer wishes to be referred to as post-Christian because she feels that this places too much emphasis on Christianity. She, like Hampson, thinks that we have to find our own meaning and values in our own time without reference to the past. Unlike Hampson she is not willing to acknowledge any Christian heritage; she wishes people to purge themselves totally of the negative influences of our Christian heritage.

POWER
Maureen McBride

IN THE patriarchal system, power is conceived as the ability to get things done. It is executed as action upon a thing or person and is exerted as authority, might, control, force, aggression, domination. Power is limited and competitive. Those who have power attempt to safeguard it either through legitimate means or through deviousness. The greatest concentration of power rests in the hands of the elites of transcorporate business, financial institutions and political and ecclesial hierarchies. This power 'trickles down' to executives, middle management and supervisors, diminishing at each level, whether in business, politics or the church. Those at the bottom and on the margins remain voiceless and powerless to affect change.

In the experience of oppression, subordinate people have been victimized by their own powerlessness and have internalized the negative image assigned to them by the dominant patriarchal society. Any claiming of power by oppressed and marginalized people is perceived as a threat to those with power and is often suppressed in one way or another. Nor is dissent tolerated within the church, as evidenced by the silencing of a number of contemporary moral and liberation theologians in the Catholic church. Consistent with this patriarchal concept of power is the image of God as male, omnipotent, omniscient, omnipresent—a demanding and exacting ruler and judge.

Throughout history, power has been used against women to tyrannize and to terrorize, to rape and to kill, to alienate and to silence, to obliterate their history and to deny their experience, to limit women's horizons and to thwart their ambitions. Women have been, and in most cultures continue to be, excluded from power and decision-making in the political, economic, legal and ecclesial spheres.

Over the centuries, the Scriptures have been used to keep women in a subordinate position within society and the church. Many passages in the Hebrew Scriptures give graphic testimony and even legitimation to the degradation, violence, rape, abuse and torture that continues to be inflicted on women to the present time (for example, the daughters of Lot, Gen. 19; the rape of Dinah, Gen. 34). As well as bringing to greater consciousness the impact of these tragic and terrible texts, feminist Scripture scholars retrieve the stories of biblical women who claim initiative and power and bring life to others (the Hebrew midwives who conspire against the power of Pharaoh to save the lives of the children, Exod. 1.15–2.10; Miriam, who leads the people in a liturgy of celebration and thanksgiving, Exod. 15.20-21; Queen Vashti, a woman of integrity who refuses to be compromised, Est. 1). In the New Testament, Mary at Cana, the Samaritan woman, Martha and Mary and the woman who anoints the head of Jesus are all examples of women who claim power and take their own initiative.

Feminists envision a very different concept of power from that of the patriarchal system. In critiquing the dominant sources and ethos of power, they retrieve the essence of the ancient Greek concept of power as 'being'. The power 'to be' is a sacred right. To recognize the power of the 'Other' is to recognize the sacredness of their being. In feminist thought power is limitless, infinite. It is not competitive and has nothing to do with control over another. When it is shared rather than being consumed, power actually regenerates and expands. There is no need to hoard or protect it, because it only increases when it is shared. The exercise of 'people power', that of the collective, enables the breaking forth from powerlessness and subordination. Women experience power in their bonding together with other women, and find liberation through the discovery that other women feel as they do. Power is re-imaged as energy, creativity, vigour, passion, wisdom, participation, mutuality-in-relation.

A revisioning of leadership in the feminist context means making use of the interests, skills, knowledge and insights of the group. To exercise the power of leadership, rather than to have 'authority over' another, means to facilitate, to enable, to energize and to empower others to articulate their intuitions, to discover and to develop their capabilities, to make their contributions, while simultaneously making one's own.

In feminist theology, God is understood as creative energy and the life-giving power of Being, Breathing, Birthing and Bursting into human history. God is the eternally creative source of relational power, our common strength, the power who fosters life rather than death. The movement of God is to empower humanity to realize their full potential as human beings. Created in the image and likeness of God, women and men are invited to collaborate in the creatorship of God and are gifted with the power of naming and acclaiming (Gen. 2.19-20). The power of God is experienced in companionship and mutual relationship (Gen. 3.8); in face-to-face encounter and dialogue (Exod. 33.11); in intervention and liberation from oppression and injustice (Exod. 3.7); in flaming fire (Exod. 3.2), raging seas (Job 26.12) and gentle breezes (1 Kgs 19.12-13).

In Jesus, the power of God breaks into human history in a profoundly new way. Anointed with the Spirit and power (Acts 10.38), Jesus images a new concept of power as mutality and relationship in a discipleship of inclusivity and equality. In the Jesus community patriarchal power as 'lording it over' and 'exercising power over' others is rejected; instead, the disciple is to respect and revere, to enable and empower others to claim the fullness of their own power of being and acting. The praxis of Jesus breaks the prevailing ethic of domination and submission. Jesus reached out to those rejected by the religious and civil elites so that the powerless—women, children, tax collectors, prostitutes, lepers and Samaritans—became the central images of the *basileia*.

Christian women, re-imaging power as spirit and passion, as intuition, sensitivity and solidarity, as affinity and facilitation, as righteous indignation that calls forth justice, as the inbreaking of God's *basileia*, seek a transformation of church into an inclusive and liberating community that is inspired by their collective experience of the vision of a discipleship of equals, and the gratuitousness and limitless nature of God's creative activity in history.

Further reading: Furlong 1991; Grey 1990; Heyward 1982; Kramarae and Treichler 1992; Wilson Schaef 1985.

PRAXIS
Maureen McBride

THE CLASSICAL use of the term by Aristotle identified praxis as one of the three general patterns of specifically human modes of activities: *theoris*—the theoretic; *praxis*—the practical; and *poiesis*—the productive.

The term was popularized in Marxist ideology, where praxis is integral and is seen as action for social transformation, specifically, action based on thinking, or theory, on an understanding of economic structures and their development. Marx, in the first of his eleven theses, criticized the writings and thought of all previous materialists, including Feuerbach, for adopting a purely theoretical attitude towards the world, and ignoring the crucial importance of human activity (praxis). Praxis is dialectical, with theory and action constantly interrelated. Neither theory nor action is prior, both are constantly modified in the light of the other and in response to changing and developing conditions and circumstances. Praxis both builds on theory and calls for changes in theory. For Marx, the need for action to change the environment is of crucial importance to human activity.

The influence of Marxist thought, with its focus on praxis oriented to the transformation of the world, has helped theology, specifically liberation, political and feminist theologies, to recognize the importance of understanding faith in the light of human praxis in history. These theologies assign primacy to the 'praxis of faith', that is, the biblical action of 'doing of truth'. The call to praxis empowers humans to take responsibility for their own lives, gives them experiences of being subjects rather than merely passive objects of their own histories. The core of the praxis of faith is integrity, that is, consistency in hearing, seeing, believing, speaking, and doing.

The vision and praxis of Jesus in his pronouncement of and commitment to the *basilea*, the Reign of God, are central to liberation and feminist theologies. For liberation theologians, Jesus' passion for life, justice and liberating hope, his concern to restore and secure life wherever it is threatened, are at the heart of his praxis. In his inclusive table-fellowship, Jesus' attitudes and actions incarnate the basilea and embody God's love for the socially and religiously marginalized—poor people, public sinners, lepers, publicans, drunkards and prostitutes. Jesus' praxis is both social and political in nature, and in his challenging of the values and institutions of his days, he quickly becomes an affront to the rich and powerful elite and a threat to their domination.

Feminist theologians and biblical scholars have further illuminated the praxis of Jesus by pointing to the liberating character of his social relationships, particularly his relationships with women. Jesus breaks through social, religious and cultural barriers to include and embrace the contribution of women at the heart of his vision and commitment to the *basilea* (for example he defended the right of Mary, sister of Martha, to assume the privileged position of disciple [Lk. 10.38-42]; his interaction with the Syro-Phoenician woman became critical to his own action–reflection process as he shifted his initial focus from the House of Israel, to include and embrace the Gentiles [Mk 7.24–8.9]; Mary, who anointed the feet of Jesus [Jn 12.1-8] becomes the symbol of loving service in action which he himself enacts at his final supper with his friends [Jn 13.1-20]; he entrusts the mission, 'Go and Tell' to Mary Magdalene).

In Jesus, God is revealed in history, in the act of accomplishing the *basilea* and thereby transforming the human situation. Jesus proposes a new image and approach to God. God is revealed in history, in the act of accomplishing the *basilea* and thereby transforming the human situation. The praxis of Jesus implies the establishment of a new kind of solidarity, one that transforms class and natural differences. Jesus' passion for establishing the *basilea* is a passion for total liberation. Thus, in the person and praxis of Jesus are found the grounds of human liberation from all oppression and discrimination, whether political or economic, religious or cultural, or based on gender, race and ethnicity (Fabella 1989).

Liberation theologians define their method of doing theology as critical reflection on praxis in the light of the Word of God. The Christian and the Christian community are called by their religious belief to a praxis that involves real charity, action and commitment to the service of women and men. In the context of the massive human suffering experienced by the majority of the world's citizens, praxis in inextricably linked with the commandment of love and the demands for justice, and becomes the attempt to live the gospel by sharing in the lives and struggles of the poor and by striving to bring about the changes needed to eliminate such suffering, and to liberate them. Thus praxis is a prophetic function. Theologizing in the light of past and present injustices and oppressions demands conversion of sinful structures and systems, and individuals and community commitment to the *basilea*. Christian praxis cannot be limited to private virtues but necessarily contains socio-political involvement.

In feminist theology, reflection and action are not separated. Praxis is action and reflection as one moment, not as a series of events. Reflection upon practice is both an individual and communal activity, and an on-going process which evolves new questions and evokes alternative actions which when reflected upon consequently create new questions and new fields of possibility. Not merely cerebral and intellectual, nor merely activist and emotional, feminist theology does not deny the necessity of either. Rigorous passionate research and intelligent passionate participation in the transformation of the world enrich and challenge each other. Praxis is 'reflection-informed-by-practice and practice-informed-by-reflection' (Coll 1994). Some Asian feminist theologians speak of theology as 'God-praxis'. Theologizing here is living the liberation of wholeness in the here and now. 'God-praxis' is not only a theoretical exercise, it is a commitment and participation to peoples' struggle for full humanity, and discernment of God's redemptive action in history. It is theology-in-action, reflective action and engaged reflection together as an integral whole (Chung 1990).

For feminine theologians liberating praxis must also be applied to the institutional church itself, where women continue to be marginalized and their experience and giftedness is largely ignored or denied.

Further reading: Hennelly 1990; McGovern 1987; Schüssler Fiorenza 1986.

PRAYER
Anne Murphy

'**PRAYER IS** that primordial discourse in which we assert, however clumsily or eloquently, our own being' (Ulanov and Ulanov 1982). Every time we call for help or understanding from forces beyond us, or deep within us, we pray, even if we do not address the God of Scriptures or traditional religion. Prayer may start without words and often ends without them. It is woven from the texture of our lives and takes many forms: personal and private, shared and vocal, public and liturgical. Prayer can be a cry of gratitude, lament or intercession; it can be an unvoiced longing of the heart, an expression of love and intimacy, or an admission of guilt seeking forgiveness. It can be childish prayer for 'what we want', a search for security and assurance; or it may be a personal encounter with an 'Other' who is the source of our being and the core of our desires, to whom the appropriate response is 'worship'. Prayer is addressed to an 'Other' in whom we may have deep faith, shaky faith or no faith at all. We may be confident that our prayer will be heard, or feel that there is nobody there to hear us, or 'somebody' who never responds.

Within Judaeo-Christian practice, the prayer of the individual has been shaped by liturgical, mystical, popular and devotional traditions which are rich and varied, but also sometimes restrictive and limiting. The great contribution of feminist theology has been to notice and challenge the over-masculinization of the God-image in traditional worship and prayer and the practical equation of the Trinity with three male persons. It has highlighted again the necessarily metaphorical nature of all language about God, whom we can only speak about indirectly and in terms of our own experience. Until comparatively recently Christians have been conditioned to accept the primacy of maleness in our image for God. God has most usually been imaged as monarch, husband, father, shepherd, warrior. God has rarely been imaged as mother, woman in labour, sister, Sophia/Wisdom, bakerwoman, though all are scriptural images. The widely-held corollary is that maleness reflects God in a way that femaleness is unable to do. This is re-enforced by reserving 'sacral offices' to men, who are seen to be more 'appropriate' representatives of the divine. It requires a real conversion of mind and heart to see that divine spirit and power are also appropriately imaged as female, and that women in their embodied and sexual existence are 'icons' of a God whose being can never be fully expressed in any one image.

The theological need to re-image God in multiple and inclusive ways, and to use inclusive language in liturgy and prayer, poses some acute problems for the *affective* prayer life of the individual. We may be convinced intellectually of the need to address God as mother, long before it becomes 'natural' to do so in prayer. We can use the alternating term God/dess in our writing, but it may not be helpful in prayer. The most radical form of feminist spirituality worships the Great Mother Goddess who is immanent, not transcendent. While this has possibilities for the empowerment of women, some would argue that such a *thealogy* is difficult to reconcile with the Christian concept of a Triune God.

An A to Z of Feminist Theology

For many there is a 'dark night' or impasse involved in a conversion to feminist prayer and spirituality (Fitzgerald 1986: 302). Traditionally prayer has had its illuminative, purgative and unitive stages; feminist prayer passes through these traditional growth points for new reasons and in unfamiliar ways. For example, passages from Scripture or the spiritual classics suddenly lose their 'hold' on us because we have begun to read them with new eyes, using a 'hermeneutic of suspicion' rather than a 'hermeneutic of assent' (why were the ten commandments addressed to the men and not the women? Why is there no mention of the mother or sisters in the parable of the Prodigal Son?). Well-loved hymns, religious poems and mystical literature no longer nourish and sustain—at least for a time. Non-inclusive language and an all-male clergy may alienate us from formal worship. And in the intimacy of personal prayer we may feel that our familiar sense of God, the core Christian symbol of Father, Son and Spirit, is in fragments.

In the experience of 'impasse' the spiritual support systems on which we have depended since childhood seem to have given way. There is a sense of inner powerlessness and alienation, often compounded by a growing anger at the injustices which women experience within society and organized religion. It is hard—though ultimately essential—to cope with anger in prayer, especially for Christians brought up to believe that passive endurance is an essential virtue. 'There is no going back to what was— what gave comfort and clarity and brought feminists to their present stage of religious development—but there is no satisfactory way of going forward either' (Fitzgerald 1986). One has to practice revolutionary patience (as Dorothee Sölle terms it), or have the courage and faith to endure what will ultimately be a 'productive disintegration', before entering more deeply into the mystery of the Divine. At this time it is important to share experiences with others who are making the same journey, and to experiment with new forms of prayer, ritual and holistic spirituality.

Some women and men move very quickly, and with evident joy, into a relationship with the Divine Other who exists beyond patriarchy. Praying with the image of Sophia/Wisdom, and experiencing God's feminine presence within, is particularly helpful. For others it is a slow and hazardous path. The feminist/womanist journey, through impasse in prayer to religious and personal transformation, has been told most movingly in Alice Walker's novel *The Color Purple* (1982), surely a new classic of spirituality. Celie, a poor and abused black woman, tries to write the story of her life in a series of letters addressed to God. But she gives up as she realizes that 'the God I been praying and writing to is a man. And acts just like all the mens I know. Trifling, forgitful and lowdown'. So she writes to her sister, supported by the love and insights of another woman, Shug Avery. As Celie grows in self-awareness, so too does her religious and contemplative awareness. Shug helps her to understand that 'God is inside you and inside everybody else. You come into the world with God. But only them that search for it inside can find it.' Celie's final letter is addressed to the God she has found again: 'Dear God. Dear stars, dear trees, dear sky, dear peoples. Dear everything. Dear God' (Walker 1982: 242).

Celie's prayer is reminiscent of John of the Cross's paean of praise: 'Mine are the heavens and mine is the earth'. It is unitive and contemplative prayer, the grace of revolutionary struggle and patience, which sees God in All, and All in God. As such, Christian feminist/womanist prayer takes its place as both radically new and, at the same time, authentically in continuity with the great traditions of Christian spirituality.

Further reading: Coakley 1990; Grey 1990; St Hilda Community 1993.

PRESBYTERA
Mary Ann Rossi

THE TERM 'presbytera' has been recovered by research of the 1980s and 1990s as a title of women priests duly ordained in communities in full communion with Rome in the early and formative period of the church. The alternative sense of this term is 'wife of a priest', a honorary title indicative of the practice of optional celibacy, also practised in the early church. Both definitions, recorded in DuCanges, s.v., as attested in the works of Atto, Bishop of Vercelli, gradually became anathema to a hierarchy determined to eradicate from church history both women priests and wives of priests and bishops.

Cogent testimony for the definition of 'woman priest' is provided by Atto, who attests that in the ancient church women, as well as men, were ordained and were the leaders of communities; they were called 'presbyterae' and they assumed the duties of preaching, directing and teaching: these three duties define the role of the sacrament of priesthood. Hence Atto disarms the most frequent excuse for the exclusion of women from the priesthood: precedent. For Atto, it was the Council of Laodicea (second half of the fourth century) that prohibited the presbyteral ordination of women: 'It is not allowed for those called "presbyterae" to be appointed to preside in the church' (Canon XI).

The method employed to 'revise' women's role in the early church was efficacious and thorough: (1) deny that women were ever ordained; (2) when presented with any evidence of women's priesthood, define the provenance of such evidence as 'heretical'. In this way the church succeeded in defacing archaeological testimony and in misreading or misinterpreting epigraphical testimony until the twentieth century, when an Italian scholar succeeded in restoring women to the early Christian perception of their humanity and equality with men (cf. Otranto 1982).

The discovery of subtle 'revisionism' in the modus operandi of the Catholic historiographers has been a striking and highly motivating catalyst for the grassroots activism of women in the Roman Catholic movement for women's ordination throughout the world. In the United States the Women's Ordination Conference was founded in 1975; in the United Kingdom, the Catholic Women's Ordination was founded in 1993; in the Republic of Ireland, BASIC ('brothers and sisters in Christ') was founded in 1993, and in France the group is called *Hommes et Femmes dans l'Eglise*. The movement for women's ordination is also active in Scotland, Australia and New Zealand.

In the current movement for women's ordination, the outdated response of the Vatican ('there were no women ordained in the early church; women do not image Christ') clearly broadcasts to all women the inability of the Pope and his officials to accept the consensus of theologians ('women and men equally image the divine'); anthropologists ('women are fully human, and not defective males'); political scientists ('women are equal under the law'); philosophers ('the Aristotelian perception of women is false'); and psychologists ('gender polarity underlies inequality of the sexes and must be recognized and corrected'). The discovery of the definition of 'presbytera' in the early church has been a liberating and insightful clue to the restoring of women to history and history to women.

PRIESTHOOD
Ronwyn Goodsir-Thomas

THE OFFICE of priesthood is found in most societies. In the very earliest communities the king and the priest were one. Later the two offices became separated and power was usually in the hands of the constitution, that is, the king and the priest. Priesthood was not only concerned with the administration of the cult; the power it represented extended over the whole of life. As power-bearer the priest was understood to be filled with the god; in the sacrificial cult the priest was regarded as the custodian of the life of the god. In more developed societies the priestly class has a characteristic structure. It consists of closed communities which tend to divide themselves and form a classified hierarchy. Each class has a different function and a fixed rank. This is just as true of the priesthood of the Catholic Church as of that of ancient Rome, Babylon or Egypt. Priesthood repeatedly shows a tendency to gain the most absolute power possible over all areas of peoples' lives.

This pattern can be seen in the development of priesthood in the Old Testament. In its earliest stages priesthood reflected the nomadic, patriarchal way of life (Gen. 12.8; 15.8-17; 22.1-3), the priestly function being undertaken by the head of the family or clan. Later the king claimed the right to perform priestly functions (David, 2 Sam. 6.17; Solomon, 1 Kgs 3.4; 8.22, 62). Although Moses exercised priestly functions, in tradition he is seen as the lawgiver. Under Mosaic law the priesthood became confined to the tribe of Levi. From very early times priesthood formed part of the messianic hope (Ps. 110), looking to the union of kingship and priesthood in a single person. The crowning

PRIESTHOOD

of the high priest signified that he was entrusted with civil power. This became a fact under the Maccabees when Simon, the high priest, was chosen to be the political and military leader of the people (1 Macc. 14.41).

Jesus was convinced that at his coming temple and cult would come to an end (Mt. 26.61; Jn 2.19) and the offices of high priest and priest were called into question. Although Jesus did not use the title 'priest', he used priestly terms in describing his mission (Mk 10.45; cf. Isa. 53). He fulfilled the Torah, but he also transcended it (Mt. 5.17-18; 5.20-48). Christ opened up a new way into the sanctuary of God for all who came to him (Heb. 9.25). He chose his apostles to continue his mission and they in turn appointed elders for the service of the people of God. No New Testament text gives the title 'priest' to any of those responsible for the churches. Christians put an end to the ancient priestly institution, seeing in Jesus the unique High Priest according to the order of Melchizedek.

The New Testament evidence shows that in the early Christian communities not only men, but also women, were leaders in the local churches (Phil. 4.2-4; Rom. 16.1-2). They established local communities, celebrated the Lord's Supper and preached in their house churches. From c. 200 CE onwards there is no evidence of women taking leading roles in mainstream churches, and the position of men accepted as leaders had been firmly bound into a hierarchical system. During the first centuries of its existence the Christian community lived in a world in which order was breaking down. This disorder was seen as a threat to Christianity itself. In the struggle to preserve the Christian message in a world in chaos an internal conflict took place within the church itself. Women, gnostics and all who refused to subscribe to the ordered patriarchal and hierarchical system were branded as heretics. The Christian church adopted the characteristics of the traditional pattern of priesthood, with its tendency to take to itself the greatest power possible. In the centuries that followed this pattern continued to flourish. Despite St Benedict's establishment of monasteries as lay communities not subject to priestly control, within a few hundred years most monasteries in Europe were dominated by a powerful priestly caste owning vast estates. By the eleventh century Pope Gregory VII was able to claim that priests stood higher than kings. From the Middle Ages and earlier the priestly caste within Christianity was able to justify the need for the church, that is, themselves, to be powerful, and to belong to the ruling classes in society. The priesthood paid lip-service to the needs of the poor while choosing to remain part of the system that oppressed them. This was done by teaching the masses to look for heavenly solutions to earthly ills. Like priesthoods within all religions, the Christian priesthood retained power over the widest possible area: power over the rich through its sacred functions which it could give or withhold at will, and power over the poor by the fostering of a cult of dependence—dependence on the priesthood for 'spiritual' nourishment, and dependence on otherworldly justice which coincided with the interests of the powerful.

Historians of religion have long recognized the power associated with the membership of priestly castes. These groups are characterized by the separation of their way of life from that of the rest of the community. This is the basis of their power:

> The priest's life is restricted, power being, as it were, confined within his life. Official costume, celibacy, regular fasts, regular reading and discharge of the breviary etc., all have the same end: the representative has to undertake all the generalities of power of which the community is incapable (van der Leeuw 1963: 220).

Within Christianity priesthood can only be exercised within the institution of the church. It is characteristic of all institutions to have a charismatic founder. After the death of the founder the leaders of the movement develop a 'routinization' of charisma and power. The charisma of Christ within the Catholic Church has 'routinized' into a hierarchically ordained structure, supported by legal sanctions and the appeal to tradition through history and dogma. As in all institutions, authority to give commands, and activities distributed as official duties, are strictly regulated. Within this institutional machine individuals are bound to the community of functionaries who are part of the system. Officials who attempt change can be marginalized. For this reason change cannot arise from within the priesthood, but must come from outside.

The violent opposition displayed by the Vatican towards feminism and any proposal to ordain women and married men arises from its recognition that positive steps in this direction would lead to a reduction in its own power. This is leading it to increasingly totalitarian treatment of theologians and others who show sympathy with such ideas.

Further reading: Mensching 1976; Schüssler Fiorenza 1983; Weber 1968.

PROCESS THOUGHT
Sheila Greeve Davaney

DURING THE last third of the twentieth century a number of new approaches, questions and substantive proposals have appeared on the theological scene. Important among these new developments have been the emergence of process and feminist theologies. Both of these theological perspectives have had broad impact across the theological spectrum, especially as they have re-examined and criticized dominant notions of God and the human self. And while they cannot be identified with one another, their common critique of the Western theological tradition and their shared commitment to its radical revision have led to a rich conversation among some of their proponents.

For feminist theologians and theorists the issue of subjectivity has been a central and problematic topic from the beginnings of feminist reflection. Questions of what it means to be a female self in a world in which male selfhood has been normative and how such subjectivity relates to history, biology and the social and political order have focused much feminist thought. In recent feminist theology this broad concern has centered on several particular issues, among them those concerning how contemporary women should relate to their pasts and whether there is such a thing as a common women's experience or only more particular and localized experience. It is in relation to these specific concerns that I will examine process thought's view of reality.

Process thinkers, developing the vision of reality articulated by such thinkers as Alfred North Whitehead and Charles Hartshorne, have grounded much of their work in a particular understanding of the self that resonates with and can be seen to contribute to certain understandings of subjectivity that are emerging from feminist reflection. Process thinkers, while they disagree on much, begin with the common assertion that in its most basic form reality consists of distinct units of concrete actuality, not abstract entities, ideas or ideal forms. Proponents of this process perspective further contend that these fundamental concrete realities are thoroughly historical and social processes, depending upon other actual entities while at the same time maintaining subjective integrity and individual value. This process interpretation of the relational, yet integrity-filled, character of reality can be elucidated in the following ways.

Most basically, to be a concrete actual reality is to be an experiencing subject in relation to other experiencing subjects; it is to be an intrinsically social being, coexisting in interdependent fashion with other equally social entities, acting and reacting, relating and being related to. This view, therefore, rejects the understanding of the experiencing subject as an isolated self in the Cartesian sense of that which requires nothing but itself in order to exist. Autonomous, self-sufficient selfhood, that ideal of much male identity, is ruled out.

But process thought not only argues for the importance of social relations; it radicalizes its interpretation of these relations. The subject is not first a subject that then experiences or relates to other realities. Instead, the subject is the experience; it is literally the synthesis of data provided by its social environment. Social relatedness is not an interesting but non-fundamental addendum to an autonomous selfhood, but rather such relatedness constitutes the experiencing subject.

The centrality of relatedness is echoed in much feminist thought. Feminists have widely, if not universally, argued against notions of subjectivity interpreted in terms of isolated and autonomous selfhood and have opted for notions of interdependence, historicity and social relatedness. But such relationality has also been interpreted, especially in the contexts of oppression, as highly problematic. That is, women find themselves not only influenced by others in their social environment and by their personal and communal histories but literally determined by others' expectations, desires, needs and definitions. Moreover, women have historically been relegated to the sphere of relationality, interpreted as having value primarily in relation to others and lacking in intrinsic worth. Thus a major concern for feminist thought has been to develop notions of the social character of subjectivity that do not merely reinscribe oppressive and legitimizing notions of women as dependent, determined by others and devoid of intrinsic value.

The process perspective is suggestive in relation to this issue. On the one hand, it acknowledges that the present context and past history do indeed shape the self and delimit the possibilities that are available for the self-constitution of any individual. In a universe that is composed of the webs of social interaction there is no escape from history or context. This inescapability suggests why oppressive consciousness, structures and modes of relationality are reconstituted generation after generation and why the stranglehold of oppression is so difficult to break. But while process thought acknowledges that determination by others, including the other who is my past self, is a component of social relatedness, it also affirms that creative freedom is an aspect of every moment of experience. While every experiencing subject must take account of its social environment, both in terms of its immediate past and its more distant history, and while that context does indeed set limits to its possibilities, this determination is never complete, especially on a human level. Each moment of experience creatively appropriates its context and in such creative appropriation lies the possibility of transformation and ultimately liberation. Thus while dependence on and determination by others are intrinsic to subjectivity, they do not tell the whole story. Equally real is a basic creativity and freedom that contributes to the constitution of each subject. Freedom and determination are, hence, both elements of subjectivity.

This view of subjectivity offers feminist theology a compelling way to interpret the dynamics of relationality in the construction of female selfhood. In particular, it presents a helpful way to consider the relation of present and past as women seek to rethink their connection to a significantly oppressive history, including those elements of the past such as the Bible that have been so determinative of women's sense of self. In this perspective, women cannot simply ignore history; for good or ill the past influences the present. But according to a process interpretation women are not forced by such a claim to assume that the past is either a fundamentally benign influence or a wholly negative one that cannot be transformed. Instead the process approach suggests that the past is plural and multivalent; it is an ambiguous heritage of possibilities and limitations. And for process thinkers the task is neither to submit to nor reject that heritage but creatively to transform it into more liberating forms of subjectivity in the present; it is to seek conditions whereby the creative possibilities of the past are maximized and the destructive ones are transmuted as best they can be into new and novel options for the present. Hence this view suggests that women, as relational subjects, are both products of history and the creative agents and constructors of new histories; they emerge from the past but are not condemned to repeat that past.

A related concern for feminists has been whether the recognition of relationality forces women once more into the role of being values for others, those selves whose primary responsibility is to enhance the possibilities for others, especially men and children. Have women not been cast as objects for others rather than subjects for themselves? Process thought has engaged this question as well by affirming that the understanding of subjectivity argued for above entails the assertion that the division of the world into self-contained subjects and other-oriented objects is misguided and that instead reality consists of subjects, bearing intrinsic worth by virtue of their sheer existence, who in turn become objects contributing to the world that other subjects must take account of. In this interpretation there are no objects that are not first subjects; there are only moments of subjective experience that endure briefly and then become part of the vast reservoir that is the past, limiting and shaping the experience of those who follow. In this manner process thinkers affirm both that each subject is an intrinsic value

PROCESS THOUGHT

in and for itself and that it is a value for others contributing to the world. Most importantly for women, however, the richness of that gift to the future depends upon the quality of the experiencing subject. Hence, women and all other subjects contribute most to others when their own experience is fullest.

Another area of intense concern for recent feminist theology revolves around the issue of 'the appeal to women's experience'. In virtually all feminist theology until recently there has been an appeal to women's experience as both the source and norm for feminist theological reflection. Most often it was assumed that the experience of women was a shared and common experience both in terms of the oppression women had suffered and in relation to the critical consciousness that was emerging. These assumptions of commonality have come under increasing criticism as various women, most notably women of colour, have asserted that the experience referred to was, when scrutinized, not a common experience at all but primarily the experience of privileged white women that failed to take into account the profound differences that exist among women and that neglected to hold white women accountable for their complicity in the oppression of other women of different races, classes, national location and so on. No consensus has emerged within feminist thought around this issue but there has been a decided move towards emphasizing the particularity of individuals and groups, stressing the multiple factors that influence the construction of subjectivity and underscoring the differences, rather than commonalities, in women's experience.

The tenets of process thought may propose some helpful directions for feminist theology around this topic as well. For process thought each moment of experience has a uniqueness and integrity that is its alone. Each moment of experience is the creative synthesis of the influences that have been inherited from its past; out of specific strands of history, each experiencing subject creatively constitutes itself. In a very real sense there are only particular and singular moments of experience. Thus attempts to homogenize women's experience in unnuanced claims of commonality are misdirected. Both the particularity of a woman's context and of the creative synthesis that is herself lead to an emphasis on singularity and uniqueness rather than sameness and shared experience.

In feminist theology and theory this turn to particularity and difference has raised questions of whether the notion of 'women' makes sense at all or whether there are grounds for women to make common cause against forces of oppression. Process thought may also contribute fruitfully to this discussion. First, the process perspective's emphasis upon the unique character of subjectivity does indeed warn against easy claims of commonality. It suggests that both oppressive experience and its transformation are always specific and that therefore any adequate understanding and response require localized analysis and strategies of change rather than generic ones. Secondly, the process perspective does not rule out the reality that women in their varied locations and strands of history have been subjected to analogous forms of experience. That is, while individual women's experiences have always been specific and unique and while different social and historical locations have bequeathed women varied legacies, women in whatever location seem to have held less power than men and to have been less valued than the males in those contexts. Such analogous experience does not lead to an automatic commonality but does suggest that out of their varied experiences women might recognize one another.

But what of the prospects for solidarity among women when differences are acknowledged, especially when those differences are tied to some women's complicity in the oppression of other women? The notion of subjectivity within process thought is instructive here. For process thinkers the experiencing subject is not a self who exists unaffected through successive changes but is rather the discrete momentary experience. The finally real is the momentary experience. There is something that might be called an enduring self, but that perduring individuality does not consist in an unchanging self behind changing experiences but in the common character that a successive line of momentary experiences share. That is, a succession of concrete moments share, through memory and anticipation, abiding characteristics, purposes and a shared history. Thus there can be understood to be a self but, as we will see, it is

An A to Z of Feminist Theology

a peculiarly open, unbounded self.

The process distinction between the enduring self and the momentary experience can be seen to have repercussions for the issue of solidarity. It implies that a self-identity, with a narrowly delineated past and future, is not ontologically given. Instead, the experiencing subject's relation to a particular past is not different in kind from its relations to other elements of a larger past, and the self-relation to a particular future is not different in kind from its relation to other elements of a wider future. Hence, at least in principle, the barrier between the self and other is not insurmountable. It is possible, within this view, to de-emphasize the past and future of what is the traditional self and to widen that self and give more emphasis to other pasts and futures. In short, it is not necessary to be locked within the confines of narrowly defined self-interest or a particular history, but rather it is possible truly to empathize with the other, to appropriate the other's interests and concerns as one's own. Solidarity, in this sense, is social awareness, the ability to see the other's perspective and to incorporate it into one's own. One does not become the other but can, from one's own perspective, share something of the other's experience. And such sharing will, in turn, alter the subject in significant ways.

The conversations between process thought and feminist theology are continuing as process theologians, especially women theologians, are exploring fruitful junctures of dialogue and mutual enhancement.

Further reading: Cobb 1976; Davaney (ed.) 1981; Keller 1986; Suchocki 1982.

PROPHETS
Susan Smith

WHEN CHRISTIAN feminists seek to define 'women prophets', they start with the Judaeo-Christian traditions. These traditions represent the prophets as faithful to the vision of the covenant community despite marginalization by the religious and political elites. A feminist understanding of 'women prophets' demands a partisan approach to those traditions which involves appropriating texts that speak to women's reality of marginalization. Feminists recognize that the received biblical tradition represents a patriarchal and androcentric distillation of experience. For Christian feminists, women prophets are those women who exemplify alternative roles to those defined for them by patriarchal society. Women prophets and more recently, women's prophetic movements, are committed to appropriating prophetic principles to critique patriarchal structures in church and society.

Women Prophets in the Hebrew Testament

Christian feminists are reclaiming the Scriptures through interpretive processes rooted in sociological analyses, historical and linguistic research. Their diligent search uncovers important models. Miriam is the first woman to be called prophet (Exod. 15.20), acquiring the title before Moses. Scholarly opinion tends to regard Exod. 15.19-21 as older than Exod. 15.1-18, an addition intended to elevate Moses as leader over Miriam. Nor do the later patriarchal redactions adequately acknowledge the triumvirate leadership of Moses, Aaron and Miriam, but her story is not totally suppressed (cf. Mic. 6.4; Jer. 31.4). For those with eyes to see and ears to hear, other women prophets emerge from the Israelite story. Deborah leads Israel to victory and is honoured as judge (Judg. 4.4-5). Her deeds are celebrated in liturgical song (Judg. 5). The unnamed and murdered mother of the Maccabees is a prophetic figure in her resistance and courage (2 Macc. 7). These women, like Huldah, Esther and Judith, embody a struggle for life over death, a resistance to oppression that threatens the Israelites. They are not defined by their relationship to men as wives and mothers, but as religious, liturgical or military leaders.

Women Prophets in the Christian Testament

In the Christian Testament, there are traditions which indicate that women are prophetic figures in the first Christian communities. Paul hints positively at the important contribution made by women ministers in the Hellenistic world (cf. Rom. 16). But Ephesians, Colossians and the Pastoral letters are concerned that the traditional hierarchy of the Hellenistic and Roman households be a model for the Christian community. This model does little to advance women's position.

Luke's Gospel, traditionally interpreted as sympathetic to women, is ambivalent because it tends to idealize women who conform to patriarchal gender expectations. In 10.38-42, Mary is praised for sitting and listening to the Lord, suggesting the Evangelist's attempt to limit women's teaching and preaching role in the church. Furthermore, Luke takes the Markan story of the woman who anoints Jesus, and reworks it so that popular understanding identifies the woman as a sinner (Lk. 7.36-50). The Markan version (Mk 14.3-9), situates the woman in the tradition of Samuel anointing Saul as king (cf. 1 Sam. 10.1). Mark's story of the Syro-Phoenician woman (7.24-30) reveals a prophetic woman who crosses cultural, ethnic and religious boundaries to pursue life for her daughter.

The Johannine Gospel emphasizes the prophetic role of women in the stories of the Samaritan woman (Jn 4.1-42), of Martha (Jn 11.27), whose profession of faith in Jesus as messiah parallels that of Peter in the Synoptic Gospels, and of Mary Magdalene, first witness of the resurrection, and bearer of good news to the disciples (Jn 20.11-18). Internal evidence suggests that women played a key role in the Johannine community. Feminist reconstruction of Christian origins argues that the early Jesus movement was an egalitarian movement whose prophetic intention was subverted by a patriarchal community.

Women Prophets in the Christian Era

Through the centuries, Christian women have continued their struggle against patriarchy. The Middle Ages gave birth to the Beguine movement, which rejected those spiritualities that belonged to the monastic, clerical world. Beguine spirituality and practical charity were not only a response to the emerging urbanization, but to church structures that did not meet women's need for participation and an affective spirituality. Its adherents were suspected of Catharism, which allowed women to preach. The lack of clerical supervision of their simple life was a further cause of suspicion which periodically overflowed into condemnation and persecution by the church. Women's challenge to ecclesiastical power structures was interpreted as heretical rather than as fidelity to the gospel imperative of 'equality of believers'. In the late Middle Ages, the contemplative Julian of Norwich attempted a theological language of God which focused on feminine attributes of the divine, anticipating the struggle to free God-language from its androcentric biases.

The seventeenth-century Englishwoman Mary Ward founded a community of uncloistered nuns who devoted themselves to the education of girls. Her refusal to identify religious life with monastic life meant that Rome suppressed her community for almost two hundred years. Mary Ward modelled a life of service by women to other women and girls that was followed by other communities.

Also in the seventeenth century, another Englishwoman, Margaret Fell-Fox of the Society of Friends, emerged as a woman prophet, persecuted and imprisoned like her foremothers. She argued from the Hebrew and Greek Testaments that women have played prophetic roles in the community. In the nineteenth century, American feminist Elizabeth Cady Stanton also sought to reverse to reverse centuries of androcentric interpretation of Scripture.

In the latter part of the twentieth century, women's movements continue to question the proclivity of patriarchal churches to define women's role. Feminist hermeneutical suspicion has led to a flowering of biblical scholarship that is liberating in its attempt to be faithful to the prophetic tradition and to the memory of Jesus. Such scholarship allows women to interpret texts as liberating, not as prescriptive. It encourages women to recognize that their experience of patriarchal oppression is the starting point for interpretation of the word. Interpretations are not be derived from the text only, but read into the text which can then become transformative for women rather than domesticating. Christian feminist scholars are radicalizing the prophetic tradition, and freeing Scripture from ideologies of patriarchy and androcentrism. Feminist re-reading of the texts becomes an 'advocacy exegesis' containing within it the seeds of women's liberation.

Women's prophetic movements denounce

exclusivism or domination of women by patriarchal structures, and proclaim a new age which postulates an equality and mutuality between women and men. Articulation of this vision empowers women to critique language which determines, controls or alienates them. It means that women are contributing to the ongoing conversation about ecology, for they recognize that their marginalization and exploitation are paralleled in the world of nature. It ensures that women are reclaiming story, dance and song as equally valid methods of theological discourse rather than following those Western philosophical systems that give priority to a presumed rationality and objectivity. This theological task is occurring among those women, irrespective of their social class or nationality, who believe that their experiences and existential reality are the true entry point into the theological task.

Christian feminists who critique the androcentrism of religion and theology as life-negating for women are recognizably prophetic in their task of reconstructing another story for women.

Further reading: Johnson 1993; LaCugna (ed.) 1993; Ruether 1983; Schüssler Fiorenza 1983; Tamez (ed.) 1989; Trible 1989.

RABBIS
Marcia Plumb

THE LITERAL translation of 'rabbi' is 'my master', but the word is more commonly used to mean 'teacher', coming from the root *rav*. The word was first used in this way in the time of Hillel (c. 30 BCE–10 CE). The fact that 'rabbi' appears in Mt. 23.7 probably reflects its recent introduction. Rabbis were ordained (given *smickha*) by other rabbis, a custom that still continues to this day.

In Talmudic times, the title was awarded to those who were sages and law-makers for the Jewish community of the day. When the second temple was destroyed in 70 CE one of the most important tasks of the surviving Jewish community was to ordain new rabbis to carry on the education and legal structure of the community.

In the Middle Ages, *ha-rav* denoted someone of great scholarly standing and social reputation. Rabbis were accorded a certain amount of religious authority. They were seen as the spiritual leaders of the people. They were also the heads of the *Yeshivot*, the study centres. In the late Middle Ages it was also the task of the rabbi to provide the stability of Judaism by responding to the legal and spiritual questions of Jews who lived in far-flung communities.

Arbiter of disputes was added to the rabbis' job description in the eighteenth and nineteenth centuries. Jews would bring their business disputes to the rabbi for resolution. The rabbi was involved in the daily life of the community. From the fourteenth century onwards, there emerged the concept of one rabbi for one locality, who was seen to be the final authority in that geographic area.

In the Hasidic movement, in the eighteenth and nineteenth centuries, the rabbi was called 'rebbe'. The rebbe had followers, disciples, who would travel for many miles to live and study at the feet of the master. Some rebbes were healers and miracle workers as well as teachers. Although many presume otherwise, there were women rebbes; for example Hannah Werbermacher.

Today, the rabbi is teacher, preacher, officiant at life-cycle ceremonies, counsellor and leader of prayer. A rabbi is hired by a specific congregation.

There are about 350 women rabbis in the world today. Lily Montagu was the first woman in England allowed to teach as if she were a rabbi. She founded a synagogue and was its spiritual leader. She also co-founded the Liberal Movement and the World Union for Progressive Judaism. Rae Frank Litman acted as a rabbi in the 1920s in the United States. She travelled around the country preaching and teaching. The first woman ordained by a Reform rabbinical seminary was Rabbi Regina Jonas, in the late 1930s in Germany. The next one was Rabbi Sally Priesand in 1975, an ordination which began the participation of women in the rabbinate. The Reform, Liberal, Reconstructionist and Conservative Movements now ordain women.

In Orthodox Judaism, women are forbidden to be rabbis primarily because women are exempt from fulfilling the religious obligation. However, even when scholars have overcome this objection, others surface. For example, women are not considered reliable witnesses, so cannot officiate at weddings, or act as judges. They are forbidden to lead prayers because their voices might sexually arouse the men, and because their knowledge might embarrass the less informed men in the congregation.

Women rabbis have added a great deal to Judaism over the years. There are now birth ceremonies for girls, as well as new rituals for the onset of menstruation, menopause and divorce.

Women rabbis encourage all members of a congregation to become ritual-makers, preachers and teachers, rather than only the rabbi. There is a greater sense of wholeness in Judaism as a result of women in the ministry—all can participate freely and creatively in Jewish life.

Further reading: Rabinowitz n.d.; Winkler 1991.

RAPE
Marie M. Fortune

A NON-THEOLOGICAL definition of rape begins with the Latin root *rapere*, 'to seize'. The focus in English is 'to seize and carry away by force' and/or 'to force another person to engage in sexual intercourse'. The more liberal legal and practical definitions are gender-neutral and clearly indicate that both rapist or victim can be of either gender. Hence the legal concern is with forced penetration of the mouth, anus or vagina by a penis or an object, regardless of gender. However, because of the social inequities imposed due to gender, race, age and sexual orientation, the most likely victims of rape are women and children of all races and non-dominant men.

The etymology of the word 'rape' is instructive as we consider the theological and ethical import of the reality of rape. It emphasizes coercion and theft and de-emphasizes the sexual circumstance of the experience. It is, however, the theft not of someone's property, but of that person's own self that is to be considered.

The reality of rape is socially constructed. Historically there have always been categories of persons viewed by the dominant society as 'unrapable', for instance prostitutes, wives, slaves, women of color. Privileged males have always regarded free sexual access to such persons as an extension of their patriarchal prerogative. There is no need to *steal* what already belongs to them. In these terms, the absence of authentic consent on the part of the other person is irrelevant. Within patriarchy, the only concern of the dominant male was/is control over his property. Rape was/is considered a property crime against the male owner, not against the person actually raped. For example, in nineteenth- and early twentieth-century United States, African American males who were accused of raping white women were frequently lynched (with or without trial) while white men who raped African American women were rarely even charged.

Likewise in Hebrew Scripture we find the Deuteronomic laws (Deut. 22) focusing on the marital status of the female victim and the circumstances of the assault. If a man 'lies with' a betrothed virgin in the city, both shall be stoned to death: the man violated his neighbor's wife, his property, and the woman must have consented or else she would have cried out and been helped. If a man seizes and 'lies with' a betrothed virgin in the country, only he will be punished because there is no one to help the woman when she cried out. The parallel is drawn here to a man attacking and murdering his neighbor. Although the violence and force are acknowledged, the concern is still for the violation of another man, not of the woman herself. If a man seizes and 'lies with' a virgin not betrothed, and they are discovered, he must give the woman's father money and marry her. He *has* taken something that did not belong to him, so he must pay for it. The woman is condemned to spend her life with her rapist.

The perspective belongs only to the male. 'It is irrelevant to Deuteronomy whether the young woman was actually raped; the issue is not crime and punishment, but wrong and compensation' (Frymer-Kensky 1992: 58). This only regards the male. In both the text and subsequent translations, the euphemistic language distracts the reader from the reality of an assault against a woman.

In the stories of rape in Hebrew Scripture, we see the ramifications of this patriarchal legal practice played out in the rape and murder of the unnamed concubine in Judges 19, the rape of Dinah in Genesis 34, and the rape of Tamar in 2 Samuel 13. In each of these stories, the assaults against women are merely the dramatic backdrop for the struggles between men over their power and property. The fact of the violation of the women is never a central concern.

The understanding of rape portrayed in the Christian tradition perpetuated a tendency to blame the victim and not hold the rapist culpable for his actions. From the *Malleus Maleficarum* (fifteenth century) to the canonization of St Maria Goretti (twentieth century) this misogyny and the lack of accountability of men prevented the addressing of the ethical or theological implications of rape (see Fortune 1983).

What is the sin of rape? Rape is an act of aggression carried out by one person against another. It is the physical, psychological and spiritual transgression of a person and as such violates the bodily integrity of the victim as well as shattering any possibility of right relationship between the victim and the rapist. Rape can destroy trust in the other person (in the case of an acquaintance or family member) or trust in the basic security of one's world (in the case of a stranger). So the secondary effect is to isolate or cut off the victim from her or his community.

RAPE - RECONCILIATION

The rhetoric of the 1970s brought with it new awareness: 'Rape is violence, not sex'. The attempt was to shift consciousness to understand that rape was not the result of uncontrollable male sexual urges toward attractive women. Rape was understood as an act of violence and aggression in which sex was used as a weapon. The 1990s bring us even further awareness: in a culture in which violence is eroticized and sexuality is largely defined by what men choose to do sexually, there is an inevitable blurring of the line between sexual activity and rape. 'The line between sex and violence is indistinct and mobile in a society in which violence means violation of that worthy of respect, and women are not' (MacKinnon 1987: 233 n. 19). This presents a particular challenge to those who want to draw a qualitative distinction between sex and rape (see Adams forthcoming).

Theologically, our understanding of rape reflects our understanding of God and of the nature of persons. If the world as we know it is the created order intended by God, then God did not create male and female in God's own image; rather God created victims and victimizers and these categories are generally gender specific. What does this tell us about God and about ourselves? Is there evidence to the contrary? Fortunately there is. There are societies in which rape does not exist; the people, male and female, do not comprehend the concept, according to anthropologists (for instance the Ashanti of West Africa [see Benderly 1982] and indigenous tribes near Mt Banahaw, in the Philippines [see Ligo 1993]). What is most interesting about these societies is the way in which their gender relationships are organized: women are respected, share power equally with men, participate fully in religious leadership that involves a female deity, and the community seeks harmony with the environment. Thus it seems possible to assert that rape is an unnatural act, not part of the created order or the nature of humans and not ordained by God as inevitable.

Within rape-prone cultures such as Western cultures today, to assert that rape is unnatural and unacceptable is a powerful political and spiritual statement. Yet this assertion is consistent with an understanding of the God of Hebrew and Christian Scriptures who stands with the vulnerable and powerless and speaks judgment against those who choose to use their power in ways that harm others. This assertion also makes it possible to distinguish between sexual violence and sexual activity and to condemn the first and affirm the second. To make this distinction, one must assert an ethical norm that affirms shared power, equality, authentic consent, and shared responsibility within a sexual relationship. This context precludes coercion, aggression, physical force and domination, which are indicators of violation of right relationship and the sin of rape.

RECONCILIATION
Linda J. Vogel

RECONCILIATION IS a way of being in relationship that links salvation and healing; it encompasses the whole creation. Sallie McFague suggests that the source of reconciliation is the 'healing power [that] comes from God, the lover of the world' (1990: 262).

Feminists use a variety of metaphors that speak to the need for and the gift of reconciliation. Letty Russell writes of the 'household of freedom' and of a 'round table' that is inclusive, honours diversity, and invites all (but especially the marginalized) to engage in the struggle toward *shalom*. Reconciliation is not possible unless we stay connected 'to our embodied selves…to our communities of faith and struggle …and to the margins'. (Russell 1993: 208). Justice, diversity, cooperation, partnership, mutuality, harmony, care, trust, and love that is all inclusive are keys to understanding reconciliation. Reconciliation is not possible until power is shared—it is not possible for those who are dominated and those who are dominators to be reconciled until a relationship of mutuality is achieved. It is not possible unless and until all persons have a place at the round table and are able to speak and listen in the community that they are both being and becoming.

For feminists, reconciliation is an ongoing process that is a part of our journey in and toward the kindom (kingdom) of God. It sometimes requires confrontation and struggle and pain. Paul understood this when he wrote to the church at Rome 'We know that the whole creation has been groaning in labour pains until now; and not only the creation, but we ourselves, who have the first fruits of the Spirit, groan inwardly while we wait for adoption, the redemption of our bodies' (Rom. 8.22-23 NRSV). Reconciliation is often painful and is an ongoing process; it is also a gift, freely given by God, which can be known in part now and will be fully known when all is made whole.

Reconciliation brings both liberation and blessing. It grows when we acknowledge that our 'circle of love' is broken because of alienation, misunderstanding, insensitivity, a hardening of hearts, and our inability to be open to and affirm differences. God's inclusive grace banishes distinctions so that all creation is included in God's circle of love (cf. Winter 1987: 185-92).

Reconciliation can begin as we move toward God's reign and realm where 'the alienating isms of exploitation and oppression' (Ruether 1983: 212) are challenged and both persons and social institutions are being transformed. Marjorie Suchocki and Catherine LaCugna find power in reclaiming a trinitarian understanding of God that they believe can challenge women and men to become embodiments of Jesus' prayer, 'thy kingdom come' (cf. Suchocki 1988: 210). It can empower us to enter into 'a life of love and communion with others' (LaCugna 1991: 382).

'There is a home in God, a home for the whole universe. In that home, multiplicity finally achieves unity; fragmentation is embraced in wholeness', writes Suchocki (1988: 190). 'God moves toward us', writes LaCugna, 'so that we may move toward each other and thereby toward God... Our relationship to others, which is indistinguishable from our relationship to Jesus Christ, determines whether we are or are not finally incorporated into God's household' (LaCugna 1991: 377-84).

Reconciliation from a feminist perspective is an empowered and empowering openness to the whole of the created order.

REDEMPTION (1)
Lucy Tatman

IN THE Judeo-Christian tradition the word 'redemption' is used to describe God's saving action on behalf of humanity. Meaning 'to buy back', as in 'to redeem', the notion of redemption presupposes that a person or a community is in a state of bondage. Further, this person or community cannot free themselves; they are stuck, powerless and enslaved. Thus 'redemption' happened for the Israelites when God led them out of Egypt and toward the promised land. Redemption became a historical fact when the Israelites were released from their enslavement to the Egyptians and became a liberated people.

In the Christian tradition redemption both has and has not yet occurred in history. Jesus' death and resurrection (together known as the atonement) are understood to have redeemed humanity from its bondage and enslavement to sin and evil. In this sense redemption has happened. However, there is a second, arguably stronger strand of thought regarding redemption, which sees redemption is something that happens after we die. God frees us from our bondage to this earth and to our mortal bodies by taking us up into heaven, into eternal life. These two strands of thought are thoroughly interconnected. The historical crucifixion of Jesus is not enough, traditionally, to redeem humanity. The resurrection of his body and, upon our deaths, our bodies or at the very least our souls, are required for redemption to be accomplished. Redemption, traditionally defined, places the emphasis on the need to overcome ordinary, human limitations. It is about God reaching into history in order to pull humanity out of history, out of this world. Always the emphasis is on God's actions, humanity's passive acceptance of 'his' actions, and (implicitly or explicitly) the wretched quality of creation as it is.

One major theme in feminist theology is that humanity is tangled up in distorted, perverse, demonic relations and unjust power structures. The very societies and institutions in which we 'live, move and have our being' are perpetuating systemic sins and evils. Sexism, racism, classism, world hunger, genocide, 'ethnic cleansing', the denial of adequate health care services to those without money, the dumping of toxic waste in oceans, deserts, quarries and the local tip, incest, rape and gay-bashing are some of the evils from which all of us need to be redeemed.

But the evils named above are not intrinsic to creation; they are 'man-made' atrocities which, unchecked, will destroy the world. Therefore the notion of redemption must be transformed,

REDEMPTION (1)

turned inside out. Instead of seeing redemption as happening apart from humanity and creation, feminist theologians assert that it must happen within and be produced by humanity and must never be separate from this world, our world. As Rosemary Ruether notes, creation and redemption are woven together (Ruether 1983). Just as we are a part of creation and creation happens around us every day, so too can redemption happen here and now—and yet, if it is to happen, we must necessarily participate in it. However, just as creation is destroyed, poisoned and denied so too can redemptive acts be rejected, denigrated, or simply go unnoticed.

Carter Heyward focuses on the utterly human nature of redemption. Within her theological framework there is no place for anything but immanent, here-and-now redemption. It is not a matter of waiting for a saviour, for someone else. It is about our refusal to settle for less than justice here on earth. According to her, redemption begins to happen when humans move from a passive or apathetic acceptance of ourselves as created, dependent beings into an understanding of ourselves as co-creative, interrelated creatures. The effort to define ourselves and to live as co-creative, responsible earth creatures is hindered firstly by our own fears. For we have been taught to fear passionate involvement, to fear our own power (strength and ability and voice and intuition and gut feeling), to fear the consequences of 'stepping out of line', in short to fear much of what it means to be human (Heyward 1989). Yet redemption, the creation of justice on earth as it is in heaven, does not happen without our active involvement, without our 'immersion in the struggle for justice, which in turn teaches us much of what we are to know of love' (Harrison 1985). Redemption rests in human hands, our hands, and according to Heyward God too must be redeemed from an other-worldly, transcendent depository for our fears and hopes and transformed into the current that flows between us, empowering us to insist on justice and love for all, including this earth our home (Heyward 1982, 1989).

I believe that for Heyward the concept of redemption includes both the process (the struggle for justice and right relations) and the end, justice realized. She would have to say that we may not be able to redeem humanity, God and creation. The destructive force of the faiths, institutions and even world-views that we must rage against might well end up crucifying us all.

This is the point at which I would shift the meaning of 'redemption'. A pragmatic, immanent conceptualization of redemption would, instead of emphasizing justice as the end result of redemption, redefine redemption so that it is *understood entirely as the movement away from injustice*. The knowledge, the conviction that where we are is not where we ought to be, is the heart and soul of redemption. When we strive to move away from abusive relationships, away from passivity, away from apathy and away from the absence of feeling, that is precisely when we embody redemption.

Redemption is both the knowing that compels us, sends us hurtling or hesitant on the journey home, and that journey (Morton 1985). It is never our arrival, for we will never finally arrive. However, along the way there can be moments, instances, of radical justice, love and right relation. Therefore redemption contains the possibility, though not the certainty, of justice. Redemption is not the end; it is the knowing that causes our beginning and sustains us on the way. It is our movement away from injustice. That is all it is.

Because redemption thus defined is not 'realized justice', redemptive acts are not necessarily 'good' or 'right'. A redemptive act is the best a person can do at the time, given her or his current situation, the influence of past experiences and the sum of the resources, strengths and relationships she or he has to draw upon. Consequently, given that most of us have been taught from birth to conform, to acquiesce, to accept what we have been handed without a murmur, to bear our burdens alone, many if not most redemptive acts go unnoticed and unnamed. A woman's steadfast refusal to do the dinner dishes until after she has watched the sunset; my friend Jean, who kept cutting herself in order to feel because a part of her insisted on the need to feel something...

Redemptive acts are stubborn acts and, I suspect, tend to be defined as irrational, mad, silly, stupid and sick far more than they are called brave, courageous, splendid or messianic. They are not about salvation; they are about making a little bit of the world a little bit better. Redeemers are born and die every day; '...there are no prodigies/in this realm, only a half-blind, stubborn/cleaving to the timbre, the tones of what we are...' (Rich 1978).

REDEMPTION (2)
Melissa Raphael

THE FEMINIST vision of redemption shows feminist theology at its most positive and constructive. Its new picture of redemption as the creation of a transformed world of non-dominative relations in turn summarizes and reconstructs our concept of community, history and ultimately God, and the meaning and purpose of the cosmos. Feminist theology does not, then, question the present need for the redemption of human society and the natural world from the real and evil 'principalities and powers' as the New Testament calls the structures of oppression. But feminists do question and seek to revise the processes by which redemption is achieved, as well as the form that a redeemed world would take.

Furthermore, the very process of such revision on the basis of women's experience is itself a part of the process of redemption. Since the verb 'to redeem' can be defined as an act of reclamation, liberation, recovery from a 'state of submersion', or extrication from meaninglessness, 'when we engage in an activity of reclaiming the lost history and experience of women this is truly a redeeming activity' (Grey 1989: 2). When women have become involved in the women's movement, their consequent sense of personal liberation may be like a conversion: a foretaste of a more global transformation of values. Through actually experiencing the feminist paradigm shift and the spiritual pain of attempting to live out traditional doctrine, Christian feminists are moved to deconstruct traditional models of salvation and so expose their political and conceptual relativity. That is, doctrines of redemption can be shown to be particular to the biographical and ideological context in which they were formulated, namely that of patriarchy.

The strenuousness of the patriarchal struggle to control and exploit nature has, it is argued, coloured men's vision of salvation as a liberation from nature. Feminist theologians are not alone in their criticism of otherworldly notions of salvation as insufficiently biophilic. And in any case there is no single doctrine of salvation in the Bible. But feminist criticism insists that too much speculation about salvation has involved not only the repudiation of nature but also the repudiation of the erotic: that energetic engagement with life of the embodied self, where the union of sexuality and spirituality constitutes human well-being or wholeness.

Salvation has traditionally been envisaged as some form of everlasting life. But drawing on the research of feminist psychologists such as Carol Gilligan and Anne Wilson Schaef, feminist theologians argue that women are either conditioned to be, or are innately, uninterested in doctrines that promise individual transcendence or immortality. Being better socialized than most men, women tend to make a far greater spiritual investment in the nurture of life rather than in the achievement of autonomy. And to some extent, female biology requires women to do so. While being wary of biological determinism, none of the feminist theologies of salvation severs the redemption of humankind from that of the whole of creation. The common feminist vision of salvation as a state of 'shalom' is inclusive not just of women but of all categories of oppressed beings, including those in nature. And just as creation is a past, present and future dynamic, so too redemption is an immanent process. It is not rescue from mortality. If God is immanent in the erotic processes of life, then the maintenance and healing of those processes, which are so often damaged by patriarchy, is also a healing of humanity's relationship with God. For as Dorothee Sölle has written, 'It is through our most humane activities, in work and in love, that we become co-creators of the new earth, the place we may finally call home' (1984: 103). But the not-yet of salvation is not lost in feminist theology. Arguably, we have not yet seen this world of non-dominative relationships, although we have had proleptic glimpses of it in pockets of resistance to exploitation, in the rediscovery of female sacrality, and in the witness of discipleship among the dispossessed.

Grounded as it is in women's experience, feminist scholarship in ethics, history, literature and psychology is helping feminist theologians to

REDEMPTION (2)

reconstruct our perception of the salvific process. And a primary task in the process of reconstruction is to use the insights of these disciplines to redeem the language of redemption. This involves the historical awareness that doctrines of salvation were generally formulated to be exclusive of non-Christians, and to reward unquestioning obedience to a male divine will. These doctrines were (and very often still are) conceived by a white male elite whose contact with women and children was usually kept to a minimum and who rarely challenged the stratifications of sex, race and class. As such, feminist consciousness cannot accept their authority, since that authority seems to be guaranteed as much or more by the social order than by divine love.

Salvation is release from a state of sin. Christian feminists are aware that 'sin' is a political term and does not refer to persons indifferently of gender. As far back as 1960 Valerie Saiving noted in her essay 'The Human Situation: A Feminine View' (reprinted in Plaskow and Christ [eds.] 1979) that men are far more likely than women to succumb to the sin of pride. More often than not, women suffer more from an under-development of the ego and, if anything, their fault is often one of passivity and triviality of life. The relative powerlessness of many women means that they are not always as accountable for evil as men though they are often guilty of complicity. But the sin of complicity has not been part of a traditional Christian characterization of sin. Christianity more commonly summarizes the state of sin as one of pride or *hubris*, that is, wanting to be as the gods, immortal and all-powerful. As a rule, it is still only men who have the opportunities to cherish such ambitions.

Christian theology, including its feminist forms, requires divine–human reconciliation— mending the rift caused by sin is the precondition for redemption. But in patriarchal theology, the need for reconciliation is premised upon a Fall for which women, in the person of Eve, have been seen to be responsible. But even when feminists have rejected this view that self-sacrifice to the needs of men is a primordial punishment for the sin of femaleness, the meaning of redemption through the suffering and death of Jesus is conditioned yet more systematically by gendered language and reasoning.

Rule-bound law is necessarily detached and 'objective'. The idea that redemption is dependent on the undifferentiated judgment of all 'sinners' by God is considered unjust by feminists. Any model of redemption in which Jesus' death is a ransom paid to God, whose dignity is offended by sin, is premised on the mathematical calculation of damages owed and the legal justification of violence, rather than on the ethical conditions for salvation which the prophets and Gospels seem to insist upon. Christian feminists might want to say instead that we will be redeemed because Jesus suffered *with* the oppressed whom he loved, not *instead* of them. Again, it may be true that concepts of atonement modelled on the proceedings of a court of law properly attempt to articulate the workings of divine justice. But law courts under patriarchy are a distorted metaphor for those women in societies where the courts are controlled by male members of the ruling classes and whose lives are insulated from those often disadvantaged persons whom they judge and punish.

Feminist scholarship has shown that classical theories of atonement might actually distort the meaning of redemption as being effected through victimization and violence against Jesus. Likewise, many Christian women's identification with Jesus' sufferings has been distorted by patriarchy. Traditionally, women's domestic self-sacrifice through their love for their family has been spiritualized as a private imitation of the life of Christ. Consequently the cross, as the central mechanism of Christian atonement and reconciliation, has become highly ambivalent for feminists. As Mary Grey puts it: 'If the central symbol of Christianity contains with it a message that keeps women impaled on that cross, with societal approval, what message of resurrected hope and redemption can it bring?' (1989: 13). It is not difficult for women to find in this language a reflection and a glorification of their own experience as victims. (Indeed, the language of vicarious punishment seems to fund the practice of powerful groups scapegoating vulnerable groups, whether wise women or Jews.) It is clear that the currency of sacrifice is easily debased. For instance, a battered woman may read the violent humiliation of Christ on the cross as the sanctification of her victimhood.

The historical and political nature of the fem-

An A to Z of Feminist Theology

inist vision of redemption has christological repercussions. The belief that one historical man, Jesus, could rescue all women from sin ignores the possibility that human and divine creativity together can co-create and transform the world. Christian women should be wary, as Carter Heyward has warned, of projecting their powerlessness onto a hero or saviour instead of transforming that power in their own lives. Similarly, the classical Anselmian atonement doctrine that God used Christ to buy us back from the devil reinforces the ideal of female passivity and obedience to husbands and fathers. But this is the very mind-set that feminists are now refusing. For Carter Heyward, redemption is not about waiting for deliverance but about becoming friends and co-creators with God/ess in a co-redemptive process (1982: 1). Women who have been commoditized in culture do not want to be bought back, as the word 'redemption' often connotes. Feminist theology of all types insists that the redemptive process of mending relationships can only be set in motion when patriarchy concedes women's personhood as full rational and moral agents and when (like the heroine in Margaret Atwood's novel, *Surfacing*) women come to refuse to be victims of patriarchy. It is not enough for a trained theologian to say that feminists may not have understood the doctrines correctly. Here we are interested in how the powerless *read* those doctrines in the context of their own situation.

Feminist theologians of liberation have a central contribution to make to the revisioning of redemption. Here redemption is a future historical possibility as the ultimate form of liberation from the oppressive patriarchal structures of domination and subordination. Like all religious feminists, Rosemary Ruether cannot accept that there can be any salvation of the soul when the present structures of injustice that cause starvation, rape, slave wages and pollution remain in place. Both she and Letty Russell look to the Jubilee tradition of Lev. 25.8-12 which depicts an ecological salvation or healing through a series of revolutionary transformations. This brings about the periodic restoration of 'life as God intended it. Each family has its own land, its own vine, its own fig tree. No one is enslaved to another. The land and animals are not overworked' (Ruether 1983: 254). According to Ruether, the historical Jesus was a prophetic critic of hierarchical power, as are feminists today. The Christ represents a new liberated humanity in which those who are redeemed redeem others. So Christ is not simply the ascended form of the historical Jesus but the true identity of the Christian community as it struggles for liberation (Ruether 1983: 138).

Those feminist theologians working in a liberation tradition are not so very far away from those who use process thought to provide a model of God and the world coming to be in a relation of mutual love. After all, loving mutuality is impossible without justice. It is here, in women's capacity (whether natural or conditioned) for relationship and mutual dependence that Mary Grey locates her hope for redemption: 'This is the insight of feminist spirituality of our particular age: that the full becoming of the universe will reach fruition not through an ethic of domination, competitiveness, individualism and military strength, but through the living out of increasing depth of redemptive relatedness' (1989: 176). It does not seem coincidental, then, that the sign language deaf Christians use for the word 'salvation' is so close to the feminist vision of salvation: it depicts the gathering into an enfolding embrace.

RELATIONALITY
Linda Hogan

RELATIONALITY EMERGES as a key concept in feminist theology, and particularly in feminist ethics. Although it has been used in the service of various schools of feminist theory, its precise meaning, and the usefulness of its employment, are often disputed. In general the notion of relationality includes a number of elements. It includes the concepts of interdependence and mutuality. In some schools of feminist discourse it also suggests a special relationship between women and nature. It also implies a call for the reconceptualization of sacred symbols to take account of immanance and to forge new relationships between the deity/deities, human beings and the earth.

Carol Gilligan (1982) argues that women have a distinctive *modus operandi* in ethics. This has become the classic statement of relationality. She shows that women display a different perspective on the self, relationships and morality from that described by traditional theories of moral development. Through her work with young women, Gilligan uncovered what she considered to be different modes of moral judgment, which she termed the ethic of justice and the ethic of care, which are gender related but not gender specific. On the ethic of care, individuals (women) define themselves as connected in relation to others, they understand relationships as response to another on his or her own terms, and they resolve moral problems with attention to maintaining the connections between interdependent individuals. A central concern therefore is not strict equality or fairness, but whether relationships are maintained or restored. While Gilligan's work remains important in itself, it has also been significant as a starting point for many feminist ethicists who depart from many elements of the original thesis.

One of the issues which this raises is the question of how wise it is for women to embrace this notion of relationality/interdependence. Katherine Zappone (1991) notes that it is important to distinguish interdependence from the passive dependency which has been encouraged of women. The autonomy or self-integrity towards which women strive is not exclusive of the promotion of relationality and interdependence. If we relate to each other with mutuality, that is, with a willingness 'to allow the other a significant, equal agency within the relationship', then, Zappone suggests, neither elements of autonomy nor relationality need be sacrificed.

This discussion is brought a stage further by ecofeminists. Mary Grey (1989) proposes a 'metaphysic of connection', which will begin with an understanding of redemption as self-affirmation and right-relation and which will empower ecological healing and growth. This is the view which emerges from the character Shug Avery in Alice Walker's much celebrated *The Color Purple* when she says 'it come to me: that feeling of being part of everything, not separate at all. I knew that if I cut a tree, my arm would bleed' (1982: 167).

A feminist vision which stresses the importance of relationality recognizes the need for the reformulation of the metanarratives of Western culture. Ruether (1992) argues that, in the quest for earth healing, we need to create new narratives which will evoke eco-justice and will endorse the metaphysic of connection. This leads naturally to the reconceptualization of primary sacred symbols, so that human talk about the divine will inspire relationality. Starhawk, Merlin Stone, Carol Christ and others use the metaphors of the Goddess(es) of a pre-patriarchal age in this reconstruction. They point to the eco-friendly and mutual practices which result from a life inspired by these metaphors. Another theologian who seeks to prioritize the notion of relationality vis-à-vis the deity is Carter Heyward (1982). She suggests conceiving of the Christian God as power-in-relation, a model which ought then to be mirrored in egalitarian and just relationships in society.

RELIGIOUS LIFE
Myra Poole SND

THE RELIGIOUS life is entered upon by taking three vows: of poverty, chastity and obedience. Some religious are called 'contemplatives', others 'apostolic'.

In his book *The Mystical Element in the Church* (1923) Von Hugel describes the church as composed of three essential elements: the institutional, the critical and the mystical. Religious life must be grounded in the latter two elements; if it is not, it ceases to be religious life. It is true to say that at the present time much of what is called religious life in fact is not; many congregations and orders are now simply arms of the institutional church and hence have lost touch with the true purpose and dynamism of their origins.

It is, then, generally recognized by feminist theologians that a radical overhaul of our ideas of religious life is required. Many metaphors are used for the process of change: re-visioning, re-weaving, re-founding, even re-dreaming. But how might the change take place, and what will the new form of religious life look life? The vows of chastity, poverty and obedience are integral to all forms of religious life, but it is their interpretation that is at stake. The insights of feminist philosophy, psychology, theology and thealogy, and ethics must be used to produce a concept of religious life in which the three central vows become liberating for women both individually and collectively.

The concept of chastity was developed by women in the early centuries of written history primarily as a means of freeing themselves from marriage, providing a space in which relationships between women could develop and flourish. It was a means of escaping from social control, in order to live under the 'liberating control' of God. This notion of chastity was as revolutionary and uncomfortable to the early church as lesbianism is to many people today, and for the same reason: both constitute a place in which women can free themselves from patriarchy, a freedom to love all women, men and children as they please and in their own way.

The concept of poverty does not mean living in total destitution; it indicates rather the sharing of goods and all that we are. Evelyn Underhill, in her book *Mysticism* (1911) talks of the poverty of the mystics as primarily conceptual. It is the emptying out of our own learned ideas—the ideas of patriarchy—to make space for God's ideas. In *The Feminist Mystic* (1986) Mary Giles argues that feminism represents a movement in this direction, towards establishing the kingdom of God for both women and men. This new emphasis will lead to a deconstruction and a reconstruction of both society and religion—in fact, to a new culture: 'I cannot conceive of working for women to have a bigger share of the existing cake. It is a new cake that I want' (Spender 1988: 15).

The vow of obedience has been particularly relevant to the oppression of women in the church, having been interpreted as requiring obedience to ecclesiastical authorities. In its true interpretation, however, as obedience to God, it allows people to emancipate themselves from social control. We can see this in the lives of female mystics such as Hildegard of Bingen, who was enabled to resist male authorities through the strength of her mystical experiences. Caroline Walker Bynum (1986, 1989) has clearly shown how religious women in medieval times relied on their own visions for authority, when the power of the church was consolidating around clericalization.

The concept of religious life as community centres on the belief in a common vision. It is from this vision, rather than from position or status, that power flows. We can see that this is very much in the tradition of the mystics. The aim of the vows of religious life must be to radicalize women and men, to enable them to see the distortions of patriarchal religion and the truth in the vision of Christian feminism. Women and men religious need to recognize that, as Adrienne Rich wrote, 'the maps they gave us were out of date by years'; only then will religious life begin to renew from its mystical source.

Further reading: Fiand 1992; Neale 1987; Schneiders 1986.

REPENTANCE
Ann Gilroy

REPENTANCE for Christians, and particularly in feminist theology, refers to the experience and hope of renewing relationship with God and within the Christian community that has been distorted by sin. Sin is understood as the breaking of relationship with both God and with human beings, which can take the form of weakness, as well as pride, in its denial of the importance of human responsibility in both the personal and the political realms (Carr 1990). Women and men come to repentance often through realizing the hurt they have caused others and want to avoid repeating in the future. Their hope for a better community rests in their changing and being healed of the attitudes and behaviour that damage themselves and others. Repentance challenges them to change, and the change of one person in the community can influence change through the community networks.

Biblical repentance is imaged as a radical change in relationships; the heart of cold stone changing into warm flesh (Ezek. 11.19; 36.26), the king dressed in sackcloth and ashes walking out weeping for sorrow in the community (1 Kgs 21.27), honouring the responsibility to provide shelter and food for widows and orphans (Isa. 9.17; Tob. 1.8), the feasting when the lost son returns home to his father's arms (Lk. 15.11-23), the neighbourhood party when the woman finds her lost coin (Lk. 15.8-10), and the woman breaking the alabaster jar of ointment over Jesus'

REPENTANCE

feet (Lk. 7.36-50). These images catch the moments of vulnerability when the person is broken open to the power of God and risks remaining vulnerable to the changes brought about in that person through the holiness of God. They underline the damage personal and social sin wreaks in the community, yet emphasize the hope and rejoicing when relationships are healed, strengthened and renewed. Repentance, then, is more of a process of healing than an instantaneous cure. It is an experience of salvation in which the possibilities of at-one-ment with God are tasted.

The repentance of either an individual or a community refers to their sorrow and conversion from sinful attitudes and behaviour to those that promote Christian morality in life-giving relationships and loving responsibility. Women and men, created in the *imago Dei*, face their life's challenge of embodying God for each other and in being a constant revelation of the divine for each other. Repentance means that the person or community, after becoming aware of the distortions in their relationships, seek to make changes to bring them closer to the gospel challenge of justice and love. They seek conversion to accept responsibility to make changes in praxis—the on-going reflection and evaluation of their practice—that help to effect change. Repentance and conversation lead to the transformation of the person and the community.

Feminists have been critical of classical categories of sin which claim that pride, inordinate self-esteem, excessive ambition and self-serving are the prime universal sins of humanity. While these may describe the immorality of men, women can be victims of this experience of sinfulness in most countries where patriarchy is endemic in society. Women have been profoundly affected by the patriarchal systems which limit and correlate their value as persons in relation to the status of their father or husband in the system. Institutional sexism, whereby women are discriminated against because of their gender, is often defined as the root sin or evil in contemporary times, because women are denied full access to their humanity by male systems designed to control and dominate women and perpetuate their oppression. The distorting effects of sexism on society were glimpsed in the United Nations survey of October 1994, which found that the world's poor had increased in the last decade so that one in five people in contemporary times lived below the poverty line. Seventy per cent of these poor are women and girls. As Janet Martin Soskice has remarked, 'Sexism is not something that hurts women's feelings, sexism kills millions and millions of girls and women each year' (1993: 110).

In such systems where women are dominated, women sin in that they have colluded with the system rather than challenged men to change and refused to cooperate with such evil. Women collude with institutional sexism by believing that they are less loveable, less responsible, less able to make decisions, and less differentiated as individuals than men. They do not take seriously the Christian ethic to love themselves. Their sin is therefore not self-pride but lack of pride in their humanity, lack of self-esteem and ambition, and lack of personal focus. When they fail to love themselves they too often perpetuate this lack of self-love in their daughters' development by allowing them to learn damaging attitudes. Through silence and passiveness, women work with men in allowing violence and abuse of women and children, and the exploitation of creation to continue.

Repentance in women, then, involves being open to the process of conscientization to sexism and its pervasive control in distorting relationships among women and men and the world. This process often builds up a fierce anger in women at the misery and suffering such distortion causes. Women need to find a way of directing their anger so that their call for urgent and radical change in women and men's attitudes and practices is heard. Many feminists have taken a moral stand and moved to a post-Christian position because they believe that forms of sexism are so intrinsic to Christianity that women have no place in Christianity (for example Mary Daly and Daphne Hampson). Others have created alternative communities of worship and praxis, for example Women-Church (Rosemary Radford Ruether, Erin White). Some challenge sexism because it perpetuates the adulation of a male idol, whereas women and men experience the divine in profoundly moving and varied ways (Grace Jantzen, Miriam Therese Winter). Others again stay within their Christian tradition and see their contribution to conversion as

An A to Z of Feminist Theology

rather like the irritant grain of sand inside the oyster that could produce a precious pearl (Joan Chittister, Janet Martin Soskice).

Repentance means a conversion to an open attitude where women choose to participate actively and in varying ways to bring about the liberation of women and men from people and structures that perpetuate suffering and pain. In their hope for inclusive communities, women take responsibility for working at developing right relationships with other women and men. Most significantly, repentance for women means that in the face of the enormous challenges to radical change they live in the hope that God is with them in the struggle, and in the experience of that hope they will persist in their praxis.

While repentance means that women face up to what promotes suffering and pain among people and in creation, it also means that they engage in worship as community to celebrate the transforming power of God's love among them. Just as feasting and rejoicing is a strong feature of repentance and forgiveness in biblical images, so too feminist theology distances itself from guilt and prefers to image repentance as learning and healing. Celebrating keeps hope alive and rejoices that God is in the midst of all life.

Further reading: Hampson 1990; Johnson 1993; Ruether 1973.

RESURRECTION
Lisa Isherwood

IT WAS the resurrection that, according to Rom. 1.3-4, turned Jesus of Nazareth into the Christ: 'regarding his Son, who as to his human nature was a descendant of David, and who through the Spirit of holiness was declared with power to be the Son of God by his resurrection from the dead: Jesus Christ our Lord'. Many Christians feel that without the resurrection there is no Christian faith at all; Jesus would be a prophet and miracle-worker, but not the Christ.

The notion of resurrection has always been hotly debated both within and without Christian circles, and even those who believe in it have disagreed over the form it may take. The biblical texts are not entirely helpful on this point since they lend themselves to a variety of interpretations.

Patriarchal theology has found it very difficult to conceive of resurrection of the body, because the body has always been viewed as inferior to the spirit. There has therefore been a very strong tradition that emphasizes the resurrection of Jesus, and consequently our own, as spiritual resurrection. When this will happen has also been debated; some believe that it occurs at the point of individual death, while others believe in the notion of the parousia or end of time when all the dead will be raised. Many believe that at that time the world, including people, will be restored to its original beauty; others believe that it will all pass into a heavenly realm where perfection will abound. These views originate from the biblical declaration that a new heaven and a new earth will come into being in the end time.

Of course, these views of spiritual renewal either in heaven or on earth show little concern for the planet: according to this doctrine we need not be vigilant about the earth since it will be renewed at the end. In terms of ecology the purely spiritual and heavenly view turns out to be the most destructive. As feminist theology includes the whole of creation in the scheme of liberation it naturally has a problem with this model.

According to one strand of the tradition we will be called out of our graves at the end of time and judged according to conduct. The good will live on the earth in a restored paradise, in a physical form, while the bad will suffer in hell. At one time it was believed that women were imperfect males, and that they would at the time of the resurrection be perfected and become males.

The Apostles' Creed states that we believe in the resurrection of the dead and the life of the world to come, although it is not exact as to how that resurrection will occur. Paul gives us another insight when he writes that the dead will be lifted up first but those who are still alive will also be lifted up into the clouds to meet the Lord in the air (1 Thess. 4.15-17). This adds a collective element to the events: we will all be resurrected together.

At the heart of feminist theology is a rejection of the dualism of spirit and matter that underlies these notions of resurrection. If there is no spiritual realm into which we pass, and if—as experience tells us—we cannot survive death in a physical form, there is no room in feminist theology for the notion of personal survival after death. Indeed Rosemary Radford Ruether (1992) has suggested that it is of fundamental inportance that we give up this notion. She suggests that this would be very healthy ecologically, since we would cease seeing ourselves as so important that the world cannot survive without us (the truth being that we cannot survive without the world, and yet we are destroying it). Ruether suggests that after death we become part of the ongoing process of the cosmos as we are enveloped by it in our decay. Her view, then, does not deny the continuation of some part of us, if not a personal and recognizable part.

Ruether's insight can also be incorporated into a feminist theology of resurrection that places adequate emphasis on the importance of the body. If we see ourselves as part of the body of the cosmos, we can give a new sense to the notion of physical resurrection—a resurrection that takes place now, in this world. If we reject the notion of a spiritual paradise in the afterlife, the emphasis is placed firmly back onto our immediate situation. The resurrection of the body can become a very powerful reality for feminist theology once it expands the understanding of body to include that of the cosmos and when it dares to imagine just how a liberated and erotically empowered world might look. That would after all be a new heaven and a new earth and would indeed appear glorified and shining in the heavens! This understanding of the resurrection can bring about a total change in our way of living.

When we place the crucifixion and the resurrection together as two related events and look to the actions in between we get an even greater understanding of what the implications are. Jesus was abandoned in his pain and suffering by his trusted male followers. The women stood and watched, made ready his body for burial and held the relationship even in the pain; the result was the resurrection. This is surely a note that rings true for all kinds of transformations: they require being present to the pain and the hopelessness. The physical resurrection of Jesus is a powerful message for the cosmos and its inhabitants; we see that even the most hopeless situations can be overcome by mutuality in relationships.

Further reading: McFague 1993; Moltmann 1985.

REVELATION
Lucy Tatman

God saw everything that (s)he had made,
and indeed, it was very good
(Gen. 1.31, NRSV).

WHAT I see today is not 'very good'. All around me creation is weeping: the earth itself, my friends, strangers whose lives I can only catch a glimpse of on the evening news. When I think and feel as honestly as I am able, I know that I am almost paralysed by the sheer enormity of the mess we humans have made of things. And this is revelation. It's not all there is to revelation, but it is revelation nonetheless. Before the work of redemption can begin, long before salvation can be conceived, what is, as it is, must be acknowledged. Prophets are peculiarly good at revelation; it's what they are called to do, and why they tend to make so many of us so uncomfortable when they do it. Prophets work on the assumption that simply knowing something makes the knower accountable for what is known. In other words, prophets insist upon the relationship between my actions and the state of the ozone layer, for example. They implicitly demand accountability from every one of us.

What this means from a feminist theo-ethical perspective is that revelation involves relation, the acknowledgment that we are in relation with each other no matter how different we are from one another, that we are in relation with this earth because we are each a part of creation, not above it or separate from it. Furthermore, the shape and nature of our relations matter. Revelation consistently points us away from an individualistic, totally autonomous notion of personhood and toward the understanding that 'the personal is political'. We are each integrally bound to the vast scheme of things, affecting and effecting that which is seen and unseen, affected and effected by people, events and forces of which we may be totally unaware. And it is this knowledge that makes revelation bearable. We can't know all the ramifications of our choices, our actions; we can only live as wisely and as care-fully as our limited, finite selves are able.

Does the concept of revelation contain any hints as to how we are to live? Once again the prophets in our midst show us by example one of the demands of revelation. That demand is passionate anger, the call to rage against the denial of our responsibility to this good creation, to rage against the destruction of peoples, species, oceans, plants, friendships. Beverly Harrison has written of 'the power of anger in the work of love', and it is exactly this loving anger, this 'fierce tenderness' (Mary Hunt) that revelation evokes. Not bitter, spiteful anger, not 'holier than thou therefore I know best' anger, but deeply loving rage against that which denies justice in its broadest sense—justice as 'right relation'. It is crucial that I, we, never become blinded by this rage, that I never assume that the revelations I experience in the course of my nice, white, middle-class life must necessarily be 'universal revelations', applicable to all for all time. This is simply ridiculous. Truthfully, the revelations of those upon whose backs I stand are the revelations I most need to hear, to heed. And this indicates another aspect of revelation. It takes time and patience and the willingness to shut up and listen to others in order to dis-cover what is, as it is. My perspective is just that, one, singular perspective. I cannot see the whole, and all that I do see I see through very particular lenses, lenses ground and shaped by my unique experiences. This means that I am dependent on others' views; in order to learn 'what is' as it is for others, I must always be a student, learning from those who know far better than I what their lives are like.

But revelation is not only about dis-covering more fully what is, as it is. Revelation is also about revelling in relation and creation. One meaning of 'to revel' is to 'take keen delight in'. When God saw everything that she had made, she saw that it was very good. As created earth creatures we are a part of what is very good. As members of a faith community that celebrates creation and our lives in relation we are called to revel in what is, to take keen delight in our ordinary days. On the seventh day God rested, enjoying all that was. Righteous anger cannot be the only consequence of revelation, for what is, as it is, is so vast, so extraordinarily complex that it demands appreciation. Revelation calls us to look up, look around in awe and thanksgiving, for we too are a part of all that is. Thus understood, revelation implies that life devoid of joy, devoid of delight in the is-ness of creation, is not life lived in the image of God. Within this aspect of revelation is the affirmation of humanity's affinity with God. We are both called and able to do what God did—to create and to cherish, not to destroy and denigrate.

Revelation happens every day: in classrooms, on the bus, within the pages of a novel, half-way up the mountain and in the middle of a picket line. In and of itself it is not an earth-shattering experience. It's more like a call, a call to pick up a bed and walk. Always, the choice is with each of us to heed that call or not, to choose a redemptive path or to ignore what we have learned. Revelation makes redemption (the movement away from injustice) possible; it does not cause redemption. Revelation marks the intersection of prophecy and celebration, urging but not requiring responsible action, seeking but not insisting on delight.

Further reading: Harris 1988; Hunt 1991; Mudflower Collective 1985; Plaskow and Christ (eds.) 1989; Harrison 1985.

THE SACRAMENTS
June C. Goudey

IN THE beginning, the Christian church was shaped by a number of simple practices: a bath (baptism), a common meal (eucharist), the washing of feet, the anointing of the sick and the casting out of demons. Over time, as the church became more hierarchical and more dogmatic, the rationale for these sacred acts was reformulated in the context of various doctrinal controversies that emerged in the second and third centuries. Some practices were discarded altogether, while others were reshaped by order and uniformity.

Defining and distinguishing what a sacrament is has been complicated by a number of factors—the realization that the word 'sacrament' is nowhere found in the New Testament, the uncertainty of the term itself, and the assumption that these rites were instituted by Christ. Despite its legalistic bias, the Latin word *sacramentum* (from *sacrare*, to consecrate) was chosen to represent the Greek *mysterion*, meaning mystery or secret. *Sacramentum* originally carried various meanings, but the most popular was a military oath of allegiance to the emperor. While it lacked the depth of *mysterion*, one of its earliest liturgical usages appeared in the writings of Tertullian (c. 160–225). Later Augustine (c. 354–430) developed the first theory of sacraments based on the conjunction of word and physical element.

In general a sacrament has been understood to be an 'outward and visible sign of an inward and spiritual (invisible) grace'. These sign-acts or 'visible words' have celebrated God's loving self-disclosure in Christ, but little agreement has existed as to how many of the church's sign-acts are truly sacraments. While the Eastern Orthodox and Roman Church have recognized Peter Lombard's (c. 1100–1160) designation of seven sacraments—baptism, confirmation, eucharist, penance, extreme unction, ordination and marriage—most Reformation churches have acknowledged baptism and the eucharist as the only true sacraments.

Until the twentieth century, sacramental theology had been shaped by a substantialistic understanding which focused on the substance and essence of the physical elements of the rite. Today, many liturgical scholars and theologians, influenced by modern physics and phenomenological considerations, stress the relational dimensions of the sacraments in community, and perceive them as profound symbols of God's dynamic presence in all of creation. There is also movement in some circles to experience the sacraments as 'rites of passage or intensification' while incorporating the insights of developmental theorists.

This sea change in sacramental theology remains largely an academic exercise, lacking a full appreciation of women's experience and having little influence on actual church practice, which is why feminists continue to question the basic nature of sacramental thought. Mary Daly (1973) was the first to call sacramental patriarchy into question and to urge women to reject the eucharist because it upholds patriarchal power while denying women's experience and power. Daly called the notion of transubstantiation in the eucharist an exercise in 'swallowing the lie', one that distances us from the truth of our bodily senses by making us believe that the elemental acts of eating and drinking are not what we think (1984).

Until recently, feminist critiques of the sacraments have been confined to the use of inclusive language and the exclusion of women from the priesthood. In the 1990s, however, this critical agenda has broadened. Catholic feminists, noting that the 'sacramental principle' in their tradition affirms that God is revealed in all of creation, argue that the sacraments must be reconnected with ordinary biological life and grounded in an incarnational theology which honors human embodiment and the bodily experiences of women as well as men. Protestant feminists, acknowledging their debt to the insights of their Catholic sisters Mary Daly, Rosemary Ruether (1985) and Elisabeth Schüssler Fiorenza (1983) have focused their call for reform on baptism and the eucharist.

Marjorie Procter-Smith (1990) argues that since the sacraments (baptism and eucharist) are acts that both bring into being and sustain the church the ecclesial context of the sacraments as well as the rites themselves must be rigorously challenged. Because the sacraments have functioned to reinforce male clerical power, the recognition of their social and political context is a crucial step in moving to an emancipatory praxis that will make the church less misogynist. For the sacraments to be 'true revelations, true *mysteria*', she argues, they must witness to 'God's self-disclosure in women's lives'. Sacraments laden with patriarchal inequities thus give the lie to the church's promise of baptismal equality and dignity (Gal. 3.27-28).

Ruth Duck (1991) explores the history of the Trinitarian baptismal formula and calls for removing the gender bias of the declarative formula through a process of threefold questioning—Do you believe in...? Noting that Trinitarian controversies played a heavy hand in reinforcing the masculine bias of the present formula—'In the name of the Father, the Son and the Holy Spirit'—Duck argues that the need for revision cannot await ecumenical consensus.

Critiques of the eucharist also push the ecumenical question to the margins. These arguments have centred primarily on the negative influence of atonement imagery and the metaphor of self-sacrifice, the recovery of the meal character of the rite, and the true nature of communion. More recently, critics have challenged the image of the divine punisher that lies at the heart of atonement theories and the influence of apocalyptic eschatology, which shapes Paul's eucharistic proclamation: 'For as often as you eat this bread and drink the cup, you proclaim the Lord's death until he comes' (1 Cor. 11.26). In effect these critiques call for less reliance on traditional 'Words of Institution' and the notion of the 'Second Coming'.

From a feminist perspective, a more faithful eucharistic praxis would build on God's self-disclosure in the risk-taking and truth-telling life praxis of Jesus rather than in Jesus' death. It would also celebrate the active presence of the risen Christ here and now, our relations with one another, and the resurrection hope we experience in communion with God's mystery in Christ. As feminist reflections on the sacraments continue to evolve, greater study is needed regarding the influential role of symbolic expression and the power of imagination in human becoming. Still one thing is clear: justice and grace are inseparable when it comes to sacramental theology and the lives of women.

Further reading: Goudey 1993; Ross 1993.

SADOMASOCHISTIC SOCIETY
Monica Furlong

A STRIKING feature of sexuality in modern Western society is the degree to which excitement is seen to be bound up in power, or the lack of it, instead of erotic arousal more directly associated with beauty, intimacy, reverence or love. Inequalities of power as shown in modern pornography, either in humiliation or pain inflicted on women, or in paedophilic material, suggest an inability to feel intimacy or straightforward eroticism, so that power becomes the substitute for this. In individuals this may be due to a lack of a satisfying physical relationship with parents, or with 'games' of exclusion played by them. As a result of disappointment in parental loving it is possible for children to develop a slavish longing, with a wish to fuse with a beloved adult, and some people, particularly women, carry this on into their adult loving at great cost to themselves, choosing unsuitable partners and loving them without the proper boundaries of self-love to protect them. Robin Norwood has dubbed them 'women who love too much', but in many ways their emotion is a travesty of love. Alongside so much 'devotion' may be fantasies of cruel revenge, and, in certain circumstances, it is easy for masochists to become sadists and vice versa. Many marriages and other close relationships show evidence of sadomasochistic 'game playing', and these are particularly difficult relationships to change or break out of.

Although Christians have sometimes suggested that the Christian religion ushered in a new era of life for women, in contrast to their subjugation in Roman or Jewish households of the first century, it now seems that, perhaps as a result of persecution, the young church quickly reverted to the familiar pattern. There probably *was* a period, soon after the death of Jesus, when women had the chance to lead a different life, but at least in the second century, if not before, they were being instructed, by the unknown author of the Letter to Timothy for one, to keep silence before their male betters in church. The silence, along with 'modestly' covered heads, and the exclusion from leadership roles, was continued for centuries.

The Church Fathers show an alarming tendency to find women dangerous, a threat to men's spiritual growth, and they use this growing split between spirituality and sexuality, or, as it often seemed to them, between intellect and nature, to insist that women must be 'controlled'—a dangerous idea. Later the 'reforms' of Pope Gregory the Great were enforced by Leo IX (1002–54), insisting that priests must be celibate. This made the implicit explicit, namely that marriage, the union with a woman, was a second best option for a 'spiritual' person, and it was only one of the innumerable ways in which women were put down and despised. Gradually this creeping hostility to women emerged in the centuries of savage persecution of witches, who were mainly women. Other forms of cruelty have also been very evident over the centuries: the torture of heretics, the persecution of Jews and 'infidels', the savage suffering some Christian saints felt it necessary to inflict upon themselves, even the routine beating of children that went on in many Christian schools. It is a worrying 'shadow' for a religion that claims to be about love.

More recently, the struggles within some churches to ordain women as priests have brought a strong strain of misogyny to light, with women seen as inferior, unclean and less godlike than men. This buried stream of misogyny within the major religion of Europe has, of course, shaped us sexually in ways in which we are only gradually becoming aware, and the churches cannot disclaim responsibility for the perversion of erotic love that is so evident in our society and which is the real threat to the sort of stable society we are always claiming to want.

Further reading: Brown 1989; Countryman 1989; Dobash and Dobash 1980; Ranke-Heinemann 1990; Stone 1979.

SAINTS
Sarah Jane Boss

'**SAINT**' is derived from the Latin word 'sanctus', meaning 'holy'. In the New Testament, 'saints' are all of God's elect, or the members of the Christian community. However, from early times, Christians sought the intercession of those members of the communion of saints who had died and whose lives were considered to have been exceptionally holy.

The primitive church celebrated the Lord's supper upon the tombs of martyrs. The vestige of this custom remains in the Catholic and Orthodox practice of enshrining saints' relics in altars.

Among the earliest Christian martyrs were Felicity and Perpetua, who were thrown to wild animals at Carthage in 203 CE. They were both very young women who had recently given birth, and their deaths were regarded by their contemporaries as particularly shocking and heroic (see Shewring [ed.] 1931: 18-20, 39-40; Atkinson 1991: 19-22).

According to tradition, the first non-martyred saint to be venerated as such was Martin of Tours (d. 397). Canonization to sainthood was carried out by public acclamation, and it was not until the high Middle Ages that the Western church instituted official procedures for the recognition of saints (Farmer 1992: xxi).

Among the different categories of saint, women have been disproportionately represented among the martyrs, and are predominantly recorded as virgins in the church calendars. It is important to understand, however, that the popularity of a given saint has not generally been related to her attractiveness as a model for imitation, but has been tied overwhelmingly to the perceived power of her intercession. St Margaret of Antioch, who was a virgin martyr, was enormously popular in Western Europe during the later Middle Ages, and was called upon especially to help women in childbirth (Duffy 1992: 181).

The legend of St Wilgefurtis recounts that she wished to remain a virgin when her father wanted her to marry. She therefore prayed for some disfigurement that would render her too unattractive to be marriageable, and her prayer was answered when she grew a beard. She was put to death by crucifixion, and was venerated in images of a bearded woman hanging upon a cross, until this depiction was forbidden by church authorities. In England, Wilgefurtis was known as St Uncumber, because women would pray to her to uncumber them of unwanted hus-

An A to Z of Feminist Theology

bands (Thurston and Attwater [eds.] 1932: 287-88). Women have also turned to male saints for assistance, as is seen in the flourishing cult of St Jude (Orsi 1991).

Christians have always believed that one of the greatest virtues is humility. This has given women an ironic advantage: since women have often been regarded as naturally inferior to men, they have correspondingly been seen as the favoured instruments of God's action in the world (MacLean 1983: 21). God loves to confound the mighty through the agency of the weak, and saints such as Hildegard of Bingen (1098–1179) have been viewed as shining examples of the operation of this principle (Newman 1987: 1-4).

During the modern period, there has been a decline in the veneration of women saints who wielded political authority during their lives, such as Abbess Hilda of Whitby (614–680); instead, there is a marked emphasis upon women who were powerless, such as the twelve-year-old Maria Goretti (1890–1902).

Feminist theology is deeply suspicious of the concept of sainthood for two reasons. First, it tends to place a negative view of women's behaviour before us—women are beatified for suffering violence at the hands of others or for inflicting violence on themselves or for passively enduring social and physical injustice. They also often exhibit disturbed behaviour. Secondly, feminist theology does not acknowledge the hierarchy of worth which sainthood implies, nor does it honour the bureaucratic process that feels able to dispense this worth. Further, the notion of intercession to find favour with God confiscates personal integrity and worth and underlines the unworthiness of humans.

SALVATION
Lucy Tatman

FOR AS long as I can remember I have 'known' that salvation means going to heaven when I die. Traditional Christian theologians may argue that the concept of salvation is far more complex than this, but practically speaking it is not. Salvation has been presented as an ultimately transcendent concept, utterly removed from life on earth as we know it. While salvation might begin in an immanent way, initially through the life and death of Jesus and then through personal baptism, it is only completed with either the resurrection of our souls into heaven or, according to some, with the physical resurrection of our bodies from this earth.

Feminist theologians have known for some time that the practical consequences of theological constructs are just as critical, if not more so, than their theoretical stability. Unfortunately, the practical consequences of Christianity's otherworldly understanding of salvation have been and continue to be devastating, both for creation and for all earth creatures, humans included. Traditional understandings of salvation always imply that the earth does not matter as much as heaven, that this life matters little when compared to the next. And so, believing that it does not matter, Christians (particularly Christians in powerful positions within governments and corporations) have not treated the earth with respect. The air, the water, the ground on which we stand have been poisoned by our carelessness and greed. Sadly, the implications of salvation as it is traditionally defined mean that the concept of salvation cannot be used theologically to speak out against these human sins, for in the end they simply 'do not matter'. Likewise, Christians have been taught to accept the unacceptable, to suffer violence against our bodies and spirits, our homes and communities without protest, to content ourselves with thoughts of a heavenly afterlife in which all will be made well. Again, from a practical perspective what this means is that the concept of salvation actually fosters a sense of personal apathy and, at worst, encourages martyrdom.

The issue facing feminist theologians today is both simple and enormous: how do we redefine salvation in such a way as to remove the devastating practical consequences inherent in traditional understandings of the term yet maintain what needs to be a viable theological and especially pastoral concept?

First, salvation must be brought down to earth; it must be an immanent, here-and-now possibility. This is not to say that there cannot be transcendent elements in new understandings of salvation, but it is to say that unless immanence is the primary focus then the old traps will catch us again. Bringing salvation down to earth means that, as Sallie McFague succinctly states, 'creation is the place of salvation' (McFague 1993: 180, emphasis original). No longer must we place salvation ultimately in heaven; if it is to happen it must happen on earth. Immediately it is apparent that the health and well-being of the earth itself must be a significant part of what salvation is about. Very simply, the growing ecological crisis also signals a theological crisis. Humans must acknowledge that the responsibility for the salvation of creation is ours, not God's. We are called, at this point in history, literally to choose between life and death. We can choose to participate in the ongoing salvation of creation, or we can choose to participate in its destruction. Humans are, so far as we know, the only earth creatures who are able to choose between persisting in the destruction of our environment or living in harmony with the earth, our global home. Those of us who live comfortably in First World countries are the ones most able to make this choice, to develop and live according to an ecological sensibility, or to base our lifestyle on non-renewable resources.

Obviously, salvation in this sense does not mean a single, once-and-for-all event. Instead 'salvation' must be re-imaged as a continual happening, an ongoing process composed of bits and pieces from all around the world. Salvation in our present context must be composed of the daily, partial and limited efforts of many. Old understandings of salvation coming to us from above simply no longer apply to our current situation. The twentieth century is unique in this regard: for the first time in history human actions can destroy almost all life on earth. Human beings have the power to 'uncreate' what has been created. But we also have the ability to re-create, to fix not all but many of our mistakes. Importantly, what is salvific in one location or one community will not be what another community needs to work on. No single solution will save the world; nor will the most appropriate solutions of today be adequate in the coming years. Therefore, while we must strive for salvation as though our lives depend on it (and they do), we must also hold on to salvation loosely, acknowledging that our descendants must redefine for themselves and their time what is most salvific.

In a word, salvation is about healing; it is about healing the hurts of our planet and, importantly, healing each other. The task seems overwhelming at times; there is just so much to be done, so many wounds to clean and bandage. It's worth remembering that no one is called to do everything, but that everything we do matters.

The question remains: but what of our souls? The truth is that no theologian writing today, feminist or otherwise, can honestly answer that question. We just do not know what happens after death. What we do know is that energy is neither created nor destroyed. The universe, as vast and complex as it is, is made up of a finite amount of 'stuff'. This stuff can take the form of matter, or can be converted from matter into energy. The shapes change; the amount of 'stuff' remains constant, and we are made of the same stuff as the stars. One way, perhaps the only way, to ensure our eternal salvation is to teach our children and their children to respect and honour all of creation, from the least to the most awesome aspects of the cosmos. For ultimately, no one and nothing ever leaves this universe without a trace.

Further reading: Ruether 1992; Sewell (ed.) 1991.

SEXISM
Lucy Tatman

'SEXISM' IS the word used to refer broadly to the entire range of ideologies, structures and institutional practices that uphold and enforce the dominance of men as a group over women as a group. Sexism is as all-pervasive as patriarchy, and appears in just as many different forms and guises. In fact, sexism apart from patriarchy (defined by Gerda Lerner as 'the manifestation and institutionalization of male dominance over women and children in the family and the extension of male dominance over women in society in general' [1986: 239]) is not sexism at all. It is rudeness, obnoxious behaviour, or bad manners, but without an underlying systemic imbalance of power between the sexes these unpleasantries are just that: unpleasant. In contrast, sexism is about power and dominance, specifically the abuse of power by those in the dominant group, men. In recent years the word 'sexism' has been used by some to describe instances of objectionable behaviour on the part of a woman or group of women. This misuse of the term serves to deny the religious, political, social, economic, mental and physical oppression of women as a group by men as a group, and this denial is simply yet another characteristic of sexism-in-practice.

What does sexism have to do with feminist theology? More accurately, what do feminist theologians do with the fact of sexism? One of the first responses to sexism in the church was (and remains) a call for the use of inclusive language. Feminist theologians and biblical scholars reasoned that the sexist exclusion of female pronouns and feminine metaphors from the prayer books and pulpits, from the hymnals and chosen Scripture readings could best be corrected by including words identified with the other half of the human race. If nothing else, the resulting hue and cry confirmed the power of language, the power of naming within a tradition that affirms the co-existence of the Word with God from the beginning. Importantly, writings such as *The Women's Bible*, commissioned a century ago by Elizabeth Cady Stanton, and more recently the *Inclusive Language Lectionary* bear witness to the ongoing creation of new, non-sexist 'beginnings'.

As crucial as the language issue is, it is nonetheless not enough to add the word 'her' and stir. The sexism of the church is as structural as it is linguistic. Are half of all priests, pastors and ministers women? Are half of all those who iron the altar cloths men? Simple questions, yes, but the answers are damning.

However, the most insidious expressions of sexism in the church are found deep within those texts and doctrines that claim to be beyond human peculiarities such as sex, race and class by virtue of their appeal to 'universal' truth. Within traditional theological texts the implicit norm is that of a privileged White male: White male authors have written of the 'universal human condition' out of the experiences of their own well-educated, well-paid, White male lives. Feminist theologians have named the dishonesty of this practice and have called for its end. Honest theology demands accountability to the awesome complexity of all our lives. Until all theologians exchange the pretension of a universal perspective for the honesty of their particular experiences Christian theology will be riddled with 'isms' of all kinds, not the least of which is sexism.

Further reading: Daly 1973; Frye 1983; Lerner 1986; Ruether 1983.

SEXUALITY
Alison Webster

MALESTREAM DEFINITIONS of sexuality have traditionally demonstrated a preoccupation with genital activity. Largely because of the influence of developments in feminist thought, however, contemporary theologians (including some men) tend to employ much more comprehensive definitions. James Nelson, for instance, says this:

> Sexuality is our self-understanding and way of being in the world as male and female. It includes our appropriation of attitudes and characteristics which have been culturally defined as masculine and feminine. It involves our affectional orientation toward those of the opposite and/or the same sex. It includes attitudes about our own bodies and those of others (1978: 17-18).

Feminist thinkers have worked to overcome patriarchal dualistic patterns of thinking which, in the field of sexuality, have encouraged the rigid separation of male from female, heterosexual from homosexual, orientation from practice, external forms of relationship from qualitative considerations, and body from spirit. The patriarchal approach has also understood sexuality to be essentially disruptive of the social order since it is characterized by feeling and emotion rather than by rationality. Male sexuality, in particular, has been deemed uncontrollable.

In contrast, feminist thinking has emphasized the fluidity of sexuality and seeks a language in which we can articulate the changing nature of relationships; it emphasizes the all-embracing nature of sexuality as that which affects all aspects of our lives; it emphasizes the value of bodiliness in contrast to the asceticism of the past, and it encourages the exercise of our moral agency and responsibility through our ethical decision- making.

With regard to affectional orientation, theological debates have mirrored those in other disciplines over the comparative roles of nature and nurture, essence and social construction. However, these debates have largely assumed heterosexual normativity so discussions have focused exclusively on the origins of same-sex attraction, with no similar scrutiny given to heterosexual attraction. The feminist rejoinder has been a critique of 'compulsory heterosexuality' (Rich 1980) as a political force, with substantial philosophical and theological work (see Raymond 1986; Hunt 1991) focusing on the important role of women's friendships (especially women's sexual friendships and lesbian relationships) in overcoming patriarchal social structures and building sexual justice. This work also challenges the traditional preoccupation with 'coupledom' which has characterized sexual ethics, and calls for an end to the tyranny of relational dyads.

A further, but closely related focus of feminist theological work has been the links between sexuality and social and political action. Carter Heyward, for example, famously defines sexuality thus:

> Sexuality is our desire to participate in making love, making justice, in the world; our drive toward one another; our movement in love; our expression of being bonded together in life and death. Sexuality is expressed not only between lovers in personal relationship, but also in the work of an artist who loves her painting or poetry, a father who loves his children, a revolutionary who loves her people (1984: 86).

An important foundation of this kind of theological perspective is undoubtedly to be found in Audre Lorde's famous and ground-breaking essay 'Uses of the Erotic: The Erotic as Power', in which she says,

> The dichotomy between the spiritual and political is also false, resulting from an incomplete attention to our erotic knowledge. For the bridge which connects them is formed by the erotic—the sensual—those physical, emotional, and psychic expressions of what is deepest and strongest and richest within each of us, being shared: the passions of love, in its deepest meanings (in Lorde 1984: 56).

Through debates about sexuality we enter the realm of shifting identities. Each person is part of a complex variety of communities which give our life structure and meaning, and which provide us with a language through which to express our identity and our aspirations. For instance, Alice Walker's definition of 'womanist' (1984) highlights the differences between white women and women of colour in their experiences of sexuality and gender. In terms of theological methodology, there is therefore a growing recognition that the pursuit of objectivity is an unhelpful diversion in the quest to understand sexuality. Rather, the most pressing need is for the location of our own subjectivity: to take account of differences in age, ability, race, sexual integrity, educational and economic background. Human experience is considered to be primary; abstract reasoning alone is considered an inadequate starting point in rethinking sexuality. In the words of pro-feminist James Nelson, the necessary move is from the 'theology of sexuality' towards 'sexual theology'—which he explains thus:

> A theology of (or about) sexuality tends to argue in a one-directional way: What do scripture and tradition say about our sexuality and how it ought to be expressed?... We need to ask also (after the manner of various liberation theologies): What does our experience as human sexual beings tell us about how we read the scripture, interpret the tradition, and attempt to live out the meaning of the gospel? The movement must be in both directions, not only in one (1992: 21).

SHECHINAH
Rachel Montagu

'SHECHINAH' is the rabbinic term for God's indwelling presence. Grammatically, it is a feminine noun. The Hebrew root 'to dwell' from which it derives is used in the Hebrew Bible to signify the residence of human beings, and also the dwelling place of God (Num. 24.2; Exod. 29.46). Over and over in the book of Deuteronomy comes the phrase 'the place where I chose to make my name dwell', referring to Jerusalem, where the temple is to be built and which will replace the shrine in the wilderness as the centre of the religious life of the community. The Hebrew word *miščan* for the shrine in which God's presence is manifest to Moses comes from the same root.

An A to Z of Feminist Theology

SHECHINAH

In rabbinic Bible exegesis 'Shechinah' is used to describe any manifestation of the divine presence; it is the Shechinah who spoke to Moses and gave him the commandments and who inspired David with those psalms which begin 'To David' (Babylonian Talmud *Šabbat* 87a; *Pesaḥim* 117a).

The rabbis believed that the Shechinah went into exile with the Jewish people after the destruction of the temple (Babylonian Talmud *Megillah* 29). The rabbis of the Talmud originated the idea, which was developed further in the Jewish mystical tradition, that in the future messianic age the Shechinah and God will be united once more. Meanwhile, on every Sabbath, in a foretaste of the future age of perfection, God and the Shechinah unite; this is why it is important for a married couple to have sexual relations on the Sabbath; they are imitating in this realm the unity of God and the Shechinah in the heavenly realm. Because of the belief that the performance of the commandments helps to bring the world into the state of perfection, Jewish prayer books which are influenced by the mystical tradition include a formula before the performance of many positive commandments: 'I am ready and prepared to perform this commandment in order to unite God and the Shechinah'. The Shechinah has been described as the 'bride of God within God, mother of the world and feminine side of the divine self, in no way fully separable from the male side of God. Indeed, the root of all evil, both cosmic and human, is the attempt to bring about such a separation' (Green 1983: 255).

Rabbinic Judaism used the word 'Shechinah' as a convenient way of describing the presence of God, for instance in *Pirke Abot* 3.3. Rabbi Hanahiah ben Teradyon said: 'But when two sit together and exchange words of study the Shechinah is present with them…'. Likewise, Rabbi Akiba expounded: 'When husband and wife are worthy, the Shechinah abides with them; when they are not worthy, fire consumes them' (Babylonian Talmud *Soṭah* 17a). However, they were also cautious about using the idea of the Shechinah in any context where this might be deemed to detract from pure monotheism, and so phrases like 'so to speak' are frequently found in personified references to the Shechinah. Despite this, the Shechinah is used to indicate an association with God and the feminine aspect of the divine; for instance, 'When Rabbi Joseph heard his mother's footsteps, he would say: "I will arise before the approaching Shechinah" ' (Babylonian Talmud *Kiddushin* 31b). The Shechinah is described as that which protects Israel; converts to Judaism are said to 'come under the wings of the Shechinah' (Babylonian Talmud *Šabbat* 31a).

In the mystical tradition the Shechinah is the lowest of the ten *sefirot*, the ten spheres of manifestation of God which surround the world, and therefore represents God in the most available and accessible aspect.

The continued association between the Shechinah as the feminine aspect of God and the manifestation of God most present with the Jewish people in their exile from the promised land can be seen in a dream recounted in a Hasidic tale:

> …and he went to the Western wall, where he wept copiously. Upon raising his eyes he saw above the wall the figure of a woman with her back toward him…he fell upon his face and cried out in tears: 'Mother Zion! Woe is me that I have seen you thus!'… Then he says in a dream that she came and put her hand on his face and wiped away his tears and said to him, 'Be comforted Abraham my son, there is hope for thy future and thy children shall return to their own border' (Freeman 1994: 45).

Modern Jewish feminist liturgies which wish to find a feminine form to address God in Hebrew, a gender-inflected language, often praise the Shechinah. For instance, the unvarying beginning of every *b'rachah*, or blessing, the form on which all Jewish liturgy is based, is *Baruch atah Hashem elokeinu melech haolam*. While this formula can be translated into English in either masculine language ('Blessed are You, Lord our God, King of the Universe') or neutral language ('Blessed are you, the Eternal our God, Ruler of the Universe') the Hebrew is definitely masculine. In a new liturgy of thanksgiving for the occasion when a woman first gives birth and becomes a mother, the writer has creatively adapted the traditional blessing said after using the lavatory. The blessing addresses the Shechinah, so the pronouns used in the Hebrew are feminine in form:

B'ruchah at Shechinah, Blessed are You, Shechinah, who in wisdom formed women's bodies and created in us unique openings, passages, organs and glands. These are known and revealed to You. If one of these opens when it should close or closes when it should open, it is impossible for us to live and sustain ourselves or to create and sustain our children. Blessed are You Shechinah, Healer of all flesh Who creates and sustains our bodies in wondrous ways. Blessed are You, Shechinah, Who has made me a woman (from the 'Simchat Yoledet, Celebrating the Birth of a Mother', in Levine [ed.] 1991: 17).

SIN
Lucy Tatman

IN 1960 Valerie Saiving published an essay, 'The Human Situation: A Feminine View' (reprinted in Christ and Plaskow [eds.] 1979) in which she noted the fact that understandings of sin as pride, will to power and self-exaltation did not reflect or characterize the experiences of women. (Saiving acknowledged that 'femininity' is defined differently in different cultures but did not, by extension, acknowledge that there could be no universally shared *social* experience. Her work was written in the context of a white, Western woman's experience.) Instead, she stated, 'women's sins' could be more accurately described as the reverse of those things: that is, as a lack of self-esteem, as self-negation, as losing one's identity in the absence of one's relations with others, as self-sacrifice to the point of losing any sense of self or self-worth apart from one's actions on behalf of others, and as not taking oneself seriously. In short, she effectively challenged the unquestioned notion of 'the universal sin of man', showing that men's sins did not apply at all equally to women, and that 'women's sins', especially those involving self-sacrifice and self-negation, had been named, traditionally, as virtues.

Saiving's essay, regarded by many as the beginning of the current wave of feminist theological scholarship, did not cause an immediate explosion of interest in the field of feminine theology or in the concept of sin, specifically. But it was there on the shelves, waiting to be rediscovered, reread and expanded upon; all of which Judith Plaskow did, publishing her 1975 doctoral dissertation *Sex, Sin and Grace: Women's Experience and the Theologies of Reinhold Niebuhr and Paul Tillich* in 1980. Just as Saiving had pointed out the imposition of culturally or socially defined attributes of masculinity and femininity upon males and females respectively so too did Plaskow raise the issue of the social or socialized characteristics of sin as a matter for further consideration by feminist theologians. However, unlike Saiving who wrote of 'women's experience' as though it were a universally shared experience common to all women, Plaskow grounded her work in the particular experiences of white, middle-class, Western women. She also further extended the comparisons Saiving initiated through her (Plaskow's) examination of Paul Tillich's definition of sin as estrangement (meaning a sense of alienation, of separation). Given that society's expectations and demands of white, middle-class Western women include caring for children, supporting partners at home and nurturing those around them, it became evident that the lived reality of these women truly did allow for the possibility of estrangement. Indeed, these women were at risk of losing their own identity if they lived too much for and through others' lives.

It is important to note that neither Saiving nor Plaskow, although they named the social, cultural and historical conditions that both created the possibility for and, in a sense, defined the limits of white Western women's sins, permitted these constructed conditions to excuse the fact of personal sin among women. In this regard their work runs parallel to traditional theology. The fact that white Western men have been taught to take pride in their work and in themselves does not excuse them from the sin of having too much pride, of trying to replace God with themselves. Similarly, the fact that many white Western women have been taught not to take themselves seriously but to live for others does not serve as an excuse for losing themselves in others' lives, though it does seem to explain why this so often happens.

Curiously, apart from Saiving's and Plaskow's work there has been little feminist theological reflection on the concept of personal sin. Carter Heyward is one theologian who has done such reflection. In her book *Touching Our Strength:*

An A to Z of Feminist Theology

The Erotic as Power and the Love of God (1989), she defines sin (both personal and systemic sin, such as sexism) as 'the violation of right relation'. Because right relations are those which are mutually empowering, sin occurs whenever a person or group use or abuse an individual, group or natural resource for their own purposes, thereby disempowering, degrading and all too often destroying who or what was used. Heyward's definition of sin is deceptively simple. Its strength lies in the fact that it does not come with detailed instruction for use; rather, she acknowledges that mutually empowering relations are known only in context. Therefore the violation of 'right relations' can be determined only in the context of each specific instance, each relation. Because of this her work has the potential to be useful to women of colour as well as white women, to women in the two-thirds world as well as 'first' world women, to men as well as women.

While feminist theologians have not written a great deal about personal sin, thorough analyses of systemic sins against women and other oppressed groups have been and continue to be developed. In the act of revealing sexism, racism, classism and religious intolerance as systemic sins theologians such as Rosemary Ruether (1983) and Susan Thistlethwaite (1989) have simultaneously transformed the entire concept of sin and pointed to ways of redemption from these sins. Their work has been transformative because they have shifted the focus on sin away from what can be described as solitary navel-gazing onto a much broader context, which is the structure of the social, political, economic and religious institutions that function to perpetuate sins such as racism and sexism. These sins are perpetuated either through practices that actively promote them (such as ordaining men but not women) or, often, through practices that do not challenge and refute them (practices that accept the status quo). Feminist theologians are calling everyone to be accountable both for their personal actions and their actions *as members of social, political, economic and religious groups*. Part of the process of accountability involves acknowledging one's complicity in the perpetuation of systemic sins and evils. For example, white women must recognize that they have benefited from the institution of racism simply because they are white, regardless of any personal feelings about members of different races. And, because everyone has spent their entire life in societies and cultures that are utterly saturated with explicit and implicit racist assumptions there is no way to be totally free of racism personally. Redemption from the sin of racism therefore includes unlearning deeply ingrained racist beliefs and working to transform the current meaning of race from that of a hierarchical ranking system to something entirely different, to something that is mutually empowering for all. In the instance of race this means firstly that white people must listen and learn how people of colour understand and define themselves.

Traditionally, women have been blamed for bringing sin into the world and for continually tempting men to sin. The refusal to accept the blame for any notion of 'original sin' and the refusal to accept responsibility for men's sins are foundational premises in most feminist theologians' work, whether these refusals are stated explicitly or implicitly. Because women, whatever their race, class and creed, have been sinned against so thoroughly and for so long one of the first tasks for feminist theologians was to uncover the nature and extent of these sins against women. However, it is not appropriate to remain theoretically caught in a women-as-victims perspective, and some have begun to explore what it means to be both a victim and a perpetrator of sin. At this point it is impossible to predict where these explorations will go or how they will affect the shape of feminist theology. However, it seems that specificity, difference and accountability will be crucial elements in newly developing feminist theological and ethical conceptualizations of sin.

SPIRITUALITY
Ursula King

'SPIRITUALITY' IS associated with a wide range of meanings relating to both religious and secular contexts. The word has its origin in the Judaeo-Christian tradition and many non-Western languages have no exact equivalent for it. The term 'spirituality' is now globally used across the religious traditions and however defined and widely varying in practice, it refers to a perennial human concern.

SPIRITUALITY

On one hand the spiritual can be seen as wider than the religious; on the other hand it can be understood as the deepest and most central element of religion, or as something which is outside and beyond religion altogether. Three different meanings of spirituality can be distinguished: (1) a lived experience or praxis within a particular religious or spiritual tradition (whether ancient or new); (2) the spiritual teaching which a particular person or school imparts; and (3) the systematic, comparative and critical study of different spiritual experiences, disciplines and teachings—a new subject matter which is sometimes described as the global study of spirituality.

Numerous publications and conference titles bear witness to the widespread interest in spirituality today. In Britain, both the 1944 Education Act and the 1988 Education Reform Act require teachers to pay attention to the spiritual development of children, not only in religious education but across the whole school curriculum. Many people today ask how spirituality can help to bring about the personal and social transformation our world needs so urgently. Spirituality is a topic as much addressed by new religious movements as it is by the women's movement, the ecological movement or by people interested in psychotherapy and consciousness, or those working towards the renewal of Christianity or in interfaith dialogue. Yet much contemporary interest in spirituality is too individualistic, static and past-oriented, too much focused on revival rather than renewal, emphasizing the individual's inwardness rather than the transformation of both the inner and outer world.

Traditional spirituality is often cast in a patriarchal and hierarchical mode in which the spiritual quest is primarily considered to be a male prerogative. One can distinguish between the pre-patriarchal spirituality of earlier historical periods, about which we have relatively little definite information, patriarchal spirituality, which has been dominant throughout most of history, and post-patriarchal spirituality, which is beginning to emerge now and whose definite form is still unclear. In the past, the search for spiritual perfection and holiness was often related to men's contempt for the body and the world, and even more to their contempt for women. The history of renunciation and asceticism is responsible for a great deal of misogyny in the world religions. Traditional spirituality separated men from women, from each other, and from the world. In this sense much of past spirituality is deeply dualistic, dividing the world of women, work and matter from that of the spirit. By contrast the contemporary revisioning of spirituality seeks holiness through wholeness and integration by reconnecting all forms of life and by transforming traditional attitudes to gender, work, the environment and many other aspects of personal and social experience.

There now exists a fast-growing women's spirituality movement, sometimes referred to as spiritual or metaphysical feminism or as the women-spirit movement or movements. Some feminist activists and radical feminists consider this a soft option while others proclaim it a necessity, not a luxury. Others again see the women's movement itself as a spiritual revolution. Whatever the case, there can be no doubt that besides the explicit developments in women's spirituality there exists also an important implicit spiritual dimension in contemporary feminism (King 1993), since the search for liberation, peace and justice, for the full humanity of women, has ultimately not only political and economic but also spiritual aims.

Spirituality is a process of inner growth in awareness and sensitivity linked to reflection and transformation which results in a growing sense of well-being, wholeness and trust, a sense of feeling connected and interdependent, of joy and graciousness, of reverence and gratitude for the wonders of creation and the mystery of life. With a new consciousness and identity, and an awareness of the new possibilities for transformation, women feel they can no longer simply practise a spirituality handed down to them from the past, but must develop their own.

Feminist spirituality involves the awareness of women's own power from within, of a new empowerment which can be nurtured to effect personal, social and political changes. Contemporary women's spirituality is a rich tapestry of many strands. Prominent among them is women's discovery of their own self and its agency, their experience of bonding and power sharing, a creative reimaging and renaming of the sacred, and a growth in sensitivity to

An A to Z of Feminist Theology

the interdependence and sacredness of all life-forms, and the importance of earth–human relationships.

Women's discovery of the self and spiritual quest has been mapped by Carol P. Christ (1986) and others as a series of steps from initiation to awakening, insight, transformation and wholeness. Much of this trajectory can be traced through the works of contemporary women writers, a rewarding research area which also yields many insights into women's intimacy and mutuality with others and the connections between sexuality and spirituality.

Following women's spiritual quest and seeking to meet women's spiritual needs is linked to the growing recognition of where to find spiritual resources. Many, but not all, can come from women's own experience, their inner power and strength. But women are now also discovering the rich spiritual heritage in the different world religions, in which countless women saints and mystics and other leading female figures provide inspiring examples for today. Much contemporary research also helps to uncover the rich female imagery and symbolism in different religions; which is, however, often profoundly ambivalent. The greatest efforts go into reimaging the divine and developing more inclusive images and metaphors for God. Central to this is the recognition of the power of the Goddess and the rediscovery of many very ancient Goddess traditions around the world. Yet however powerful, these do not necessarily have a direct bearing on the status of women in society. Some women prefer an androgynous or monistic conceptualization of divine reality over either a matriarchal or patriarchal expression.

The term 'feminist spirituality' can be understood in a wider sense as the spiritual quest and creativity of contemporary women, pursued in diverse traditional and non-traditional ways, or in a more specific sense as a new movement outside traditional religions altogether. Its primary sources then consist in women's own experience and in newly created rituals drawn from Wicca and folk traditions celebrating life and nature cycles. Similar themes are found in ecofeminist spirituality.

The rich patterns of the newly created feminist spirituality are evident from Plaskow and Christ, *Weaving the Visions* (1989) and Eller (1993), whereas Christian themes of women's spirituality are dealt with by Conn ([ed.] 1986) and Fischer (1989). Zappone (1991) deals with both Christian and wider aspects of women's spirituality, as does King (1993). Christian women's spirituality has traditionally been much constricted and often been confined to an 'ideology of obedience' (Dorothee Sölle [1984]). Contemporary Christian women who want to combine their faith with feminism need to construct a new, more woman-defined and woman-oriented spirituality from the resources within the Christian tradition and themselves. The heart of the Christian story is not self-development, so central a theme in contemporary feminist spirituality, but is much more community-oriented. Its central paradigm of death, resurrection and life celebrates the universal experience of birth, death and regeneration which belongs to both sexes. Incarnate Christian spirituality is truly holistic, widely connected and empowering, but in practice the embodiment of the Christian vision often falls far short of the hope for wholeness which is such an integral part of its own foundation.

Women's spirituality is an important theme in contemporary Christian feminism. Spirituality understood as the struggle for life, and all that this entails, is central to feminist theology in the Third World, where women speak of a newly emerging spirituality born out of the encounter of Christian women with the spiritual heritage of indigenous civilizations and cultures. This may lead to a rich, new synthesis in spirituality in the future, as yet difficult to predict.

Further reading: Leonard 1990; *Women's Studies Quarterly* 21.1, 2 (Spring/Summer 1993), special issue on *Spirituality and Religions*.

SUFFERING
Lucy Tatman

AT THE centre of the Christian tradition is the Son of God, suffering and dying on a cross. Historically, his suffering and death may have been presented to all Christians as necessary, salvific, and *something to be emulated*. When these theological and pastoral interpretations of suffering are combined with Gen. 3.16, in which God

SUFFERING

'greatly increase[s] [Eve's] pangs in childbearing' (NRSV) because of her perceived sin, an enduring and entangled double message is sent to women. First, it is both good and God-like to suffer, and secondly, suffering is the inevitable consequence of personal sin. As Christians women are called to suffer as Jesus suffered; as daughters of Eve women are eternally punished with suffering.

When Christian feminist theologians name this double bind unacceptable, unjust and evil they are both calling into question the theological foundations of the Christian tradition and pointing out the horrifying implications *for women especially* of the theological glorification of suffering.

Theories of the Atonement, interpretations of the crucifixion, doctrines of salvation and theological answers to the question of theodicy traditionally have accepted, either implicitly or explicitly, the correlation between sin and human suffering. Likewise, divine suffering has been interpreted as the necessary response to the problem of humanity's sinfulness. Traditionally, redemption from sin occurs by and through the God-demanded suffering and death of God's own son. Joanne Carlson Brown and Rebecca Parker have named this paradigmatic justification of suffering 'Divine child abuse' and, in accordance with their veil-rending statement that 'suffering is never redemptive', have called for the transformation of Christian theology, flatly refusing to honor or emulate suffering any longer.

Many Christian feminist theologians, ethicists and pastors have named the harmful effects the traditional justifications of suffering have on women who are victims or survivors of childhood incest, rape or assault. When suffering is understood as punishment for personal sin Christian women who are victims or survivors must either blame themselves for their attacker's actions (and forgive the attacker[s]), embrace their suffering (like Christ), or reject their faith tradition. None of these 'options' has to do with real healing, love or justice. From a pastoral perspective there is a dire need for alternative understandings of suffering within the Christian tradition. It is not acceptable to blame the victim, nor is it acceptable to tell the victim or survivor to embrace her suffering as a sign of her faith.

It is important to note that the refusal to allow suffering salvific status does not deny the existence of suffering in the world. It is a crucial first step toward establishing a Christian feminist framework within which the problem of individual and mass suffering can be re-worked, re-asked and re-answered in ways that are meaningful and helpful to all of us who have suffered and will suffer.

Christian feminist responses to the fact of suffering can be expressed in two words: justice and love. When suffering happens as a result of systemic evil (a political power-play, war, the genocide of a people on the basis of religion or race, the Holocaust) then as Christians we are called to fight against injustice, to resist evil, to attempt to liberate the suffering ones from that which is oppressive. In and with and through the struggle for justice runs another thread, inseparable. Out of love we are called to mourn, to grieve, to remember, to feel. Love compels us into and sustains us through the struggle for justice; justice requires love, for where love is not there reigns despair and the distance between despair and apathy is short indeed.

More difficult is a response to individual suffering, when we are forced to bear or watch another bear intolerable pain for whatever reason, or no reason at all. In these instances the response is love, compassionate love sustained by eternal justice, the eternal validation and remembrance of the sufferer. The forms love-with-passion can take are many and varied: visible and outward, silent, inward, voiced or felt. The one commonality, necessity, is that all forms of love-with-passion allow the reality of the suffering. Finally, the profound effect the reality of suffering has upon an individual never goes away; the effects of suffering can be transformed, or muted, but they never disappear. Jesus' wounds sent him into the tomb; when he left it they were with him still.

Further reading: Sölle 1975; Brown and Bohn (eds.) 1989; Brown and Parker 1989; Redmond 1989; Fortune 1989.

SUFFRAGETTES
Sue Morgan

THE TERM 'suffragette' was coined by the *Daily Mail* in 1906 to denote and distinguish a woman active in the most militant wing of the overall campaign for female parliamentary suffrage. The notion that women might exercise the right to vote can be traced back at least as far as Mary Wollstonecraft's *A Vindication of the Rights of Women* (1792), but it was not until the mid-nineteenth century that women began in earnest to organize themselves around the issue. A nationwide network of regional suffrage organizations (the earliest, the Manchester Women's Suffrage Society, having been established by Lydia Becker in 1867) became affiliated to the National Union of Women's Suffrage Societies (NUWSS) in 1897 under the presidency of Millicent Fawcett (1847–1929). The NUWSS was the largest of all Edwardian suffrage organizations with a membership of over 50,000. A non-militant society, its leadership was comprised of predominantly middle-class women of liberal, non-conformist inclinations.

Couching their protests in a language evocative of previous abolitionist struggles, suffragists drew upon libertarian concepts of the rights of the individual, equality of representation and political justice as they sought to expose the inherent hypocrisy of a parliamentary system that described itself as democratic while simultaneously proffering a blatantly imbalanced representation of the population. They also reinterpreted dominant cultural ideologies of womanhood, transforming them into a powerful argument for the vote. Such were the superior moral and nurturing qualities of the virtuous Victorian wife and mother, it was contended, that female suffrage would both humanize politics and purify the state.

The latter half of the nineteenth century witnessed a gradual concession of the franchise to women in municipal and county elections. The ability to vote and be elected for town councils (1868), local school boards (1870), county councils (1888) and parish councils (1894) significantly heightened the visibility of publically and politically accountable women. There is no doubt that success at local government level fuelled feminist aspirations towards the national scene as well as emphatically refuting the anti-suffrage argument that women were mentally and emotionally unequipped for the harsh realities of political life. By the 1890s, the campaign for the vote had emerged as the dominant and unifying feature of the women's movement. Yet despite persistent petitioning, lengthy courtroom battles seeking to expose inconsistencies in legal practice and efforts to enlighten public opinion via the dissemination of educational tracts, the NUWSS made little headway against governmental apathy and ridicule.

In 1903, Emmeline Pankhurst (1858–1928) founded the Women's Social and Political Union (WSPU) along with her daughters Christabel (1880–1958) and Sylvia (1882–1960) in order to further the concerns of women within the nascent labour movement. Profoundly disillusioned with the decorous but ineffective strategies of the respectable NUWSS, the Pankhurst leadership aimed to break the political impasse spawned by parliamentary indifference, embarking upon a campaign of disruptive militancy. A dramatist with a real flair for publicity, Mrs Pankhurst moved the WSPU headquarters from Manchester to London in 1905 and set out to promote female suffrage in vigorous fashion. 'Deeds not Words' was the motto of the WSPU members or 'suffragettes', who heckled individual politicians, demonstrated vociferously on street corners, attacked public buildings and underwent imprisonment for refusing to pay court fines.

Such confrontational tactics quickly distanced the WSPU from older suffrage societies. Support from the Liberal Party so fervently hoped for in the landslide election victory of 1906 had not been forthcoming and the suffragettes found themselves faced with entrenched hostility from male political opponents who regarded any woman's transgression of her appointed domestic sphere as threatening the very sanctity of the home. They determined to increase the scale of their agitation in an effort to prevail against the evasive and vacillatory tactics of Asquith's Liberal government. From 1909 onwards art treasures were defaced, pillar boxes vandalized and a policy of window-smashing launched. Suffragette prisoners also resorted to hunger striking so as to secure their release more rapidly. Parliament responded by introducing forcible feeding and, despite public consternation at this brutal measure, implemented the 'Cat-and-Mouse Act' of 1913 which allowed the women hunger strikers to be released for short periods to regain their health before being rearrested.

The preparedness of the suffragettes to undergo this type of physical and mental anguish cannot be interpreted as a simple question of greater intensity of commitment to the cause. Suffragism had functioned as an all-consuming endeavour for Fawcett and the constitutionalist arm of the campaign as well, for all their perceived timidity and moderation of strategy. Rather, the answer lies in the passionate and charismatic appeal of the Pankhurst administration. Emmeline Pankhurst exerted a particularly powerful and autocratic influence over the membership of the WSPU. Extolling the impact of the individual upon the course of political history, she imbued her followers with a sense of destiny and personal empowerment through militant activity. It is perhaps not insignificant that her own personal heroine was Joan of Arc. The Pankhursts' ability to inspire commitment and devotion in those previously indifferent to women's enfranchisement was in evidence throughout the entire suffragette years, attracting people of great energy and talent into the movement such as Annie Kenney and the Pethick-Lawrences. The bitter experiences of physical struggle, police arrests, incarceration, forcible feeding, permanent impairment to health and martyrdom, as was the fate of Emily Wilding Davison, all served to bond the small cadre of suffragettes together and galvanize them on to further endeavour.

It is clear with hindsight that the WSPU overestimated the effect of their militant activities. Even during the period 1912–14, which witnessed the most violent phase of the suffragettes' history and may well have damaged their reputation among enemies and allies alike, Asquith's power as prime minister was sufficient to prevent any concessions from the Liberal Party against his intransigent opposition to the suffragettes' cause. In many ways, the onset of World War One heralded a welcome respite from what had become a highly destructive course of action. The WSPU was disbanded and the majority of the suffragettes (with the exception of Sylvia Pankhurst and her East London Federation who were bitterly opposed to the war) adopted a highly patriotic stance, encouraging women to place the interests of the nation first. To what extent the contribution of women's labour during the war enabled the eventual gaining of limited female suffrage in 1918 is a contested point. It has been argued that ultimately the acquisition of the vote was as much a gesture towards postwar principles of democracy as to the women's movement itself. Nevertheless, the fundamental principle had been ceded, with the deep-seated male fear of government by women reflected in the age and status limitations of the 1918 Act. The franchise was given to all remaining adult males but only to women over thirty who were local university graduates, government electors or the wives of electors. This age qualification was dropped in 1928 when the vote was extended to all adult women.

Initially anticipated as a swift and decisive campaign, women's suffrage was one of the fiercest and most divisive struggles undertaken. In addition to the strength of external resistance, the movement itself was beset by irreconcilable differences as to how extensive a female franchise to demand, tensions surrounding factors of wealth, class and marital status. Considering the very real minority of women suffragists that comprised the membership of the WSPU suffragettes, however, it is remarkable that this brief period in feminist history has come to overshadow most of its predecessors' activities.

The struggle to attain the vote has tended to dominate feminist accounts of the period, yet it is important not to regard it in complete isolation but as a key component in a series of interlocking nineteenth-century women's campaigns surrounding female sexuality, rights within marriage and access to improved education and employment. The issue of female suffrage functioned above all as a consolidating factor that drew together the various themes and challenges of the first wave of feminism. That the suffragists' demand for political recognition and inclusion was an implicit acceptance of orthodox structures of power cannot be denied. It is highly unlikely, however, that tactical success could have been achieved in any other way.

The suffragettes themselves were responsible

for successfully re-energizing the flagging spirits of earlier participants in the campaign and for single-mindedly focusing the related interests of the women's movement onto the parliamentary franchise. While there appears to have been no predominant religious affiliation among WSPU members, the suffragettes viewed their cause as a fundamentally quasi-spiritual one, a sort of holy crusade. It is worth noting for example that Christabel Pankhurst, who had begun to display an apocalyptic drift during the war, was afterwards to find an outlet for her oratorical abilities as a Second Adventist, preaching on the second coming of Christ. Above all, the suffragettes catalysed a mass movement of women that identified the vote not only in symbolic terms as an important intrusion into the inner sanctuary of the male sphere, but as the pre-eminent tool with which to create a more just and egalitarian society.

Further reading: Harrison 1987; Liddington and Norris 1978; E. Pankhurst 1914; E.S. Pankhurst 1977 [1931]; Rubinstein 1986; Tickner 1987.

SYMBOLS
Ronwyn Goodsir-Thomas

SYMBOLS CAN be creative. They can also be dangerous when, as in Christianity, specific meanings have been attached to certain symbols, restricting their meaning and damaging their validity as symbols. Symbolism and imagery are closely related. If images are over-defined they may cause difficulties which obstruct a person's development. An individual may be burdened with a collection of antiquated and obsolete views of the world, leading to conflict and confusion. This is the case for many women today. Before we can reinterpret symbolism we must first change the image.

The meaning that a symbol has is not the same for every generation or for every culture. Images with a meaning peculiar to their own time and place, once created, can suddenly be forgotten, and then remembered again after centuries of oblivion. Symbols arise naturally out of human experience; they cannot be artificially constructed. (Although some scholars have attempted to create 'modern' symbols for contemporary religion, these are not true religious symbols and it is not possible for them to function as such.) The fact that a symbol is used in one culture does not preclude its use in another culture so long as the symbol is a familiar part of the everyday life of that culture. Symbols that arise across the world are as old as the human race. These are traditional symbols. The Great Mother (see Neumann 1974) refers to an inward image at work in the human psyche, which is expressed in rites, myths and images. If they are to be really effective such symbols must act as links between two worlds—the world of everyday life and the world of unconscious depths hidden below the surface of our lives.

Natural symbols reach down to and express the unconscious in primitive fashion; at the same time they correspond to the highest intuitions of consciousness. Mary Douglas (1973) describes natural symbols drawn from the physical personality, with its flesh, blood, breath and orifices, ingestions and secretions. Robertson Smith's natural symbols (1889) are things in the external environment which have independent existence unaltered by human beings, such as rocks, trees, mountains and sacred stones.

The most basic symbols of Christianity are bread and wine. A recent study of the use of food as a symbol in religion has shown it to be related to basic needs within the human psyche. The human psyche has a need for transformation; it has creative, protective and nourishing needs; it also has a need to engage in confrontation with the dimension of the terrible. The most potent symbols are polyvalent: they may be open to a number of different interpretations and may answer a number of different psychological needs. For this reason it is not possible to measure or analyse the content, meaning and truth of symbols by something which is supposed to be reproduced in them. The same symbol may express different things to different people or to the same person on different occasions. The essential characteristic of a symbol is that it should be transparent and not need to be translated. Symbols are not signs, nor do they have interpretative meanings. They only have value for those who can recognize and appropriate them.

THEOLOGY
Nicola Slee

'THEOLOGY' MEANS 'God-talk' (from the Greek *theos* + *logos*), and has been well defined by David Jenkins as 'disciplined and responsible reflection and argument on the beliefs and traditions of a faith considered from within' (1984: 344). Christian theology always has the task of interpreting anew the inherited wisdoms of Scripture and tradition for fresh times and fresh situations. All Christians are called to engage in this lively and critical task in order that the fullness of lived experience and human wisdom may be engaged with the richness of past understandings of God's ways. This is not to say that all theological activity is undertaken at the same level or within the same context. The Boff brothers (1987) distinguish between three ways of doing theology necessary to the life of the church: the *professional*, which refers to the work of full-time, trained theologians, who earn their living by teaching and writing theology; the *pastoral*, which refers to church leaders and workers who reflect, teach and preach; and the *popular*, which consists of ordinary people living and working in the world who are called to reflect on their day-to-day experience in the light of the gospel. Each of these three aspects of theology employs different discourses, methods and tools, yet essentially they are engaged in the same task: the critical reflection on experience in the light of the gospel.

The assertion that theology is an activity of the whole church in which every Christian is called to participate has clearly not been reflected in official doctrine of the church, which has been perpetuated by a male clerical elite. Women, who constitute the majority of faithful worshippers within the churches, have been systematically excluded from the authoritative and interpretive task of theology. Although there have always been individual women who have railed against this injustice, it is only in the last two or three decades that feminist theology has emerged as a self-conscious challenge to the male bias of church doctrine and teaching, first in the United States, and then more widely in Europe and, more recently still, across the globe. The publication of Mary Daly's *The Church and the Second Sex* in 1968 ushered in a new era of theological activity marked by the systematic critique and reformulation of every aspect of Christian doctrine from the perspective of women's experience. Among the leading pioneers of this movement in the United States were Rosemary Radford Ruether (1983), Phyllis Trible, Elisabeth Schüssler Fiorenza, Sallie McFague (1983), Carol Christ and Judith Plaskow. Feminist theology then took root in Britain and the continent of Europe. The distinctive voice of black and Asian feminist theologians, while present from the beginning, began to find fuller expression only in the 1980s in the work of such women as Mercy Amba Oduyoye, Rita Nakashima Brock, Jacquelyn Grant and Chung Hyun Kyung.

From the beginning, feminist theology has incorporated a broad range of perspectives. There seem to be two main issues which divide feminist theologians and which operate as ideological axes marking off what might be described as different 'schools' (although in practice the boundaries between the various 'schools' are extremely fluid). First, while all feminists are agreed that religion has been profoundly shaped and distorted by sexism, they are divided on the question of how far patriarchal religious traditions are capable of reform. Christian feminists, or revisionists (such as Schüssler Fiorenza, McFague, Grey and Trible), affirm that Christianity is capable of being reformed so that it may become truly inclusive of all humanity; they thus work within the tradition to seek to change and renew it. On the other hand, post-Christian feminists, or revolutionaries (such as Daly and Daphne Hampson [1990]), argue that Christianity is irredeemably sexist and that the only viable solution is to abandon the tradition completely and forge a new religious consciousness based on women's contemporary religious experience.

Secondly, while all feminists are agreed that there is a fundamental injustice in the relationship between the sexes, they analyse that injustice differently and recommend different solutions to it. Some, such as Hampson, affirm the basic equality of all human beings, who share a common human nature characterized by reason and moral conscience, and they seek to work by social reform to extend the rights enjoyed by men to women. Daly and other separatists believe that the male has become so corrupt and malign through the false exercise of power that it is only the female who represents salvation and wholeness; they seek a reversal of the traditional male–female hierarchy so that the female principle can restore healing to the world. Others, such as Ruether and Grey, affirm humanity as male and female, both of whom are potentially revelatory of the image of God, but assert that male and female exist in a structurally unjust relation such that they both represent different types of alienation of humanity from its original potential. Only a total restructuring of social reality will release women and men to become a 'new humanity'.

Despite the important ideological differences between feminist theologians one can also identify certain common characteristics. Like other forms of liberation theology, feminist theology tends to be strongly contextual, drawing on women's concrete, lived experience in particular historical contexts as the locus for the revelation of the divine. While not all feminists eschew systematic thought, many feminist theologians have developed ways of writing and thinking which are more strongly narrative, metaphorical and imagistic, rooted in the stories and images created by the female imagination. They have also sought to develop theologies which are strongly holistic, holding together in creative tension opposites which traditional theology has often forced apart, such as body and spirit, emotion and rationality, individual and community, personal and political, humanity and nature, sacred and profane.

As feminist theological research increases there are several encouraging signs that it is achieving a new level of maturity and recognition. First, there is developing a much more nuanced and critical differentiation of women's experience in recent debate than characterized the early years. Black feminist theology has shown that 'women's experience' cannot be assumed to be global and undifferentiated, but is always profoundly shaped by other factors such as race, class, culture and context (see Thistlethwaite 1990). Feminist theology must take this with absolute seriousness if it is not to be guilty of projecting onto all women everywhere what is, in reality, the limited and privileged experience of white, Western, middle-class women. Secondly, there is a broadening and deepening of the range of critical issues. While feminists have never been narrowly concerned with questions of sex and gender in isolation from other structural realities, recent work has addressed the connections between sexual oppression and other forms of injustice, for example, in the development of eco-feminism, which demonstrates the profound connection between the pillage of the earth and the oppression of women. Thirdly, there is a gradual recognition of feminist theology in 'mainstream' theology. Until recently, feminist theology has been largely regarded as a separate strand, a kind of minor tributary of the mainstream of white, Western, man-made theology which impinges little on the ideas and methods of those outside its ideological community. As feminist scholarship extends to every area of theological discourse, it becomes increasingly difficult to marginalize it. There is a more serious engagement by theologians, whatever their personal convictions, with the fruits of feminist research and theory. This may provide some hopeful pointers to a time when women's experiences will become central to theology.

Further reading: Loades 1990.

TRANSCENDENCE
Lisa Isherwood

FEMINIST THEOLOGY rejects the Greek dualism of spirit and matter and so finds problematic the notion of a transcendent God. Patriarchal religion has been keen to preserve the transcendence of God as a central component in creating a religious hierarchy on earth. Those who move from the attachment to earthly things and towards the transcendent God are seen as worthier than those who remain connected with the earth. Christianity has labelled women 'earthy' and therefore claimed that since they are lower in the hierarchy they cannot reflect the transcendent God. The transcendent God has to be mediated to the world and this is usually done by those who most represent him, those who are most removed from the earthly order, such as monks, hermits and celibate priests.

The emphasis on transcendence has also had negative effects on the understanding of nature and its respect in patriarchal theology. The

Christian creation myth tells us that we can rule over the earth; indeed, we even have the power of naming. If God is above creation then nature becomes yet another aspect to be subdued and ruled over by God and his representatives. This approach has led to near ecological disaster.

Even Augustine was aware that we look the wrong way for God: we look outside when if we were to look within we would find the true God. He was not including the whole of nature in this, but perhaps we can do so. Feminist theology considers personal experience to be the starting point for theology and this has implications for our view of transcendence. We experience in and through our bodies, and so experience the immanence of the divine; to suggest that God is ultimately transcendent is perhaps the greatest illusion of all.

Further reading: McFague 1987.

TRINITY
Ann Loades

THE DOCTRINE of the Trinity is a significant mark of Christian identity. Both in the New Testament and in second- and third-century writings of the Christian era three-part confessions of belief emerged, as a result of the question-and-answer preparation of adult candidates for baptism and in order to distinguish true from false teaching. The pattern reflects belief in God as 'three in one' as indicated in forms of blessing (for example 2 Cor. 13.14) or in the so-called Nicene creed associated with the Council of Constantinople of 381, extending the formula of the Council of Nicea in 325. There are many Christian confessions of belief, but the Nicene creed has been used in the liturgy of the Eucharist from about the sixth century onwards.

Christian belief is in God who is a Trinity of love, active both towards the world and within itself in its internal relations between Father, Son and Holy Spirit. Allowing for all the qualifications to be made for a God who exists outside human space and time, it is worth attending to the notion of *perichōresis* (co-inherence, mutual loving interchange) used from the seventh century onwards in respect of the Trinity; that is, the 'dance' of divine love which flows in constant motion from and through one to the other of the divine 'persons'. God is ultimately unhindered in love, in the divine life itself, in creation, incarnation and in the liturgy and sacramental life of the church.

The fourth-century theologians known as the Cappadocians worked out a way of conceptualizing God as 'unoriginate' (coming to be from no one), but also as originating and related, that is, 'Son' and 'Spirit' equal in glory. Augustine explored the possibility of discovering the traces of the Trinity within oneself (made in the 'image' of God), crucial to the way in which he saw the conversion of the heart to God as becoming possible. The Trinity has thus been associated *both* with the intra-personal *and* with the personal self-in-relation.

The dynamics of tradition-making, which requires both attention to markers of truth and identity and responsibility for those markers in widely differing contexts, may take arguably malign forms; for example, the notion of Trinitarian co-inherence may be compromised by notions of hierarchy and subordination, which may in turn impinge on human political and social order. Thrashed out in controversies about the understanding of Christ, to which the doctrine of the Trinity is intimately connected, then as now the fundamental Christian principle of inclusively *human* salvation and of God-likeness may not be put in jeopardy by some forms of Trinitarian theologizing, and these are now being scrutinized afresh as a result of feminist theological sensitivity.

One important theological rule is that God transcends both sex and gender. By the latter term we may mean (1) what any given society makes of the complexity of biological differences between women and men and (2) gender as grammatical classification. Just as some of us balk at a New Testament which accepts slavery as part of the social order and employs it metaphorically, but can cope with it (more or less) because we do not have to live in that social order, we may also balk at the use of 'Father' for the first person of the Trinity because we cannot cope with its use or misuse in legitimating demeaning understandings of women, and understandings which privilege men over women within the church. Since (as attention to Trinitarian doctrine reveals) there is no necessary association of

An A to Z of Feminist Theology

'Father' with being dominant, implacable, distant, unrelated and controlling, it may well be possible both to be faithful to the language of Christian doctrine and to find imaginative and refreshing ways of reappropriating it.

This is particularly important given some of the goals of feminist theology. One is to find the mesh and web of connection between formal theology and lived experience, so that the church may become the institution in which women and men find enrichment and reconciliation in their differences. They are given the Spirit and give Spirit to one another in creative compassion and the seeking of justice. This is why the language of Trinitarian doctrine is no merely 'verbal' matter, since it is arguable that it contributes to the devaluation of women as co-procreators and co-nurturers of human life. A second goal of feminist theology is to overcome the deep unease in formal expressions of belief about the association of the female and the feminine with the godlike. The claim to be sustained is to the effect that the 'feminine' can of and by itself image God *in as full and in as limited a way as God is imaged by the masculine*, which is *not* a matter of simply adding a 'feminine' dimension to a God basically imaged as 'masculine'. A third goal must be to negotiate the associated difficulty about thinking that divine transcendence is compromised by associating God with the 'feminine', which in turn genderizes appropriate ways of thinking and experiencing divine presence and immanence, sacramental or otherwise.

We might, for instance, agree that 'mother' cannot be accepted as a substitute name for the first 'person' of the Trinity (thus avoiding bowdlerization), and agree that calling on God as 'father' cannot absolutely exclude calling on God as 'mother', least of all in public worship. The kind of tradition-making which continues to flower as it has through the centuries in gender-fluid devotion and prayer without inevitable error and irretrievable spiritual corruption should make it possible both to revitalize the Trinitarian tradition and to praise God in a proliferation of ways.

Further reading: Soskice 1992; 1994; Williams 1992; Lacugna 1993; Johnson 1993.

TRUTH
Lisa Isherwood

FEMINIST THEOLOGY asks a fundamental question about truth: who decides what is true? We have been led to believe that a small group of clerical males can decide on universal truths which will benefit all of us. The lessons of church history show how devastatingly wrong this can be. Feminist theology is questioning the notion of absolute truth and the idea that it can be applied in a standard form to all peoples.

Feminist theology recognizes the fundamental problem to be that of power; those who feel able to define ultimate truth for others ascribe to themselves a great deal of power and they will not easily relinquish this status. The history of Christianity shows the penalties imposed on those who would question the authority of the definers of truth. While people are no longer sent to the flames by the clerical hierarchy they are suspended from teaching and preaching positions.

The challenge of feminist theology to this way of being is to declare that truth is found by living in relation to one's community and environment. This gives truth a new face: it is no longer something declared from on high but is found between people as they deal with the challenges of everyday life. Truth is found not by asking the question, 'what is truth?' but by pursuing right-relation with the whole of the created order. This living experience gives us an embodied truth that far outweighs abstract concepts. On this model, the notion of universal truth is inapplicable. Living in an empowered way in the pursuit of right relation and therefore truth is a liberating way of being, since we can explore all aspects of ourselves and the world in order to find the best way. The imposition of truth is not a liberating way to live because it assumes that all is known and that people have to mould themselves to fit with the already revealed path.

Further reading: Sölle 1984.

An A to Z of Feminist Theology

VIOLENCE (1)
Maureen McBride

VIOLENCE AS brutality, force, destruction, or the unjust use and abuse of power is pervasive at all levels of society. The diverse issues of conflict and violence, including powerlessness and addictions, violence against women and children, graft and corruption, destruction of the environment and over-exploitation of the world's resources, militarism and state repression, must be recognized as being interrelated.

Violence always provokes violence and irresistibly engenders new forms of oppression and enslavement. At the personal level, direct physical violence is manifest in the alarming rate of suicides, and the attraction to violence-spawning addictions such as drug and alcohol abuse and gambling is not only endemic in Western societies, but increasingly is an indication of hopelessness and alienation that threatens poverty-stricken communities in developing nations as well.

At the interpersonal level, physical violence against women and children takes a myriad of forms: domestic violence, wife-battering, rape, child abuse, incest; the widespread practice of female genital mutilation across a huge tract of Africa and into the Middle East; female foeticide and infanticide in cultures where male children are favoured; the resurgence of sati, or wife-burning, in parts of India; the brutal use of power and humiliation of women through the billion-dollar pornography industry; the compulsory sterilization of poor women in countries with high population growth; life-threatening work conditions in women-intensive, multi-national industries.

At local, national and global levels, violent crimes, kidnapping and hostage-taking, state terrorism and abuse of human rights proliferate. Armed conflicts create a spiral of violence that destroys civil societies, devastates cities, towns and villages, and cuts down young people in the full flower of their youth. The overwhelming majority of the civilian victims of armed conflicts are women and children. Of the survivors, many endure gang rape and torture, while millions are forced as refugees to flee national borders or travel dangerous distances seeking safer ground within their own territory. Women bear the trauma of seeing husbands, brothers, sons, transformed into killers or being detained or killed, while at the same time they must function as the sole providers for their families. The psychological effects of living for decades in militarized areas, or situations of low-intensity conflict, are either acceptance and resignation to a culture of violence, or the inability to envision any peaceful alternative. Of the children born into war zones, many have the aspiration to become soldiers to 'get even' or to 'kill the enemy'.

One of the most insidious forms of violence is structural or institutional violence, because it is accepted as the 'legal order'. Social inequalities and massive unemployment are not only tolerated, but are generated to protect the interests of wealthy elites. Militarization is used to quell dissent and uprisings and peoples' movements for liberation and transformation. Poor people, especially women, bear the burden of the debt owed by developing nations that has already been repaid by decades of slavery, graft and corruption, inequitable prices paid for labour and resources, exorbitant interest, the impoverishment of peoples and the environment. The globalization of economies and finances, the internationalization of trade and industry and the 'structural adjustment programmes' euphemistically imposed by the World Bank or the IMF on faltering economies result in severe cuts to health, education and social service budgets.

Sociocultural and psychological violence is implicated in the globalization of culture which is propagated through entertainment, advertising and the mass media, provoking new forms of racism and the cultural alienation of minority groups. Religious discrimination and intolerance impose violent forms of evangelization and legitimate terrorism, while fundamentalism creates a climate for doomsday cultist massacres and mass suicides.

Sexual harassment, the commodification of women through beauty contests and the movie industry, sex tourism and the mail order bride trade combine with the forces of spiritual and social control heaped on women which violate their human rights in the name of decency and moral values. Inflicted through government and church sanctions, social pressure and stigmatization, camouflaged violence strips women of their voices and deadens their sense of outrage.

Today ecological violence threatens the environment on a global scale. Acid rains, smog alerts, deforestation and desertification, depletion of the ozone layer, dynamite and drift net fishing, destruction of corals, the diminishment of bio-diversity and the destruction of the rainforests for the profit of plunderers devastate the fabric and integrity of creation. The deprivation in developing countries has led to the destruction of natural resources. On the other hand, the affluence and over-consumption of industrial nations have largely depleted our limited energy supply and created ecological imbalance by polluting, congesting and poisoning the environment with toxic waste.

Any form of violence is an attack on life. In those contexts where all the above faces of violence are inserted into the fabric of everyday life, no community, family or individual is untouched by its tentacles: Red Alerts, Armelite-toting youngsters in army fatigues, reverberating helicopters, rumbling tanks on city streets, checkpoints and on-the-spot searches, barrios and villages exploding with refugees of forced evacuations; congested squatter areas teeming with vermin, the pungent smell of bad sanitation, the bulging eyes and bellies of the malnourished; the fear, mistrust, insecurity that is etched on children's faces, become masked by apparent passivity or resignation in women and the elderly; scarred hillsides, silted rivers, diesel-laden air, tribal peoples bewildered and dispossessed.

Nevertheless, there is rarely a fatalistic submission to the death-dealing despair promoted by violence. Rather there remains a profound hope and trust in the passionate God of life who eschews violence and injustice. The paradigm of Jesus who preached human solidarity and who proclaimed that love should configure all our social structures is imaged in the signs of hope abounding in sectors that are disadvantaged but not discouraged, in the poor who are dispossessed but remain undaunted, in women who are abused but not broken, in the youth who are restless and have kept their ideals; in children and women who are celebrated as primary 'zones of life' or bridges to peace.

Further reading: Barbe 1989; Bautista and Rifareal (eds.) 1990; Burgos-Debray (ed.) 1984; Tamez 1982.

VIOLENCE (2)
Dorothy Coxon

VIOLENCE IS usually understood as 'unlawful exercise of physical force' (*OED*) and most articles or books (by men) about violence deal with the psychology of aggression or the issues of war and pacifism. Typically, feminists have derived their interpretation of violence from the lived-out experience of women and pointed to its more personal nature. Oppression by means of domination would be classed as violence in a feminist interpretation, so that the model of male superiority and female subservience, bolstered by the paradigm of male rule in Gen. 3.16 and linked to Eph. 5.21-33, would fall within this interpretation.

A further feminist interpretation of violence would include a critique of the patriarchal assumption of male dominance that leads to a misogynistic mindset, and would claim that a potential victim is the object of violence. This may seem a far cry from actual physical violence, but it follows the model set up in the Sermon on the Mount, in which identification of the root of the problem replaces dealing with the extreme end of the continuum (Mt. 5.21-22). So, just as Jesus saw anger against a brother as the root cause of murder, feminists see the routine definition of women by their gender as the root of potential violence. If we want to avoid the obvious violence of gang rape and the effectiveness of the symbolism of the unnamed concubine of Judges 19 we must begin with an elimination of the violence of sexist dualism.

Institutionalized Christianity has fuelled male privilege at the expense of women, denigrating them as second-best; this has resulted in a violation of the lives and self-esteem of women who have learnt the path of self-rejection via a religion whose central figure symbolizes liberation, not control or dependency; this is violence.

Feminists claim that the prevalence of rape in the culture in which we live is the result of the way that men see and relate to women normally; a comment from Brian Wren (1989: 42) seems appropriate here: 'Few men commit rape, but all benefit from the violence of those who do, since it instils in women the need for male protection, thus helping to keep them in a subordinate place'. An extension of the definition of violence to include the imposed subordination is the point at issue. To many this may smack of diluting the definition of violence beyond common recognition—Katie Roiphe's book *The Morning After* (1994: 172) implies that feminists have reduced the definition of rape to leering and pinching and are identifying with passivity and victimhood. But it is precisely the urge to break out of the passive mode that is at the root of feminism; some would argue that leers and pinches are flea-bites compared to the violence of the rejection of skills and gifts that many women have suffered because of their gender. The blow of being refused the possibility of priesthood in the church is the type of violence that feminist theologians recognize as valid.

History has also provided us with evidence of the extent to which the rejection of women and their gifts led to violence, notably in the witch-hunts of the fifteenth to seventeenth centuries throughout Western Europe. The impetus for the wholesale murder of hundreds of thousands of women with the collaboration of church and state was their supposed demonic power over men. The *Malleus Maleficarum* exhibits the views that women are more sexual, more earthly and bodily than men, and that they have insatiable sexual appetites which threaten men.

The defeat of the witch was one of the worst manifestations of Christian misogyny. Mary Daly reinforces this judgment (1985: ch. 6) while exposing another aspect of the witch-craze—the claim by church and state that they were 'purifying' society and the body of Christ (behaviour precursive of Nazism?). They focused on spinsters and widows—those who had rejected or survived marriage. Stripping and gang rape were not counted as torture, merely a preliminary exercise of authorized abuse. In the twentieth century the rape atrocities performed by the Filipino military, exposed by Amnesty International as weapons of repression intended to punish, humiliate and intimidate women, have a paradigm in Renaissance and Reformation Christianity; it is difficult to remain less than cynical when we realize how little this violence towards women has been publicized in the accounting of history. After the elimination of witches, survivors were encouraged to renounce independence, so that ideologically both the virtuous woman and the witch were domesticated. Overt and implied violence formed an ideal of domesticity with chastity and complete dependence on the male as its hallmark; this Puritan paradigm lived on in the respectability afforded white middle- and upper-class 'ladies' of the nineteenth century who afforded no challenge to the status quo.

While the easy stereotyping of man as potential rapist and woman as potential victim is an over-simplification of the power structure that resulted, the ideology of female innate inferiority nevertheless is an invitation to denigrate women's achievements and their worth as individuals. Feminist theologians point to the harm that is done to the self-esteem of females who from infancy have imbibed the idea that being 'only a girl' is in some way an inherent failure; the mental 'slaps' provoked by gender constitute an insidious violence that can inhibit self-love.

In conclusion, an emphasis on violence against women in this definition does not denote ignorance of other areas of abuse; rather it is a focus on the type of power structure that has lent itself easily to violence and is an indictment of the domination model that was so positively rejected by Christ (Lk. 4.5-8).

VIRGINITY
Sarah Jane Boss

History

WITHIN CHRISTIANITY, the choice of living a celibate life goes back as far as New Testament times. St Paul commended the unmarried over the married state (1 Cor. 7.32-40), on the grounds that married people's obligations mean that they cannot be entirely devoted to the work of the Lord. Paul is evidently speaking of both women and men, and celibacy was chosen by both sexes from this time onwards. Nevertheless, within the Western church nuns, rather than monks, have been understood as typical representatives of the lifelong celibate state. Compared with other religions, this fact seems to be exceptional (see Brown 1989: 262-63).

Widows and virgins who dedicated their lives to the service of God came to be called 'brides of Christ', since they had chosen a heavenly spouse, with whom they could not consummate their marriages. In the early centuries, they lived either within their relatives' households, or in communities with one another. They were held in high esteem by the Church Fathers (see Brown 1989: 264-65), many of whom wrote treatises on virginity (for example, St Gregory of Nyssa).

The rite of virginal consecration, which is at least as old as the fourth century (see Camelot 1967), was maintained as an option in many religious orders until recent decades. The Roman Catholic church's current Code of Canon Law makes provision for lay women to become consecrated virgins. Carthusian nuns retain the rite of consecrated virginity, and consecrated virgins in the Order may also effectively become deaconesses (see *Moniales Chartreuses*: 53; Boss 1988: 979-80, 985).

Symbolism

Christian authors of the Middle Ages frequently praised the fruitful virginity of the Virgin Mary, as in St Hildegard of Bingen's hymn *O Virga Viridissima* (in Page [ed.] 1983: 24). The idea that virginity is a condition of abundant fertility has more recently been taken up by Jungian writers, who point out that the 'virgin forest' is a place of lavish fecundity (Layard n.d.: 290-91; Horrocks 1991: 110-11). Nor Hall describes what such symbolism might mean in women's lives: 'The word *virgin* means 'belonging-to-no-man.'... To be virginal does not mean to be chaste, but rather to be true to nature and instinct' (1980: 11). However, the symbolic associations of virginity with both fertility and female independence have historically been tied to the condition of not having had sexual intercourse with a man. The virgin is viewed as especially fertile because her store of fertility, as it were, has not yet been tapped.

In societies in which women are normally under the economic and political control of men, the avoidance of marriage and childbearing may be the only means by which a woman can acquire control of her own affairs and exercise influence over others. The virginal consecration of the Byzantine empress Pulcheria can be seen in this light (Limberis 1994: 42-43).

Female virginity has also been associated with power of other kinds. In antiquity, large crowds of virgins became 'an integral part of a bishop's show of power' (Brown 1989: 260), as though his authority was somehow vested in the women's bodily integrity. The virginity of the Virgin Mary has likewise been seen as the guarantor of the inviolability of cities or armies (for example at Chartres; see Le Marchant 1983: 217-21), or in recent liberation theology—as a sign of the potential restoration of social and economic integrity to dispossessed peoples (Elizondo 1983: 62). Andrea Dworkin draws attention to the sense of awe which St Joan of Arc's virginity inspired in those who knew her (1987: 83-105).

In theology, however, the intention to remain a virgin—and thus to be dedicated entirely to Christ—takes precedence over a person's physical condition, and the most important aspect of virginity is therefore not compromised by rape (see Aquinas, *Summa Theologica* 2a 2ae, 152.1).

WHOLENESS
Joan James

'NOT THE holiness of the elect, but the wholeness of *all* is the central vision of Jesus' (Schüssler Fiorenza 1983: 121). Wholeness is a central theme in feminist theology: in terms of wholeness of the individual, integration of the human community, health of the planet, inclusivity of language about God.

From the nineteenth century onwards it was realized that theology had been written by men for men, with a totally androcentric perspective. Half of humanity—the male—had been taken to represent the whole. Female experience had been totally ignored, thus creating distortions of perception very costly for humankind and for the planet.

In 1885 the American campaigner for women's rights, Elizabeth Cady Stanton, headed a team of women scholars who caused scandal by bringing out *The Women's Bible*, a commentary from a female standpoint on texts and chapters of the Bible which directly referred to women and 'those in which women are made prominent by their exclusion' (Cady Stanton 1985 [1895]: 5). Thus began the first feminist critique of the Bible, continued today by feminist theologians all over the world. Their work is liberating and healing for both women and men, although the mainstream of academic theology is reluctant to accept it.

In patriarchal cultures the growth towards wholeness of the individual person is made almost impossible by the gender stereotypes which are imprinted upon women and men from birth onwards, resulting in unbalanced and wounded beings. The Bible and androcentric theology have both been used to reinforce these stereotypes and to confer gender inappropriately on qualities that are common to all human beings. Thus qualities such as gentleness, nurturing, passivity, receptivity, weakness and emotionality are deemed to be 'feminine', while strength, aggression, ambition, initiative and reason are called 'masculine'. The consequence of these distortions is the disastrous inability of much of humankind to achieve maturity and to maintain healthy relationships. Feminist theology explores and develops more holistic theories of what it means to be fully human: 'there will be a concept of God which unites feeling, energy and action for justice. God will be a God of wholeness of being and doing' (Grey 1989: 88).

For feminist theology, therefore, the healthy society is one of justice-making relatedness: it is non-hierarchical, interactive, and empowers the participation of *all* members of the community including those who are oppressed, marginalized, poor and discriminated against because of their race, class, sex, sexuality or disability. This holistic vision necessitates the transformation of the very structures of church and society and is therefore fiercely resisted by all who hold, or aspire to, power in hierarchical systems.

The wholeness of the planet is a major concern of feminist theology, which understands the systematic exploitation and devastation of delicately balanced ecosystems as being a direct consequence of belief in an almighty, victorious, male God, which has encouraged and validated the belief that conquering maleness must be the norm for human life. Consequently, men in turn have believed it right to use and abuse the earth.

Theologians such as Sallie McFague reject these imperialistic and triumphalist images of God and experiment with new metaphors, such as the world as the body of God, God as mother, God as passionate lover, God as friend. They feel that it is imperative in this dangerous nuclear age that our language about God and our attitude to the planet must become inclusive, holistic and appropriate to our time:

> we belong, from the cells of our bodies to the finest creations of our minds, to the intricate, constantly changing cosmos. The ecosystem of which we are a part is a whole: the rocks and waters, atmosphere and soil, plants, animals and human beings interact in dynamic, mutually supportive ways (McFague 1987: 7-8).

Further reading: Primavesi 1991; Ruether 1983.

WICCA
Sabrina Woodward

WICCA IS a form of neo-paganism whose adherents declare it to be the pre-Christian 'Old Religion' of Northern Europe. Its etymology is disputed. *Chambers Etymological Dictionary* derives the word from Anglo-Saxon *wicce, wicca*, noting that according to Grimm, this is associated with Gothic *veihan* (German *weigen*), to consecrate, to do or perform rites; later scholars, including Goldenberg (1979: 96), suggest that it has to do with bending or turning and is similar to 'wicker', basket-work that is turned or shaped. Wicca's followers usually call themselves witches, and often suggest that the derivations have in common the syllable *wi*, which may derive from Anglo-Saxon *witan*, to know, which is also the origin of 'wisdom', 'wise' and 'wit'.

All these suggested meanings can be conflated into the beliefs and practices of Wiccans, who are one of the oldest and largest of several sects of modern witches. They declare themselves the inheritors of the historical wise women who were healers and practical helpers of all kinds; they perform sacred rites, and they take part in exercises to help shape or turn energy and events to promote beneficially the affairs of individuals or of society, even the earth itself. It is important at this stage to note that popular concepts of evil, ugly old women muttering curses, or of Satanists and so-called 'Black' magicians (itself now coming to be recognized as a racist term) have no part in Wicca.

Whether the current movement actually is the inheritor of an unbroken line of age-old pagan traditions is open to doubt. Starhawk (1979: 5, 9), an influential modern American witch, writes of the long lineage of those who could 'shape the unseen to their will. Healers, teachers, poets, midwives, they were central figures in every community'. Their work lives on: 'somehow in secret, in silence, over glowing coals, behind closed shutters, encoded as fairy tales and songs, or hidden in subconscious memories, the seed was passed on'. This may be so, but there are strong indications that modern Wicca as an organized religion was invented, or reinvented, in the mid-twentieth century.

Gerald Gardner, a writer and practitioner in magic (see Gardner 1947), set up what came to be known as the Gardnerian (Wiccan) Craft. Covens and groups throughout Britain sprang up in the middle years of this century. Their religion appeared to be pantheistic; deities of the land and of Nature were invoked and worshipped, energies were raised to promote healing and nurture.

The Gardnerian Craft has as its background a powerful modern history of magic and magic-working personalities. It calls upon the work of a nineteenth-century society called The Hermetic Order of the Golden Dawn. Gareth Knight (1978: 157-59) describes this as an expression of the Western tradition of magic as compared with many ideas emanating from the East. Its principal founder, S.L. McGregor Mathers, used his researches in the British Museum to construct an amalgam of tradition and magic, including what Knight calls 'ceremonies of ritual initiation' (p. 157). Added to these was instruction in the Kabbala, astrology, alchemy and various forms of psychic working, including divining, use of Tarot cards and the making of talismans. In addition, there is available as a resource to Wiccans the long underground tradition of magical working in Britain and elsewhere, described by, among others, the distinguished scholar Frances Yates (1964, 1969).

Most present-day magical and occult practices owe much to the Golden Dawn. The Order included notable people in the artistic, literary and political worlds, including W.B. Yeats, Maud Gonne, Annie Horniman and Florence Farr, and was much involved in the so-called Celtic Revival that was important at the time. This became infused with themes from the Renaissance magical tradition and entered mainstream artistic and even academic life.

Gardner synthesized such material with elements from various other sources. Important contributions were made by people identifying themselves as witches or inheritors of witches' heritage, and included practices claimed to be derived from long-held family traditions.

Other branches of Wicca today include the Alexandrian, founded by Alex Sanders, self-styled 'King of the Witches'. This, like a number of other branches, is based on modifications of Gardnerian Wicca. Some people still claim to belong to hereditary, pre-Gardnerian traditions; such claims may be valid, but have not been substantiated.

The Craft venerates deities generically called the Goddess and the God as a sacred pair, served in each coven by the High Priestess and High Priest and their followers. Emphasis is placed on the importance of the Goddess and, through her, of women's spiritual experience; on the sacrality of matter, on a holistic approach to both the material and spiritual world, and on what Knight has called 'the development of a higher type of awareness, the steady light of intuition, of pure reason, or the secondary imagination' (1978: 177). Groups or covens include initiates and those who are in training to be so (there are also solitaries working alone).

It is only since 1951 that Wiccan activities have been legal in Britain and memories of widespread persecution of witches are very strong. Such fears have been strengthened by the recent rise of fundamentalist branches within Christianity which apparently seek to re-create the witch-hunting hysteria of earlier centuries.

So far Wicca has been described in its traditional or neo-traditional form, where both women and men comprise its practitioners. The term has also been used, however, particularly in the US, to refer to women, relating to a concept of a Goddess religion. Naomi Goldenberg (1979: 96-97) writes: 'I see nothing inappropriate in referring to a witch as "wicca". We can consider the Old English term as having been reborn, so that it actually does mean "wise woman" in current usage.' She continues: 'All witchcraft begins with a psychic picture that a woman works to weave into reality', and declares that 'the first thing a woman learns to visualise and bring to birth in the world is herself. She needs to have a positive image of herself at all stages of her life'. Zsuzsanna Budapest, a leading witch in the US, defines a similar position:

> We believe that feminist witches are wimmin who search within themselves for the female principle of the universe and who relate as daughters of the Creatrix. We believe that just as it is time to fight for the right to control our bodies it is also time to fight for our sweet womon souls…without a secure grounding in wimmin's spiritual strength there will be no victory for us (Budapest 1979: 9).

She was also instrumental in creating a women-only type of Wicca known as the Dianic Craft. The form of worship and ritual acknowledged the Goddess by various names, but did not include the God.

In a survey of publications on feminist spirituality 1975–81, A.P. Long (1982: 103-108) commented that the major aspect of feminist Wicca that contrasts it with the neo-pagan revival is that it identifies a strong connection between spiritual and political action (p. 105). She points out that while traditional rituals and festivals are celebrated by today's women Wiccans, major attention is also given by teachers such as Budapest and Starhawk to modern needs, for instance, freeing political prisoners, countering the effects of nuclear energy production, or, more personally, introducing a new baby to its community, celebrating a young woman at her menarche, and an older one at her menopause.

In a later survey, Long (1994: 11-39) emphasizes that two decades of the Goddess movement in Britain have centred on the building up of women's self-worth. The Goddess, she affirms, has become a powerful symbol for the rebuilding of women's confidence in their bodies, their minds, spirits and general powers. The situation concerning actual praxis—celebrations, rituals, magical working and so on—is not structured as in Wicca itself, but depends on its practitioners. Goldenberg comments that 'the witches use their goddess concept to give women positive self images in all stages of life' (1979: 97), and continues: 'witchcraft is the only Western religion that recognises woman as a divinity in her own right' (p. 98).

In a wide-ranging critique of Goddess spirituality among women, Pam Lunn (1993) sums up many objections and warns that however attractive such beliefs may be, they tend to suffer from a romantic and sentimental view of history and of politics. She writes:

> It may be that strong, powerful, even divine images of women from the past can be a positive force now…but the danger in them is that if we depend on images from the past to validate or uphold present aspirations or goals then we are vulnerable to any re-evaluation of history which may undermine our present view; or if we resist such interpretations of the past we may find ourselves trapped in an eccentric backwater of quaint beliefs, tenaciously held but irrelevant to the political realities for women at the end of the twentieth century (1993: 35).

She quotes Angela Carter's dismissal of the theme: 'Mother goddesses are just as silly as Father Gods. If a revival of these cults gives women emotional satisfaction it does so at the price of obscuring the real conditions of life' (p. 36).

Wiccans of all descriptions would object to this on the grounds that their praxis is based on today's needs, while women find their consciousness of their own current position highlighted by revisionist history. But there are criticisms of neo-traditional Wicca that are harder to counter. These may centre on its heterosexism, since the pairing of the genders is an integral part of the belief and ritual. There is also a widespread objection to its Eurocentrism, its lack of interest in or respect for the huge reservoir of history, practice and belief from all parts of the world, most notably Africa and Asia. To this must be added the racist connotations of the terminology of 'White magic' and 'Black magic'. Some efforts have been made in the USA to counter these practices, and in Britain there is a small but growing awareness, certainly among women's groups, of a need for humility and a broadening of their world outlook.

Yet another warning concerns the possibility of anti-Semitism in both Goddess circles and Wicca proper. Susannah Heschel, in her account of patriarchy and Nazism in German feminist thought (1995), points to the continuing blame put on the Jews by spiritual feminists for the introduction of patriarchal monotheism and thus for the destruction of Goddess culture and the world introduction of misogyny (1995: 138). This is all the more troubling since Carol Christ (1987) wrote a magisterial piece entitled 'On Not Blaming the Jews for the Death of the Goddess', quoting earlier warnings of the anti-Semitism arising among Goddess women by both Judith Plaskow (1980) and Annette Daum (1980a, 1980b). Recently Katharina von Kellenbach (1994) has outlined the resurgence of anti-Judaism among feminists, this time placing it firmly among writings of feminist theologians. In contrast to this are cautions from some German Christian feminists that connections have been made between spiritual feminists, many of them claiming to be witches and to practice Wicca, and neo-Nazi political groups, the relationship being based on similar views of the necessity to preserve 'the Land' from outside 'foreign' influences and to dismiss in the same way pagan deities other than those associated with Northern Europe.

Alongside these very disturbing criticisms come those from traditional Christian, Jewish and Islamic sources who still hold age-old views and fears about the supposed evil that witches do, and do not wish in any way to associate themselves with any of the practices or activities. This is despite the fact that much is held in common. Healing by laying on of hands and of the spirit is only one example; the celebration of the sacred festivals at much the same time is another (for instance, Christmas/winter solstice, All Souls Day/Samhain, the day when the dead are nearest to us, Candlemas/Brigid, the great Irish triple goddess often conflated with St Brigid, and many others).

Feminist theologians often find that their work in revisioning the Bible, in seeking out strong ancient women, in discovering Goddess material and above all in countering traditional misogyny brings them very near the Wiccan and Goddess feminists. The latter find that similar studies make for similar results. It is possible that the coming together of these two paths is one of the most important directions that women can follow. Reconciliation between the descendants of the witch persecutors and those of the persecuted is slow and painful; this is a route of great difficulty, but also of exceeding promise.

Further reading: Farrar and Farrar 1984; Hole 1977; Lethbridge 1972; Liddell 1994; Valiente 1974.

WISDOM
Lucy Tatman

This piece is dedicated to the memory of Nelle Morton, a wise and courageous feminist theologian to whom credit must be given for the phrase 'hearing into speech'.

AS I began my search for feminist theological interpretations of Wisdom what I found amazed me; silence, almost total theological silence on the subject. There has been an abundance of feminist spiritual reflection on Wisdom, mostly with the biblical, female personification of Wisdom/Sophia as its root source. Womanist ethicist Katie Geneva Cannon has named the

WISDOM

ethical qualities of moral wisdom within Black women's literature, drawing ethics from story, and her work is brilliant. But spirituality and ethics are not theology, and it was Wisdom as a theological subject that I was determined to find. At last I came across one glowing sentence. 'Wisdom is feminist and suggests an existence earlier than Word' (Morton 1985: 175). As I tried to write out the implications of this sentence in a somewhat traditional manner I began to understand the presence of such silence about Wisdom. I simply could not find the words to say what I needed to say. I thought again of Cannon's work, of how her ethical reflection depended on the prior existence of the stories in which she found such moral wisdom. Finally I realized that until I heard Wisdom's story as told by a woman I could not write a feminist theological definition of Wisdom. Having come to understand that it is not by choice but by necessity that most feminist theologians are also storytellers, perhaps you will understand when I tell you that I held Nelle Morton's words very, very still and waited, waited for the beginning.

Once upon a time long, long ago there was Wisdom. There was Wisdom, and she was present everywhere with all the desire and all the intensity of all there was. The stars and planets were not yet separate, each from the others; creation before creation was a timeless, limitless whole, bound yet boundless in itself. Was it good, this infinite presence of the not-yet created? It simply was, it was everything all at once and once was all there was. Wisdom alone knew something of its possibilities.

Though time did not pass Wisdom waited, imbuing herself ever more deeply throughout the uncreated whole. At last, in time-without-time, it happened. The Word was spoken. Heard into speech by all the desire and all the intensity of all there was. At the sound of the Word the uncreated whole drew back, rejoicing yes, but also, for the very first time, confused, afraid. Spinning, rushing, echoing the Word, above all else feeling the pain of birth. For the Word was birthed from uncreation as surely as a woman births a child. And just as at the time of her first birth a woman bears herself into a mother so too did uncreation bear itself into creation at the birthing of the Word.

And what of Wisdom during this first time? She was everywhere all at once, rushing, spinning into brand new space with the now created not-yet whole. Quietly coaxing the dust to settle into planets in their courses, setting alight the stars burning through their necessary paths. She became for the first time gentle and for the first time fierce, insisting on cooperation, coaxing harmony out of chaos. Ceaselessly she loved creation out of uncreation, as stern and tender as a midwife, a lioness, a strong and stubborn woman. For she and she alone knew that the Word arrived as both gift and burden. She knew that soon, very soon, wherever creation was not known by Word it would not be known at all, but Word alone would collapse upon itself, spoken yet unheard.

As the Word became words uncreation knew itself no more as one but as many. For the first time distinctions were made clear. And as uncreation rushed and spun its now defined selves through spaces and times as new as each distinction Wisdom alone dived into the distance, making holy the necessary silences between the words of new creation. Into the vast, unutterable space Wisdom poured herself, now silent, hearing, all intensity and all desire.

Time grew, widening and deepening, and with it new creation became a different kind of whole. Stars continued to be formed, and earths. Each named, each known by Word and Wisdom. And where the words were not, not-yet, or passed and long forgotten still there was Wisdom, her presence knowing whole.

At last the time for stories came, for telling and remembering. But the storytellers took for granted the present-filled silence between their words. It was to the Word, to the Word that wrought the definition of sun from moon and earth from sky and story from teller and each from other that they prayed over and over until at last they knew of nothing but the Word. Knowing only words, they did not grasp that it is within the spaces between the words where lies the Wisdom of all creation. They did not grasp that Word alone collapses upon itself, its unheard weight bowed infinitely meaningless.

This is the truth of burden and gift; Word without Wisdom will unhear itself and all it has named; through Word, Wisdom's story may be

An A to Z of Feminist Theology

told and creation may remain as many, infinitely listening each to all.

Once upon a time there was Wisdom. There was Wisdom, and she was present everywhere with all the intensity and all the desire of all there was. And once the Word was spoken she and she alone dived into the spaces between the words, blessing the silence out of which new worlds are born. Now, as it was in the beginning, Wisdom is hearing all creation into speech. She alone knows something of its possibilities.

Further reading: Morton 1985; Cannon 1989; Cady, Ronan and Tussig 1989; Rupp 1990.

WOMANIST THEOLOGY
Toinette M. Eugene

IN THE preface to her collection of womanist prose entitled *In Search of Our Mothers' Gardens*, Alice Walker defines a 'womanist' as a black feminist or feminist of colour who, among other things, is wilful, serious, loving, and 'committed to survival and wholeness of entire people, male and female'. A womanist is an African American feminist who claims her roots in black history, religion and culture. This concept has generated attention from theologians and ethicists because its inherent claims seem to resonate in the plurality of life and faith experiences of black women which are clearly in contradistinction to white feminist cultural, social and theological perspectives. Alice Walker's literary use of a folk expression common among African American communities has become the foundational source for identifying womanist theology.

At issue in the appropriation of the term 'womanist' as a descriptive genre for theology is the power of self-definition, of self-naming. 'Womanist theology' is a signification for a theology which permits African American women to define themselves, to embrace and intentionally affirm their cultural and religious traditions, and their own embodiment. Thus, womanist theology taps directly into the roots of the historical liberation capability of black women according to the derivation of Walker's definition.

Informed by biblical, theological, historical and economic bases, womanist theology searches in particular for the voices, actions, opinions, struggles and faith of African American women in order to shape a distinctive perspective that takes seriously their experiences and traditions in response to the liberating activity of God. Womanist theology, as a disciplined commentary about the nature of God, intimates a critical posture towards sexism, towards misogyny, towards the objectification and abuse of black women within African American communities and within the dominant patriarchal culture.

Womanist theology takes seriously the sociohistorical context in which African American women have found themselves as moral agents, using this context as an operative norm for ethical praxis and reflection. Womanist theology not only proceeds from the particular context of the suffering and experience of African American women, but that context, which brings together issues of race, sex and class, also provides the most comprehensive foundation for liberation theology.

Womanist theology agrees with the critique of white racism and the need for black unity expressed in black theology, and it agrees with the criticism of sexism and the need for unity of women in feminist theology. Methodologically, womanist theology moves beyond both by providing its own critique of racism in feminist theology and of sexism in black theology. It also emphasizes the dimension of class analysis since, historically, most African American woman have been poor or are negatively affected by the unequal distribution of capital and gainful employment as a direct consequence of the economic system operative in the United States. Consequently womanist theology must be based on a tridimensional analysis of racism, sexism and classism. Womanist theology is usually non-separatist and dialogical; it welcomes discourse with a variety of theological voices including non-feminist, non-womanist expressions. Womanist theology considers one of its primary tasks to be to dialogue with the church and with other disciplines.

In addition to the experiences and activities of African American women in society and in the church as points of departure for womanist theology, it is also important to cite a distinctive use of the Bible and the role and significance of Jesus in the womanist tradition as distinguishing char-

An A to Z of Feminist Theology

acteristics and marks of uniqueness. Indeed, whether one considers African American women's history from the perspective of North American women's history or that of African American history, one discovers that the Bible has been the book most consistently and effectively used by those in power to restrict and censure the behaviour of African American women. When the Bible has been able to capture the imagination of African American women, it has been and continues to be able to do so because significant portions speak to the deepest aspirations of oppressed people for freedom, dignity, justice and vindication. Womanist theology relies on the Bible as a principal resource for its purposes because of its vision and promise of a world where the humanity of everyone will be fully valued. Womanist theology engages in a liberationist hermeneutical interpretation of the Bible as a major method for religious validation, in spite of numerous voices from within and without the Christian tradition that have tried to equivocate about that vision and promise made to African American women and all other oppressed and marginalized persons and communities.

The prominence given to Christology by womanist theology discloses a perspective which is congruent with and flows from its liberationist interpretation of biblical revelation. For womanist theology, it is the humanity, the wholeness of Christ, which is paramount, not the maleness of the historical person Jesus.

This peculiarly egalitarian Christology evokes a womanist commitment to struggle not only with oppressive symptoms, which are abundantly extant for African American women within church and society, but with causes of pervasive inequality and disenfranchisement. Such a Christology challenges womanist theology to forge a distinctively different genre as required by the particular constraints and contexts in which it finds a locus.

Womanist theology attempts to help black women see, affirm, have confidence in the importance of their experience and faith for determining the character of the Christian religion in the African American community.

Further reading: Cannon 1988; Eugene 1994; Grant 1989; Weems 1988; Williams 1993.

WOMEN AND LITURGICAL MUSIC
June Boyce-Tillman

ALTHOUGH OFTEN absent from the formal liturgical music of the established churches, women have nevertheless played a significant part in the musical worship of churches. Their contribution has been made in hidden ways and unpaid positions, by offering their time and talents without public reward or profit. Formal education for women in music was in the past seriously deficient and so they lacked the formal grasp of notation necessary in the Western European classical tradition. As the tradition moved from monophony (a single line melody) to a contrapuntal and harmonic tradition, women became isolated from the mainstream of liturgical music until the late nineteenth century. By then the hierarchical structures of the churches worked as powerfully against the inclusion of women in any position whatsoever in musical hierarchies as they did against women's participation in the ordained ministries of Orthodox, Roman Catholic and Anglican denominations. The extension of the ministerial role to women in the emerging Protestant traditions was paralleled in music and in the Salvation Army, which had women in leadership roles from the outset.

In the Orthodox tradition there are the works by the ninth-century poet Kassia (born in 810), whose short hymn 'The Fallen Woman' for Holy Wednesday is fairly well known. In the Catholic tradition Hildegard of Bingen is outstanding with her *Symphonia Armonie Celestium Revelationum*. Women religious and women Sunday school teachers have had a certain degree of musical authority. However, in the formal worship of the Anglican cathedrals and many Roman Catholic ones, girls were excluded from the choirs and therefore excluded from the possibility of an excellent free musical and general education in the cathedral choir schools. Even today there are only a few girls' schools in the Anglican tradition and very few women are cathedral organists.

In the folk traditions which rose in popularity in the 1960s, women have been the musical directors of independent groups. In the charismatic traditions, more women have been involved in writing and music making. Feminist worshipping groups have chosen the simpler, more improvisatory style of the Taizé chants, with their stress on contemplation through musical repetition, and simpler melodies of folk-type origins. Many of these groups still lack the confidence to create their own music, so they rely on taped recordings and oral transmission. It is to be hoped that today when musical education is available to everybody, women will take their rightful place in music-making. The move towards inclusive language in liturgy will necessitate new settings of texts and may also promote the composition of new tunes. These are surely areas in which the contribution of women will become increasingly important.

WOMEN-CHURCH
Mary E. Hunt

WOMEN-CHURCH is a global, ecumenical movement of feminist base communities which gather in sacrament and solidarity to express their religious faith in egalitarian, democratic styles. While this is impossible in a patriarchal context, women-church as a concept and as a reality is a horizon over against which to measure feminist progress. Women-church is not a new denomination, sect or organization. It is a movement expressed in many forms around the world.

The term 'women-church' originated in US Roman Catholic circles among feminists so scandalized by the exclusion of women from ordination to the priesthood that a new religious expression was necessary. It has become increasingly ecumenical in usage and development. Elisabeth Schüssler Fiorenza coined the term *ekklesia gynaikon* in 1983, and it was translated into English as 'woman church'. It was changed to the plural and hyphenated form by 1987 when the 'Women-Church: Claiming Our Power' conference was held in Cincinnati. This change reflected increased sensitivity to the errors of essentialism, specifically, a rejection of the notion that any 'woman' could be construed as representative of all women. This was an error common among the predominantly white, Euro-American women who began the movement, but one which is mitigated by the increasing diversity among adherents.

Diversity remains a central issue as the spirit of women-church, the effort to live out what Schüssler Fiorenza calls a 'discipleship of equals' (1993), spreads throughout the world. Womanist, *mujerista*, Asian and other perspectives challenge Euro-American feminist understandings. Hence it is important to note that women-church is but one of a range of women's spiritual expressions emerging in patriarchy.

Particularly active groups are found in Canada and the United States, Western Europe, Australia, New Zealand and parts of Asia and Latin America. Most of the groups are small, autonomous gatherings which focus primarily on liturgy and ritual. Work for social change and the building of community among members are equally important components. In some countries, Switzerland for example, there are coalitions of member groups which sponsor periodic national gatherings, educational programs and publications. The Women-Church Convergence is a coalition of such groups in the United States which meets twice a year for education and strategizing. It sponsors occasional conferences such as 'Women-Church: Weavers of Change' in Albuquerque in 1993.

The term 'women-church' is mistakenly understood by some to mean a church for women only. It really means an inclusive community in which feminist women, men and children join together in what Schüssler Fiorenza calls 'emancipatory communities'. These are envisioned as groups in which women as well as men are part of a democratic process of decision-making and leadership. This is not currently the case in the vast majority of Christian churches, just as in the vast majority of societies in the world. Another popular interpretation of the term is Rosemary Radford Ruether's vision (1986) of women-church as a 'feminist exodus community' from patriarchy, taking the eucharist and feminist forms of ministry into a promised land of equality.

In the US, what began as primarily Roman Catholic-rooted groups are now increasingly ecumenical in heritage and eclectic in content. Wicca, Goddess worship, Native American and New Age as well as feminist Christian sources feed into the theological mix. Some members

An A to Z of Feminist Theology

belong simultaneously to women-church and to a Christian denomination or other religious tradition; some people have moved away from institutional churches into women-church groups as their spiritual base. This dynamic varies throughout the world with women-church as a movement having no membership requirement as such.

Women-church signals a commitment to actualize the vision of equality and participation in both church and society. Far from being a separatist reaction to injustice in the church and a theological solution to what is a wider social problem, women-church is a political movement which sees patriarchal religious institutions as discriminatory and in need of substantive structural change. Schüssler Fiorenza observes correctly that not all women-church groups or members have understood this important political dimension (1993: 344-52), but it is increasingly clear to feminists in religion that changes in society will not be accomplished without changes in the fundamental belief systems which undergird patriarchy, and vice versa. This means that the concerns of women-church groups must include economic, political, sexual and spiritual matters, with specific attention to eradicating the ways in which patriarchal religious ideologies bolster discrimination.

Women-church is distinct from 'women and church' or 'women in church' efforts in that it signals that the agenda is set by those who have been marginalized, not by those who have discriminated. The term 'women-church' signals a desire to 'be church' on women's terms rather than trying to change hierarchical churches on patriarchal terms. There is a fair amount of overlap in the efforts, but the power dynamic signaled by the term 'women-church' is key to understanding what feminist faith looks like.

This primary focus on women, and decidedly secondary focus on institutional churches, is why the women-church movement has been made up predominantly of women who are faced with strong opposition in their churches, such as Roman Catholics. Likewise, the women and church efforts have been more readily engaged in by those who can find ways to be church in their respective denominations, whether as ordained or lay members, and thus have the possibility to renew from within. The scandal of patriarchal discrimination is such that for many Roman Catholic women it is women-church or no church; for many Protestant women, especially clergywomen, being part of the women-church movement is a way to avoid being coopted by their institutions, a way to assure that feminist agendas hold sway, indeed for many a source of spiritual nourishment they no longer find in their churches.

Women-church adherents recognize that patriarchal models of church, like patriarchal models of society, keep women and other non-privileged persons, especially those from oppressed racial, ethnic and class groups, from being protagonists of their own spiritualities. In women-church, women are religious agents who seek nothing less than the human right to spiritual integrity, and nothing more than the opportunity to pursue it. That is a threat to patriarchal religions.

In the near future, women-church needs to pay serious attention to global networking so that local and national groups can learn from one another. It needs to pay attention to the religious development of children whose formative religious experience is in women-church. It needs theological and ethical reflection, liturgical development and attention to the pastoral needs of its members. These are challenges which await the movement in what is only its second decade. The remarkable progress of the women-church movement in its first decade suggests that it has its roots in the centuries of women who have struggled in patriarchal cultures to be religious on their own terms. That is a struggle well worth continuing.

Further reading: Neu and Hunt 1993; Schüssler Fiorenza 1992.

WORK
Elizabeth Nash

WORK IS the 'expenditure of energy to some purpose' (*Concise Oxford Dictionary*) and the 'central reality of existence' (Macquarrie [ed.] 1967: 362). Its purpose is to sustain and renew human life. Some work is enjoyable and some is not, some is paid and some is not, some is creative, some sustains life and some destroys it either by design or by accident. According to the United Nations women do seven tenths of the world's work, but earn only one tenth of the world's income. Economics takes account only of work which has monetary value.

The biblical doctrine of work, as illustrated by the story of the Garden of Eden, shows work as both a blessing and a curse. The Christian doctrine of work sees it as pleasing to God, but also, of necessity, hard labour. The Reformation discovered a doctrine of vocation in everyday life and this developed into capitalism, which demands hard work for the lowest pay possible. Communism glorified in the labour of human hands but also required hard work, including that done in labour camps. In both systems, those who are poor or dissidents pay the price of their sin with hard labour while those who are rich or acceptable are accorded righteousness and servants to do the work.

The traditional Christian understandings of work are all male centred. Our theology reflects the sexual division of labour. Across the world women begin their work long before the men, and continue long after, as they work a double shift, to care for home and family as well as earning money or growing crops.

Women's work…is vital to the survival and ongoing reproduction of human beings in all societies. In food production and processing, in responsibility for fuel, water, health-care, child-rearing, sanitation, and the entire range of so-called basic needs, women's labour is dominant (Sen and Grown 1988: 23-24).

Yet, despite the importance of women's work, they are undervalued, underpaid and under-trained. In Britain in 1996, 26 years after the Equal Pay Act (1970), women's average weekly earnings are only 71 per cent of men's and women still work predominantly in those areas which relate to their traditional domestic responsibilities—cooking, cleaning, clothes and caring.

A feminist theology of work begins from a different place. It centres on the following concerns.

Life and Work as a Whole

Life is not a series of compartments in which we are here a worker, there a mother, here a homemaker or a wife, there a friend or a lover. Wherever we are, whatever we are doing we are all these things at once. At work we do not cease to be everything else although we (especially men) sometimes behave as if this were the case. Employers expect our undivided attention and unlimited time. It is, in general, only men with wives to cope with all the home responsibilities who can work like this. For women, life cannot be divided in this way. We are whole people and paid work cannot be allowed to win in the competition for the needs of those we love and care for, whether they are young or old.

A feminist theology of work needs to include all work, paid and unpaid, and to see each person as a whole person.

Valuing Work

Capitalist societies value people and the work they do by how much they are paid. Thus a city broker is of more value than a works manager, who is of more value than a cleaner, who is of more value than a housewife. But this does not reflect the true worth of those people, nor does it reflect the personal importance of the housewife or cleaner to their family and workplace. Work should be valued in terms of the relationships it builds and creates and the life that it sustains. To make a billet of steel has no value in itself, but to make steel which makes a washing machine which relieves women of the drudgery of washing is valuable. To clean a house is of no particular value in itself, but the pleasure of a comfortable clean home in building family relationships and preventing disease is valuable.

A feminist theology of work gives value to work which is life-enhancing and which enables relationships.

Caring Versus Servicing

All Christians have a responsibility to love and care for one another, but we have had a different expectation of what this means for men and women. Men are expected to serve by exercising power and responsibility and women are expected to serve in the domestic role by servicing people and churches. If loving care is not received with respect for the person giving it and if there is no mutuality in sharing power as well as care then the serving is made servile.

A feminist theology of work implies that ser-

An A to Z of Feminist Theology

vicing is not right for women or men, but rather mutual serving and loving care are the responsibilities of everyone.

Valuing Women and their Work

The sins of men and women are not identical. Women are more likely to sin by undervaluing themselves than they are to sin by being too proud of their achievements. This is particularly true in the arena of working life because of the way in which society values work. A woman cleaner is unskilled because she has done this job all her life, while a male builder is skilled because he has done this job all his life. Women often fail to recognize and value their skills because their paid work is connected with their domestic role and that is not valued.

A feminist theology of work requires women to give full value to themselves and their work.

Further reading: Borrowdale 1989; Bryan, Dadzie and Scaffe 1985; Coyle 1984; Templeton (ed.) 1993.

WORSHIP
Lala Winkley and Veronica Seddon

WORSHIP IS a public or semi-public action celebrating our search for and finding of meaning in the mystery of life. It is the way in which a group of people give expression to their deeply held beliefs. When women and men gather to engage in the liturgical activity which we call worship, they are giving it a special moment, recognizing a special significance in what they are doing. It is done not from obligation or through coercion but because there is a deeply felt need or wish for it. Through worship we acknowledge God's presence and importance in our lives.

Women have challenged the churches' view that only specially ordained ritual agents—priests or ministers—are authorized to initiate and lead acts of worship. In a feminist understanding of worship, all present are able to influence the whole and contribute creatively. Because each person is important to any group, then a different group would result in a different act of worship even though the basic framework is the same. Each person brings her or his history, experience and knowledge to the act of worship. Every person contributes creatively to the whole which is about discovering our nature and our understanding of God. In the feminist understanding, an individual may be the initiator and leader of any particular occasion of worship. The group, by their presence, empower the person for that moment. Feminist women have also challenged the patriarchal nature of their religious traditions and seek to uncover the hidden roles of women throughout religious history. They seek to use inclusive language so that God is not seen only as a white male. They seek to recognize and remember the contribution made by women in and beyond Scripture.

On an everyday level, everyone engages in rituals such as birthday parties and the celebration of the special events in our lives. A great deal of thought, care and preparation goes into these events. We are able to do what is appropriate for the occasion. We are not intimidated by the magnitude of the task. Often we will enlist the help of friends in the preparation, sharing the work. Similarly, everyone should be able to prepare and lead worship. It is up to us to empower each other to be able to prepare worship that is authentic and meaningful for the group. We need to give each other confidence. If some part is not totally successful, failure can be accepted and we can learn from it. It is important to prepare something from the heart and for the participants to give themselves to it with integrity.

Acts of worship or liturgy have some basic elements. First, acknowledging God, secondly, searching for understanding of and learning about God. These two elements are combined and expressed through action and ritual. In this way we are adding to tradition, evoking meaning, inspiring commitment and above all encouraging hope.

Acts of worship lift up everyday events to particular significance or focus by making use of familiar contexts. This enables the participants to connect in a special way, thus bonding the group. For instance, in the sharing of bread we are physically connected to each other. There is something very basic or elemental about eating together. A shared meal to which everyone has contributed takes us beyond the narrow space of the individual. The ordinary act of eating, taking food, sharing drink becomes endowed with symbolic meaning.

Symbols in worship are another kind of language and have many depths of meaning. They 'speak' beyond the confinements of words. They engage with us at the place where we are in our understanding or belief. The same object can have different meanings at different times, even within the same group. A symbol should only be used as long as it is helpful. Likewise, metaphors and stories can communicate truth in a gentler way than dogmatic assertions. They 'allow' our understanding and comprehension to grow organically, gradually. Indeed the revelation of God always involves more than that which is immediately obvious; but through symbols and images, metaphors and stories, and by trusting our own life experience we can deepen and extend our search for an understanding of and our relationship with God.

On a practical level, time needs to be given to the preparation of worship. It is often helpful to work in a group of two or three who share ideas. In this way, those who have experience of preparing liturgy can share their expertise and confidence with anyone to whom this is quite new. Care needs to be taken in working out the framework, paying attention to how and where participants will be contributing and following through a theme with consistency. It takes time and effort, but is a rewarding and renewing task.

Worship is a dynamic, symbolic act. The enactment can take many different forms. We need to find the appropriate moment and the appropriate form in order to nurture our very being and our soul. Then we shall enlarge our understanding of ourselves, of God and our community. We shall become more ourselves, more whole and more truly human, 'finding joy in the midst of sorrow, hope at the edge of despair, witness to a Christian courage that offers New Life to all' (Winter 1987).

Further reading: Boyce-Tillman and Wootton (eds.) 1993; Briscoe (ed.) 1987; McDade 1986; St Hilda Community 1991.

YHWH: A WOMAN'S PERSPECTIVE
Sylvia Rothschild

BIBLICAL NAMES denote something of the essence of the persons to whom they belong, and thus are intensely personal and revealing. The unique name of God is a four-letter word, apparently composed of the three tenses of the verb 'to be', an amalgamation of the past, the present and the future. Thus it is a name which reveals that a basic principle of God in the Hebrew Bible is that of eternal existence. It is traditionally believed that the vowels which accompany the four consonants are lost to us, although several early Greek Christian writers testify that the name was pronounced Yahweh. Assuming that the first syllable is pronounced Yah (as found in shortened form in, for example, Exod. 15.2), it is possible to make the case that the verb is used in the *hiphil* (causative) form, meaning 'The One who Causes Existence'. However, the tetragrammaton, while open to the possibility of being deconstructed, is traditionally viewed as the personal name of God, and is qualitatively different from any other name of God in biblical and rabbinic literature.

The tetragrammaton YHWH is known in Hebrew as HaShem ('The Name par excellence'), and observant Jews will substitute the word 'HaShem' for any name of God. Until the destruction of the First Temple in 586 BCE the tetragrammaton was regularly pronounced with its proper vowels (as is clear from the Lachish Letters), but by the third century BCE pronouncing the name was avoided and the word 'Adonai' ('my Lord') was substituted (see Babylonian Talmud *Kiddushin* 71a). In pointed texts the vowels of the word 'Adonai' are attached to the consonants YHWH to remind the reader not to pronounce it in any way, but to say instead 'Adonai'. In the Middle Ages this was misunderstood by Christian scholars, who read it as written, and so created the hybrid name Jehovah. While there are many names for God, all of which denote some particular attribute, the four-letter name of God is, as Maimonides wrote, the only one which does not derive from actions, but gives instead a clear and unequivocal indication of God's essence.

It would be difficult, then, to relate to the tetragrammaton strictly in feminist terms. Unlike *shechinah*, or *ha-rachaman* (both of which have specifically female connotations), or *adonai tzeva'ot* (which has masculine imagery), the tetragrammaton is above issues of gender or of imagery. Translated as 'The Eternal One', 'Being', 'The One Who Is', 'The Omnipresent', 'You', or even 'Source of Life', it transcends the sexual politics inherent in many of the other names of God, which by describing particular attributes become available to gender manipulation.

It is unfortunate that the word 'Adonai' has been the traditional substitute for the tetragrammaton, because that word is loaded with gender-specific imagery, and removes the specialness of the all-inclusive tetragrammaton. Other names or attributes would also interpret and so unbalance the perfectly made Name. Using HaShem, or the rabbinic HaMakom ('the place'), might be suitable alternatives when reading the ineffable Name, since they also clarify the sense of immanence invoked by the tetragrammaton.

Further reading: Plaskow 1990; Magonet 1991.

BIBLIOGRAPHY

Adams, C.
1995 'Toward a Feminist Theology of Religion and the State', in C. Adams and M.M. Fortune (eds.), *Violence against Women and Children: A Theological Sourcebook in the Christian Tradition* (New York: Continuum).

Adams, C. (ed.)
1993 *Ecofeminism and the Sacred* (New York: Continuum).

Aguilar, D.
1988 *The Feminist Challenge* (Manila: Asian Social Institute).

Allchin, A.M.
1988 *Participation in God* (London: Darton, Longman & Todd).

Anderson, B., and J. Zinsser
1989 *A History of Their Own* (London: Penguin Books).

Arai, T., and W. Ariarajah
1989 *Spirituality in Interfaith Dialogue* (Geneva: World Council of Churches).

Arbuckle, G.
1986 *Strategies for Growth in Religious Life* (London: St Paul's).

Archer, J., and B. Lloyd
1992 *Sex and Gender* (Cambridge: Cambridge University Press, 2nd edn).

Ardener, S.
1978 *Defining Females* (London: Croom Helm).

Arendt, H.
1961 *Between Past and Future: Six Exercises in Political Thought* (New York: Meridian).

Armstrong, K.
1993 *A History of God* (London: Mandarin).

Association for Inclusive Language
1990 *Women, Language and the Church* (London: AIL).

Aswynn, F.
1988 *Leaves of Yggdrasil: A Synthesis of Magic, Feminine Mysteries, Folklore* (London: Aswynn).

Atkinson, C.W.
1991 *The Oldest Vocation: Christian Motherhood in the Middle Ages* (Ithaca, NY: Cornell University Press).

3Bacon, M.H.
1993 *One Woman's Passion for Peace and Freedom: The Life of Mildred Scott Olmsted* (Syracuse: Syracuse University Press).

Baker, D.
1978 *Medieval Women* (Studies in Church History, Subsidia, 1; Oxford: Basil Blackwell).

Bal, M.
1987 *Lethal Love: Feminist Literary Readings of Biblical Love Stories* (Bloomington: Indiana University Press).

Bal, M. (ed.)
1989 *Anti-Covenant: Counter-Reading Women's Lives in the Hebrew Bible* (Sheffield: Almond Press, 1989).

Barbe, D.
1989 *A Theology of Conflict and Other Writings on Nonviolence* (New York: Orbis Books).

Baring, A., and J. Cashford
1993 *The Myth of the Goddess: Evolution of an Image* (Harmondsworth: Penguin; New York: Viking).

Barter, D.
1993 *Grace Abounding: Struggling with Sin and Guilt* (London: Darton, Longman & Todd).

Bautista, L., and E. Rifareal (eds.)
1990 *And She Said No! Human Rights, Women's Identities and Struggles* (National Council of Churches of the Philippines).

Beard, M.R.
1962 *Woman as Force in History* (New York: Collier Books).

Beauchamp, T.L., and J.F. Childress
1989 *Principles of Biomedical Ethics* (Oxford and New York: Oxford University Press, 3rd edn).

Beauvoir, S. de
1949 *The Second Sex* (London: Picador).

Begg, E.
1985 *The Cult of the Black Virgin* (London: Arkana/Routledge & Kegan Paul, 1985).

Bem, S.
1993 *The Lenses of Gender* (New Haven and London: Yale University Press).

Benderly
1982 'Rape Free or Rape Prone', *Science* (October).

Benhabib, S.
1992 *Situating the Self: Gender, Community and Postmodernism in Contemporary Ethics* (London: Polity Press).

An A to Z of Feminist Theology

BIBLIOGRAPHY

Bentley, L.
1987 *The Gnostic Scriptures* (London).

Berry, P., and A. Wernick (eds.)
1992 *Shadow of Spirit: Postmodernism and Religion* (London: Routledge).

Bertell, R.
1985 *No Immediate Danger* (London: The Women's Press).

Best, T. (ed.)
1988 *Beyond Unity-in-Tension: Unity, Renewal and the Community of Women and Men* (Faith and Order Paper, 138; Geneva: World Council of Churches).

Biale, R.
1984 *Women and Jewish Law* (New York: Schocken Books).

Binch, C.
1987 *Passionate Politics* (New York: St Martin's Press).

Blumberg, R.L. (ed.)
1988 *Gender Stratification, Economy, and the Family (Journal of Family Issues* 9.1 [March]; London: Sage).

Boff, L.
1980 *Jesus Christ Liberator* (London: SPCK).
1985 *Church, Charism, Power* (New York: Crossroads).

Boff, L., and C. Boff
1987 *Introducing Liberation Theology* (Tunbridge Wells: Burns & Oates).

Bondeson, W.B., et al. (eds.)
1984 *Abortion and the Status of the Foetus* (Dordrecht: D. Reidel).

Booth, C.
1870 *Female Ministry or Woman's Right to Preach the Gospel* (London: Morgan & Chase).

Børresen, K.E. (ed.)
1991 *Image of God and Gender Models* (Oslo: Solum Forlag).

Borrowdale, A.
1989 *A Woman's Work: Changing Christian Attitudes* (London: SPCK).

Boss, S.J.
1988 'The "Weakness" of Women', *The Month* (November): 979-85.

Bowie, F.
1989 *Beguine Spirituality: An Anthology* (London: SPCK).

Bowie, F., and O. Davies (eds.)
1990 *Hildegard of Bingen: An Anthology* (London: SPCK).

Boyce-Tillman, J.
1995 *Singing the Mystery: 28 Liturgical Pieces by Hildegard of Bingen* (London: Association for Inclusive Language and the Hildegard Press).

Boyce-Tillman, J., and J. Wootton (eds.)
1993 *Reflecting Praise* (London: Stainer & Bell/Women in Theology).

Braidotti, R.
1991 *Patterns of Dissonance: A Study of Women in Contemporary Philosophy* (London: Polity Press).

Bredow, W. von
1983 *Moderner Militarismus* (Stuttgart: Kohlhammer).

Brenner, A.
1985 *The Israelite Woman: Social Role and Literary Type in Biblical Narrative* (Biblical Seminar, 2; Sheffield: JSOT Press).

Briscoe, J. (ed.)
1987 *Historical Anthology of Music by Women* (Bloomington: Indiana University Press).

Brock, R.
1988 *Journeys By Heart: A Christology of Erotic Power* (New York: Crossroad).

Brooke, E.
1993 *Women Healers* (London: The Women's Press).

Brown, J.C., and C.R. Bohn (eds.)
1989 *Christianity, Patriarchy, and Abuse: A Feminist Critique* (New York: Pilgrim Press)

Brown, J.C., and R. Parker
1989 'For God So Loved the World?', in Brown and Bohn (eds.): 1-30.

Brown, P.
1986 *The Body and Society: Men, Women and Sexual Renunciation in Early Christianity* (New York: Columbia University Press; London: Faber & Faber [1989]).

Brown, R.E., K.P. Donfried, J.A. Fitzmyer and J. Reumann (eds.)
1978 *Mary in the New Testament* (London: Geoffrey Chapman).

Browning, D.S.
1991 *A Fundamental Practical Theology* (Minneapolis: Fortress Press).

Bryan, B., S. Dadzie and S. Scaffe
1985 *The Heart of the Race: Black Women's Lives in Britain* (London: Virago).

An A to Z of Feminist Theology

BIBLIOGRAPHY

Buckley, J.J.
- 1988 'The Holy Spirit is a Double Name', in King (ed.) 1988: 211-27.

Budapest, Z.
- 1979 *The Holy Book of Women's Mysteries*, I (Los Angeles: Susan B. Anthony Coven 1).
- 1980 *The Holy Book of Women's Mysteries*, II (Los Angeles: Susan B. Anthony Coven 1).

Burgos-Debray, E. (ed.)
- 1984 *I, Rigoberta Menchu: An Indian Woman In Guatemala* (London: Verso).

Butler, J.
- 1990 *Gender Trouble: Feminism and the Subversion of Identity* (London: Routledge).

Bynum, C.W.
- 1982 *Jesus as Mother: Studies in the Spirituality of the High Middle Ages* (Berkeley: University of California Press).

Byrne, L. (ed.)
- 1992 *Directory of Women's Organisations and Groups in Churches and Ecumenical Bodies in Britain and Ireland* (London: CCBI Publications).
- 1993 *Christian Women Together: The Durham Quilt* (London: CCBI Publications).

Cady, S., M. Ronan and H. Tussig
- 1989 *Wisdom's Feast: Sophia in Study and Celebration* (San Francisco: Harper & Row, 1989).

Cahill, L.S.
- 1993 'Feminist Ethics and the Challenge of the Cultures', *CTSA Proceedings* 48.

Caird, G.
- 1980 *The Language and Imagery of the Bible* (London: Duckworth).

Cambridge Women's Peace Collective
- 1984 *My Country is the Whole World* (London: Pandora Press).

Camelot, P.T.
- 1967 'Virginity', in *New Catholic Encyclopedia* (New York: McGraw–Hill), XIV: 703.

Campbell, J.
- 1976 *The Masks of God: Occidental Mythology* (Harmondsworth: Penguin).

Cannon, K.G.
- 1988 *Black Womanist Ethics* (Atlanta: Scholars Press).
- 1989 'Moral Wisdom in the Black Women's Literary Tradition', in J. Plaskow and C.P. Christ (eds.), *Weaving the Visions:*

New Patterns in Feminist Spirituality (San Francisco: Harper & Row).

Carmichael, A.
- 1992 *Carmina Gadelica: Hymns and Incantations collected in the Highlands and Islands of Scotland in the Last Century by Alexander Carmichael* (Edinburgh: Floris Books).

Carmody, D.
- 1992 *Biblical Women* (New York: Crossroad).

Carr, E.
- 1990 *Transforming Grace: Christian Tradition and Women's Experience* (San Francisco: Harper & Row).

Carr-Gomm, P.
- 1991 *The Elements of the Druid Tradition* (Shaftesbury: Element Books).

Certeau, M. de
- 1986 *Heterologies: Discourse on the Other* (trans. B. Massumi; Manchester: Manchester University Press).

Chesler, P.
- 1989 *Women and Madness* (New York: Harcourt Brace Jovanovich, 2nd edn).

Chopp, R.
- 1987 'Feminist Theological Pragmatics: A Social Naturalism of Women's Experience', *Journal of Religion* 67: 239-56.
- 1989 *The Power to Speak: Feminism, Language, God* (New York: Crossroad).

Christ, C.P.
- 1986 *Driving Deep and Surfacing: Women Writers on Spiritual Incest* (Boston: Beacon Press).
- 1987 'On Not Blaming the Jews for the Death of the Goddess', in *The Laughter of Aphrodite* (San Francisco: Harper & Row): 83-92.

Chung, H.K.
- 1990 *Struggle to be the Sun Again: Introducing Asian Women's Theology* (Maryknoll, NY: Orbis Books; London: SCM Press [1991]).

Church of England General Synod
- 1986 *Towards a Theology for Interfaith Dialogue* (Church of England: Board of Mission and Unity).

Church of Scotland Women's Guild
- 1984 *Motherhood of God* (Edinburgh: St Andrews Press).

Cixous, H.
- 1979 *Vivre l'orange/To live the orange* (Paris: des Femmes).

BIBLIOGRAPHY

Clayton, M.
1990   *The Cult of the Virgin Mary in Anglo-Saxon England* (Cambridge: Cambridge University Press).

Clebsch, W.A., and C.R. Jaekle
1964   *Pastoral Care in Historical Perspective* (London: J. Aronson).

Cline, S.
1993   *Women, Celibacy and Passion* (London: Andre Deutsch).

Coakley, S.
1990   'Creaturehood before God: Male and Female', *Theology* 93: 343-54.

Cobb, J.B., Jr
1976   *Process Theology: An Introductory Exposition* (Philadelphia: Westminster Press).

Coll, R.
1994   *Christianity and Feminism in Conversation* (Connecticut: Twenty-Third Publications).

Colledge, E., and J. Walsh (eds.)
1978   *A Book of Showings to the Anchoress Julian of Norwich* (Toronto: Pontifical Institute of Medieval Studies).

Collins, A.Y. (ed.)
1985   *Feminist Perspectives on Biblical Scholarship*, 10 (Chico, CA: Scholars Press).

Conley, V.A.
1992   *Hélène Cixous* (Hemel Hempstead: Harvester Wheatsheaf).

Conn, J.W. (ed.)
1986   *Women's Spirituality: Resources for Christian Development* (New York: Paulist Press).

Connell, R.W.
1987   *Gender and Power* (London: Polity Press).

Coon, L.L., et al.
1990   *That Gentle Strength: Historical Perspectives on Women in Christianity* (Charlottesville and London: University Press of Virginia,).

Cotter, J.
1988   *Prayer at Night: A Book for the Darkness* (Exeter: Cairns Publications).

Countryman, L.W.
1988   *Dirt, Greed, and Sex: Sexual Ethics in the New Testament and their Implication for Today* (New York: Fortress Press; London: SCM Press [1989]).

Courtenay, A.
1991   *Healing Now* (London: Dent & Sons).

Cowan, M.
1987   'Sacramental Moments', in R.A. Duffy (ed.), *Alternative Futures for Worship*, I (Minnesota: Liturgical Press): 35-62.

Coyle, A.
1984   *Redundant Women* (London: The Women's Press).

Crowley, V.
1986a   *Principles of Paganism* (London: Thorsons).
1986b   *Phoenix from the Flame: Living as a Pagan in the Twenty First Century* (London: Thorsons).

D'Costa, G.
1986   *Theology and Religious Pluralism* (Oxford: Basil Blackwell).

Dahlberg, A.
1987   'Transcendence of Bodily Suffering: An Anthropological Study of English Catholics at Lourdes' (PhD thesis, University of London).
1991   'The Body as Principle of Holism: Three Pilgrimages to Lourdes', in J. Eade and M.J. Sallnow (eds.), *Contesting the Sacred: The Anthropology of Christian Pilgrimage* (London: Routledge): 30-50.

Dale, J., and P. Foster
1986   *Feminists and State Welfare* (London: Routledge & Kegan Paul).

Daly, M.
1968   *The Church and the Second Sex* (Boston: Beacon Press).
1973   *Beyond God the Father: Toward a Philosophy of Women's Liberation* (Boston: Beacon Press; London: The Women's Press [2nd edn, 1985]).
1978   *Gyn/Ecology: The Metaethics of Radical Feminism* (Boston: Beacon Press; London: The Women's Press [1985]).
1984   *Pure Lust: Elemental Feminist Philosophy* (Boston: Beacon Press; London: The Women's Press).

Daly, M., with J. Caputi
1988   *Wickedary of the English Language* (London: The Women's Press).

***Daughters of Sarah* (journal)**
1992   18.3 (Chicago, IL).

Daum, A.
1980a   'Blaming Jews for the Death of the Goddess', *Lilith* 7: 12-13.
1980b   'Feminists and Faith. A Discussion with Judith Plaskow and Annette Daum', *Lilith* 7: 14-17.

BIBLIOGRAPHY

Davaney, S.G. (ed.)
1981 *Feminism and Process Thought* (The Harvard Divinity School/Claremont Center for Process Studies Symposium Papers; Lewiston, NY: Edwin Mellen).

Davis, E.G.
1971 *The First Sex* (New York: Putnam's Sons).

De Waal, E.
1991 *A World Made Whole* (London: HarperCollins).

Deen, E.
1955 *All of the Women of the Bible* (New York: Harper & Row).

Delumeau, J.
1990 *Sin and Fear: The Emergence of a Western Guilt Culture 13th–18th Centuries* (New York: St Martin's Press).

Dickey Young, P.
1990 *Feminist Theology/Christian Theology: In Search of Method* (Minneapolis: Fortress Press).

Dobash, R.E., and R.P. Dobash
1980 *Violence against Wives: A Case Against Patriarchy* (Shepton Mallet Open Books).

Douglas, M.
1970 *Purity and Danger* (Harmondsworth: Penguin Books).
1973 *Natural Symbols* (London: Penguin Books).

Dowell, S.
1990 *They Two Shall Be One: Monogamy in History and Religion* (London: Collins).
1993 'A Feminist Critique', in *Celibacy* (*The Way* Supplement, 77): 76-86.

Dowell, S., and L. Hurcombe
1987 *Dispossessed Daughters of Eve* (London: SPCK).

Dowell, S., and J. Williams
1994 *Bread, Wine and Women* (London: Virago).

Doyle, J.A., and M.A. Paludi
1991 *Sex and Gender: The Human Experience* (Dubuque, IA: W.C. Brown).

Duck, R.
1991 *Gender and the Name of God: The Trinitarian Baptismal Formula* (New York: Pilgrim Press).

Duffy, E.
1992 *The Stripping of the Altars: Traditional Religion in England, 1400–1580* (New Haven and London: Yale University Press).

Dworkin, A.
1981 *Pornography* (London: The Women's Press).
1987 *Intercourse* (London: Secker & Warburg).

Eaton, J.
1990 'Kingship', in R. Coggins and L. Houlden (eds.), *A Dictionary of Biblical Interpretation* (London: SCM Press): 379-82.

Ecumenical Association of Third World Theologians
1991 *Women in the Philippines and Asia: Patriarchy in Asia and Asian Women's Hermeneutical Principle* (Theology/Spirituality of Struggle Series; Manila: EATWOT).

Edwards, B.
1989 *The Case for Women's Ministry* (London: SPCK).

Ehrenreich, B., and D. English
1974 *Witches, Midwives and Nurses* (New York: Feminist Press).

Eisler, R.
1982 'Women and Peace', *Women Speaking* (Oct.–Dec.).

Elizondo, V.
1983 'Mary and the Poor: A Model of Evangelising Ecumenism', in H. Kung and J. Moltmann (eds.), *Mary in the Churches* (Concilium, 168; Edinburgh: T. & T. Clark).

Elizondo, V., and N. Greinacher
1980 *Women in A Men's Church* (Concilium; Edinburgh: T. & T. Clark).

Eller, C.
1993 *Living in the Lap of the Goddess: The Feminist Spirituality Movement in America* (Boston: Beacon Press).

Ellis, P.F.
1976 *The Men and the Message of the Old Testament* (Collegeville, MN: The Liturgical Press).

Engelsman, J.C.
1987 *The Feminine Face of the Divine* (Wilmette, IL: Chiron).

Epstein, C.F.
1988 *Deceptive Distinctions: Sex, Gender and the Social Order* (New Haven: Yale University Press).

Eugene, T.M.
1994 *Lifting as We Climb: A Womanist Ethic of Care* (Nashville: Abingdon Press).

An A to Z of Feminist Theology

BIBLIOGRAPHY

Evans, M.
1983 *Woman in the Bible* (Exeter: Paternoster Press).

Fabella, V.
1989 *We Dare to Dream: Doing Theology as Asian Women* (Hong Kong: Asian Women's Resource Center for Culture and Theology).
1990 'A Theological Framework from the Woman Question' (paper presented at the Annual Convention of the Association of Major Religious Superiori for Women of the Philippines, Tagaytay, January 28, 1990).
1993 *Beyond Bonding: A Third World Women's Theological Journey* (Manila: Ecumenical Association of Third World Theologians and Institute of Women's Studies).

Fabella, V., and M.A. Oduyoye (eds.)
1988 *With Passion and and Compassion: Third World Women Doing Theology* (Maryknoll, NY: Orbis Books).

Faith and Order Committee of the Methodist Church
1992 *Inclusive Language and Imagery about God* (London: Methodist Publishing House, 1992).

Farmer, D.H.
1992 *The Oxford Dictionary of Saints* (Oxford: Oxford University Press).

Farrar, I., and S. Farrar
1984 *The Witches' Way* (London: Robert Hale).

Fatum, L.
1989 'Women, Symbolic Universe and Structures of Silence: Challenges and Possibilities in Androcentric Texts', *Studia Theologica* 43: 61-80.

Fee, G.D.
1983 *New Testament Exegesis: A Handbook for Students and Pastors* (Philadelphia: Westminster Press).

Fewell, D.N.
1993 'Reading the Bible Ideologically: Feminist Criticism', in S.R. Haynes and S.L. McKenzie (eds.), *To Each its own Meaning: An Introduction to Biblical Criticisms and their Application* (Louisville, KY: Westminster/John Knox Press): 237-51.

Fiand, B.
1992 *Living the Vision* (New York: Crossroad).

Filoramo, F.
1991 *A History of Gnosticism* (trans. A. Alcock; Oxford: Oxford University Press).

Fischer, K.
1989 *Woman at the Well: Feminist Perspectives on Spiritual Direction* (London: SPCK).

Fitzgerald, C.
1986 'Impasse and Dark Night', in J.W. Wolski-Conn (ed.), *Women's Spirituality: Resources for Christian Development* (New York: Paulist Press): 287-309.

Flax, J.
1990 *Thinking Fragments: Psychoanalysis, Feminism and Post-Modernism in the Contemporary West* (Berkeley: University of California Press).

Fortune, M.F.
1989 'The Transformation of Suffering: A Biblical and Theological Perspective', in Brown and Bohn (eds.): 139-47.

Fortune, M.M.
1983 *Sexual Violence: The Unmentionable Sin* (New York: Pilgrim Press).

Foucault, M.
1984 *The History of Sexuality III. 'The Care of the Self* (trans. R. Hurley; New York: Pantheon, 1984).

Fox, M.
1979 *A Spirituality Named Compassion* (Scranton, PA: Harper & Row).
1983 *Original Blessing: A Primer in Creation Spirituality* (Santa Fe, NM: Bear & Co.).
1988 *The Coming of the Cosmic Christ* (Scranon, PA: Harper & Row).

Fox, M. (ed.)
1985 *The Illuminations of Hildegard of Bingen* (Santa Fe, NM: Bear).

Fox, R.L.
1992 *The Unauthorized Version: Truth and Fiction in the Bible* (Harmondsworth: Penguin Books, 1992).

Freeman, A.
1993 *God in Us* (London: SCM Press).

Freeman, H.
1994 'Chochmah and Wholeness: Retrieving the Feminism in Judaism', *Journal of Progressive Judaism* 2 (May): 35-48.

Frend, W.H.C.
1967 *Martyrdom and Persecution in the Early Church: A Study of a Conflict from the Maccabees to Donatus* (New York: New York University Press).

BIBLIOGRAPHY

Friedman, M.
1989 'Feminism and Modern Friendship: Dislocating the Community', *Ethics* 99 (Jan. 1989): 275-90.

Frye, M.
1983 'Sexism', in *The Politics of Reality: Essays in Feminist Theory* (Freedom, CA: The Crossing Press): 17-40.

Frye, N.
1982 *The Great Code: The Bible and Literature* (New York and London: Harcourt, Brace, Jovanovich).

Frymer-Kensky, T.
1992 'Deuteronomy', in Newsom and Ringe (eds.) 1992: 55-62.

Fuchs, E.
1983 *Sexual Desire and Love* (New York: Seabury).

Furlong, M.
1991 *A Dangerous Delight: Women and Power in the Church* (London: SPCK).

Fuss, D.
1989 *Essentially Speaking: Feminism, Nature and Difference* (London: Routledge).

Gage, M.J.
1985 *Woman, Church and State* (repr. Salem, NH: Ayer Company [1900]).

Gardner, G.B.
1951 *Witchcraft Today* (London: Rider).
1959 *The Meaning of Witchcraft* (London: Aquarian Press).

Gebara, I.
1994 'The Face of Transcendence as a Challenge to the Reading of the Bible in Latin America', in Schüssler Fiorenza (ed.)1994: ch.12.

Gebara, I., and M.C. Bingemer
1989 *Mary, Mother of God, Mother of the Poor* (London: Burns & Oates).

Gershon, W.
1991 *They Called Her Rebbe: The Maiden of Ludomir* (New York: Judaica Press).

Gilchrist, C.
n.d. *The Circle Nine* (Dryad Press).

Giles, M.
1986 *The Feminist Mystic* (New York: Crossroad).

Gilligan, C.
1982 *In A Different Voice: Psychological Theory and Women's Development* (Cambridge, MA: Harvard University Press).

Gimbutas, M.
1982 *The Goddesses and Gods of Old Europe, 6500–3500 BC* (London: Thames & Hudson; Berkeley: University of California Press).
1989 'Women and Culture in Goddess-Oriented Old Europe', in Plaskow and Christ (eds.) 1989: 62-71.

Glaz, M., and J.S. Moessner (eds.)
1991 *Women in Travail and Transition* (Minneapolis, MN: Fortress Press).

Gnanadason, A.
1993 *No Longer a Secret: The Church and Violence against Women* (Geneva: World Council of Churches).

Goerhring, J.
1988 'Libertine or Liberated', in K.L. King (ed.) 1988: 329-44.

Goldenberg, N.
1979 *Changing of the Gods* (Boston: Beacon Press).

Goodison, L.
1990 *Moving Heaven and Earth* (London: The Women's Press).

Goudey, J.
1993 'Atonement Imagery and Eucharistic Praxis in the Reformed Tradition: A Feminist Critique' (ThD dissertation, Boston University).

Graham, E.L.
1995 *Making the Difference: Gender, Personhood and Theology* (London: Mowbrays; Minneapolis: Fortress Press).
1996 *Transforming Practice: Pastoral Theology in an Age of Uncertainty* (London: Mowbrays).

Graham, E.L., and M. Halsey (eds.)
1993 *Life-Cycles: Women and Pastoral Care* (London: SPCK).

Grahn, J.
1982 'From Sacred Blood to the Curse and Beyond', in C. Spretnak (ed.), *The Politics of Women's Spirituality: Essays on the Rise of the Spiritual Power within the Feminist Movement* (Garden City, NY: Doubleday).

Grant, J.G.
1989 *White Women's Christ and Black Women's Jesus: Feminist Christology and Womanist Response* (Atlanta: Scholars Press).

Gray, E.D. (ed.)
1988 *Sacred Dimensions of Women's Experience* (Wellesley, MA: Roundtable Press).

BIBLIOGRAPHY

Green, A.
- 1983 'Bride, Spouse, Daughter: Images of the Feminine in Classical Jewish Sources', in S. Heschel (ed.), *On Being a Jewish Feminist* (New York: Schocken Books).

Greenberg, B.
- 1983 *How to Run a Traditional Jewish Household* (New York: Simon & Schuster).

Grey, M.
- 1989 *Redeeming the Dream: Feminism, Redemption and Christian Tradition* (London: SPCK; also published as *Feminism, Redemption and the Christian Tradition* [Mystic, CT: Twenty-third Publications (1990)]).
- 1990 'The Core of Our Desire: Re-Imaging the Trinity', *Theology* 93: 363-72.
- 1993 'Have the Wellsprings Run Dry? Re-sourcing Tradition in Feminist Theology', *Feminist Theology* 3: 38-52.
- 1993 *The Wisdom of Fools? Seeking Revelation for Today* (London: SPCK).

Griffin, S.
- 1981 *Pornography and Silence: Culture's Revenge against Nature* (London: The Women's Press).

Haight, R.
- 1979 *The Experience and Language of Grace* (New York: Paulist Press).

Hall, N.
- 1980 *The Moon and the Virgin: Reflections on the Archetypal Feminine* (London: The Women's Press).

Hampson, D.
- 1990 *Theology and Feminism* (Oxford: Basil Blackwell).

Hampson, D. (ed.)
- 1996 *Swallowing a Fishbone? Feminist Theologians Debate Christianity* (London: SPCK).

Hampson, D., and R.R. Ruether
- 1987 *Is There a Place for Feminists in a Christian Church?* (Oxford: New Blackfriars).

Hannaford, R.
- 1989 'Women and the Human Paradigm: An Exploration of Gender Discrimination', *New Blackfriars* 70.827: 226-33.

Harris, M.
- 1988 *Women and Teaching: Themes for a Spirituality of Pedagogy* (New York: Paulist Press).

Harrison, B.W.
- 1983 *Our Right to Choose: Towards a New Ethic of Abortion* (Boston: Beacon Press).
- 1985 *Making the Connections: Essays in Feminist Social Ethics* (ed. C.S. Robb; Boston: Beacon Press, 1985).
- 1987 'Two Models of Feminist Leadership: Millicent Fawcett and Emmeline Pankhurst', in *Prudent Revolutionaries: Portraits of British Feminists between the Wars* (Oxford: Clarendon Press): 17-44.

Hart, C.
- 1980 *Hadewijch: The Complete Works* (New York: Paulist Press; London: SPCK).

Hart, C., and J. Bishop
- **1990** *Hildegard of Bingen: Scivias* **(New York: Paulist Press).**

Haskins, S.
- 1994 *Mary Magdalene* (London: HarperCollins).

Hayes, J.H., and C.R. Holladay
- 1987 *Biblical Exegesis: A Beginner's Handbook* (London: SCM Press, 2nd edn).

Hennelly, A.T. (ed.)
- 1990 *Liberation Theology: A Documentary History* (Maryknoll, NY: Orbis Books).

Herzel, S.
- 1981 *A Voice for Women* (Geneva: World Council of Churches).

Heschel, S.
- 1995 'Configurations of Patriarchy, Judaism and Nazism in German Feminist Thought', in T.M. Rudavsky (ed.), *Gender and Judaism* (New York: New York University Press): 135-54.

Heyward, I.C.
- 1982 *The Redemption of God: A Theology of Mutual Relation* (Lanham, MD: University Press of America).
- 1984 *Our Passion for Justice: Images of Power, Sexuality and Liberation* (New York: Pilgrim Press).
- 1989 *Touching Our Strength: The Erotic as Power and the Love of God* (San Francisco: Harper & Row).
- 1993 *When Boundaries Betray Us: Beyond Illusions of what is Ethical in Therapy and Life* (San Francisco: Harper Collins).

Hill, P.R.
- 1985 *The World Their Household* (Ann Arbor: University of Michigan Press).

Hillman, J.
- 1978 *The Myth of Analysis* (New York: Harper & Row, Harper Colophon Books).

BIBLIOGRAPHY

Hite, S.
1994 *The Hite Reports* (London: Hodder & Stoughton).

Hole, C.
1977 *Witchcraft in England* (London: Batsford).

Holmes, H.B., and L.M. Purdy (eds.)
1992 *Feminist Perspectives in Medical Ethics* (Bloomington: Indiana University Press).

Hooker, M.D.
1963–64 'Authority on her Head', *New Testament Studies* 10: 410-16.
1990 'Kingdom of God', in R. Coggins and L. Houlden (eds.), *A Dictionary of Biblical Interpretation* (London: SCM Press): 374-77.

Hooker, R., and C. Lamb
1986 *Love the Stranger: Ministry in Multi-Faith Areas* (London: SPCK).

Horrocks, R.
1991 'The Divine Woman in Christianity', in A. Pirani (ed.), *The Absent Mother: Restoring the Goddess to Judaism and Christianity* (London: Mandala): 110-11.

Hull, G.G.
1989 *Equal to Serve* (London: Scripture Union).

Hunt, M.E.
1991 *Fierce Tenderness: A Feminist Theology of Friendship* (New York: Crossroad).

Iannello, K.P.
1992 *Decisions Without Hierarchy: Feminist Interventions in Organization Theory and Practice* (London: Routledge).

Ingram, A., and D. Patai (eds.)
1993 *Rediscovering Forgotten Radicals: British Women Writers 1889–1939* (University of North Carolina Press).

International Reports
1981 'Change, Military Ideology and the Dissolution of Democracy: Women in Chile', *International Reports* 6: *Women and Society* (London).

Irigaray, L.
1985 *Speculum of the Other Woman* (trans. G.C. Gill; Ithaca, NY: Cornell University Press).
1993 *An Ethics of Sexual Difference* (trans. C. Burke and G.C. Gill; London: Athlone Press).

Isasi-Díaz, A.M.
1989 'Mujeristas: A Name of Our Own', *The Christian Century* (May 24-31): 560-62.
1992 E. Olazagasti-Segovia, S. Mangual-Rodríguez, M.A. Berriozábal, D.L. Machado, L. Arguelles, and R. Rivero, 'Who We Are and What We Are About', *Journal of Feminist Studies in Religion* 8.1 (Spring, 1992): 105-25.
1993 *En La Lucha—In the Struggle: Elaborating Mujerista Theology* (Minneapolis: Fortress Press).

Isasi-Díaz, A.M., and Y. Tarango
1993 *Hispanic Women: Prophetic Voice in the Church* (repr.; Minneapolis: Fortress Press [1987]).

Isherwood, L. and D. McEwan
1993 *Introducing Feminist Theology* (Sheffield: Sheffield Academic Press).

Jagger, A.
1983 *Feminist Politics and Human Nature* (Sussex: Harvester Press).

Jantzen, G.
1984 *God's World, God's Body* (London: Darton, Longman & Todd).
1992 'Connection or Competition: Identity and Personhood in Christian Ethics', *Studies in Christian Ethics* 5.1: 1-21.

Jenkins, D.S.
1984 'Theology', in J.M. Sutcliffe (ed.), *A Dictionary of Religious Education* (London: SCM Press): 344.

Johnson, E.A
1992 *She Who Is: The Mystery of God in Feminist Theological Discourse* (New York: Crossroad).
1993 *Women, Earth and Creator Spirit* (New York: Paulist Press).

Jonas, H.
1958 *The Gnostic Religion: The Message of the Alien God and the Beginnings of Christianity* (Boston: Beacon Press, 2nd edn).

Jones, L. (ed.)
1983 *Keeping the Peace* (London: The Women's Press).

Jones, N.
1994 *Power of Raven, Wisdom of Serpent* (Edinburgh: Floris Books).

Jordan, J.V., A.G Kaplan, J.B. Miller, I.P. Stiver, and J.L. Surrey
1991 *Women's Growth in Connection: Writings from the Stone Center* (New York/London: Guilford).

An A to Z of Feminist Theology

BIBLIOGRAPHY

Joseph, A. (ed.)
1990   *Through the Devil's Gateway: Women, Religion and Taboo* (London: SPCK, 1990).

Katoppo, M.
1979   *Compassionate and Free: An Asian Women's Theology* (Geneva: World Council of Churches; Maryknoll, NY: Orbis Books, 1980).

Kellenbach, K. von
1994   *Anti-Judaism in Feminist Religious Writings* (Atlanta: Scholars Press).

Keller, C.
1986   *From a Broken Web: Separation, Sexism, and Self* (Boston: Beacon Press).

Kelly, J.
1984   *Women, History and Theory* (Chicago & London: University of Chicago Press).

Kelly, J.N.D.
1958   *Early Christian Doctrines* (London: SPCK).

Kelly, K.
1992   *New Directions in Moral Theology: The Challenge of Being Human* (London: Geoffrey Chapman).

King, K.L. (ed.)
1988   *Images of the Feminine in Gnosticism* (Philadelphia: Fortress Press).

King, U.
1993   *Women and Spirituality: Voices of Protest and Promise* (London: Macmillan; University Park, PA: Penn State Press, 2nd edn).

King, U. (ed.).
1994   *Feminist Theology from the Third World: A Reader* (London: SPCK; Maryknoll, NY: Orbis Books).

Kissling, F.
1994   'For Catholics, it's "Happy Martyr's Day" ', *Los Angeles Times* May 8: M5.

Klein, V.
1989   *The Feminine Character: History of an Ideology* (3rd Edn, with Introduction by J. Sayers; London: Routledge).

Knight, G.
1978   *A History of White Magic* (London: Mowbrays).

Knitter, P.F.
1985   *No Other Name? A Critical Survey of Christian Attitudes Toward the World Religions* (London: SCM Press).

Kramarae, C., and P.A. Treichler
1992   *Amazons, Bluestockings and Crones: A Feminist Dictionary: A Woman's Companion to Words and Ideas* (London: Pandora Press).

Krieger, D.
1986   *The Therapeutic Touch* (New York: Prentice Hall).

Kristeva, J.
1980   'Motherhood according to Bellini', in *Desire in Language* (ed. L.S. Roudiez; New York: Columbia University Press): 237-70.
1983   *Tales of Love* (trans. L.S. Roudiez; New York: Columbia University Press).
1986   'Stabat Mater', in T. Moi (ed.), *The Kristeva Reader* (Oxford: Basil Blackwell): 160-86.

Kyung, C.H.
1991   *Struggle to be the Sun Again* (Maryknoll, NY: Orbis Books; London: SCM Press).

Lacan, J.
1982   'Encore', in J. Mitchell and J. Rose (eds.), *Feminine Sexuality: Jacques Lacan and the école freudienne* (London: Macmillan): 137-48.

LaCugna, C.M.
1991   *God for Us: The Trinity and Christian Life* (San Francisco: Harper).
1993   'God in Communion with Us: The Trinity', in idem (ed.), *Freeing Theology: The Essentials of Theology in Feminist Perspective* (New York: HarperCollins): 83-114.

LaCugna, C.M. (ed.)
1993   *Freeing Theology: The Essentials of Theology in Feminist Perspective* (New York: HarperCollins).

Laws, S.
1990   *Issues of Blood: The Politics of Menstruation* (London: Macmillan).

Layard, J.
n.d.   'The Incest Taboo and the Virgin Archetype', *Eranos JahrBuch* 12: 290-91.

Le Marchant, J.
1973   *Miracles de Notre Dame de Chartres* (ed. P. Kunstmann; Chartres: Société Archéologique d'Eure-et-Loir; Ottawa: Editions de l'Université d'Ottawa).

Leeuw, G. van der
1963   *Religion in Essence and in Manifestation* (London: George Allen & Unwin).

An A to Z of Feminist Theology

BIBLIOGRAPHY

Lennon, P.
1994 'The Fear and the Faith', *The Guardian*, 8th April.

Leonard, J.
1990 'Teaching Introductory Feminist Spirituality: Tracing the Trajectory through Women Writers', *Journal of Feminist Studies in Religion* 6.2: 121-35.

Lerner, G.
1979 *The Majority Finds its Past* (New York: Oxford University Press).
1986 *The Creation of Patriarchy* (New York and Oxford: Oxford University Press).

Lethbridge, T.C.
1979 *Witches* (Secaucus, NJ: Citadel Press).

Levin, D.M.
1988 *The Opening of Vision: Nihilism and Postmodernism* (London: Routledge).

Levine, E.R. (ed.)
1991 *A Ceremonies Sampler* (San Diego: Women's Institute for Continuing Jewish Education).

Liddell, E.W.
1994 *The Pickingill Papers: The Origin of the Gardnerian Craft* (Newbury: Capal Bann).

Liddington, J., and J. Norris
1978 *One Hand Tied Behind Us: The Rise of the Women's Suffrage Movement* (London: Virago).

Ligo, A.
1993 'Banahaw Women's Religiosity', *In God's Image* 12.3 (Autumn).

Limberis, V.
1994 *Divine Heiress: The Virgin Mary and the Creation of Christian Constantinople* (London: Routledge).

Liturgical Commission of the General Synod
1988 *Making Women Visible* (London: Church House Publishing).

Loades, A.
1993 'Introductory Address', *Feminist Theology* 3: 12-22.

Loades, A. (ed.)
1990 *Feminist Theology: A Reader* (London: SPCK).

Long, A.P.
1982 'Feminism and Spirituality: A Review of Recent Publications', *Women's Studies International Forum* 5.1: 103-108.
1992 *In a Chariot Drawn by Lions* (London: The Women's Press).
1994 'The Goddess Movement in Britain Today', *Feminist Theology* 5 (January): 11-39.

Lorde, A.
1978 *Uses of the Erotic: The Erotic as Power* (Freedom, CA: The Crossing Press).
1984 *Sister Outsider: Essays and Speeches* (Freedom, CA: The Crossing Press).
1984a 'The Uses of Anger: Women Responding to Racism', in *Sister Outsider*: 124-33.
1984b 'Eye to Eye: Black Women, Hatred and Anger', in *Sister Outsider*: 145-75.

Lunn, P.
1993 'Do Women Need the Goddess?', *Feminist Theology* 4 (September): 17-38.

MacHaffie, B.J.
1986 *Her Story: Women in Christian Tradition* (Philadelphia: Fortress Press).

MacKinnon, C.
1987 *Feminism Unmodified* (Cambridge, MA: Harvard University Press).
1989 *Toward a Feminist Theory of the State* (Cambridge, MA and London: Harvard University Press).
1994 *Only Words* (London: Harper Collins).

MacKinnon, M., and McIntyre, M.
1995 *Readings in Ecology and Feminist Theology* (Kansas City: Sheed & Ward).

MacLean, I.
1983 *The Renaissance Notion of Woman: A Study in the Fortunes of Scholasticism and Medical Science in European Intellectual Life* (Cambridge: Cambridge University Press).

Macquarrie, J. (ed.)
1967 *A Dictionary of Christian Ethics* (London: SCM Press).

Magonet, J.
1991 *A Rabbi's Bible* (London: SCM Press).

Maitland, S.
1983 *A Map of the New Country: Women and Christianity* (London: Routledge & Kegan Paul).

Marshall, C.B.
1987 'The Future of Women in Politics' (originally published 1916; repr. in M. Kamester and J. Vellacott [eds.], *Militarism versus Feminism: Writings on Women and War* [London: Virago]).

Martin, E.
1989 *The Woman in the Body* (Milton Keynes: Open University Press).

BIBLIOGRAPHY

Matthews, C. (ed.)
1991 *Voices of the Goddess* (London: Aquarian).

McAllister, P.
1988 *You Can't Kill the Spirit* (New Society).

McBrien, R.
1994 *Catholicism* (London: Geoffrey Chapman, 3rd edn).

McDade, C.
1986 *This Tough Spun Web* (Plainville, MA: Womancentre at Plainville).

McFague, S.
1983 *Metaphorical Theology: Models of God in Religious Language* (London: SCM Press).
1987 *Models of God: Theology for an Ecological, Nuclear Age* (Philadelphia: Fortress Press).
1990 'The Ethic of God as Mother, Lover and Friend', in A. Loades (ed.), *Feminist Theology: A Reader* (London: SPCK).
1993 *The Body of God: An Ecological Theology* (Minneapolis: Fortress Press; London: SCM Press).

McGovern, A.
1987 *Marxism: An American Christian Perspective* (Maryknoll, NY: Orbis Books).

Melichar, J.
1993 'Rights for Humans' (editorial), *Peace Matters* (Peace Pledge Union, July).

Mellor, M.
1992 *Breaking the Boundaries: Towards a Feminist Green Socialism* (London: Virago).

Mensching, G.
1976 *Structures and Patterns of Religion* (Delhi: Motilal Banasidass, Delhi).

Merchant, C.
1980 *The Death of Nature: Women, Ecology, and the Scientific Revolution* (San Francisco: Harper & Row).

Meyers, C.
1988 *Discovering Eve* (Oxford: Oxford University Press).

Miegge, G.
1955 *The Virgin Mary: The Roman Catholic Marian Doctrine* (trans. W. Smith; London: Lutterworth).

Mies, M., and V. Shiva
1993 *Ecofeminism* (London: Zed Books).

Miles, M.
1989 *Carnal Knowing: Female Nakedness and Religious Knowing in the Christian West* (Boston: Beacon Press).

Milhaven, A.L. (ed.)
1991 *Sermons Seldom Heard: Women Proclaim their Lives* (New York: Crossroad).

Miller, A.
1991 *Banished Knowledge: Facing Childhood Injuries* (London: Virago Press).

Miller, J.B.
1986 'What Do We Mean By Relationships?', *Work in Progress*, 22 (The Stone Center Working Paper Series; Wellesley, MA: The Stone Center).

Mollenkott, V.R.
1983 *The Divine Feminine: The Biblical Imagery of God as Female* (New York: Crossroad).
1988 *Godding: Human Responsibility and the Bible* (New York: Crossroad).

Moltmann, J.
1985 *God in Creation* (London: Scm Press).

Moltmann-Wendel, E.
1982 *The Women around Jesus* (London: SCM Press; New York: Crossroad).

Moore, G.
1992 *The Body in Question: Sex and Catholicism* (London: SCM).

Morgan, D.H.J.
1992 *Discovering Men* (London: Routledge).

Morley, J.
1992 *All Desires Known* (London: SPCK).

Morton, N.
1985 *The Journey is Home* (Boston: Beacon Press).

Moss, R.
n.d. *The I That Is We: Awakening Higher Energies through Unconditional Love* (Celestial Arts).

Mudflower Collective
1985 *God's Fierce Whimsy: Christian Feminism and Theological Education* (New York: Pilgrim Press).

Murphy, D.
1995 *The Death and Rebirth of Religious Life* (Dublin: Columba Book Service).

Naipaul, S.
1986 *An Unfinished Journey* (London: Hamish Hamilton).

National Catholic Reporter
1991 Vol. 30 no. 27 (May 6): 10.

Neale, M.A.
1987 *The Just Demands of the Poor* (New York: Paulist Press).

BIBLIOGRAPHY

Nelson, J.
1978 *Embodiment: An Approach to Sexuality and Christian Theology* (Minneapolis, MN: Augsburg).
1992 *Body Theology* (Lousville, KY: Westminster/John Knox Press).

Nelson, J., and S. Longfellow (eds.)
1994 *Sexuality and the Sacred: Sources for Theological Reflection* (London: Mowbrays).

Neu, D.L., and M.E. Hunt
1993 *Women-Church Sourcebook* (Silver Spring, MD: WATERworks Press, 1993).

Neumann, E.
1974 *The Great Mother* (Princeton, NJ: Princeton University Press).

New Shorter Oxford Dictionary, The
1993

Newman, B
1987 *Sister of Wisdom: St Hildegard's Theology of the Feminine* (Aldershot: Scolar Press)
1988 *Saint Hildegard of Bingen: Symphonia* (New York: Cornell University Press).

Newsom, C.A., and S.H. Ringe (eds.)
1992 *The Women's Bible Commentary* (London: SPCK).

Nicholson, E.W.
1986 *God and His People: Covenant and Theology in the Old Testament* (Oxford: Clarendon Press).

Nussbaum, M., and G. Sen (eds.)
1993 *The Quality of Life* (Oxford: Clarendon Press).

Oakley, A.
1972 *Sex, Gender and Society* (Aldershot: Gower).

O'Carroll, M.
1982 *Theotokos: A Theological Encyclopedia of the Blessed Virgin Mary* (Dublin: Dominican Publications).

O'Murchu, D.
1995 *Reframing Religious Life* (London: St Paul's).

Ochs, C.
1983 *Women and Spirituality* (New Jersey: Rowman and Allanheld).

Oddie, W.
1984 *What Will Happen to God?* (London: SPCK).

Oduyoye, M.
1992 *Who Will Roll the Stone Away? The Ecumenical Decade of Churches in Solidarity with Women* (Risk Books, Geneva: World Council of Churches, 1992).

Oduyoye, M.A., and M.R.A. Kanyoro (eds.)
1992 *The Will to Arise: Women, Tradition and the Church in Africa* (Maryknoll, NY: Orbis Books).

Okin, S.M.
1989 *Justice, Gender and the Family* (New York: Basic Books).

Oldfield, S.
1989 *Women against the Iron Fist: Alternatives to Militarism 1900–1989* (Oxford: Basil Blackwell).

Omerod, P.
1994 *The Death of Economics* (London: Faber & Faber).

Ormerod, N.
1992 *Grace and Disgrace: A Theology of Self-Esteem, Society and History* (Newtown, New South Wales: E.J. Dwyer).

Orsi, R.A.
1991 ' "He Keeps Me Going": Women's Devotion to Saint Jude Thaddeus and the Dialectics of Gender in American Catholicism, 1929–1965', in T. Kselman (ed.), *Belief in History: Innovative Approaches to European and American Religion* (Notre Dame: University of Notre Dame Press): 137-69.

Orsy, L.
1992 *Theology and Canon Law: New Horizons for Interpretation and Legislation* (Collegeville, MN: Liturgical Press).

Ostriker, A.
1989 'Entering the Tents', *Feminist Studies* 15: 541-47.
1993 *Feminist Revision of the Bible* (Oxford: Basil Blackwell).

Otranto, G.
1982 'Note sul sacerdozio femminile...', *Vetera Christianorum* 19: 341-60 (et M.A. Rossi, 'Priesthood, Precedent, and Prejudice', *Journal of Feminist Studies in Religion* 7.1: 73-94).

Otto, R.
1923 *The Idea of the Holy* (London: Oxford University Press).

Pagan Federation
1992 *The Pagan Federation Information Pack* (Pagan Federation, BM Box 7097, London WC1N 3XX).

An A to Z of Feminist Theology

BIBLIOGRAPHY

Page, C. (ed.)
1982 *Abbess Hildegard of Bingen: Sequences and Hymns* (Newton Abbott: Antico Edition).

Pagels, E.
1982 *The Gnostic Gospels* (London: Weidenfeld & Nicholson).
1988 'Adam and Eve and the Serpent', in King (ed.) 1988: 412-23.
1988 *Adam, Eve and the Serpent* (London: Weidenfeld & Nicolson; New York: Random House).

Pahl, J.
1989 *Money and Marriage* (London: Macmillan).

Pankhurst, E.
1914 *My Own Story* (London: Eveleigh Nash).

Pankhurst, E.
1977 *The Suffragette Movement: An Intimate Account of Persons and Ideals* (London: Virago [originally published 1931]).

Pattison, S.
1993 *A Critique of Pastoral Care* (London: SCM Press, 2nd edn).
1994 *Pastoral Care and Liberation Theology* (Cambridge: Cambridge University Press).

Pellauer, M.D., B. Chester and J. Boyajian (eds.)
1987 *Sexual Assault and Abuse: A Handbook for Clergy and Religious Professionals* (San Francisco: Harper & Row)

Perrin, N.
1976 *Jesus and the Language of the Kingdom* (London: SCM Press).

Petchesky, R.P.
1986 *Abortion and Women's Choice* (London: Verso).

Pétrement, S.
1991 *A Separate God* (trans. C. Harrison; London).

Philibert, P.R.
1987 'Readiness for Ritual', in R.A. Duffy (ed.), *Alternative Futures for Worship*, I (Minnesota: Liturgical Press): 63-121.

Phillips, A., and J. Rakusen (eds.)
1989 *Our Bodies, Ourselves: A Health Book by and for Women* (Boston Women's Health Book Collective; London: Penguin Books, 2nd British edn).

Phillips, J.A.
1984 *Eve: The History of an Idea* (San Francisco: Harper & Row).

Plaskow, J.
1980 'Blaming the Jews for Inventing Patriarchy', *Lilith* 7: 9-11 (originally published as 'Christian Feminism and Anti-Judaism', *Cross-Currents* 28 [1978]: 306-309).
1980 *Sex, Sin and Grace: Women's Experience in the Theologies of Reinhold Niebuhr and Paul Tillich* (Lanham, MD: University Press of America).
1990 *Standing Again at Sinai: Judaism from a Feminist Perspective* (London: HarperCollins).

Plaskow, J., and C.P. Christ (eds.)
1979 *Womanspirit Rising: A Feminist Reader in Religion* (San Francisco: Harper & Row).
1989 *Weaving the Visions: New Patterns in Feminist Spirituality* (New York: HarperSanFrancisco).

Plaut, W.G.
1981 *The Torah: A Modern Commentary* (New York: Union of American Hebrew Congregations).

Plumwood, V.
1993 *Feminism and the Mastery of Nature* (London and New York: Routledge).

Poling, J.N.
1991 *The Abuse of Power: A Theological Problem* (Nashville: Abingdon Press).

Porete, M.
1981 *A Mirror for Simple Souls* (ed. and trans. C. Crawford; Dublin: Gill and Macmillan).

Primavesi, A.
1991 *From Apocalypse to Genesis: Ecology, Feminism and Christianity* (London: Burns & Oates; Minneapolis, MN: Fortress Press).

Procter-Smith, M.
1990 *In Her Own Rite: Constructing Feminist Liturgical Tradition* (Nashville: Abingdon Press).

Rabinowitz, L.I.
n.d. 'Rabbi', *Encyclopedia Judaica*, XIII (Jerusalem: Encyclopedia Judaica).

Radcliffe Richards, J.
1980 *The Sceptical Feminist* (London: Routledge & Kegan Paul).

Raming, I.
1976 *The Canons Excluding Women from the Priesthood* (New Jersey: Scarecrow Press).

An A to Z of Feminist Theology

Ranke-Heinemann, U.
1990 *Eunuchs for Heaven* (London: Andre Deutsch).

Ranke-Heinemann, U.
1990 *Eunuchs for the Kingdom of Heaven* (Garden City, NY: Doubleday).

Raphael, M.
1994 'Feminism, Constructivism and Numinous Experience', *Religious Studies* 30: 519.

Raymond, J.
1986 *A Passion for Friends: Toward a Philosophy of Female Affection* (Boston: Beacon Press; London: The Women's Press).

Redmond, S.A.
1989 'Christian "Virtues" and Recovery from Child Sexual Abuse', in Brown and Bohn (eds.): 70-88.

Religious Network for Equality for Women
1988 *Learning Economics: Empowering Women for Action* (New York: Women's Collective Project in Economic Literacy).

Rhode, D.L. (ed.)
1990 *Theoretical Perspectives on Sexual Difference* (New Haven: Yale University Press).

Rich, A.
1978 'Transcendental Etude', in *The Dream of a Common Language* (New York: Norton).
1980 'Compulsory Heterosexuality and Lesbian Existence', *Signs* 5.4: 631-60.
1984 'Twenty-One Love Poems: XIII', *The Fact of a Door Frame: Poems Selected and New 1950–1984* (New York: Norton).

Roberts, M.
1984 *The Wild Girl* (London: Methuen).

Robinson, J.M. (ed.)
1988 *The Nag Hammadi Library in English* (Leiden: Brill, 2nd edn).

Rodríguez, R.
1991 'La Marcha de las Mujeres…', *Pasos* 344 (March–April).

Roiphe, K.
1994 *The Morning After* (London: Hamish Hamilton).

Rose, R.S.
1991 'A Feminist Response to the Eucharist Section of *Baptism, Eucharist and Ministry* (BEM) of the World Council of Churches' (DMin dissertation, San Francisco Theological Seminary).

Ross, S.A.
1993 'God's Embodiment and Women: Sacraments', in C.M. Lacugna (ed.), *Freeing Theology: The Essentials of Theology in Feminist Perspective* (San Francisco: HarperSan Francisco): 185-209.

Rubinstein, D.
1986 *Before the Suffragettes: Women's Emancipation in the 1890s* (Brighton: Harvester).

Rudolph, K.
1988 'Response to J.J. Buckley', in King (ed.) 1988: 228-38.

Ruether, R.R.
1974 'Virginal Feminism in the Fathers of the Church', in idem (ed.), *Religion and Sexism* (New York: Simon & Schuster): 150-83.
1979 *Mary: The Feminine Face of the Church* (London: SCM Press).
1981 *To Change the World: Christology and Cultural Criticism* (New York: Crossroad).
1983 *Sexism and God-Talk: Towards a Feminist Theology* (Boston: Beacon Press; London: SCM Press).
1985 *Women-Church: Theology and Practice* (San Francisco: Harper & Row).
1991 'Women's Difference and Equal Rights in the Church', in A. Carr and E. Schüssler Fiorenza (eds.), *The Special Nature of Women?* (Concilium, 6; London: SCM Press, 1991).
1992 'Renewal or New Creation? Feminist Spirituality and Historical Religion', in S. Gunew (ed.), *A Reader in Feminist Knowledge* (London: Routledge).
1992 *Gaia and God: An Ecofeminist Theology of Earth Healing* (San Francisco: Harper & Row; London: SCM Press).

Ruether, R.R. (ed.)
1985 *Feminist Interpretation of the Bible* (Philadelphia: Westminster Press).
1996 *Women Healing Earth. Third World Woman on Ecology, Feminism and Religion* (London: SCM; Maryknoll, NY: Orbis Books).

Ruether, R.R. and E. McLaughlin
1979 *Women of Spirit: Female Leadership in the Jewish and Christian Traditions* (New York: Simon & Schuster).

BIBLIOGRAPHY

Rupp, J.
1990 *The Star in My Heart: Experiencing Sophia, Inner Wisdom* (San Diego, CA: LuraMedia).

Russell
1980 *A History of Witchcraft* (London: Thames & Hudson).

Russell, D. (ed.)
1993 *Making Violence Sexy* (Buckingham: Open University Press).

Russell, L.
1974 *Human Liberation in a Feminist Perspective* (Philadelphia: Westminster Press).
1987 *Household of Freedom: Authority in Feminist Theology* (Philadelphia: Westminster Press).
1993 *Church in the Round: Feminist Interpretation of the Church* (Louisville, KY: Westminster/John Knox Press).

Russell, L. (ed.)
1985 *Feminist Interpretation of the Bible* (Oxford: Basil Blackwell).

Ruston, R.
1982 'Religious Celibacy and Sexual Justice', *New Blackfriars* (June): 260-74.

St Hilda Community
1991 *Women Included: A Book of Services and Prayers* (London: SPCK [new edn, 1993]).

Saiving, V.
1979 'The Human Situation: A Feminine View', in Plaskow and Christ (eds.) 1979: 25-42.

Sattel, J.W.
1983 'Men, Expressiveness, and Power', in Thorne, Kramarae and Henley (eds.), *Language, Gender, and Society* (London: Newbury House).

Schillebeeckx, E.
1985 'Eager to Spread the Gospel of Peace', in *The Church and Peace* (Concilium, 164; Edinburgh: T. & T. Clark).

Schneiders, S.
1986 *New Wine Skins* (New York: Paulist Press).
1991 *Beyond Patching* (New York: Paulist Press).

Schüssler-Fiorenza, E.
1981 'Toward a Feminist Biblical Hermeneutics: Biblical Interpretation and Liberation Theology', in D.K. McKim (ed.), *A Guide to Contemporary Hermeneutics: Major Trends in Biblical Interpretation* (Michigan).
1982 'Tablesharing and the Celebration of the Eucharist', in M. Collins and D. Power (eds.), *Can We Always Celebrate the Eucharist?* (Concilium, 152; New York: Seabury Press): 3-12.
1983 *In Memory of Her: A Feminist Theological Reconstruction of Christian Origins* (New York: Crossroad; London: SCM Press).
1984 *Bread Not Stone: The Challenge of Feminist Biblical Interpretation* (Boston: Beacon Press).
1987 'The "Quilting" of Women's History: Phoebe of Cenchreae', in P.M. Cooey, et al (ed.), *Embodied Love: Sensuality and Relationship as Feminist Values* (San Francisco: Harper Collins).
1992 *But She Said: Feminist Practices of Biblical Interpretation* (Boston: Beacon Press).
1993 *Discipleship of Equals: A Critical Feminist Ekklesiology of Liberation* (New York: Crossroad).
1994 *Searching the Scriptures. I. A Feminist Introduction* (London: SCM Press).

Sears, M.
1989 *Life Cycle Celebrations for Women* (Mystic, CT: Twenty-Third Publications).

Sen, G., and C. Grown
1988 *Development Crises and Alternative Visions: Third World Women's Perspectives* (London: Earthscan).

Sewell, M. (ed.)
1991 *Cries of the Spirit: A Celebration of Women's Spirituality* (Boston: Beacon Press).

Shewring, W.H. (ed.)
1931 *The Passion of Ss. Perpetua and Felicity Mm.* (London: Sheed & Ward).

Shuttle, P., and P. Redgrove
1978 *The Wise Wound: Menstruation and Everywoman* (London: Victor Gollancz, 1978).

Simons, M.A., and J. Benjamin
1979 'Simone de Beauvoir: an Interview', *Feminist Studies* 5.2: 330-45.

Smith, W.R.
1889 *Lectures on the Religion of the Semites* (Edinburgh: A. & C. Black).

Sölle, D.
1974 *Political Theology* (Philadelphia: Fortress Press).
1975 *Suffering* (trans. E.R. Kalin; Philadelphia: Fortress Press).

An A to Z of Feminist Theology

BIBLIOGRAPHY

1984 *The Strength of the Weak: Toward a Christian Feminist Identity* (Philadelphia: Westminster Press).

Sölle, D., and S.A. Cloyes
1984 *To Work and to Love: A Theology of Creation* (Minneapolis, MN: Fortress Press).

Sölle, D., and F. Steffensky
1983 *Nicht nur Ja und Amen: Von Christen im Widerstand* (Rowohlt Rotfuchs TB, 324; Reinbek, 1983).

Soskice, J.M.
1933 'Women's Problems', in A. Walker (ed.), *Different Gospels: The New Edition* (London: SPCK, 1933).
1992 'Can a Feminist Call God Father?', in A.F. Kimel (ed.), *Speaking the Christian God: The Holy Trinity and the Challenge of Feminism* (Leominster: Gracewing): 81-94; and in T. Elwes (ed.) *Women's Voices: Essays in Contemporary Feminist Theology* (London: Marshall Pickering): 15-29.
1993 'Christ in Feminist Context', in H. Regan (ed.), *Christ and Context* (Edinburgh: T. & T. Clark).
1994 'Trinity and "the Feminine Other" ', *New Blackfriars* 75: 2-17.

Southern, R.W.
1970 *Western Society and the Church in the Middle Ages* (Harmondsworth: Penguin Books).

Spender, D.
1980 *Man Made Language* (London: Routledge & Kegan Paul).
1988 *Women of Ideas and What Men Have Done to Them* (London: Pandora Press).

Spretnak, C.
1991 *States of Grace: The Recovery of Meaning in the Postmodern Age* (San Francisco: Harper & Row).

Stanton, E.C.
1985 *The Woman's Bible* (repr.; Edinburgh: Polygon Books [1898]).

Starhawk
1979 *The Spiral Dance* (San Francisco: Harper & Row).
1987 *Truth or Dare: Encounters With Power, Authority, and Mystery* (San Franscisco: Harper & Row).

Stendahl, K.
1962 'Biblical Theology, Contemporary', *The Interpreter's Dictionary of the Bible* (New York: Abingdon Press), I: 418-32.

Stone, L.
1979 *The Family, Sex and Marriage in England* (London: Pelican).

Storkey, E.
1985 *What's Right with Feminism?* (London: SPCK).
1989 'The Significance of Mary for Feminist Theology', in D. Wright (ed.), *Chosen by God: Mary in Evangelical Perspective* (London: Marshall Pickering): 184-99.

Strehlow, V., and G. Hertzka
1988 *Hildegard of Bingen's Medicine* (Santa Fe, NM: Bear).

Stuart, E.
1995 *Just Good Friends: Towards a Lesbian and Gay Theology of Relationships* (London: Mowbrays).

Stuart, E. (ed.)
1992 *Daring to Speak Love's Name: A Gay and Lesbian Prayer Book* (London: Hamish Hamilton).

Suchocki, M.H.
1982 *God–Christ–Church: A Practical Guide to Process Theology* (New York: Crossroad).

Swantz, M.L.
1989 'Miscalculated Economics', in Commission on the Churches Participation in Development, *For a Change No 2* (Geneva: World Council of Churches): 8-11.

Swimme, B., and T. Berry
1992 *The Universe Story* (New York: HarperCollins).

Tamez, E.
1982 *Bible of the Oppressed* (New York: Orbis Books).

Tamez, E. (ed.)
1989 *Through Her Eyes: Women's Theology from Latin America* (Maryknoll, NY: Orbis Books).

Tamez, E. (ed.)
1989 *Through Her Eyes: Women's Theology from Latin America* (Maryknoll, NY: Orbis Books, 2nd edn).

Templeton, E. (ed.)
1993 *A Woman's Place? Women and Work* (Edinburgh: St Andrew's Press).

Thistlethwaite, S.B.
1989 *Sex, Race and God: Christian Feminism in Black and White* (New York: Crossroad; London: Geoffrey Chapman [1990]).

An A to Z of Feminist Theology

Thompson, D. (ed.)
  1983 *Over Our Dead Bodies: Women against the Bomb* (London: Virago).

Thurston, H., and P.T. Slater (eds.)
  1904 *Eadmeri Monachi Cantuarensis: Tractatus de Conceptione Sanctae Mariae* (Freiburg-im-Breisgau).

Thurston, H.S.J., and D. Attwater (eds.)
  1932 *Butler's Lives of the Saints*, VII (London: Burns, Oates & Washbourne).

Tickner, L.
  1987 *The Spectacle of Women: Imagery of the Suffrage Campaign 1907–14* (London: Chatto & Windus).

Tilley, M.A.
  1991 'The Ascetic Body and the (Un)Making of the Martyr', *Journal of the American Academy of Religion* 69.3: 467-79.
  1995 'One Woman's Body: Repression and Expression in the Passio Perpetuae', in P. Phan (ed.), *Ethnicity, Nationality and Religious Experience* (Lanham, MD: University Press of America).

Tither, M. (ed.)
  1994 *English Nature* 11 (January 1994) (Peterborough: English Nature).

Tolbert, M.A.
  1990 'Protestant Feminists and the Bible', in A. Bach (ed.), *The Pleasure of Her Text* (Philadelphia: Trinity Press International).

Tong, R.
  1989 *Feminist Thought: A Comprehensive Introduction* (Sydney: Unwin Hyman).

Trevett, C.
  1991 *Women and Quakerism in the Seventeenth Century* (York: Sessions Book Trust).

Trible, P.
  1978 *God and the Rhetoric of Sexuality* (Philadelphia: Fortress Press).
  1984 *Texts of Terror: Literary-Feminist Readings of Biblical Narratives* (Philadelphia: Fortress Press).
  1989 'Bringing Miriam out of the Shadows', *Bible Review* 5.1 (February).
  1993 'Treasures Old and New: Biblical Theology and the Challenge of Feminism', in F. Watson (ed.), *The Open Text: New Directions for Biblical Studies* (London: SCM Press): 32-56.

Tronto, J.
  1993 *An Ethic of Care: Feminist and Interdisciplinary Perspectives* (London: Routledge).

Uhlein, G.
  1983 *Meditations with Hildegard of Bingen* (Santa Fe, NM: Bear).

Ulanov, A., and B. Ulanov
  1982 *Primary Speech: A Psychology of Prayer* (London: SCM Press).

Underhill, E.
  1911 *Mysticism* (London: Methuen).

Ussher, J.
  1991 *Women's Madness: Misogyny or Mental Illness?* (Amherst: The University of Massachusetts Press).

Valiente, D.
  1974 *The ABC of Witchcraft* (London: Robert Hale).

Vergote, A.
  1988 *Guilt and Desire: Religious Attitudes and their Pathological Derivatives* (New Haven: Yale University Press, 1988).

Walker, A.
  1982 *The Color Purple* (New York: Harcourt Brace Jovanovich; London: The Women's Press [1983]).

Walker, A.
  1984 *In Search of Our Mothers' Gardens: Womanist Prose* (London: The Women's Press).

Walker-Bynum, C.
  1982 *Jesus as Mother* (Berkeley: University of California Press).
  1987 *Holy Feast, Holy Fast* (Berkeley: University of California Press).

Walker, B.G.
  1990 *Women's Rituals: A Sourcebook* (San Francisco: Harper & Row).

Walker, M.
  1990 *Women in Therapy and Counselling: Out of the Shadows* (Milton Keynes: Open University Press).

Waring, M.
  1968 *If Women Counted: A New Feminist Economics* (London: Macmillan).

Warner, M.
  1976 *Alone of All Her Sex: The Myth and the Cult of the Virgin Mary* (London: Weidenfeld & Nicolson).

Warren, K.J.
  1994 *Ecological Feminism* (London and New York: Routledge).

Weber, M.
1968 *On Charisma and Institution Building* (ed. S.N. Eisenstadt; Chicago: University of Chicago Press).

Weems, R.J.
1988 *Just a Sister Away: A Womanist Vision of Women's Relationships in the Bible* (San Diego: LutaMedia Publishers).

Weideger, P.
1978 *Female Cycles* (London: The Women's Press).

Weiner, E., and A. Weiner
1981 'Change, Military Ideology and the Dissolution of Democracy: Women in Chile', *International Reports: Women and Society* (London): 6.
1990 *The Martyr's Conviction: A Sociological Analysis* (Atlanta: Scholars Press).

Weinreich-Haste, H.
1986 'Brother Sun, Sister Moon: Does Rationality Overcome a Dualistic World View?', in J. Harding (ed.), *Perspectives on Gender and Science* (London and New York: Falmer).

Weir, A., and J. Jerman
1986 *Images of Lust: Sexual Carvings on Medieval Churches* (London: Batsford).

Welch, S.
1975 *Communities of Resistance and Solidarity* (New York: Orbis Books).
1990 *A Feminist Ethic of Risk* (Minneapolis, MN: Fortress Press).

West, A.
1990 'Sex and Salvation: A Christian Feminist Bible Study on 1 Corinthians', in Loades (ed.), *Feminist Theology: A Reader*: 72-80.

Whitehead, A.N.
1978 *Process and Reality* (New York: The Free Press).

Whitford, M.
1991 *Luce Irigaray: Philosophy in the Feminine* (London: Routledge).

Williams, D.S.
1993 *Sisters in the Wilderness: The Challenge of Womanist God-Talk* (Maryknoll, NY: Orbis Books).

Williams, J
1992 'The Doctrine of the Trinity: A Way Forward for Feminists', in T. Elwes (ed.), *Women's Voices: Essays in Contemporary Feminist Theology* (London: Marshall Pickering): 31-43.

1993 *First Lady of the Pulpit* (The Book Guild).

Willis, E.
1987 'Nothing is Sacred, All is Profane: Lesbian Identity and Religious Purpose', in L. Hurcombe (ed.), *Sex and God: Some Varieties of Women's Religious Experience* (London: Routledge & Kegan Paul): 104-24.

Wilson Schaef, A.
1985 *Women's Reality: An Emerging Female System in a White Male Society* (San Francisco: Harper & Row).

Wiltshire, A.
1985 *Most Dangerous Women: Feminist Peace Campaigners of the Great War* (London: Pandora).

Winter, M.T.
1987 *Woman Prayer Woman Song: Resources for Ritual* (Oak Park, IL: Meyer Stone Books).

Witherington, B.
1990 *Women and the Genesis of Christianity* (Cambridge: Cambridge University Press).

Women's Environment and Development Organization
1992 *Official Report of the World Women's Congress for a Healthy Planet* (New York: WEDO).

Woolf, V.
1938 *Three Guineas* (London: The Hogarth Press).

World Council of Churches
1990 *Guidelines on Dialogue with People of Living Faiths* (Geneva: WCC).

Wosein, M.-G.
n.d. 'On the Sacred Origins of Dance', in J. King (ed.), *Dancing Circles* (privately published).

Wren, B.
1989 *What Language Shall I Borrow? God-Talk in Worship: A Male Response to Feminist Theology* (London: SCM Press; New York: Crossroad).

Yarbro Collins, A.
1985 *Feminist Perspectives on Biblical Scholarship* (Chico, CA: Scholars Press).

Yates, F.
1964 *Giordano Bruno and the Hermetic Tradition* (London: Routledge & Kegan Paul).
1969 *The Rosicrucian Enlightenment* (London: Routledge & Kegan Paul).

Young, P.D.
1990 *Feminist Theology/Christian Theology: In Search of Method* (Minneapolis, MN: Fortress Press).

Zappone, K.
1990 'Is there a Feminist Ethic?', in Freyne (ed.), *Ethics and the Christian* (Dublin: Columba Press): 110-27.

Zappone, K.
1991 *The Hope for Wholeness: A Spirituality for Feminists* (Mystic, CT: Twenty-Third Publications).

Zárate Macías, R.M.
n.d. 'Canto de Mujer', in *Concierto a Mi Pueblo* (tape available from R.M. Zárate Macías, PO Box 7366, San Bernadino, CA 92411, USA).

Zeitlin, I.
1984 *Ancient Judaism* (Cambridge: Polity Press).